HITCHCOCK'S MUSIC

HITCHCOCK'S MUSIC

jack sullivan

yale university press / new haven and london

Copyright © 2006 by Yale University.

Designed by Mary Valencia.
Set in Minion type by The Composing Room of Michigan, Inc.

Printed in the United States of America by Sheridan Books.

The Library of Congress has cataloged the hardcover edition as follows:

Sullivan, Jack, 1946–
    Hitchcock's music / Jack Sullivan.
        p. cm.
    Includes bibliographical references and index.
    ISBN-13: 978-0-300-11050-0 (cloth : alk. paper)
    ISBN-10: 0-300-11050-2
    1. Motion picture music—History and criticism.   2. Television music—History and criticism.   3. Hitchcock, Alfred, 1899–1980—Criticism and interpretation. I. Title.
    ML2075.S89 2006
    781.5′42—dc22

                                                                    2006010348

ISBN 978-0-300-13618-0 (pbk. : alk. paper)

A catalogue record for this book is available from the British Library.

The paper in this book meets the guidelines for permanence and durability of the Committee on Production Guidelines for Book Longevity of the Council on Library Resources.
10 9 8 7 6 5 4 3 2 1

For Robin, Geoffrey, and David

CONTENTS

ACKNOWLEDGMENTS

I would like to express deep appreciation to Sidney Gottlieb for his gracious assistance and meticulous criticism; to John Waxman and Christopher Husted for their seasoned advice and expert help establishing contacts; to Harry Haskell for his early support; to Elisabeth Weis for sharing her remarkable knowledge of film sound; to Jacques Barzun for his inspiration and encouragement; to Seymour Solomon for recounting his vivid memories of Bernard Herrmann; to Art Paxton and George Chastain for help with images; to Sedgwick Clark for sharing his vast collection of recordings; to Jules Feiffer for his witty insights shared in our children's schoolyard; to John Fitzpatrick for information about *Spellbound;* and to David Lehman for the title. A special thanks goes to Joseph Stefano, whose amazing memory and warm friendship brought the Herrmann-Hitchcock era to life.

I am grateful to Rider University for grant support and for colleagues who helped with the project, especially Katherine Maynard, James Guimond, and Cynthia Lucia. I am indebted to the many librarians and scholars across the country and in London who helped me unearth materials; they include Kyle Barnett, Steve Wilson, David Peers, Barbara Hall, Jenny Romero, Warren Sherk, Shari Weid, Julie Heath, Tegan Kossowicz, Heather Schwartz, Carolyn Davis, and Ned Comstock.

Portions of this book have appeared in the *Chronicle of Higher Education,* the *Hitchcock Annual, Opera* magazine, and the *American Record Guide.*

OVERTURE

Alfred Hitchcock employed more musical styles and techniques than any director in history, from Marlene Dietrich singing Cole Porter in *Stage Fright* to the revolutionary electronic sound track of *The Birds*. For nearly half a century he created films full of gripping and illuminating music. *Rebecca, Spellbound, Notorious, Rear Window, Vertigo, North by Northwest,* and *Psycho* are landmarks in the history of film music, unsurpassed in their power to hypnotize and bring to life ideas and emotions that cannot be captured by dialogue and images. Hitchcock's most radical experiments— *Rope, The Wrong Man, The Birds*—redefine film music altogether. The sustained quality of his music over such a long period—from *Blackmail* in 1929 to *Family Plot* in 1976—is a unique phenomenon.

Although music is essential in Hitchcock's concept of pure cinema, it is largely unexplored. The scores to *Vertigo* and *Psycho* have certainly received attention; indeed, a remarkable consensus among moviegoers and critics holds that the collaboration between Hitchcock and Bernard Herrmann was the greatest director-composer partnership in film history. But the special connection Hitchcock had with music began much earlier, with the dawn of movie sound, and continued until his final collaboration, with John Williams.

The premise of this book is that one cannot fully understand Hitchcock's movies without facing his music. Music is an alternate language in Hitchcock, sounding his characters' unconscious thoughts as it engages our own. What follows is an exploration of its meaning and an account of how Hitchcock interacted with its creators. Based on archival material and interviews with Hitchcock's composers, writers, and actors, including John Williams, Maurice Jarre, Joseph Stefano, Teresa Wright, and Janet Leigh, this book examines not only Hitchcock's scores but all the ways he used this most elusive and personal of the arts. Many of Hitchcock's most original films make music a crucial part of the narrative—sometimes the key to the mystery—and many more comment on his musical tastes and prejudices.[1] His characters are often musicians who play or sing music central to the story, sometimes in operatic set pieces; heroes and villains alike ally themselves with songs and musical themes, much like characters in opera or musical theater.

Hitchcock changed the way we think about film music. Films like *Vertigo, Psycho,* and *The Man Who Knew Too Much* are indivisibly linked in the popular imagination with their scores; *Rebecca* and *Spellbound* were among the first to successfully use complex orchestral suites as marketing tools.[2] With lesser directors, music is often a form of hyperbole, blasting defensively onto the sound track to make up for a lack of pictorial distinction; with Hitchcock, the latter is taken for granted, and music is freed up to create its own realm of meaning, deepening or counterpointing memorable images with sounds that are far more sophisticated than what we hear in standard Hollywood scores. This phenomenon characterizes other directors who use music effectively—Curtiz, Fellini, Kubrick, and Spielberg, for example—but Hitchcock's innovations span a uniquely long period and have a dazzling variety. From the beginning, he ignored the convention that film music should stay in the background. Often its presence is so strong that it behaves like a character in the drama. In the rarely shown *Waltzes from Vienna,* a cinematic operetta about the Strauss family, he dramatized ideas about music that he would use for the next forty years. He also established a consistent pattern of shots that he would reprise in numerous films depicting orchestras and singers. Even Hitchcockians neglect *Waltzes;* here I shall try to bring it back to life.

Hitchcock rarely spoke on the record about music, but when he did, his words were incisive. Clearly, he regarded music as much more than accompaniment or an easy way to generate suspense. Like Erich Korngold, he compared film to opera. By the early 1930s, he was calling music a revolutionary medium with the potential to destroy or enhance a film, a counterpoint to the power of silence.

This book examines the full range of Hitchcock music used in his productions, including *Alfred Hitchcock Presents,* which unleashed a black humor new to television. I strongly agree with Peter Conrad in his riveting book *The Hitchcock Murders* that "anyone who is genuinely fascinated by Hitchcock will find all his work indispensable."[3] Even movies Hitchcock himself panned, like *Jamaica Inn, Stage Fright,* and *Topaz,* have superb scores and songs, impeccably woven into their textures. Rather than succumb to the temptation of covering the half-dozen films with the most famous scores, I launch into all of them. Leaving any out would be painful, and a disservice to Hitchcockians, who value detail and thoroughness.

The importance of music in Hitchcock has been acknowledged in a general or metaphorical way. The French compare Hitchcock's creation of an alternate universe of games and illusions to the state of music; the 1999 Hitchcock exhibit at the Museum of Modern Art compared his "no-accidents-permitted" storyboards to musical composition; Hitchcock himself connected his role as director to that of orchestrator and composer, commenting that he cut the picture beforehand in his imagination "just like a composer makes those little black dots to make music."[4]

Hitchcock's first image was a musical one: the frantic, spinning jazz dancer in the opening shot of *The Pleasure Garden*, his debut film from 1926. Beginning with his earliest talkies, he presented music as a mysterious force, something almost preternatural that floats over the action, influencing it for good or ill, sometimes dominating it completely. Its impact can be sexual, paternal, healing, or demonic; Orpheus's lute and Paganini's fiddle are equally resonant. Despite his reputation as a classicist, Hitchcock's vision of music was surprisingly Romantic: he felt no need to explain how a waltz travels from the villain's head to the heroine's or how the Prelude to *Tristan* playing on the radio causes a juror to have multiple epiphanies; and he did not regard having a song save a life as farfetched. Although Hitchcock's musical designs often depict an outer world of action and drama, providing a rhythm for his kinetic images—the sounds commonly associated with the "master of suspense"—the deepest, most original kind of Hitchcock music evokes inner turmoil and ambivalence, pitting subconscious desires and anxieties against behavior enacted on the screen.

If Hitchcock's underlying concept of music was Romantic, his openness to new sounds was refreshingly modern. He was knowledgeable about many kinds of music, from tonal British composers like Vaughan Williams to nontonal avant-gardists like Pierre Boulez and Karlheinz Stockhausen. Like John Cage, Hitchcock viewed music in extremely broad terms; his definition encompassed street noise, dialogue (especially voice-over), sounds of the natural world, and sonic effects of all kinds, including those produced by electronic instruments. It also included silence, the sudden, awesome absence of music, capable of delivering the most powerful musical frisson of all.

He also used every conceivable kind of dance music, among them waltzes, jazz, samba, and swing. He paid affectionate tribute to each of these even as he used them for distinctive, often ironic purposes. As early as his silent films such as *Downhill* and *The Ring*, he depicted dancers, dance halls, and stages as backdrops to disaster. Dancers and singers party on as their world crumbles beneath them, reinvoking Stephen Spender's haunting metaphor: "The war had knocked the ball-room floor from under middle-class English life. People resembled dancers suspended in mid-air yet miraculously able to pretend that they were still dancing."[5] Hitchcock's use of the dance as a cover for calamity began in England, during the period Spender was writing about, and continued in Hollywood, where it became a counterpoint to the gathering Nazi threat.

In other instances, Hitchcock adheres to the Shakespearean theme of music as healer: a close-up of a drummer's eye saves an innocent man on his way to the gallows; a song wafting up a staircase saves a child and reunites a family; a vision of flames on a ballet stage gives a trapped American agent a life-saving idea for escape; a promise of music lessons helps keep two young boys sane after their musician-father is falsely imprisoned. Hitchcock's music can go either way, toward tragedy or restoration, as can the quality of its performance: a hesitant rendering of a song can bring on violence or guilt; a confident one can restore life and sanity.

Hitchcock's career was an unending search for the right song, whether a serenade, a music-hall ditty, a cabaret routine, a carousel tune, or a rock track. These are an essential part of his atmosphere, characterization, and story line. The attempt to find a felicitous song often resulted in tense behind-the-scenes negotiations and confrontations, many of which have never been recounted; they are an important piece of Hitchcock's commitment to creating a compelling sound world and a barometer of the increasing corporate pressure he found himself under as movies entered the modern era. Many of these searches ended in failure, though not necessarily to the detriment of the film; others resulted in successes that were the movie's crowning glory.

Hitchcock used the best composers of his various eras, among them Arthur Benjamin, Franz Waxman, Miklos Rozsa, Roy Webb, Alfred Newman, Richard Addinsell, Hugo W. Friedhofer, Dimitri Tiomkin, Bernard Herrmann, Maurice Jarre, and John Williams. How these artists collaborated or fought with him is part of this story. Critics tend to ignore or dismiss Hitchcock's music, but composers viewed his involvement with their art as deep and intense. Herrmann stated that there were only "a handful of directors like Hitchcock who really know the score and fully realize the importance of its relationship to a film"; Williams said that Hitchcock's mastery of music was a boon to all film composers. That Hitchcock knew the score is evident in his involvement in the earliest stages of the scoring process, providing his composers with detailed, sometimes witty music notes, an unveiling of which constitutes a significant part of this book. Hitchcock scores were often the defining moments in his composers' careers. That many of them were fellow émigrés was a subtle advantage: the rich blend of Hollywood glamour and European formality is precisely in tune with Hitchcock's sensibility and with the films themselves—with their casting, story lines, and Hitchcockian combination of Old World sophistication and New World brashness.

His music presents a fascinating tension between calculation and freedom, fanatical preparation and breakneck creativity. His work with composers resembled his method with actors, which, according to James Stewart, Hitchcock described as "planned spontaneity." After elaborate calculation and storyboarding, "he preferred to let the actor figure things out for himself. . . . Hitchcock believed that if you sit down with an actor and analyze a scene you run the danger that the actor will act the scene with his head rather than his heart, or guts."[6] It was much the same with music. Some of the richest scores were written the most quickly, under fantastic pressure, but only after Hitchcock made the concept forcefully clear. Others were brought to fruition only after behind-the-scenes machinations and close calls. Using detailed music notes, Hitchcock plotted sounds, effects, musical emotions, and even technical devices, then let the composer "figure things out for himself." This legendary control addict knew when to get out of the way.

But not always. His opinions about music were so specific and his need for control so large that he sometimes fought bitterly with composers. He quarreled with Franz Waxman on the set of *Rear Window,* angrily rejected Henry Mancini's score for *Frenzy,* and fired Bernard Herrmann in front of their colleagues, a tragic severance that ended a mutually enriching collaboration and a drama of clashing egos that I explore in this book. Yet with others he was so serene and sunny that the music process seemed like an extension of endless dinners and wine tastings; Chasens and other Hitchcock hangouts became the composer's conference room. Whether stormy or smooth, these relationships produced decisive music. *Psycho* might never have appeared on the big screen had its composer not insisted that Hitchcock listen to the terrifying, secretly composed shower cue; *Spellbound* reached a mass audience through advance radio broadcasts of the theremin-haunted score and championing by Leopold Stokowski.

Although this book is not a psychoanalytical exploration, it is fair to assume that Hitchcock's music reflects his own psychological conundrums as well as his characters'. As Donald Spoto eloquently shows in *The Dark Side of Genius,* Hitchcock was a complex person afflicted with doubts, phobias, and anxieties that he projected in his art; the blocked desire of Roy Webb's *Notorious,* the longing and loneliness of Bernard Herrmann's *Vertigo,* and the claustrophobic anxiety of the same composer's *The Wrong Man* were expressions of Hitchcock's inner turmoil. With source music and electronic sound—the macabre jocularity of Gounod's "March of a Marionette," the impassioned panic of Tchaikovsky's *Francesca da Rimini,* the sinister chatter of *The Birds*—he could express his emotions more directly.

I have been greatly influenced by *Hitchcock/Truffaut,* François Truffaut's book-length interview with Hitchcock. Truffaut established once and for all that Hitchcock was an artist as well as an entertainer, and his insights into Hitchcock's films are more acute than anyone's. This compulsively readable book has a surprising number of musical ideas, many articulated for the first time. I have also, since I was very young, followed Royal S. Brown's innovative work on Bernard Herrmann, especially his pieces in *High Fidelity* magazine and his authoritative program notes. Another important resonance from the past is Donald Spoto's spellbinding Hitchcock class, which I was fortunate enough to take at the New School for Social Research in 1974, and which planted the seed of my own Hitchcock work.

The organization of this book is both chronological and topical, the latter occasionally interrupting the former; Hitchcock tended to make movies in pairs or threes, with musical strategies to match, but since he was so prolific, other projects often intervened. I have tried to incorporate this pattern by organizing the 1940s wartime dramas and the films incorporating waltzes in their own chapters (to cite two examples), even though doing so violates strict chronology. In general, I have presented the movies in chronological order. Hitchcock was involved with music for so long that it seems essential to tell the story from the beginning; there is a deepening musical richness and subtlety reflected in more detailed music notes as he gains experience with composers and new technologies, even though his themes and obsessions remained constant.

This is a book about Hitchcock for those who want to experience his work from a different point of view—to listen as well as watch. It is not about movie composers, though their careers and dealings with Hitchcock are an important part of the story. Nor is it about scores or harmonic analyses, though musicians will, I hope, find it interesting. I have pitched it to all who love Hitchcock, whether general readers and moviegoers or academics.

Hitchcock is unusual in that he appeals to both intellectuals and a larger public. My students, whatever their majors, revere Hitchcock and instantly recognize the shower cue from *Psycho,* a film they uniquely regard as a classic, not as a stuffy old movie; my colleagues in the literary world who sniff at the notion of taking movies seriously make an exception in Hitchcock's case. Jacques Barzun, normally skeptical about film, told me he regarded Hitchcock as "highly intelligent," one of the few directors "whose work holds up." Cynthia Ozick is "not even sure movies are art" but believes that in this case "the music is artful."

It is ironic that literary people applaud a moviemaker who had such a profound skepticism about language. A product of the silent era, Alfred Hitchcock distrusted words but came to trust music; it spoke a language deeper than dialogue, allowing the world of obsession and longing, his favorite subject, to have its say. Music "can tell you what people are thinking and feeling," observed Bernard Herrmann, who worked with Hitchcock over a greater length of time than any other composer, "and that is the real function of music. The whole recognition scene of *Vertigo,* for example, is eight minutes of cinema without dialogue or sound effects—just music and picture. I remember Hitchcock said to me, 'Well, music will do better than words here.'"[7] It does better in dozens of other Hitchcock films as well.

1

the music starts

Play something!
—The circus manager following the trapeze suicide in *Murder!*

John Williams, the last composer to work with Alfred Hitchcock, has stated that music is a key ingredient in Hitchcock's work, indeed, "almost his signature pattern."[1] In *Blackmail*, Hitchcock's first movie with sound, that pattern is already dramatically present.[2] This revolutionary 1929 film, which he called a silent talkie, was among the first to blend sound and visual techniques in a personal, sustained, and sophisticated manner that became an intrinsic part of the atmosphere, psychology, and action.

Coming only a year after Sergei Eisenstein's hotly debated "Statement" on film sound, *Blackmail* exemplified many of this director's principles. Eisenstein declared that "the dream of a sound film has come true" but cautioned that "photographed performances of a theatrical sort" would "destroy the culture of montage." He warned that "every adhesion of sound to a visual montage piece increases its inertia." Eisenstein's manifesto called for a dynamic, nonimitative interaction between what the audience sees and hears. Only a "contrapuntal use of sound in relation to the visual montage piece" would "give the necessary palpability which will lead to the creation of an orchestral counterpoint of visual and aural images."[3]

Eisenstein's swipe at "photographed performances" bears a startling resemblance to Hitchcock's well-known aversion to "photographs of people talking." Eisenstein's insistence on "orchestral counterpoint" rather than "adhesion" was Hitchcockian as well. In *Blackmail*, even scenes that initially appear to be mere talking photographs are elaborately contrapuntal: the

1

opening talkie sequence has the heroine saying one thing, the restaurant music another, the suggestive glances at her secret admirer from across the room still another. As we shall see, this kind of complex interaction is a hallmark of the film, especially in the "Miss Up to Date" musical murder and the famous breakfast knife scene.

Just as Hitchcock learned the art of visuals from German expressionists in the 1920s, he picked up musical traits from the same aesthetic: looming shadows, tilted angles, sinister staircases, high-contrast lighting, and anxious close-ups are paralleled by discordant harmonies, astringent orchestration, nervous silences, sudden dynamic contrasts, minimalist chord repetitions, and spectral pizzicato. Expressionist modernism is powerfully present in chromatic ascending scales that take us up a nightmarish Hitchcockian staircase; in a tremulous high pedal as the landlady who discovers the body frantically calls the police; in the quavery organ that slinks with the heroine into her bed after the crime; in the crazed repetitions of the main title theme during the "Wanted" poster montage and the chase up the dome of the British museum. This vivid, original soundscape, created before the establishment of movie-music clichés, became a template for Hitchcock's musical experiments throughout the next five decades.

Blackmail's score evokes the world of Alban Berg, Arnold Schoenberg, and early Kurt Weill, especially Weill's symphonies and Schoenberg's "Music for a Cinematographic Scene." Only when he began working for Gaumont in the mid-1930s did Hitchcock, with Louis Levy as his musical director, begin using a more British musical language, with firmer harmonies and Elgarian rhetoric. In all these styles, the fundamental way that sound and silence interact with imagery—from the most Romantic to the most avant-garde scores—is consistent. Despite inevitably crude moments (given British cinema technology in 1929), the music in *Blackmail* is already thoroughly Hitchcockian, not only in the basic contrapuntal approach but in numerous details. Scholars marvel at how many characteristic touches— the amusing cameo, the Hitchcock blonde, the transfer of guilt, the wrongman theme, the young female point of view, the conflict between love and duty, the climactic chase on a public monument, indeed, the whole Hitchcockian world of sex and suspense—were already present in this silent talkie. The same wonder holds for music. *Blackmail* unveils an array of Hitchcockian signatures, including musical irony, vertiginous arpeggios, fateful chimes, unresolved chord chains, popular song as a narrative device, and a dreamlike merging of real music with the invisible score.

Blackmail even has distinctive Hitchcockian instrumental touches: a demonic use of the (normally) celestial harp, creepy organ sonorities, dis-appearing brass fanfares, and distant timpani to announce a death. Also typical is Hitchcock's immersion in the vanguard musical styles of the pe-riod, in this case Noël Cowardesque pop combined with expressionist clas-sical, so that the music is an exact reflection of the cultural moment, even though it never sounds dated. Most striking of all is Hitchcock's uncanny use of music to establish a subjective point of view, a one-to-one correspon-dence between sound and psyche as tightly organized as opera.

Hitchcock was fortunate to get a unified effect from his production team. The experimental hybrid in *Blackmail* was the combined effort of composer Henry Stafford and arranger Hubert Bath.[4] The gruffly effective performance was by the British Symphony Orchestra conducted by John Reynders, who would go on to write the music for *Murder!* and conduct the rich and strange panoply of sounds in *Rich and Strange*. The prelude to *Blackmail*'s violence, "Miss Up to Date," was written by Billy Mayerl and Frank Eyton for a Cyril Ritchard stage vehicle, *Love Lies*. Hitchcock's film appeared the same year as the play, and the song is therefore up-to-date in-deed, as Hitchcock always insisted his pop songs should be.[5]

It is difficult to pin down Hitchcock's exact contribution and degree of control in the final musical mix, especially given the lack of archival mater-ial on music in British Hitchcock.[6] Nonetheless, the musical patterns are so astonishingly consistent with Hitchcockian music in later films—music frequently cued by Hitchcock's extensive, immaculately preserved music notes—that it is reasonable to assume he controlled a great deal. Movies are a collaborative enterprise, of course, but the Hitchcock musical universe, using a variety of composers and songwriters over five decades, has a com-pelling unity. However his films got created, through whatever combina-tion of accident, improvisation, and preplanning, Hitchcock's musical pat-tern is unique. "It's *there*," said Elizabeth Weis, author of *The Silent Scream*, and its palpability is the important element; the issue of precisely how it got there may well remain a mystery, at least in the British films.[7]

The opening combination of imagery and music, a hubcap spinning with tense discords, is the first instance of a design Hitchcock would con-tinue to favor, most strikingly in the wheels of the grim police van in *The Wrong Man* and the spirals and arpeggios of *Vertigo*. Whirling anxiety linked with a circular visual element is therefore apparent from the begin-ning of Hitchcock's music. Also present in this debut score is music that re-lies on disorienting harmonies and angular motifs rather than melody. The harmonies are tonal, but barely so. Like the deceptively ordinary lives of

Hitchcock's characters, the tonal center feels a bit unstable, as if it could disintegrate at any moment. The Hitchcockian world of normality about to collapse is given a powerful musical voice.

What we hear during the documentary-style arrest and booking scenes in the film's "silent" opening has a Weillian starkness. The anxious main theme follows a speeding police van with swirling strings and spitting trumpets over a brass chorale that strives upward, then disintegrates into fragments. This is an early version of Hitchcockian chase music, a burst of kinetic energy that sputters and dies out. Here, it lurches to half speed with tense pizzicato and a mournful oboe as police invade the suspect's dingy flat. When they grab his gun, the music erupts into what seems a climax, then collapses into a desolate timpani roll. Surrounded, the doomed man dresses to the strains of a melancholy cello. He may well be guilty, but the tragic music makes us sympathize with him nonetheless, an early example of Hitchcock humanizing the villain. As the prisoner is taken outside, the title theme reappears in terse fragments, continuing through the trip to Scotland Yard, the interrogation, the lineup, and the booking. At the moment the prisoner is locked in his cell, the chorale returns in a claustrophobic variation that plummets into darkness.

Then, for the first time in British film history, the characters suddenly, miraculously, start talking. The silent movie is over, the talkie begins. Always fascinated by new technology, Hitchcock could not bear to wait until the next project to use sound. Once it became available in 1929, in the middle of shooting *Blackmail*, he was compelled to exploit it immediately.[8] Already, in his first talkie sequence, dialogue and music counterpoint what we see on the screen rather than imitating it. As the police chatter moves into the restroom, the music is transformed into a perky, major-key variation on the main theme, a moment of Orwellian irony in which music establishes a distance between the characters and their harrowing profession: the talk is cheery and banal, about tailors and business transactions, far removed from the grim business we have just witnessed. This toilet could just as easily be in a pub as in Scotland Yard. As the camera moves toward the introductory shots of Alice and Frank, the music fades and vanishes, without resolution or cadence.

Already we are witness to many of Hitchcock's musical preferences: lonely solos where we might expect dramatic climaxes, anguished harmonies when a character is locked in a cell, ironic cheer in the most cheerless situations. The opening scene with the lead characters inaugurates a Hitchcock tradition as well. As he would do in *Rich and Strange, Rebecca,*

Notorious, North by Northwest, and many other films, Hitchcock uses restaurant music in the beginning of the narrative as a blandly ironic backdrop to deceit and betrayal. Alice White, the beautiful young working-class heroine played by Annie Ondra, is shown in profile with her detective boyfriend, Frank, on location at Lyons Corner House, waiting for Cyril Ritchard's character, Crewe, a secret admirer, to show up at the restaurant so she can sneak away with him. "Girl of My Dreams," a popular song crooned by a jilted lover, is the tune playing in the restaurant—a deft ironic touch. Alice's catty back-and-forth manipulations and Frank's mounting exasperation are depicted against a sudsy backdrop of strings, giving the scene a special brittleness and tension. When Frank leaves the restaurant in disgust, the music stops, but when he sees Alice and Crewe coming out the door together, it wafts out into the street with them until the door closes, a bitter coda for Frank.

Alice goes away with Crewe, an artist from a different social class, someone she doesn't know how to read. Her naïveté versus the audience's awareness of her vulnerability is signified by increasingly ominous music, a counterpoint to the gathering shadows on Crewe's face. "I know instinctively if I can trust a man," she says, but as she climbs Crewe's dark staircase, a chromatic scale suggests otherwise. Once she is in his studio, he sits at the piano and sings "Miss Up to Date," a song Cyril Ritchard himself performed in 1929, the first instance of Hitchcock's fondness for working a central musical theme into the narrative by casting a singer or musician—for example, Marlene Dietrich in *Stage Fright* or Bernard Herrmann and Doris Day in the remake of *The Man Who Knew Too Much.* Hitchcock opts for popular song over "scary" suspense music, a technique that would reverberate through the next several decades in astonishing ways: redemptively in *Rear Window* and the 1956 *Man Who Knew Too Much,* ironically in *Saboteur* and *The Birds,* malevolently in *Shadow of a Doubt* and *Strangers on a Train.*

Here we have a forecast of all these methods: played twice, with piano riffs between the two performances, the song first seems to brighten the tone of the scene but gradually becomes a sinister prelude to Crewe's assault. The scene illustrates Hitchcock's early ability to manipulate music in a thoroughly cinematic way, matching a musical design with a visual one; Crewe creates a musical portrait of Alice as he guides her through the sketching of a nude self-portrait.[9] His mounting excitement and aggression in his musical performance is in tune with his manipulation of Alice's sketch of the "naughty child" in the song lyric.

The song goes through telling transformations. At first, "Miss Up to

Date" offers welcome relief from the brittle score, but we soon realize that its fizz is all on the surface. In a breezy prelude, Crewe whistles the tune, accompanied by Alice playing a piano scale. He then plays a rendition full of music-hall exuberance; if this is a come-on, it is charming and inviting, not aggressive. Indeed, the two make gleeful eyes at each other across the keyboard, much as they did in the restaurant. "You're absolutely great, Miss up to date," croons Crewe, "and that's a song about you, my dear." It is about her indeed: the song accurately characterizes her as flirtatious, willing to take chances, a bit duplicitous, basically childlike.

Alice seems charmed by Crewe's musical portrait. Changing into a girlish costume at his skillful coaxing, she fails to get the hint. The audience, however, watches Crewe's cheery smile transform into a shadowy leer as he steals her clothes. When he plants an unwanted kiss, she finally gets it, pulling away and insisting, "I'd better go." But Crewe's next performance implies that he is not about to allow her to. This rendition of "Miss Up to Date," the terrible turning point in the scene, abandons lyrics; he flails at the tune with quickening tempo, aggressive body motion, and a decidedly less delicate touch. By the end of this demented solo, he is banging, betraying his longing and impatience. As he would do in *Young and Innocent* and *Rope,* Hitchcock uses an out-of-control musical performance as a signifier of violence, either past or to come. The playing is ugly, obsessively repetitive, interrupted by outside car horns. Alice begins to panic after this performance, but it is too late. Crewe concludes the song by pounding a cluster in the bass, a startling dissonance rather than a triumphant flourish, ripping apart the illusory cheeriness of the scene and setting up his assault.

In a startling contrast, the behind-the-curtain knifing, silent and unseen, has no music at all. From the beginning, Hitchcock knew the power of silence, of counterpointing music with emptiness. As Alice defends herself behind the curtain, a scene presented solely as a gigantic shadow on the wall, the silence continues. We hear only her screams, providing their own expressionist "music" before Crewe's lifeless arm thrusts out from behind the curtain, much like the anguished cries in the sound montage in *The 39 Steps* and the Statue of Liberty finale of *Saboteur.* (Even in *Psycho,* Hitchcock wanted Janet Leigh's screeches to have no music; he laid in Bernard Herrmann's iconic music only at the last minute.)

Immediately after the killing, the music takes us from outside the action into Alice's head. The unforgettable image of the traumatized heroine staggering in slow motion with the knife, unable to take in what she has done, is caressed first by a delicate, enchanted version of Crewe's song, a daring way

"Miss Up to Date." The debut of Hitchcockian opera.

of registering Alice's bewilderment and shock through musical irony. As the jester on the easel mocks her disaster, Hitchcock delivers his first intrusion of source music into a score: the fake-cheery motif of "Miss Up to Date" is heard as distant, bleak piano notes that infiltrate the orchestra, becoming a recurring wind tune; originally in a major key, "Miss Up to Date" darkens into somber diminished chords and anxious whole-tone scales. The lonely piano sounds originate in Alice's haunted psyche, linking the violence with its warning in the song and its aftermath in her numbed brain as she attempts to dress.

As she staggers from Crewe's flat and creeps back down the stairs, icy chord clusters, macabre pizzicato notes, and shivery string tremolos merge with insistent car horns, a realism effect Hitchcock would continue to favor. She moves trancelike into the street, the blackmailer's shadow looming over her—one more nightmarish indication that her life will never be the same. Her one decisive act is to obliterate her signature under her nude sketch; that "naughty child" identity is forever gone, along with her musical portrait in the upbeat, music-hall version of "Miss Up to Date."

In 1929, Hitchcock's music was thus already an organic part of a psychodrama rather than an outside effect or accompaniment. Alice's distraught mind conjures this increasingly tragic version of "Miss Up to Date" and links it with surreal images: the cocktail billboard in Piccadilly Circus that becomes a stabbing knife, the actual hand that transforms into that of the dead Crewe, the jostling crowds that dissolve into transparent ghosts. In a sardonic moment, a "COMEDY" marquee mocks her in the same manner as the jeering jester, an image made more bitter by a suddenly cheerful variation on her fatal song.

These hallucinated visions move through the street as Alice begins her all-night journey through London's West End, a cinematic descent into the underworld. She wanders through a mist of posttraumatic shock, drifting on the notes of a spectral nocturne that blends "Miss Up to Date" with snatches of the title music in creepy counterpoint. Now she will become a hunted criminal, much like the anonymous suspect whose arrest is signaled by the doom-laden theme. "Miss Up to Date" has become distorted into repeating, unresolved fragments that wind and unwind obsessively, monotonously, a vicious circle that merges with the repetitious patterns of the main title.

Only for a moment does Hitchcock relieve the claustrophobic subjectivity: an aerial shot of London in a foggy dawn. This brief omniscience is turned into delicate poetry by a seductive harp glissando, much like the "Dawn" cue in *Vertigo,* also a moment of repose in the midst of death and madness. These gripping sounds and images combine with the somber ringing of Big Ben, a pealing that would continue to clang through Hitchcock's movies; they culminate in Alice's scream transforming into that of the concierge, who discovers Crewe's body, a sound montage that springs from Alice's confusing a memory of Crewe's limp hand with that of a sleeping derelict.

Blackmail's psychological and musical transferences are so fluid that the famous knife montage emerges organically rather than as a sudden gimmick. This early experiment in sound was an avant-garde musical concept that anticipated by two years the symphony of noises in the opening of Rouben Mamoulian's *Love Me Tonight,* not to mention the scoreless "music" for the train scenes in *The Lady Vanishes,* the factory sequence in *The Secret Agent,* and the entirety of *The Birds.* The voice of the gossipy cockney woman describing the murder, spoiling Alice's already unpleasant breakfast, is essentially a pedal point over which a disturbing "note" is played in crescendo, as Hitchcock implied in an interview: "As her voice went on, it became a drone, but the clearest word was 'knife' all the time, and it was played over the girl's face."[10] A close-up of Alice's twitching brow and rolling eyes as she tries to handle the breakfast knife cues subjective musical effects evoked from the woman's rambling soliloquy: "Knives is not right, That's what I think, and that's what I feel. . . . Whatever the provocation, I could never use a knife. . . . A knife is a difficult thing to handle." From here on, the speech is a series of inaudible babblings punctuated by the clearly articulated "knife!" rising in a terrifying crescendo, culminating in a traumatic screech that causes Alice's knife to fly out of her hand and the audience to jump out of its seat. "You might have cut somebody, Alice," says her father, in an apt coda.

These subjective effects continue in the unnerving "bing!" that announces "another customer, Alice"; in the unnaturally loud birds singing in her morning bedroom scene—the first instance of sinister bird sounds in Hitchcock; in the terrible silence when Frank produces the gloves ("For God's sake, Alice, say something!"); and in all the other instances where *Blackmail* unveils a troubled sound track of the subconscious. What we hear is real, at least at first, but Alice reinvents and distorts sounds from her frantic point of view, much as Jeffries does when Thorwald ascends the stairs with fortissimo thuds in the finale of *Rear Window*.

Before his spectacular death, the blackmailer Tracy contributes one more type of music that would become a Hitchcock signature: the jeering, insistent whistling of a cocky villain. Tracy whistles "The Best Things in Life Are Free," a sarcastic jibe as Alice serves him breakfast, but the joke turns out to be on him: Tracy pays dearly for his free meal and cigar, becoming the rare instance of a Hitchcock "wrong man" who is actually hunted down and killed. Tracy's doomed whistle contrasts with Frank's confident whistling of Al Jolson's "Sonny Boy," a troubling juxtaposition given that the representative of law and order covers up for the real killer.

Hitchcock originally wanted *Blackmail* to end with Frank booking Alice, recapitulating the arrest scene in the opening. This ending, in addition to delivering perfect cinematic symmetry, would have provided one more opportunity for an inventive variation on the music in the first booking and fingerprinting. He was prevented from doing so by what he called the "disciples of the happy end," producers who worried the coda would be too downbeat and uncommercial.[11] The conclusion Hitchcock created under duress is still far from cheery. Alice will continue obsessing about a crime she committed in self-defense: "I was defending myself . . . I didn't know what I was doing!" She must repress the truth as part of the cover-up perpetrated by her detective boyfriend.

In an early piece of Hitchcockian musical symmetry, the dizzying arpeggios that spin the movie into motion during the chase-arrest scene also wind it down. But Alice's haunted mind will spin on, despite the red-herring death of her blackmailer, Tracy, announced by muffled timpani as he falls through a glass dome of the British Museum. The vicious circle in Hitchcock, a Poe-like musical design connoting a mental maelstrom, would continue to spiral into the collapsing waltz in *Young and Innocent,* the "Merry Widow" dancers in *Shadow of a Doubt,* the repeating theremin in *Spellbound,* the convoluted "love" theme in *Strangers on a Train,* the obsessive spirals in *Vertigo,* the lost highway in *Psycho.* The human psyche spinning its wheels, a central Hitchcockian concept, was set in motion by Hitchcock's music in 1929.

Blackmail ends with a volley of forced laughter that resembles the banal joking in the first talkie scene. "Did she tell you who did it?" asks Frank's older colleague. "Yes, she did" is Frank's factual answer. "Look out, you'll be losing your job, my boy," the questioner continues, blurting out awkward jokes about "lady detectives" that Alice must pretend to find funny. Her uneasy laughter becomes excruciating when the jester, carried by workmen, gloats at her one more time. Irony and Eisensteinian counterpoint continue right to the end. Even in the final fade-out, Hitchcock's music repudiates imitation; "The End" appears over fake laughs and an effulgent, obscenely inappropriate version of "Miss Up to Date," now for full orchestra. The music delivers an ironic cadence, a promise of closure unsupported by the images and the rest of the sound track.

For Hitchcock's new identity as a musical manipulator of emotion, *Blackmail* was only the beginning, an auspicious debut that became a template for further experiments. His basic drama of sudden catastrophe, repressed guilt, and blocked emotion—all cued by a haunted interior music—would continue to resonate throughout his career.

FROM *TRISTAN* TO TRAIN WHISTLES: EARLY EXPERIMENTS IN SOUND

The riveting musical experiments inaugurated in *Blackmail* continued in *Murder!, Number 17,* and other early talkies. *Murder!,* Hitchcock's most overtly Shakespearean film, is the most satisfying of these, as well as the earliest example of music functioning as an independent force that hovers over the action and shapes its outcome.

Murder! commences with Beethoven, collapses into band-music cacophony, and ends with schmaltz that turns out to be a devious joke. The main title is Beethoven's Fifth Symphony, which Hitchcock would bring back in *Saboteur,* where the famous victory motif would again signify a struggle against injustice and adversity. As the credits roll, the first movement segues into the scherzo taken at a slow, sinister tempo, forecasting the many harrowing moments before the last-minute happy ending.

The precision of art versus the chaos of life, a theme Hitchcock pursued throughout his career, is enacted throughout this dark yet curiously sentimental drama about a juror who falls in love with the accused, then, after helping convict her, uses his skills as a professional actor to get her off the hook. This is a movie full of self-references and intertextual jokes. Herbert Marshall's actor-hero Sir John asserts that for this life crisis "art for once can bring its technique to bear." By reenacting act 3, scene 3, of *Hamlet*, a play within a play that catches a villain, Sir John enlists drama to fool the real criminal, solve the crime, and get the girl. At the end, he is able to say to the self-incriminating villain: "Mr. Fane, you've forgotten your script," an eerie premonition of the detective's final line in *Frenzy:* "Mr. Rusk, you're not wearing your tie."

Sir John gets the idea from a previous role, "what the critics would call a highbrow shocker," precisely what *Murder!* is. Because it's Hitchcock, who always focuses on the interior drama, the play within a play is "the inner history of the Baring case." This is an artful version of the real drama, which is chaotic, tedious, and inartistic. "The law has no sense of drama," says Sir John, despairingly.

But Hitchcock gives the Baring case all the drama it needs, including Wagnerian music-drama. The most memorable touch is Hitchcock's employment of *Tristan,* establishing an "inner history" through music and inaugurating a storytelling device more compelling than words. It happens as Sir John is shaving in front of a mirror, pondering the guilty verdict he was so instrumental in obtaining. This is a vivid example of Hitchcock the modernist, creating a revelation from something resolutely ordinary. Sir John hears the Prelude to *Tristan and Isolde* playing on the radio, its swelling suspensions filling him with mysterious, guilty passion. Wagner's music, surely the most sensuous ever written, forces Sir John to confront the wrenching reality that he has convicted a woman to whom he is intensely attracted: "That manner of hers . . . very attractive," says his voice-over, with British propriety. Wagner is more explicit.

But rather than blinding him, as love traditionally does, this eruption of passion brings him to devastating truth, forcing him to see Diana in a clear light, both legally and erotically. Raising a glass at the precise moment Wagner's strings move toward their exquisitely unresolved climax, he remembers Diana's adamant insistence that she didn't drink the incriminating brandy, even though she wasn't sure she committed the murder. "Whoever drank that brandy?" blurts his voice-over, by now a vocal obbligato, its crescendo in sync with Wagner's.

This Wagnerian stream of consciousness, a new mode of cinematic revelation, does not end with the moment of truth. The radio continues playing as Sir John frantically scribbles a note, his epiphany souring into self-blame: "Why did I send her away?" By now, *Tristan* has ceased behaving as an internal storyteller and is acting like a score, its resolute irresolution mirroring agitation and excited dialogue. But unlike a score, it is heard by the character, altering his consciousness and behavior as well as establishing atmosphere and tension for the audience. It becomes all-enveloping, as Wagnerian music-drama should.

Hitchcock would return to *Tristan and Isolde* twenty-eight years later in *Vertigo,* in which Bernard Herrmann's *Tristan*-haunted score would become an emblem for doomed love. *Murder!,* however, is tragicomedy with a last-minute upbeat ending; *Tristan* begins in Sir John's shaving scene as a signifier of painful longing, as it should, but moves the drama through moral ambiguity toward light and resolution, uniting the lovers rather than presiding over their doom. This scene was the launching pad for other source-music revelations, many using radios, in movies as diverse as *Young and Innocent, Saboteur,* and *Rear Window,* all of which would elevate the status of source music to that of a score.

Most important, it was Hitchcock's first treatment of music as a powerful, mysterious force, for good or ill. Here, as in Shakespeare, it is a bearer of truth and a restorer of order. This occurs not only in the radio epiphany but in the climactic trapeze suicide. "Play something!" shouts the circus manager to the band leader following this traumatic scene; without music, the screams of the horrified circus fans, like those of the music-hall audience in the last scene of *The 39 Steps,* would be intolerable. When the band commences, it transforms horror into healing, as a revelatory letter reading rescues the falsely accused heroine just in time to avoid the gallows.

It is fascinating to watch Hitchcock's careful but dramatic sonic experiments in his early talkies. The shaving scene comes a year after the innovation in *Blackmail* in which Alice is haunted by piano fragments of "Miss Up to Date" following her crime. There the music is purely subjective, a memory rather than something heard on-screen in the present moment. Even so, the motif begins as Cyril Ritchard's piano source music before uniting with Hubert Bath's score. In *Murder!,* Hitchcock took the use of actual music a decisive step further.

Despite the crude production values of early British cinema, Hitchcock was playing with all manner of subtle transferences between scores and real sounds, psyches and musical associations. In these scenes, he could manipulate sounds rather than give up control to a composer. In *Murder!* these include ominous chimes followed by screams and a little girl practicing piano with excruciating inaccuracy as Sir John begins the decidedly awkward process of trying to rescue the woman he has helped condemn. In the mock-sentimental ending, a schmaltzy score accompanies Sir John and Diana, finally united, as the camera pulls back to reveal that it is really source music after all: a theater performance with applause, a curtain, a timpani roll, and a final cadence. "This is not a play," Sir John has always insisted; "this is life." By now, the two are delightfully intertwined.

Hitchcock's love of theater would continually manifest itself in films with stages, music halls, plays within plays, and depictions of orchestras. His next attempt at bringing these elements together would be *Waltzes from Vienna*, in 1933. Between *Murder!* and *Waltzes*, he found himself in a holding pattern, with a series of flops that offer scant music. (The same year as *Murder!*, he collaborated in a British musical revue, *Ellstree Calling*, but directed the bridging segments rather than the musical numbers.) Nonetheless, when music does appear, it is surprisingly compelling. A deceptively pastoral waltz opens the tragic Galsworthian class warfare in *The Skin Game*, one that dissipates into a bleak silence broken only by sounds of aggression and dislocation: screaming landlords, blaring horns, barking dogs, bleating sheep, and the final ugly sound of a tree being felled. Like *Juno and the Paycock* from two years earlier, this is more of a filmed play than a drama re-created cinematically. *The Skin Game* was an ill-fated project in every way. During Hitchcock's visit to Galsworthy's country estate, Mrs. Galsworthy asked him what music he liked. "Wagner," he replied, still immersed in *Tristan;* "he's so melodramatic." "Oh, no," sniffed Mrs. Galsworthy, "we like Bach."[12]

Number 17, a thriller burlesque, is far more entertaining. A. Hallis's score is a danse macabre full of spectral pizzicato, crunching strings, multiple stinger chords, and sinister midnight chimes, a Gothic fun house that admirably suits *Number 17*'s thunder, howling wind, creepy shadows, vanishing corpses, and expressionist staircases. In the breathless train-race finale, the score vanishes, leaving explosions, piercing whistles, and clattery railroad percussion, the *mécanique* effects Hitchcock would continue to mine in *The Lady Vanishes* and other train thrillers: noise music par excellence.

Hitchcock had not yet hit upon the precise romance-comedy-suspense formula that would make his career; *Blackmail, Murder!* and *Number 17* are fascinating precisely because they are eccentric, daredevil experiments. After the last, Hitchcock took an intermission from suspense altogether in a gloriously odd excursion into tragicomedy followed by a Viennese operetta.

RICH AND STRANGE: "I WANT LIFE!"

The music in *Rich and Strange,* Hitchcock's quirkiest, most original comedy, is exactly what the title promises. Rich in every conceivable type of music—symphonic, burlesque, ragtime, pop, and much else, erupting on and off camera—this strange little gem is a kaleidoscope of sound and fury signifying who knows what? The meaning of this movie's gloomy exuberance is much debated by the few who have seen it, but it leaves a greater residue of enigma than many of Hitchcock's serious masterworks. A voyage of discovery following a vicious circle, it is full of light and black humor, absurdly amorous escapades, and oddly humiliating epiphanies. The music is as hard to pin down as the tone and narrative: this is a romantic comedy, but it offers little straightforward love music; nor does the music cue the laughs (Hitchcock being far too shrewd to fall into that cliché). The best gags—the drunken bedtime prayer scene, the surreal menu presented during Fred's seasickness—are without music.

Hitchcock's music is associated with thriller effects. But the comedies, underrated in other ways as well, provided fertile ground for some of the master's most original sonic experiments. (It should not be forgotten that the first and most unusual Bernard Herrmann score was *The Trouble with Harry.*) In *Rich and Strange,* music is released from its traditional mission to set the mood; instead, it provides ironic commentary and counterpoint, "speaking" slyly to the audience during the many scenes without dialogue that seem to invade the screen from Hitchcock's silent era. Occasionally, it assumes an utterly self-contained life quite separate from the mise-en-scène. Hitchcock would continue to explore these effects with increasing subtlety, culminating in comic masterpieces like *North by Northwest* and *Rear Window.*

A tragicomedy that flirts with disaster before a provisional happy ending, *Rich and Strange* feels experimental from beginning to end. It is often close to silent film, a category always congenial to Hitchcock's most dazzling musical innovations. The opening is stunning: an exotic, romantic title theme by Hal Dolphe (a.k.a. A. Hallis) evaporates into the chimes of Big Ben, a favorite Hitchcock sound, then crashes into dissonance as the camera cranes down into the hero's workplace: a pen in close-up scrawls down an accounting ledger, workers chained to partitioned desks suddenly barrel downstairs at six o'clock, the camera following them without cuts, then flying ahead to view them from outside the window, their frantic scurryings made more so by mad, Antheilian *ballet mécanique* music. Low woodwinds snort, announcing rain; string glissandos sweep open umbrellas in pairs, all except our hero's, which refuses to open. The music rises and topples on itself as the mob surges into the tube station from the point of view of the train swerving into the station. Inside the train, the camera crowds in with the workers to claustrophobic chords as Fred whacks his fellow passenger in the face with a newspaper and watches a man gnawing a sandwich; the camera then looks up with Fred to a succession of banal ads, then down at his newspaper: "Are You Satisfied with Your Present Circumstances?" A wistful close-up of Fred accompanied by a bittersweet brass chorale tells us the answer to this cruel question. Arriving home exhausted, to rows of interchangeable suburban houses, Fred finally opens his umbrella successfully, and the sweet strings from the opening return, adding a snippet of "Home Sweet Home." By now, we don't believe a note of it: it's all mockery.

This Hitchcockian ballet is one of his most original openings. There is no dialogue, just an Ivesian collage of impressionist, Romantic, and pop-song motifs leading a queasy succession of images. It takes the breath away—but what is the tone? The frenetic topplings and circlings are a bleak portrait of the modern workforce, but we also get a winning energy and charm from Fred's mock-heroic attempts to open his umbrella; his weary tenacity is beguiling, like the relentlessly cheery music that moves him through claustrophobic space.

But this is a talking picture, after all; once the talk finally (reluctantly) starts, it is a verbalization of the haunting chorale playing during the "Are You Satisfied?" ad. Fred's wife, Em, played by an exquisite Joan Barry, offers steak-and-kidney pie, discourses on the comforts of home, speaks eagerly of the cinema and the wireless—but Fred will have none of it: "Damn the pictures and the wireless," he shouts; "I want some life, life I tell you!" He stares wistfully at a picture of a ship and grumpily pitches something at their black cat. The music disappears, replaced by alienated, disconnected chatter.

Then, everything changes. A sudden inheritance from Fred's uncle sends the couple on a world cruise. The life sought by Fred exuberantly splashes across the screen with an elaborate musical montage that rivals the opening. "To get to the Folies Bergère, you have to cross Paris," the title tells us, and brilliant carnival music (sounding oddly like *Petrouchka*) propels us from the Eiffel Tower and Arc de Triomphe into a crowded theater with the naïve, newly flush couple: Fred nursing a cigar, Emily embarrassed by her provocative, Paris-friendly outfit. Dramatic aerial shots of a symphony orchestra playing a combination of burlesque and pseudo-Gershwin alternate with swift images of seminude dancers, a boisterous audience, and a black boy playing a banjo. In a dynamic deep-focus shot, jazz players lean eagerly up to the front of the screen, as if wanting to break through it. A conductor in close-up—a forecast of Bernard Herrmann in *The Man Who Knew Too Much*—presides over this sexy cacophony—"life!" indeed. But when overorchestrated ragtime leads the couple into a bar, things get out of hand, as a squealing clarinet dramatizes Em being pinched in the behind. After they down two large drinks, the music turns woozy, a drunken fiddle competing with the blurring camera; when it cuts to the street outside, symphonic car horns synchronize with the preceding music, an effect Hitchcock would continue to exploit in later films.

In this vividly detailed depiction of the pleasures and perils of a crowded music hall, Hitchcock captures both the excitement and underlying anxiety of the Paris jazz scene between the world wars, when thousands of African Americans poured into Paris to escape Jim Crowism and establish a new jazz community. Beginning with the silent film *Downhill*, of 1927, and continuing through *The Wrong Man*, in 1956, Hitchcock exploited the duplicity of jazz, the note of danger just under the surface of boozy insouciance. His view of jazz was close to that of his fellow Englishman Constant Lambert, who in his 1934 essay "The Spirit of Jazz" spoke of the genre's "intoxicating melancholy." The latter phrase is a good description of the jazz scene in *Rich and Strange*, which communicates an aura of desperate gaiety masking impending collapse. The year of its release, 1932, marked the apex of African-American domination of nightclubs—what displaced French musicians called the "jazz peril"—just before the Great Depression reached across the Atlantic to bring it down (at least for awhile). According to William A. Shack in *Harlem in Montmartre*, black jazz in the early 1930s had "spread like wildfire arranged to a musical score in the age of *le tumulte noir*. But the popularity of making noise and stomping feet masked the precariousness of the black jazz scene that the Great Depression now pushed to the edge of the economic abyss."[13] By the summer of 1933, Paris was in a jazz drought. Fred and Em, it seems, made the scene just in time.

The umbrella and jazz sequences—twin musical kaleidoscopes—set us up for what we would expect to be a series of wild comic adventures around the world. What transpires is far more cranky, ambiguous, and eventually

Rich and Strange. Jazz as anxious exuberance.

harrowing, cued by swiftly changing music. Following a long stretch of source music from hotels and bars, Hal Adophe's score reemerges to accompany the cruise to Marseilles, but now it is strangely gruff and sinister.

The remainder of the film ingeniously mingles and exchanges on- and offscreen music. The big kissing scene is always charged with meaning in Hitchcock, even if it's a dark one, but these kisses are strangely unfulfilling. Fred and Emily both become involved in romantic dalliances; in each case, the crucial kiss has real music hovering in the background. Fred's involvement with the ludicrous "Princess" merits, appropriately, cheap carnival music. Emily's "marvelous night" with Captain Gordon begins with a cruise-ship version of "Danny Boy." But the romantic mood dissipates when she sees Fred and the Princess waltzing by to happy dance music: her stricken look contrasts touchingly with the music's upbeat quality. Her kissing scene with Gordon is juxtaposed with boisterous singing, accordions, and men playing cards. We don't see the source, shown in a subtle long shot in the left corner of the screen, until well into the scene. When Captain Gordon and Emily finally kiss, the accordion suddenly goes off-key, an unsettling effect registering Emily's unease with what she is getting into. "Let's get back!" she snaps.

The refusal of the music to deliver the expected romance—the luscious main melody teasingly appears in the "Mediterranean" title, only to vanish—is echoed in the unconventional way Hitchcock treats the "Port Said" sequence. Filled with a sense of wonder, Emily marvels that this extraordinary place has always been there, unbeknownst to her, but Fred, crabby as ever, sneers at this epiphany. The music, an absurdly repeating wind motif, seems to support him, not her. But it continues for so long, after Fred's snort and during his infatuated eye contact with the Princess, that it takes on a crazy life of its own, an example of a kind of omniscient Hitchcock music that parallels similar moments with his camera.

The music throughout *Rich and Strange* reflects Emily's "love is dangerous" speech to Captain Gordon. The difficulties of love, she says, are made endlessly more so because "everything is multiplied by two." Everything happens to both partners, and everything is two-sided. From the bitterly comic opening through Fred's absurd yet sexy seduction scenes to the bickering reconciliation of the estranged couple, everything is double. The music is much the same; motifs repeat, then generate a contradictory idea: romantic point, ludicrous counterpoint. The return of the lyrical title music during the "Mediterranean" scene, more luscious than ever, is ruined by mechanistic noise music as the camera cuts to a close-up of the ship's engine. "He's a Jolly Good Fellow" and "Auld Lang Syne" echo boisterously through the ship during romantic scenes with Fred and the Princess, and Emily and Gordon, respectively, contradicting the wistful ambivalence of both marriage partners: Fred's grim face indicates he doesn't feel like a jolly good fellow at all for leaving Em; the latter seems to be hearing "Auld Lang Syne" as a bitter commentary on deserting Fred.

These strangely beautiful twin scenes are elaborated in the confrontation between the couple after they break up with their illicit lovers. Hitchcock uses ironic background source music with exquisite counterpoint. When Fred tries to go back to the Princess a final time, even after Em comes back to him, the latter breaks down in tears as a haunting North African chant drifts through the hotel (a striking forecast of the Moroccan chant floating around the hotel in *The Man Who Knew Too Much* remake); when she reads Gordon's passionate farewell letter revealing how much he really loved her, the camera blurs, her sadness turns to despair, and the background music transforms into a remembered dance tune from her courtship scenes with Gordon on the ship; when Fred slinks back to admit he's been had by the fake "Princess," a band marches outside the window, returning the musical commentary to a mode of mocking irony from one of haunted regret. When Emily finally sees Fred as the outer world perceives him, realizing she really did miss a big chance at happiness by going back to him, but deciding to stay anyway, now having no illusions, the background music continually changes from real sounds to psychological ones, exterior music to interior, creating an alternate world of subjective commentary.

The terrifying perils of the shipwreck—a peek at the kind of effects Hitchcock might have refined had David Selznick not abandoned the *Titanic* project Hitchcock was originally slated to direct—are unleashed in breathless quiet, with no music at all. After these traumas cause the couple to put everything in perspective and realize they have each other, they go back to bickering off camera as "The End" appears on the screen. The final snatch of lively street music rather than romantic strings is a clue that at least they are arguing with a new honesty and sense of reality. Em knows what she wants, a new house, and has no more of the phony banalities she once used to cheer Fred up. In music, as in life, romantic delusion is gone; the bickering is offscreen as the carnival of life blares on.

2

waltzes from vienna:
hitchcock's forgotten operetta

It may sound far-fetched to compare a dramatic talkie with opera,
but there is something in common.

—Alfred Hitchcock

Waltzes from Vienna, Hitchcock's affectionate musical comedy about the
Strauss family, is his rarest movie. Infrequently screened and notoriously hard
to find, it would seem to be not worth looking for. Donald Spoto and other influential Hitchcockians have always panned it as worthless; François Truffaut
told Hitchcock he had difficulty believing the project was his own choice.

The film was actually chosen by the independent producer Tom Arnold, who offered a depressed Hitchcock the project after the commercial
failure of *Rich and Strange.* Although most commentators regard Hitchcock's association with this project as an anomalous act of desperation, it is
not hard to see why he would find the subject congenial: Strauss waltzes, like
Hitchcock movies, combined popular entertainment with high art; they
were crowd pleasers that also offered classical construction. *Waltzes* was a
hard movie to make. Despite elaborate costuming, casting, and music, the
budget was stingy, even for British cinema. Its production difficulties may
partly explain Hitchcock's grumpy attitude toward the film, though, as we
shall see, he was excited about its musical aspects. Esmond Knight, who
plays the younger Strauss, reports in his memoirs that after a particularly
hard day of shooting in a stuffy studio full of extras, Hitchcock threw up his
hands and declared, "I hate this sort of thing. Melodrama is the only thing I
can do."[1] In later years Hitchcock called this venture a "musical without
music" and told commentators that it was the low point in his career.

Those of us who are charmed by *Waltzes from Vienna* find its dismal reception and continued neglect sad and astonishing. This depiction of the conception, composition, and debut of "The Blue Danube Waltz" explores the creative process in music, something Hitchcock would return to in *Rear Window*, and poignantly portrays father-son conflicts, something rare in the Hitchcock canon. It also became a laboratory for musical experimentation, the predecessor of numerous musical effects and designs, one of which Hitchcock would launch a year later in *The Man Who Knew Too Much*. Most striking of all, it marks the beginning of an obsession with waltzes that would continue throughout Hitchcock's career.

As in *Blackmail* and *The Man Who Knew Too Much* remake, Hitchcock found his musical star on the stage. Esmond Knight, who combines comic fizz with romantic intensity, created the role of Johann Strauss Jr. in a popular West End play called *The Great Waltz* (in America, the title of the film was *Strauss's Great Waltz*). Strauss's younger girlfriend, Rasi, is played with spirit and luminosity by the celebrity actress Jessie Matthews, who, like so many others, spurned the movie, accusing Hitchcock of being "an imperious young man who knew nothing about musicals."[2] (The bad feeling was mutual; Hitchcock thought Matthews, Britain's most popular musical star, was an overrated diva and treated her roughly on the set.)

The real stars of the show, however, are Erich Wolfgang Korngold and Hubert Bath, who contributed vivid arrangements of Strauss waltzes that play elegantly through the film, on and off camera, in windows and from orchestra pits.[3] Bath, who had arranged the music for *Blackmail* and adapted Korngold's orchestrations for the screen, was a minor figure who was becoming a known quantity in the film world. Korngold was another matter entirely. In Vienna, he was widely regarded, along with Arnold Schoenberg, as one of the world's two greatest composers: Schoenberg was the guru of the New Viennese School; Korngold the standard-bearer of the old, the avatar of Strauss and Mahler. *Waltzes from Vienna* marked an important transition in his journey from concert to movie composer; his Strauss arrangements, which originated with the stage version of *Waltzes*, came a year before Max Reinhardt summoned him to Warner Brothers to create the scintillating Mendelssohnian pastiche for *A Midsummer Night's Dream*, the movie that launched his career as one of Hollywood's star film composers.

Hitchcock and Korngold had striking similarities. Both pioneered genres—Hitchcock the suspense film, Korngold the movie score—that became respectable to intellectuals only in the late twentieth century; both struggled with the need to be taken seriously as artists while appealing to large audiences; and both were grudging Hollywood émigrés. In the early 1930s, they swore they would have nothing to do with America or Hollywood. Korngold turned down Hal Wallis's offer to score *The Adventures of Robin Hood*, stating in an impassioned letter that the notion of writing for Hollywood was painful and pleading with him to stop making tempting offers. Then his father called with the news that the Nazis had confiscated everything they owned in Vienna; his world collapsing, he and his family immigrated to Hollywood the next year. Hitchcock too belittled Hollywood, insisting that he was perfectly happy to remain in Britain: while shooting *Waltzes*, he gave an interview to the *Daily Herald* comparing Hollywood to an asylum taken over by the inmates.[4] Like Korngold, he changed his mind, but it was a choice—the lure of money and glamour from the Selznick Studio—rather than a deadly necessity. As we shall see, Selznick considered Korngold for Hitchcock projects once he had the latter under contract. The collaboration never came off, but it is fascinating to contemplate what Korngold, with his complex chromaticism, dreamlike lyricism, and unsurpassable professionalism, would have brought to Hitchcock.

Hitchcock's quip about *Waltzes* being a musical with no music is belied by the film itself, though it does renounce the traditional number musical for a sparer, more organic concept based on the interaction of dramatic scenes and musical fragments. Depending on the dramatic situation, the waltzes and songs appear, at subtly varying volume levels, as tiny motifs or full-blown excerpts for orchestra, voice, and piano solo, creating a dreamlike backdrop that grabs the foreground in the big orchestral set piece at the end.

Hitchcock opens with a surreal blend of street music and other sounds coming in windows, much as he would do in *Rear Window*. In the startling first image, a bugle of the Vienna Fire Brigade, in close-up, blares into the ear of a carriage driver. Fanfares compete with excerpts from waltzes by Johann senior as the younger Strauss, "Schani," plays piano and sings a duet with Rasi, belting out "With All My Heart" through the window; half-dressed girls in the corner dress shop listen rapturously with their rear underclothes to the camera, and Fay Compton's Countess, soon to be Rasi's love rival, fantasizes about the handsome young composer across the way. Occasionally, Hitchcock ventures into traditional musical theater, substituting song for dialogue: after Schani hooks up with the Countess, he sings a duet with her, a paean to the rising sun; the camera then cuts to Rasi singing the same song in a lonely solo.

This combination of cinema and operetta broadens into an examination of musical composition and its effect on human relationships, a forecast of *Rear Window*. The younger Strauss's composition of "The Blue Danube" is part of a larger drama involving his relationships with both a younger and older woman and his struggle for identity against his over-bearing father who, desperate to maintain his rule as the Waltz King, does everything he can to undermine his son's confidence. By the time the narra-tive reaches its dramatic and musical climax, which are exactly the same, the central oedipal conflict has become entangled with eros and art. The erotic energies of Schani's simultaneous love pursuits fire the composition of his innovative waltz; its triumphant performance at his father's concert is cun-ningly arranged by his well-connected older lover, who uses a white lie to manipulate Schani into upstaging his father.

The motifs of "The Blue Danube" gradually accumulate from these parallel plots. Human drama drives the show rather than tagging on to songs. The 1933 *Observer* ran one of the few reviews that celebrated this achievement, noting that the film "presents a 'musical' unlike any other that has ever been filmed, in which the rhythm and melody spring directly from the action, instead of the action being used to amplify the song."[5] (Only the climactic concert scene, as we shall see, reverses the dynamic.)

Typically, Hitchcock subverts the distinction between underscore and source music. After the opening slapstick routine involving botched fire-rescue attempts and Rasi losing her underwear, the band plays on as the café owner serves canapés and Schani scurries into a dressing-room alley door with Rasi's skirt. It continues as the Countess seductively eyes Schani and suggests a quid pro quo: through powerful friends, she can get his music played by his father's orchestra if he agrees to set her verses.

The waltzes seem to come from street players outside the window, for none of them is synchronized with the action. But suddenly, one is; it com-mences with dreamy chords when Schani and the flirtatious Countess say their good-byes, then falters into embarrassed oblivion when Schani awk-wardly introduces Rasi to the Countess. This fusion of a theatrically syn-chronized score with the sounds of real life was increasingly becoming a Hitchcock trademark. In another, more dramatic example, Schani unthink-ingly dedicates "The Blue Danube" to each of his girlfriends. First he plays the waltz on the piano to the adoring Countess as she kisses him, then, in a dissolve, to Rasi as she hugs him from behind. The scene concludes with al-ternating close-ups of Schani's dedications, one to each girlfriend, as the visible waltz played on the piano blooms into an invisible version for full or-chestra.

Not all the musical manipulations are this fresh. Hitchcock resorts to comic imitation as the Prince smokes a cigar in front of mirror; and he uses a downward-spiraling piano glissando to punctuate the Prince kicking the valet down the stairs. But these are clichés only in hindsight; they were relatively new tricks in 1933, and most of *Waltzes* eschews such gimmicks altogether.

The center of the film is the young Strauss's composition of "The Blue Danube," depicted comically and dramatically, without a hint of sentimentality or Music Appreciation didacticism, incorporating intimate shots of musical epiphanies set against dense crowd scenes, small solos against big orchestras, long pan shots against staccato montage. The prelude is the humiliating encounter between Schani and his father during a rehearsal. The scene begins with a point-of-view shot from outside the door, a seemingly serene orchestra in the Staatstheater led by an imperious Johann Sr.; as in *Murder!* the camera moves slowly in the door to reveal behind-the-scenes conflicts. Close-ups of father and son show mutual frustration: Schani, playing violin, thinks his father needs to get beyond the success of the ever-popular "Lorelei," which has become a tired cliché; Johann, shocked and hurt by his son's insubordination, yanks away the music stand separating them and dares Schani to play a better waltz on the piano. With his furious father towering over him in a crowded hall, Schani can, of course, do no such thing. His disastrous performance—"aborted improvisations," in his father's contemptuous words—causes him to lose face in front of his colleagues and sinks his self-confidence to a new low. All he can do is slink from the hall in despair.

This humiliation sets the scene for a dramatic comeback, which begins, typically for Hitchcock, with a kiss. Schani and Rasi are clearly meant for each other, as demonstrated by their spiritual connection with the same tune, a fragment of the enchanted introduction to "The Blue Danube." (In *Shadow of a Doubt,* young Charlie speaks of waltzes "jumping from head to head," a peculiarly Hitchcockian form of musical telepathy.) Their embrace is initially accompanied by standard Viennese waltzes, but suddenly they hear a far-away vision of something dreamlike and original. The camera closes on them in an ecstatic close-up as they have a duel epiphany of "Blue Danube," singing its first halting phrases in a duet as they kiss again.

Hitchcock's vision of musical inspiration is both modern and Romantic, practical and spontaneous. We know that the title of the waltz and its verses come from the Countess, who in a Joycean transference gets "The Blue Danube" label from her maid's suggestion that she wear a blue outfit; we know that Schani remembers one of Rasi's tunes that she reluctantly offers as a good fit for her love rival's verses. But precisely how the first fitful rhythm and phrases erupt in the couple's head is a mystery.

The remainder of the "Blue Danube" conception, much less mysterious, is shown with comic precision in a remarkable bread-baking scene that mixes slapstick comedy, a quirky dramatization of the compositional process, and Hitchcock's obsession with food. Rasi's father shows his probable son-in-law the family business as "The Blue Danube" Prelude, already in Schani's head from his duet with Rasi, takes on rhythms suggested by bakers frenetically tossing dough back and forth. The waltz itself begins with barely coherent distortions, some for orchestra, others for piano, as the bread throwing becomes more animated. It quickens and begins to cohere as Schani's face transforms from pensiveness to ecstasy. His excited singing is interrupted by the continuing sounds in the bread bins and Rasi's querulous father, who dismisses his song as stupid, much as his own father did. But Schani is now bursting with confidence; no yelling from a father figure can repress him. As bread flies in different patterns, like the umbrellas in the balletic opening of *Rich and Strange,* dissonant "Blue Danube" fragments— made more so by Schani singing in a different key than the orchestra in his head—gradually melt into consonance.

The turning dough machine then inspires the middle section of the waltz, its rhythms again creating musical correspondences in a zany *ballet mécanique.* By now, Schani is not only singing but conducting, clearly a man deranged. His subjective orchestra, one only he hears, plays the piece with robust confidence, filling the room more vividly than Johann's orchestra in the Staatstheater. Overcome with excitement, Schani rushes upstairs, jumping over the maid to share the new waltz with Rasi, who admonishes him for singing in her father's bakery. When she tells him that commerce is as important as art, bread as significant as song, he abruptly abandons her for the Countess, whose love and lyrics first sparked his muse.

"The Blue Danube" comes to fruition at the St. Stephen's festival concert, the film's big set piece. With the exception of the two versions of *The Man Who Knew Too Much,* this is Hitchcock's most intricate depiction of a concert. In the background are parental and romantic manipulations— Schani's dedications and undedications to his quarrelling girlfriends; the setting back of Johann senior's watch by Drexler, the Countess's coconspirator, so he will arrive after "The Blue Danube" is sneaked onto the musicians' music stands; and the Countess lying to Schani before the concert, assuring him that his father has consented to his conducting "The Blue Danube." The same betrayals and machinations that characterize Hitchcock's thrillers, exercises in moral relativity, also play through his musical comedies; a larger truth, in this case a musical one, triumphs through chicanery and subterfuge. "The Blue Danube" takes flight through lies and betrayals.

The concert is preceded by a sad, tersely edited prelude. Unaware that his son is in the process of usurping him, Johann plays "Lorelei" on the piano at the behest of the Prince at a private party, a wan performance that shows Schani's accuracy in asserting that the famous waltz has become formulaic. There are no adoring crowds; nobody cares.

The film cuts to a devastating contrast: Schani conducting "The Blue Danube" in its debut, before a huge audience. The initial shots are subjective, with characters watching the bandstand from varying points of view: Drexler and the Countess anxiously waiting to see their scheme enacted, Rasi in shock as she sees the Countess, the irritable audience banging on beer tables for the show to begin.

In this breathtakingly long take, we finally get to hear "The Blue Danube" straight through, with point-of-view shots from all the principals as well as objective views of the orchestra. The camera swivels languidly through the mesmerized crowd, then through the ensemble, section by section, at one point closing on the horns' valves, looking down on Schani conducting with violin in hand, concluding with his point of view, then traveling through the ensemble again. As the waltz quickens and builds toward a crescendo, Hitchcock switches to quick montage, as he would in the mounting agitation of the *Storm Clouds* Cantata scene in *The Man Who Knew Too Much.* Hitchcock described this sequence in detail. Normally, he explained, he had "the action . . . be the inspiration of the music. But in this case, the music had to inspire the action. All the camera has to work with is the orchestra, the conductor and the audience. The human angle is the conductor—the younger Strauss—and the people of the story who are listening. So I required the cutting to match the rhythm of the music. . . . In the slow passages the cutting is slow; when the mood quickens the mood of the melody is followed by the quick cutting."[6]

The human angle is indeed paramount. The camera captures the ambivalent face of Rasi, thrilled by Schani's great moment even as she is enraged by the omnipresence of the Countess, who watches the result of her manipulations with radiant glee. Overwhelmed by conflicting emotion, Rasi finally collapses in tears at her table as others rise to dance, first one couple—who seem moved by musical powers beyond themselves—then everyone, as the film spins into ballet.

The scene concludes with spiky counterpoint between the human and the musical dramas. Arriving too late, Johann Sr. moves slowly through the crowd, which is now mad for his son, looking lonely and stricken, "The Blue Danube" swelling triumphantly against his despair. The exuberant final cadence is followed by stunned silence, then by a standing ovation as the overthrown father continues stalking through the audience in shock.

When Johann recovers, he explodes into fury, projecting his rage onto the Prince, intimidating him with gossip about his son's affair with the Countess. Rasi is also furious with the new Waltz King, who has reacted to her tantrums by going away with the Countess. As in *Stage Fright,* artistic triumph has a human cost; the perfection of art and the chaos of artists inhabit two very different realms.

But in musical comedy, anger is the first stage of reconciliation. The reuniting of Schani and Rasi is a bit formulaic, but the father-son rapprochement is implied with great delicacy. The film concludes at the near-deserted festival with a melancholy Johann wandering among empty chairs. When a young girl asks for his autograph, he obliges, then, with a wistful look, takes the program back and adds "senior" under his name, proud of his son in spite of himself. The lights go down on the bandstand, and the movie ends with a bittersweet fragment of "The Blue Danube." The harmonies resemble those of Maurice Ravel, who used Viennese waltzes to mark the passing of an era. It is a touching coda portending the end of one Strauss generation and the beginning of another.

Sooner than anyone thought, these glorious waltzes would become a subject of nostalgia and pastiche, a metaphor for a vanished past, an emblem of grace and elegance (probably an imagined one) lost in the onslaught of modernism and two world wars. A year after *Waltzes from Vienna* debuted, another British film about Viennese waltzes appeared called *Blossom Time,* part of a popular mini-genre that included *Heart's Desire* and *Goodnight Vienna.*[7] All these films appeared during Klemens Krauss's celebrated Strauss concerts at the Salzburg Festival, which blossomed into the New Year's Day Strauss celebrations at the Musikverien, a continuing tradition that began as a reaffirmation of Old World Austria before its destruction by the Nazi nightmare. Hitchcock himself became a Strauss collagist, but not in a sentimental way; he used real and invented Strauss waltzes, often ironically, especially when presenting one of his favorite themes, the pull of the past. Like Berg and Ravel, he subjected them to surreal distortions in stories about the treachery of nostalgia.

In *Waltzes from Vienna,* however, he served them straight up. Whatever one makes of the movie, it focused Hitchcock on waltzes as an art form available for multiple uses. More broadly, it inspired musings about music in general. He didn't say much about this elusive art, at least not on the record, but when he did, his words were authoritative.

Making *Waltzes from Vienna* was the impetus for a new poetics of cinema music, setting a direction for future ideas and experiments. Hitchcock enunciated his vision of music not in a formal manifesto but in a laid-back conversation, one that was typically full of striking ideas beneath surface banter. While editing *Waltzes,* he gave an interview with Stephen Watts for *Cinema Quarterly,* a bit of advance public relations that was both practical and theoretical, revealing none of his grumpy feelings about the film itself. "I am simply experimenting in theory," he told Watts, "as I have done in practice in *Waltzes from Vienna.*"[8]

For a director who was allegedly indifferent about music, Hitchcock demonstrates broad knowledge, insight, and excitement about the subject. He begins by ticking off several functions of film music that we now take for granted, though in 1933 they were by no means formularized. First, film music is fundamental in setting atmosphere and tone, "the mood of a scene." In love scenes, the score usually delivers "conventional soft music," though he regards this as a "crude instance"; in action scenes, music can "heighten intensity" and "build up to a physical climax." Hitchcock had already done the latter, particularly in *Blackmail* and *Number 17.*[9]

Hitchcock also makes the now-commonplace comparison between movie music and opera, though this interview took place half a dozen years before Erich Korngold's dramatic pronouncements on the subject: "It may sound far-fetched to compare a dramatic talkie with opera, but there is something in common. In opera quite frequently the music echoes the words that have just been spoken. That is one way music with dialogue can be used." Throughout *Waltzes,* Hitchcock indeed echoes dialogue with Strauss numbers; in later films like *Shadow of a Doubt* and *Strangers on a Train,* he would use waltzes and other music for more subtle projections and transferences. Even in the interview, he anticipates this increasing refinement; what he would like to do is find a way to make music "subtly comment" on the movie rather than imitate it.[10]

For Hitchcock, music was always a choice. No music at all was preferable to the "wrong music." Indeed, a sense of when to leave music out was critical: "Silence is often very effective, and its effect is heightened by the proper handling of music before and after."[11] *Waltzes from Vienna* demonstrates the power of silence in Schani's excruciating introduction to the

Countess and in the lonely absence of music in the final scene with Johann Strauss Sr. Later, Hitchcock would demonstrate the "proper handling" of silence versus sound with devastating power in *Notorious, Psycho,* and *The Birds.*

Hitchcock instinctively knew that music could provide an emotionality otherwise lacking in his cool approach to moviemaking. In the interview, he recognizes that "the basis of the cinema's appeal is emotional" and that "music's appeal is to a great extent emotional too." Still, he remains a classicist in regard to technique and is excited about the capacity of music to make filmmaking more incisive and economical. Through sound, a director can achieve greater precision by displacing images with music. The scene with Schani, the Countess, and the approaching Count is a good example: "It is a quiet, tender scene. But the woman's husband is on the way. The obvious way to get suspense is to cut every now and then to glimpses of the husband traveling toward the house. In the silent days, when the villain was coming, you always had the orchestra playing quickening music. You *felt* the menace. Well, you can still have that and keep the sense of the talk scene going as well. . . . You don't need to insist pictorially on the husband's approach. . . . I used about six feet of film out of the three hundred feet used in the sequence to flash to the husband. The feeling of approaching climax can be suggested by the music."[12]

In Hitchcock's judgment, none of these techniques—all of them means to "improve the scene"—has been handled with much subtlety by moviemakers: "Music as an artistic asset of the film is still sadly neglected." This he hopes to remedy, but his main interest lies in something deeper, music that does not enhance what is on the screen but establishes a deeper subtext. This he calls the "psychological use of music," the sound *beneath* the scene. A product of the silent era, he had always preferred pictures over talk; images, he liked to say, are universal, sound merely local. Here, he acknowledges that music, a different kind of sound, is not only universal but the door to the unconscious. He even admits the "limitations" of the moving image, its need to unite with a score: "Film music and cutting have a great deal in common. The purpose of both is to create the tempo and mood of a scene." Here is one of the earliest instances of Hitchcock linking music and cinema, a fusion he would return to in later statements comparing movie-making to musical composition and the director to a maestro.[13]

As demonstrated in *Blackmail,* counterpoint was already part of Hitchcock's aesthetic. Here, in the most crucial part of the interview, he lays out the concept in practical terms: "Two people may be thinking one thing and saying something very different. Their looks match their words, but not their thoughts. They may be talking politely and quietly, but there may be a storm coming. You cannot express the mood of that situation by word and photograph. But I think you could get at the underlying idea with the right background music."

The storm that was coming in Hitchcock's next movie would be a decisive one. Its underlying idea would be expressed not only by background music but by something very much in the foreground, blasting away for full orchestra at Royal Albert Hall in Hitchcock's most ambitious musical experiment yet.

3

the man who knew too much:
storm clouds over royal albert hall

I don't think that any great director appreciates the use
of music as much as he does.

—Arthur Benjamin, on Hitchcock

The Man Who Knew Too Much, Hitchcock's first symphonic thriller, presents a daring musical conceit: a grandiose cantata cuing an assassination
during a concert in which a member of the audience must decide between
saving her kidnapped daughter and preventing the murder. The new cantata provides spectacular concert music—surely the most ambitious in any
film prior to 1934—linked with Hitchcock's most sustained suspense montage.

In *The Man Who Knew Too Much,* Hitchcock took a large step in his
quest to make music a central player in his cinema. Unlike *Waltzes from Vienna,* with its musical innovations but bad press, this bold experiment paid
off at the box office and became a template for Hitchcock suspense. He continued to refine the film's innovations, ultimately reshooting the whole project in the 1950s with the benefit of more experience, new technology, and a
formidable underscore by Bernard Herrmann. It became a launching pad
for *The 39 Steps,* which also employed music in a suspense narrative, but endeared itself even more to audiences by adding comedy and romance to the
formula.

The underrated *Waltzes from Vienna* was an important overture to the
cantata sequence. Its big set piece, the premiere of "The Blue Danube," is
a symphonic montage blending music and performance with personal
epiphanies in a rising crescendo of emotion. That is precisely what the

31

Royal Albert Hall scene does in *The Man Who Knew Too Much,* though in a thriller context, and it is hard to imagine its existing at all without "The Blue Danube" experiment. Even prominent details—the close-ups of the heroine caught between conflicting emotions as the music swells and erupting into tears, the stately shots of every section of the orchestra from varying and dizzying points of view—are strikingly similar.

Arthur Benjamin, who was commissioned to write the *Storm Clouds* Cantata for the film, was a serious artist who worked in a popular idiom, much like Hitchcock himself. He was a virtuoso pianist (he premiered Constant Lambert's swingy Piano Concerto) and a concert composer who infused his works with jazz and Latin dance rhythms. His style was unapologetically effulgent, yet snappy enough for a suspense narrative, as evidenced by the cantata's exciting finale. Benjamin was continually grateful for the commission; featured in not one but two big Hitchcock movies, the *Storm Clouds* Cantata is easily his best-known score.

Much has been made of Hitchcock's statement that the first *Man Who Knew Too Much* was the work of an amateur, the second that of a professional. But the context is important: he made the remark to Truffaut after the latter belittled the original and praised the remake for having more drama and irony. "That's true," Hitchcock concurred, "but aside from this difference, the scene in Albert Hall is similar in both versions, don't you agree? The cantata is the same." Truffaut bulldozed on: "But the second orchestration, by Bernard Herrmann, is far superior. . . . There's a three-hundred meter reel that's entirely musical, with no dialogue. . . . In the construction as well as the rigorous attention to detail, the remake is far superior." Only after this manifesto did Hitchcock, clearly wishing to end the conversation, conclude, "Let's say that the first version is the work of a talented amateur and the second was made by a professional."[1]

The critics demurred; by the 1970s they had inverted Truffaut's verdict, finding the first version brilliant and quirky, the second overstuffed and glitzy (a microcosm of opinion regarding British versus American Hitchcock among those who prefer the former). As Hitchcock indicated, reshooting the cantata montage mainly involved fussing over details: according to Benjamin's partner, Jack Henderson, Hitchcock went back to the original 1934 storyboards when he shot the *Storm Clouds* scene in 1955.[2] (The extent of Herrmann's reorchestration may be exaggerated as well, as we shall see in Chapter 15.)

As a result of the surging popularity of Bernard Herrmann and a melting of the prejudice against the remake, in the late twentieth century opinions shifted regarding the relative merits of the two films. The sequel wasn't as slick and superficial as critics had thought, said revisionists, who began discovering all sorts of subtleties in the remake, especially the music. (This second look resembled the new cachet of *Spellbound* in the late 1990s after a mounting interest in the theremin and the scores of Miklos Rozsa.) Actually both versions offer unique pleasures: the first is scruffier and more energetic, the second sleeker, yet more compassionate. The two have radically different métiers, atmospheres, settings, characters, and musical values. The more complicated remake involves symphonic music versus pop, music as an instrument of violence versus healing; the original is a showcase for musical irony and the power of source music. Both explore a key Hitchcock theme, public versus private duty, an idea that reverberates through *Saboteur, Notorious, North by Northwest,* and other films; in both versions, the *Storm Clouds* Cantata provides the vehicle for the heroine's moment of decision.

The original version opens with a seven-note fanfare from the *Storm Clouds* Cantata that builds in splendor through a montage of Swiss travel brochures and mountain vistas. The upbeat mood is deceptive—this will not be a jolly travelogue—a trick that Hitchcock would continue to play in several main titles, most strikingly in *To Catch a Thief* and *Frenzy*. The motto is followed by a lush countermelody for strings, a straight-ahead, heroic theme rather than the droopy and morose countersubject in Bernard Herrmann's main title for the remake. The fanfare rises in ecstasy, leading directly into the dramatic double opening of ski and shooting matches. Hearing the *Storm Clouds* theme in the title prepares us subconsciously for the Royal Albert Hall scene, producing a double frisson when it occurs halfway through the movie.

In the remake, Hitchcock hired Herrmann to write a noirish counterscore to the Benjamin cantata. Here, he used only found music, the ruckus of street life, in one quirky musical experiment after another—a symphony of source music. Swiss folk songs play after Louis Bernard's near-fatal ski mishap, suggesting all is well. We suspect otherwise when a leering Peter Lorre as Abbott interrupts Edna Best as Jill, a Hitchcock blonde who is also a dead shot; Abbott plays a chiming watch for Betty, her daughter, at the critical moment during Jill's shooting match with Ramon, who turns out to be Abbott's hit man. The chimes disrupt Jill's aim, but she blames her defeat on her "brat" of a child (charmingly played by Nova Pilbeam, who would go on to become the heroine in *Young and Innocent*). At the end of the film, Jill defeats Ramon in a real shooting match, this time saving rather than renouncing her child.

As in *Blackmail,* Hitchcock uses bells and chimes as fateful leitmotifs and popular song as an ironic backdrop for disaster. Abbott's chimes announce his sinister presence throughout the movie. The sound track is also filled with foghorns, whistles, and other impeccably manipulated sounds from real life: sleigh bells during young Betty's ghostly kidnapping (with lighting supplied by Nova Pilbeam's huge, terrified eyes); a foghorn during the establishing shot of Westminster and Clive's horrific encounter with the "dentist" (forerunner of Laurence Olivier's ghastly dentist in *Marathon Man*); a Dixieland band for a scary ascent up a dingy staircase; a dreadful off-key chorus in the Tabernacle of the Sun, where Bob sings an equally out-of-tune warning ("There's trouble coming soon!"), then hears Nurse Edna ask those "not in tune" to submit to "a very simple process of control." The process, hypnotism, is accompanied by the church organ playing a hymn that later covers a chair-throwing melee, a brief moment of slapstick.

In an elegant echo of *Waltzes from Vienna,* an ensemble plays dance music during the strangely formal assassination of Louis Bernard in the Swiss hotel. Shot from the rear, the orchestra frames a tableau of dancers, the camera panning through the room before resting on the two couples who dominate the scene: the father and daughter in the foreground at a table, the mother dancing with Bernard (played with dapper understatement by Louis Fresnay, a French stage actor Hitchcock admired), the tumbling skier from the opening scene. The dancers are just close enough for a mischievous, jealous Bob to secretly tie a piece of Betty's unraveling yarn to Louis's tailcoat, a joke that plays out with Chaplinesque comedy until interrupted by the gunshot that brings Louis down. He sinks languidly into Jill's arms, whispering to her the fatal secret on which the plot turns, the music dying with him. Has anyone in a movie ever expired with such refinement and grace?

This poetic assassination scene is an understated contrast to the later, more dramatic one in Royal Albert Hall, the film's centerpiece. Nothing quite like this had ever appeared on the big screen. The setup for the killing is odd and revealing. "Music is less in your line than marksmanship," Abbott cheerfully tells the assassin in a room full of thugs, as Leslie Banks embraces his traumatized daughter in the back of the frame. Nonetheless, Abbott shows the killer the musical cue through a recording, the "exact moment when you can shoot"—clearly having more confidence in the killer's musical prowess and memory than he at first indicates, since he plays the brief snippet only once. Hitchcock presumes at least a modicum of musical sophistication from everyone, even low-life villains; one drop of the needle is enough. (In the remake, this oddity is covered by having someone who can read a score and sit by the murderer and by having the recording played twice.) Here the director pays his composer the highest compliment, implying that Benjamin's piece is so memorable that the assassin needs no other rehearsal; this is a killer cue that can't miss: "I think the composer would have appreciated that," Abbott says proudly, hurrying the killer out so he won't miss a note: "It's impolite to be late for a concert."

During postproduction of *Family Plot*, Hitchcock told John Williams how he conceived of the Albert Hall montage: "What he told me at one of our lunches was that he saw a cartoon in the London *Times* about a man who gets up in the morning—he lives out in a suburb—he gets dressed, and he has his case with him, and he goes down to the corner and takes a bus to Albert Hall. He gets off the bus, goes backstage, puts on his tails, unpacks his cymbals, and walks on stage. The concert is in progress. The next shot is the conductor pointing to the man, who hits the cymbals once, leaves the stage, dresses, packs his cymbals, gets back on the bus and goes back to the suburbs. 'That's where I got the idea for when the killer pulled the trigger in Albert Hall.'"[3] (Hitchcock told Truffaut that the musician played a flute; by 1975, the cymbals from the film had apparently displaced the original in his memory.)

This droll story is an example of the fundamental comic element even in Hitchcock's most serious ideas. What emerged from the cartoon is a spectacular montage, which builds as the heroine struggles with an excruciating choice. In one of the cinema's most innovative musical moments, Jill opts for public over private responsibility, screaming at the precise moment the cymbals crash in Royal Albert Hall during the cantata, deciding to risk her daughter's life to save a diplomat she has never met. "All save the child," the climactic line in Wyndham Lewis's libretto, was cut in the remake to replace its obvious correspondence to the heroine's dilemma with an abstraction—"pure cinema" over clunky allegory. But the connection between sound and sense is subtle to begin with, for Jill in effect renounces the line for a larger political good. "All save the diplomat" is where she finally comes down.

How much of Jill's decision is conscious we cannot know. It could be that her scream emerges from a welling up of the agony presented by an insoluble dilemma. Her unconscious does the right thing, but only because she can no longer stand the tension of her impossible predicament, a moral conundrum intensified by the anguished chromaticism of Benjamin's music. Unlike the Wagnerian epiphany in *Murder!*, this scene has no voice-over to clarify what the character is thinking. Here, the score does all the talking, much like a character, without the aid of interior monologue. By trusting music to carry the scene, Hitchcock increases its teasing ambiguity; an advance in sonic sophistication is also one for psychological complexity.

The grainy black-and-white version lacks the glamour of Technicolor and the elaborate ballet movements of the 1955 improvement, where the camera cuts rhythmically back and forth between the heroine moving through the hall, her husband dashing from box to box, and the maestro sweeping his arms in broad gestures, as if he is directing a much bigger show than the one onstage. Still, this is far from the work of a "talented amateur." As John Russell Taylor points out, it is one of Hitchcock's great storyboards: "Considering that the film was made on a very restricted budget, it looks surprisingly elaborate, especially in the Albert Hall sequence. . . . Here, Hitch's detailed pre-planning helped enormously. He decided in advance exactly how he was going to shoot the sequence, from eight distinct viewpoints."[4] After a close-up of the concert hall and the heroine crossing the street to blasting car horns (repeated in the remake), we get an establishing shot inside the hall. The killer presents Jill with Betty's brooch in the lobby, an ominous and silent threat, without the threatening words tacked on in the remake. Jill makes her existential choice in complete isolation, without a know-it-all husband to contend with (Leslie Banks would be no competition for Edna Best, in any case). Unlike Doris Day, who stands shakily in the rear orchestra, a 1950s female striving to assert her power, Jill quickly sits down and surveys the scene, taking in the orchestra and chorus, soon spying the ambassador's box and the ominously empty one from which the killer will take his shot.[5] She eyes Betty's brooch, shown in repeating close-ups, with a single tear in her eye, and goes semiconscious for a moment, the camera blurring with her vision. Then, as her brief panic segues into a looming gun in close-up, she rallies. As the chorus screams of saving children, she screams to save a stranger, but unlike Doris Day's, her cry is clipped, coming a second before the cymbal crash, blending, in one of Hitchcock's wittiest sound montages, into a gloating Peter Lorre at dinner, surrounded by his sycophants, stuffing himself. The *Storm Clouds* Cantata is his dinner music, and since Edna Best's scream is less bloodcurdling than Doris Day's, it isn't clear anything is amiss. "Sounds like it went off all right," says his assistant, making sure Lorre's dinner is not disturbed.

The cantata is heard inside the great hall from Jill's seat, moving outside only during the finale, intercut with a montage of Lorre's sumptuous meal, a typical Hitchcockian linkage of food, black humor, and danger. There is

none of the remake's surreal blasting of music into the lobby to cover dialogue, for there is none to begin with. This is what Hitchcock spoke about
following *Waltzes from Vienna:* music communicating ideas and sensations
beyond the realm of talk. With rapid, rhythmic close-ups of orchestra, chorus, soloists, score, timpani, and cymbals, the montage is precise and riveting. Benjamin's cantata, anxious but stately, is an early example of Hitchcock's ability to inspire a composer to give him a sound that fit a complex
visual and emotional design. The broad declamations leave room for multiple camera shots between each phrase as thick chords and a lightning Allegro Agitato build toward the killer's cue to fire on the diplomat.

The London Symphony and Chorus under Wynn Reeves plays at a
faster clip than the same orchestra in 1955, with a gruff momentum that
perfectly mirrors the difference between the two movies. We get no dramatic close-up of the conductor, as we do of Bernard Herrmann, just a
modest long shot of the maestro from the rear, the LSO spread out to frame
the composition; the remake is an overt celebration of the art of music, even
as it presents that art as a camouflage for murder, with a longer cantata
blasting into every corner of Royal Albert Hall, including the lobby, with
loving attention to every musical detail. That extra care and nuance bring
home the ironic disparity between the majesty of the cantata and its evil use
by the killers. The leaner original uses music as a means to an end, the
drama at hand, which moves with exciting swiftness.

When the radio announces that the diplomat has survived, Abbott is
told "it was that damned woman's scream" that caused Ramon to miss.
Frantic, swirling strings accompany the bad news, a recommencement of
the Albert Hall broadcast so rudely interrupted by the botched assassination. What should be a tense moment from a suspense score is actually radio
music, a technique Hitchcock would refine in *Rear Window.* When Abbott
sees the police outside the window, he suddenly clicks the piece off in preparation for the climactic shoot-out; his perverse attempt to use music as an
evil enabler has failed.

Though now severed from violence, music continues to reverberate
with malevolent ironies and symmetries. A policeman who plays an out-of-
tune piano in a flat across the way is reprimanded by his superior, who tells
him a shoot-out is about to ensue, not a concert. The piano is then expro-
priated as a gun barrier; a musical instrument now aids police rather than
criminals. The moral order is back where it should be; the battle can begin.

The percussive pops and whistles of gunshots crack against a backdrop
of tense silence interrupted by Abbott's chiming watch, which betrays his

hiding place in a closet and allows the police to finish him off. At the beginning, chimes were used by Abbott to throw off Jill's aim in the shooting match. Here, in a real gun battle, they betray him. In a similar turnaround, Jill shoots Ramon, who had defeated her before, as he attacks her child, whom she had blamed for losing the match. This elegant reversal fulfills Jill's request in scene 1—"We must have another battle someday"—and inverts Ramon's haughty retort: "I shall live for that moment."

Jill's reunion with her child is heralded with a final peal of the *Storm Clouds* fanfare, now in a major key, a proper symphonic coda—indeed, the only invisible music in the film (a trick Hitchcock would use again at the end of *Rear Window*): the clouds have lifted.

In the remake, Doris Day desperately revived her suppressed singing career in a complicated and far-fetched stratagem to save her child. Edna Best simply swipes the bobby's rifle and blasts the villain off the roof, a cathartic reversal of her terrible powerlessness in the cantata scene. Little more need be said about these divas and their respective cultures. Jo is the repressive fifties, Jill the rowdy thirties, the era of the fast-talking dame. Fast-shooting, it seems, as well.

4

musical minimalism: british hitchcock

> I must get that damned tune out of my head!
>
> —Hannay, in *The 39 Steps*

"I HEARD IT AT THE MUSIC HALL": *THE 39 STEPS*

In *Murder!*, *Waltzes from Vienna*, and *The Man Who Knew Too Much*, symphonic music became a force for romance, revelation, or murder. In his next several films, Hitchcock would show that a musical trifle—a guitar serenade, a music-hall band number, a Disney cartoon song—could, if carefully worked into the texture of the story, have equal resonance. Indeed, the most ordinary noise could take on powerful musical and dramatic properties.

In *The 39 Steps*, Hitchcock's comedy-suspense breakthrough, the musical design is visual as well as aural. Accompanied by a jaunty band overture, the movie opens with a "MUSIC HALL" sign gliding across the screen in close-up, each letter lighting up one at a time so that when the image is finally complete, it is subconsciously imbedded in our memory. Its significance is not apparent until the end, when in another venue, the Palladium, the hero experiences a musical epiphany that brings the film to closure.

The vehicle of that revelation is "Mr. Memory's Theme," a rollicking piece of vaudeville cued by a conductor in the bandstand who raises his baton after Robert Donat's Richard Hannay, the first in a long line of Hitchcock's innocent heroes on the run, enters the music hall and sits down during the final cadence of the overture. As in *Waltzes from Vienna*, the maestro is filmed from rapidly shifting points of view, including the perspective of a

39

double bass player's back, so that the director seems to be conducting us. The tune may sound banal, but the dramatic camera work portends something important.

Because we don't know its significance until the final scene, it appears for a long time to be merely an ironic prelude to Hannay's sudden Hitchcockian plunge into chaos. But Mr. Memory's tune is the key to the movie's secrets and conspiracies. Once Hannay hears it, he can't get it off his mind; he keeps humming and whistling it during his misadventures on the moors, to the great annoyance of his put-upon girlfriend, Pamela, the Hitchcock blond to whom he is united by the master's quintessential romantic bond—handcuffs. Hannay's problem is that he forgets where he heard the melody and therefore can't fathom its significance; he needs to hear it again to make sense of a world gone mad. When he finally does, just in time, the deadly pieces of the espionage narrative come together and order is restored.

Mr. Memory's music picks up where *Rich and Strange* left off, displacing the formal score with spirited source music blasting away from an on-stage band. But *The 39 Steps* is comedy-suspense rather than comedy-drama, the first masterpiece in a genre that would endear Hitchcock to audiences for forty years. It is one of Hitchcock's wittiest entertainments, offering more thrills, chases, and romantic fireworks in its hour and twenty minutes than do most movies twice its length. As usual in comic Hitchcock, there are unexpected depths and nuances. The loneliness and isolation of the crofter's wife, whose bleak scenes have no music, and the final, fatal recitation by Mr. Memory, the obsessive-compulsive walking encyclopedia, give the film a poignant undertone. The emotional subtlety is increased by the sound track: this was the beginning of Hitchcock's fondness for cheerful, everyday vernacular music playing against suspense rather than telegraphing it, a concise way of creating his signature idea, terror in the ordinary.

As he had done in *Murder!,* Hitchcock uses band music to cover up the violence it unwittingly introduces. Music traditionally signifies civilization and order, the taming of savagery, but in Hitchcock it often represents the illusion of stability. The chaos that threatens the seemingly ordered Hitchcock world can't be kept at bay forever; the band can't cover it indefinitely. Hitchcock emphasizes this point by making it twice, in the film's overture and coda. In the first scene, Mr. Memory desperately cues the conductor to strike up the band after the unexplained gunshot and ensuing riot: "For God's sake, play something!" he shouts, as the maestro's hands emerge above the heads of the fleeing mob to strike up Mr. Memory's tune once again. (In a bizarre duet, Mr. Memory grabs the maestro's hands and con-

The 39 Steps. **Music as a cover for catastrophe.**

ducts the band with him.) At the end of the film, the Palladium emcee does exactly the same thing after the gunshots in that scene.

So riveting is Mr. Memory's prelude and its dramatic associations in the plot that it pushes the formal score into the background. The film begins with Jack Beaver's striving five-note motif, which darkens into a striking main title, registering the bright energy and spooky intrigue of the typical Hitchcock chase picture. Shadowy chromaticism vies with heroic fanfares to create the double effect of comedy-suspense that became a Hitchcock signature from here to *Family Plot.* This music returns with darker harmony and speedier rhythm to power the chase across the moors, a thrilling sequence climaxing in a shocking dissonance at the appearance of a helicopter hovering over the doubly harried hero, who must run from both police and foreign agents.

A charming contrast is provided in the music for the Highland Hotel romance scene. This theme is generally credited to Louis Levy, although in some quarters his authorship is controversial.[1] A fixture in the film industry since 1916, Levy, the musical supervisor at Gaumont-British and Gainsborough, was a significant force both in Hitchcock's British career and during his return to London in the late 1940s. Here he (or one of his associates) created the first of Hitchcock's characteristic love themes, at once lyrical and understated, full of sentiment but slightly cool. Elegant woodwinds sing the tune, as they do in the love theme for the Hollywood variation on *The 39 Steps, North by Northwest*. Hitchcock used these romance themes sparingly, here only once. Typically, the melody is used not merely for romantic atmosphere but as a key to character development: Pamela has just realized the innocence of her lover-nemesis and has decided to stand by his side. The realization is a close call, owing entirely to accident, a Shakespearean overheard conversation in a hotel lobby. Pamela could just as easily have gone on despising Richard and trying to turn him over to the police. Indeed, like all Hitchcock couples, Richard and Pamela begin bickering again soon after their rapprochement. But the final close-up of entwined hands shows that the bond endures after the handcuffs are removed; the score captures a genuine, if brief, romantic moment.

Still, most of the musical interest has less to do with the score, which is spotted sparingly, than with clever references, jokes, and special effects. Assuming the name of "Hammond," Richard is saved by a hymnal, which protects him from a fatal bullet wound: "Hymns That Helped Me," he labels it. He escapes the police by joining a Salvation Army street band, hiding his handcuffs in his pocket as the band music covers the police's futile search. In a piece of Hitchcockian wizardry, the tune he obsessively whistles, the musical ID that turns out to be Mr. Memory's ditty, is a variation on both the bold Gaumont fanfare at the beginning and Jack Beaver's symphonic theme. Hitchcock typically collapses the distinction between on- and off-stage music, creating a rich tapestry of musical identities and operatic gestures.

At the end, music brings everything together for a stunning finale. In bed with Pamela, Richard whistles Mr. Memory's tune again, an obsession from which he can't escape: "I must get that damned tune out of my head," he grumbles, anticipating Charlie's similar statement in *Shadow of a Doubt*: "I wonder when I heard it." He can't remember that it comes from Mr. Memory himself. But once he is in the Palladium, everything changes. The musical design from the opening is recapitulated, the scene introduced by blinking neon lights on the marquee, this time promising a show that is "crazy." Hannay enters to another bubbly overture, enlivened by comic tap dancers; the conductor and band are shot from numerous points of view, this time with enraptured reaction shots from the audience, including the police, whose heads bob and sway with the rhythm.

The scene has a goofy cheerfulness that seems right out of musical comedy, a mood belying the grim proceedings, including Hannay's desperate struggle to piece together a deadly puzzle as he spies, through binoculars, the villain's hand with the missing finger. Suddenly, the cliché that music is the door to memory comes true: "I heard it at the Music Hall!" Hannay's memory is awakened by a new tune playing from the bandstand, bringing on the film's epiphany: "Do you hear that tune?" he shouts at Pamela, his eyes blazing with relief. "It was that damned thing I couldn't get out of my head." Now it's out, a terrible itch scratched, but the secret formula is still inside Mr. Memory's head. Releasing it, he pays with his life. In *The Man Who Knew Too Much*, music brought on the assassin's bullet that missed its victim; this time, it doesn't.

Nonetheless, the dying Mr. Memory is relieved to get the complex formula out of his head and finish his "hardest job." "I'm glad it's off my mind at last," he says in his final speech. Like many Hitchcock characters, he is in the grip of a compulsion. Once Hannay hears Mr. Memory's tune, understands its significance, and shouts the fatal, "What are the thirty-nine steps?" Mr. Memory must blurt out the memorized answer. "He is *compelled*," Hitchcock emphasized; the issue goes beyond psychology to the central idea of a man "doomed by his sense of duty. . . . The schoolteacher in *The Birds* dies for the same reason." For Truffaut, Mr. Memory is an essential Hitchcock touch: "Mr. Memory was a wonderful character . . . quite literally, the victim of his own professional conscience. . . . It's this kind of touch that gives so many of your pictures a quality that's extremely satisfying to the mind: a characterization is developed to the limit—until death itself. . . . The incident is handled in the light of a relentless logic that makes the death ironic and yet grandiose, almost heroic."[2]

In *The 39 Steps*, which (like *Murder!* and *Stage Fright*) concludes on a stage, music turns out to be a healing force, but only provisionally. The forces of good are saved because Hannay remembered the tune, but the source of his epiphany, the victim of a "relentless logic," lies on the stage gasping his last breath as the orchestra frantically plays another vaudeville number and dancing girls kick up their heels to hide his death.

The pattern in *The 39 Steps* continues through British Hitchcock: music used sparingly but tellingly, bouncing back and forth between real sounds and the score, creating a subtle tension between life and art. During the Gaumont era, music acts as an obsession in the narrative, something mysteriously connected to a deadly secret. The truth will out, but only when music releases it.

A CORPSE AT THE ORGAN: *SECRET AGENT*

Like his modernist colleagues in the composing world, Hitchcock regarded noise as an intrinsic part of music. As early as *Blackmail,* where the unnerving knife monologue is "scored" as a rhythmic crescendo, nonpitched sounds take on musical properties. Charles Ives, George Antheil, Henry Cowell, and Edgard Varèse strove to bring the racket of modern life into the concert hall, often in spite of fierce audience resistance. In cinema, noise and music were never so far apart: as far as Hitchcock was concerned, movies *automatically* blurred the distinction between music and sound. "When you put music to film, it's really sound," he said. "It isn't music per se."[3] The entire spectrum of sound, both in the city and in nature, was part of Hitchcock's music. The merging of noise effects with musical ones is clear in a film like *The Birds,* but *Rope, Rear Window,* "Four O'clock," and others incorporate a similar unity.

One of the earliest examples is *Secret Agent,* an exploration of the devastating effects of "long-range assassination" on the human conscience. To evoke the shadowy spy-assassin world of Somerset Maugham, who inspired the screenplay (anticipating John Le Carré, Gerald Seymour, and other writers), Hitchcock created a rackety ambiance as carefully worked out as an avant-garde concert piece.[4] The sonic world of *Secret Agent* approaches what Bertolt Brecht called "musuk," a sound beyond noise but not quite music. The composer Frederic Rzewski likens this aesthetic to "driving along the road and seeing a heap of mangled metal and carcasses from an accident. Then you drive on to something else. It's a vision of life as a tangled mass of order and disorder which somehow adjusts itself as you drive along."[5]

Secret Agent, which has its share of mangled metal and carcasses, often feels like a terrible car accident; by the end of their morally repellent spy assignment, John Gielgud's Richard and Madeleine Carroll's Elsa try to adjust to the tangled morass but finally decide to get off the road altogether, vowing never to return. Fresh from the comedic romp of *The 39 Steps,* Carroll plays Elsa, a spy new to the trade who thinks the road is a joy ride, that spying is a thrill—until she has to participate in a series of killings that turn her stomach. "All you can see in it is fun," sneers Richard, her pretend husband and fellow spy, who becomes as morally sickened as she.

The movie opens with a heroic main title, credited to Louis Levy, set against an art deco design of World War I soldiers, its Elgarian splendor undermined by chromatic fragments and desperate military fanfares. This ambiguous opening segues into a solemn funeral march for a fallen hero who has "unaccountably succumbed" to a bad cold while on leave. It too is subverted, this time by a caustic woodwind cadence following the funeral as a one-armed attendant, after showing the grieving family out the door, knocks over a coffin while lighting a cigarette. The casket crashes down and pops open, revealing its contents—nothing. Filmed with dignified, gliding camera movements, the funeral turns out to be a fraud, like the music that graces it; the coffin with no corpse sets up a world where life and death are equally empty.

In the exposition, Richard, who turns out to be the "fallen" hero, plots an assassination as bombs and gunfire explode outside his window. The appropriateness of these ominous rumbles is noted by Richard's supervisor. He doesn't have to tell Richard what to do about a certain agent heading for Constantinople; the explosions do it for him. "Sounds like a gunshot" is his concise summary, giving Richard a deadly glance. Later, in a Swiss hotel, away from threatening gunshots, Richard receives the official assassination order, this time to the counterpoint of bland lobby music.

The remainder of the noise track—for music proper quickly vanishes—continues to embody fatal secrets and betrayals. White noise grinds and an alarm screams in a chocolate factory that turns out to be a "German spy post office"; the racket covers not only deadly machinations but also frantic dialogue, making the scene seem like a moment out of silent cinema, a trick Hitchcock would continue to use throughout his career. A dog howls pitifully at the door during the assassination of his innocent master far away on a mountain top, apparently possessing more feeling than the humans in the scene. The animal's long wail becomes a bridge linking the stricken reaction of the victim's wife—she senses what the dog does when she hears his whimpers—with the delayed attack of conscience experienced by Richard and Elsa, who helped plot the killing. Chimes ring out during the central Hitchcockian kiss as Richard decides to quit the spy business; a sustained phone ring signals his change of mind and his terrible separation from Elsa.

These and similar scenes constitute a bleak noise track set against the seamier aspects of espionage. The most striking of these, the Langenthal Church scene, is an early specimen of Hitchcock's fascination with organs and church bells. As Richard and the General, impishly played by Peter Lorre, approach the church to distant goat bells, they hear an eerie organ chord; as they enter the church, the sound grows in volume; as they approach the organist, his back to the camera, it gradually clarifies as a massive, dissonant cluster. Why? This is not a venue for avant-garde organ recitals, but a bucolic Swiss church in the mountains.

The organist turns out to be a double agent—a corpse grasping a button implicating his killer—his body lying against the keyboard to produce the horrific sound. Hitchcock sustains the violent chord long enough for us to experience it as shuddery, Gothic atmosphere music, especially when Richard and the General light candles in the vast shadows and peer suspiciously about the church. Here, the unpredictability of *Secret Agent* takes its most dizzying turn: spectral terror abruptly crashes into comedy as the two bumbling spies flee into the tower, where their ears are assaulted by a pealing bell rung by a villager. For a delightful moment, the somber tone of *Secret Agent* disintegrates into the Gothic burlesque of *Number 17*.

Secret Agent continues Hitchcock's experiments with waltzes. In *Waltzes from Vienna*, these were the crowning glory of Old World European culture, a force uniting eros and art. Here they represent that order as teetering on the verge of collapse. Robert, Elsa, and the General plot to kill a suspected German agent who turns out to be a likeable, gentle man with a wife and dog; during the elaborate machinations of the three assassins, waltzes play from a casino band elegantly positioned in the back of the frame, a veneer for a "simple murder," in Robert's words. "He looks so harmless," says Elsa of the intended victim, whose dog's happy barks blend with the waltzes. As the killers dine with the victim and his wife, the contrast between warmhearted music and the cold-bloodedness of what is being planned becomes excruciating, all the more so as Robert and the General flirt with Elsa and joke about whether the Geneva Convention applies to dogs.

The irony darkens further during the village yodeling scene in the beer garden following the assassination, when a telegram reveals that the trio have killed the wrong man, someone who is harmless indeed. Hitchcock's camera circles the singers as a coin spinning in a vase brings back the fatal button to Elsa's already guilty conscience. The yodels have a jarring effect against the ashen expressions of Richard and Elsa. In another turn of the musical screw, the General views the wrong-man assassination as a wonderful joke, a "beautiful accident." His mirth spills over as the chorus sings "Taler Schwingen," a song full of lonely melancholy, before the scene concludes with "Edelweiss," a final mocking commentary.

In the concluding scenes, as the husband-and-wife spy team unite in their determination to leave the espionage business, source music attempts to unite with what is on the screen. The threatening interrogation of Elsa on the train takes place against the distant singing of German soldiers; martial music sounds against the closing desert-camel montage announcing Allied victory. The Elgarian score, on hold for so long, gets a triumphant reprise in a dissolve to the finally united couple. This upbeat coda is a bit late: "Home again," reads the final message from Richard and Elsa, "but never again."

Hitchcock's foray into moral ambiguity was not quite over. After *Secret Agent* came *Sabotage,* his blackest British film, a masterpiece mixing Joseph Conrad and Walt Disney.

HUMAN BOMBS AND DEADLY DISNEY: *SABOTAGE*

Based on Conrad's *The Secret Agent,* the grandfather of the modern espionage novel, *Sabotage* is the most uncompromising film from Hitchcock's British period. Although he adds a movie theater to Conrad's narrative— an emblem of cheerful normality hiding terrorist menace—he is faithful to Conrad's vision of banal evil trumping ineffectual goodness. The noirish score, conducted by Louis Levy, stands in for Conrad's fog to evoke a claustrophobic London in the grip of terrorism. This is a world of inertia and unreality, of panic masked by false cheer. With its ascending chromaticism, stabbing repetitions, and obsessive octaves, the spare music builds to climaxes that sputter out; it's a score that goes nowhere, like the society it enshrouds.

Mr. Verloc, the film's ambivalent and incompetent saboteur, lumbers through the film's shadows to music so sluggish and opaque it seems to further slow him down. In the opening, he causes a massive yet strangely inept city blackout that produces apprehension followed by uneasy laughter among the populace; he then sneaks home and collapses in bed with a newspaper over his head as the film's minimalist score disintegrates into dissonance and cymbal crashes. His theme alternates with snatches of cinema music, brief moments of respite, as characters pass in and out of the Verlocs' Bijou cinema on their secret, murderous errands. In addition to imparting a surreal atmosphere, this juxtaposition contributes to the film's despair: here is a Hitchcock movie where even the magic of movies is ineffectual.

Indeed, in the central cinema scene, Hitchcock uses movie images and cartoon music as a catalyst for dark revelation and revenge. Verloc's botched blackout is succeeded by a far more tragic blunder, a planted bomb that goes off prematurely in a crowded bus. In shock from the news that her little brother Stevie was among the victims—that he has been blown to pieces by her husband—Mrs. Verloc watches Walt Disney's animated film "Who

Killed Cock Robin?" This disturbing movie-within-a-movie begins benignly: the Disney cartoon does what it should, providing momentary cheer and relief. Mrs. Verloc's tragic face momentarily brightens, her tears dissolving into a relieved smile. But as the robin tumbles down, pierced by an arrow, her emotion plummets with it: the childlike music suddenly seems morbid and mocking; the cartoon violence having re-evoked her stunned grief, she blazes with rage at her husband, who has just shrugged off his crime and blamed it on meddling police.

In one of Hitchcock's most sustained exercises in silence, Mrs. Verloc leaves the unbearable music behind, enters her kitchen, and, in an excruciatingly long take, kills her husband with the dinner knife. As in Conrad's novel, the obese Verloc is too slothful to save himself; he sees precisely what's coming, and how to avoid it, but can't move.

The juxtaposition between jeering cartoon music and prolonged quiet typifies this alienating, strangely powerful movie. Although equally grim in its content, *Secret Agent* has a whiff of heroism and humor in its sound track, both in Levy's orchestra and Hitchcock's inventive noise effects; the tone makes the film easier to bear. Here the score, like Conrad's mechanical piano, is as desolate as the silence, providing no whimsy or respite; the effects are limited to ugly urban noise and the somber tolling of Big Ben through the corridors of Scotland Yard as the chief inspector informs Ted, the detective tracking Verloc, that apprehending the master saboteurs behind Verloc is beyond police powers.

In the bomb sequence, *Sabotage* slips beneath irony into despair. The bus explosion that kills Stevie (and dozens of others) following his humiliation by a sadistic hawker in front of a mocking crowd rips apart the whole idea of innocence and order. The terrorists are bringing down a society that is already cruel, trivial, and crumbling. This scene—so devastating that Hitchcock regretted making it—is preceded by agonizing suspense sustained by source music that keeps Stevie from delivering his deadly package in time to save his and others' lives: first, the obnoxious, repetitive tune of the quack salesman, then the endless marching bands and bagpipes of a patriotic parade, which ten-year-old Stevie watches in enchanted wonder. Once Stevie is on the bus, smiling at an elderly lady and her dog as the bomb ticks on, the score returns, building with Hitchcock's most powerful clock montage to a grim climax timed with the exploding bomb.

Birdsong, always suspicious in Hitchcock, heralds tragedy. The "Cock Robin" scene is a climax of canary songs building through the film. In his first scene, the bomb maker, who owns a bird shop, argues with a customer about how to make birds sing. The kind of song he produces in his "other department" is mass murder, indicated by his note to Verloc: "The birds will sing at 1.45." The latter appears in surreal close-up, a moment of harrowing omniscience in this deeply subjective film, seconds before the bus explodes. Stevie unwittingly participates in this projection of human depravity onto the animal world by singing to the canaries before closing a cage wrapped up with the bomb. The avian denouement comes when the long silence of the knife killing is broken by a close-up of chirping canaries.

This depiction of a corrupt, cold-hearted society ripe for sabotage was too alienating for Hitchcock's audience. Moviegoers could simply not deal with the bus montage—the killing of a little boy, a kind old woman, a little dog, and numerous other innocents set to music so grim it seemed to welcome the catastrophe. *Sabotage* was a dismal flop. For a brief while, the director who prided himself in having his finger on the public pulse was in danger of losing it. Instinctively, he followed up with one of his great charmers, *Young and Innocent*.

"NO ONE CAN LIKE THE DRUMMER MAN": *YOUNG AND INNOCENT*

Young and Innocent, Hitchcock's second in a long line of wrong-man road movies, begins with a clap of thunder and ends with an out-of-control percussionist: in the beginning, nature, a force of chaos, heralds a violent crime; in the end, art, represented by music, restores order by establishing true guilt and innocence.

This film is another brilliant excursion in vernacular source music—perhaps the most satisfying example of music solving a crime—and also a triumph for the music department, a refreshing lift after the barren expressionism of *Sabotage*. The love theme for violins in the old mill recalls the romance music in *The 39 Steps;* the harp-studded suspensions when the falsely accused Robert breaks into his girlfriend Erica's flat through the window to tell her that he is turning himself in to the police have a Wagnerian sense of desire and longing. The score is used mainly for romantic moments rather than suspenseful ones, a hallmark of Hitchcock-Levy; as usual, it is spare, supplying just enough sentiment to warm Hitchcock's cool images. Indeed, much of the film plays without music; the *Vertigo*-like image of Erica's hands clutching a precipice into which her car has collapsed, for example, is terrifyingly quiet.

The frequent silencing of the score in suspense scenes makes the ones that do have music more vivid. A powerful example is Robert's discovery of the victim's body washing up on the beach, the beginning of his wrong-man nightmare, propelled by wavelike violin figures. When accusing women appear—harbingers of Manny's accusers in *The Wrong Man* and Melanie's in *The Birds*—the music churns into frenzy. Gulls, shrieking and flying in front of the camera, add a touch of poetry and menace, one of Hitchcock's early bird-phobic moments.

By 1937, the release date of *Young and Innocent*, Hitchcock was beginning to develop a consistent repertory of musical devices. The use of players and singers as characters in crucial parts of the narrative is the most obvious; others include sinister birdsong, claustrophobic discords, sustained bell and percussion effects, songs entangling with the underscore, and suspensions (chords that droop down rather than resolve) to evoke romantic anxiety. Following the beach discovery, a piercing dissonance over a newspaper montage registers Robert's entrapment, an echo of *Blackmail*. Chimes and trains blend with the score in an impressionist haze as Robert, full of anxiety for Erica, leaves her to hide out at the lodging house; as she falls asleep, a dreamy voice-over establishes her connection to him: "I don't want anything to happen to you, either." As in *Spellbound* and *Vertigo*, voice-overs tap into the subconscious and establish erotic connections.

We also get an ingenious instance of a source tune penetrating the score, as "Three Blind Mice" jumps from a children's game at Erica's aunt's house into Levy's music. During the same nerve-jangling party, Robert claims he "can read at sight" but misses a musical cue and nearly gives himself away to the suspicious aunt. Here is the beginning of two music-related patterns, one in which musical botches indicate guilt, whether actual or erroneous, and another in which ironically apt children's songs provide mocking counterpoint during tense scenes.

The "Three Blind Mice" near disaster forecasts the justly celebrated finale, where the real killer blows his cues while attempting to play the Lerner-Goodheart-Hoffman song "The Drummer Man" during the ballroom climax. This tune is built into the film's design from the beginning: the art deco title credits appear with a straightforward orchestral statement of the song, subtly preparing us for its fateful distortions in the finale. The latter opens with a memorable track shot sweeping through the Grand Hotel, taking in dancing couples, gradually closing on the house band in blackface, its singer performing "The Drummer Man," and finally landing on a close-up of the drummer's eye spasmodically twitching, like his increasingly unsteady playing. This is the crucial clue, telegraphed in the killer's eye spasm from the film's opening scene. But Erica can't see the twitch, the one thing that can save Robert. Nor can she appreciate the lyrics, which comment sardonically on the drummer's peculiarly wild performance: "When it comes to doing tricks, with a pair of hickory sticks, I'm right here to tell you sister, no one can like the drummer man. . . . When it comes to make that music hot, make you give it all it's got, I'm right here to tell you mister, no one can like the drummer man."

Musical performance is the key to the mystery. In Hitchcock, staying in tune and on the beat are matters of life and death, as he explained to Truffaut: "The jittery drummer sees the policemen talking with the tramp and the girl at the other end of the ballroom. He thinks they're looking for him, and his nervousness is reflected in the drumbeat, which is out of tune with the rest of the band. The rhythms get worse and worse."[6]

The shots in this scene are similar to musical designs in *Waltzes from Vienna, The 39 Steps,* and *The Man Who Knew Too Much:* the camera restlessly pans through the orchestra and crowd, sweeping through oblivious dancers, sometimes taking the player's or maestro's point of view, one agitated, the other irritated. "I pay someone else to make the orchestrations!" shouts the bandleader after a particularly bizarre percussion riff. First his cacophony mars a waltz—as usual, counterpoint for impending chaos—which Erica dances as she looks nervously for the villain. The deterioration continues through a reprise of "The Drummer Man"; as the camera gradually pulls back for a panoramic shot, a reverse of the initial tracking shot, the wacky percussion performance finally goes insane, with xylophones and cymbals crashing into a massive Varèsian breakdown of the entire orchestra, followed by the crunch of the drummer falling into his instruments.

Still, the killer almost gets away with it, and Robert almost hangs. It is only the heroine's compassion—poignantly projected by Nova Pilbeam—that saves the day, for it is she, moving beyond her own predicament, who comes forward from the crowd to help the collapsing drummer (just as earlier she had moved in to help Robert after he fainted). At the last second, she discovers the telltale twitch. As in *The Man Who Knew Too Much,* Hitchcock links a percussive sound with the heroine's natural goodness; a performance collapses into chaos but saves an innocent man.

Music provides the healing energy of comedy, allowing the truth to emerge, lovers to come together, and children to be reunited with their parents despite the relentless bumbling of the police. After the tragic starkness of *The Secret Agent* and *Sabotage, Young and Innocent* walks the tenuous tightrope of tragicomedy, its grim wrong-man narrative and its indictment of a criminal justice system bent on hanging an innocent man brightened by the lyricism of the score and the exuberant madness of the drummer man's nervous breakdown. In his next film, Hitchcock again used music to reveal truth and unite lovers, with a poise that marked the culmination of his Gaumont-Levy period.

"EVERYONE SINGS HERE": *THE LADY VANISHES*

The Lady Vanishes is Hitchcock's most charming movie and one of his most subtle in the handling of music. It might well be called "Louis Levy Vanishes," so thoroughly does the score conducted by Levy disappear along with Dame May Whitty's undercover spy. But even as the film eschews conventional movie music, it absorbs us in musical jokes, games, stratagems, and atmospheres.

The importance of music in the narrative was not lost on reviewers. An anonymous critic for *Hollywood Reporter* wondered whether this "very British affair" would "appeal to American audiences. . . . It's all about the extremely complicated—and often illogical—scheme of certain European government agents to prevent a British spy from returning to the home office with some valuable information conveyed, believe it or not, by way of a melody."[7] The reviewer might have believed it easier had he listened to *The Man Who Knew Too Much, The 39 Steps,* and *Young and Innocent,* which all hinge on musical motifs, performances, and secret codes.

Like *The 39 Steps, The Lady Vanishes* is a giddy combination of love story, comedy, and spy suspenser, all connected by music. The genre hopping starts with a comic prelude introduced by a delicate yodel for harp and winds followed by Levy's main title, a serene string serenade. The camera tracks through the snowy Alps to a hotel where a waltz is noisily interrupted by a call to arms from a cuckoo clock jumping at the screen in close-up. Miss Froy introduces herself as a governess and music teacher, proclaiming her delight with the musicality of the locals: "The people here are just like happy children, with laughter on their lips and music in their hearts." Gilbert, played with a spiky charm by Michael Redgrave, his first lead in a film, is an ethnomusicologist working on a book. His signature is folk music: when Iris, the young heroine, asks, "Who are you?" he answers by playing his clarinet. His heroic dependability once fascism rears its sinister head is connected with his love of music, which he views as his sole quality and legacy: "I couldn't help inheriting my father's love of music. It's all he left me." A passionate preserver of Old World culture, Gilbert is committed to saving the lost folk music of central Europe from extinction. By the end of the film, as Dr. Hartz and his coconspirators attempt to seize a deadly military secret, the stakes become much higher.

"Everyone sings here," says Miss Froy, and indeed, *The Lady Vanishes* feels for a long time like one of Hitchcock's most lyrical romantic comedies. The two cricket nuts, Caldicott and Charters, provide the best laughs, railing against the *Herald Tribune* when it carries no scores of the games and hanging up on a hotel guest's long-awaited call from London when the caller doesn't have them either. Confused musical cues are their reason for being stuck in the hotel, a premonition of the botched musical cues at the end of the picture. Caldicott bitterly reminds his friend that they missed the train "because you insisted on standing up when they played their national anthem." Charters counters that "you must show respect," but Caldicott has the last word: "It's always been my contention that the Hungarian Rhapsody is not their national anthem. In any case, we were the only ones standing."

Much of the comedy continues to turn on music. Performed no longer by the orchestra but by a tenor with a guitar, the serenade floats into the night air, to the delight of Miss Froy, but is raucously upstaged by Gilbert's folk dancers clomping on the floor. These performances brutally collide, instigating a wonderful slapstick routine. Margaret Lockwood's Iris, traveling to London to her doom—marriage to a dullard—sends the manager upstairs to silence whoever is "playing musical chairs with an elephant," but Gilbert indignantly refuses to stop, insisting that he is recording "the ancient music with which your peasant ancestors celebrated every wedding." When Iris bribes the manger to kick Gilbert out of his room, he invades hers, singing in her shower and threatening to tell everyone that she invited him there: "And when I say everyone, I mean everyone. I have a powerful voice." Iris calls Gilbert the most contemptible person she has ever known. "Confidentially," he answers, "you're a bit of a stinker yourself." In Hitchcockian comedy, insult is part of flirting; the seeds of romance have been planted.

Music provides the transition from comedy to thriller. Suddenly, the tone changes, as Miss Froy listens out the window to take in the haunting guitar serenade drifting through the night air. She has a look of enchantment, but the audience sees a close-up of the singer surrounded by menacing expressionist shadows; one of them becomes a gangsterish figure with two large hands, slowly moving to the middle of the frame to grab him by the neck and pull him down into darkness. To Miss Froy's bewilderment, the music stops. This choked-off serenade thus joins a long list of slaughtered Hitchcockian performances.

Shortly after the lost serenade, Miss Froy vanishes as well. Thereafter, the film relies on subtle source music. An accordion announces the arrival of the train, on which Gilbert reprises his folk dances. Railroad sounds pro-

The Lady Vanishes. **A dangerous serenade.**

duce a mesmerizing clatter hauntingly in tune with Iris's sleeping and waking and Miss Froy's disappearances and resurrections. Whistles, rattles, and
screeching brakes continue during Iris's frantic search through claustrophobic cars. Like Josef von Sternberg, Hitchcock knew the cinematic value
of trains. A train was to him what a stagecoach was to John Ford, a microcosm of life, a focused drama within strict limits, stasis in tension with
movement—what Hitchcock would later call suspense versus the chase.
Like any good fun-house manager, he keeps changing his effects. The rackety poetry of train sounds is ominously silenced when Dr. Hartz transfers
Miss Froy's double and when the train suddenly stops, the prelude to the climactic gunfight. As the reluctant heroes Gilbert and Caldicott get the train
started again in the nick of time, the resumption of its chugging sounds is
exhilarating.

Through frenzied searches and gunfights floats the serenade: Miss Froy
hums it as Iris falls asleep; she sings it in duet with Gilbert, breaking down
its structure, trying to implant it in his memory during the gunfight,
prompting Caldicott to comment that "the old girl's gone off her rocker."
The melody is finally revealed by Miss Froy to be a state secret, "the vital
clause of a pact between two European countries." After she transfers this
life-or-death tune to Gilbert before her dramatic escape, she worries that he

will not remember it. "I was brought up on music," he assures her; "I won't forget it."

He does, of course. "It's gone!" he cries in despair as he and Iris stand at the door of the foreign office. Here is the film's most subtle joke: a musicologist can't remember a simple tune. When he hums it, Iris snaps, "No, that's the wedding march!" Not to worry: from behind the door, Miss Froy bangs it sonorously on the piano, flooding the final scene with music before she embraces the relieved couple.

The Lady Vanishes sets the instability of perception against the stability of music, again Hitchcock's stand-in for art. Through the dizzying chaos of shifting identities and disguises, appearances and disappearances, culminating in Iris vanishing from her betrothed into a car with Gilbert, the all-important melody has remained firmly in Miss Froy's memory. It has vanished from Gilbert's, an inversion of the epiphany in *The 39 Steps,* where the hero remembers Mr. Memory's all-important tune at the critical moment. This lapse should not be surprising: Gilbert is so entranced by suddenly getting the girl that his head has room only for Mendelssohn's "Wedding March." And there is another reason: Gilbert and Miss Froy have strongly differing musical tastes. Gilbert is a folk musicologist whose specialty Miss Froy denounces as a "horrible noise." He shows no interest in the serenade when it wafts ravishingly through the night air; but aside from its political importance, the serenade obviously appeals to Miss Froy in a way that makes its imprinting absolute.

At the end, Louis Levy is freed up, along with everyone else, his orchestra playing the serenade with the wedding bells Gilbert has subconsciously invoked. Bells are usually somber and fateful in Hitchcock; here, they peal out jubilantly; the thwarted lovers come together, the antifascist forces prevail, and *The Lady Vanishes* returns to comedy. As Miss Froy embraces Iris and Gilbert from the piano bench, a glissando from the orchestra reaches up in ecstasy, finally having the last word after being shoved aside by sounds from the world of suspense and death.

The resplendent end title music was the last composition for Hitchcock by the Gaumont music department. From the spooky expressionism of *Sabotage* to the lilting serenades here, these subtle musicians proved resourceful. In five deftly understated scores, they showed that less can be more. But Hitchcock was growing tired of less. Caldicott speaks for him when, on observing Iris and her two companions waltzing into the hotel and getting immediate attention from management, he says "Those girls must be American—you know, the almighty dollar." Floated his way by

David O. Selznick, the almighty American dollar would soon lure Hitchcock to America, where he would vanish from England as thoroughly as Miss Froy does from her train. Indeed, Hitchcock was already negotiating with Selznick in May 1938, in the middle of shooting *The Lady Vanishes;* by the time he began editing it, he had already settled on *Rebecca* as his Selznick debut, a lavish project that would mark the end of serenades and spare source music. Soon, he was to be maestro of far more lavish scores from Hollywood's Golden Age. The challenge would be not austerity but excess.

A GRUMPY GOOD-BYE TO THE BRITISH CINEMA: *JAMAICA INN*

Jamaica Inn, Hitchcock's costume-pirate movie, opens with stirring title music by Eric Fenby, the lifelong champion of composer Frederick Delius, who would become a heroic template in *Saboteur.* This music holds great promise: a tempestuous chromatic idea surges against a sweeping modal melody; orchestral waves crash over a sea montage, then recede for a lyrical meditation over a Cornish prayer for storm victims. The music then vanishes, replaced by the sound of real storms and cries of terror in the first pirate scene. Fenby's music makes such a vivid impression that we expect it to return after Charles Laughton's scruffy pirates have done their worst.

But it doesn't. The rest of this curious movie, loathed by Hitchcock so much that he tried unsuccessfully to get out of his contract, and rated even by fanatical Hitchcockians as a failure, has no music, only blasting wind, screaming seamen, and crashing surf. Ocean montages would continue crashing a year later in *Rebecca,* though softened by Franz Waxman's score. In *Jamaica Inn* the tempests blow with lonely, uncompromising blasts, a sound consistent with Hitchcock's ominous vision of nature, and with Daphne du Maurier's Bronte-like novel, which, in a striking coincidence, was offered to Hitchcock just before he began *Rebecca.* (Du Maurier hated *Jamaica Inn* as much as Hitchcock did.)

What happened to Fenby's magnificent score? Hitchcock distanced himself from *Jamaica Inn* so fast that we'll never know. Whatever the reason, the dramatic title music followed by sustained sounds of a threatening sea turned out to be an effective device, giving *Jamaica Inn* a bleak power in its sound track that is only occasionally matched by the visuals. A further development of Hitchcock's noise-music experiments, *Jamaica Inn* is the forerunner of *Lifeboat,* which also begins with a stunning main title score, only to collapse into a threatening sea for the scoreless remainder.

This pirate melodrama is actually more fun than its reputation would suggest. Maureen O'Hara, in her screen debut, projects considerable beauty and heroism; Leslie Banks's apelike pirate underling is bizarre beyond belief; and Laughton's menacing waddle, over-the-top line readings, and gigantic faux eyebrows are high camp even for him.

His most marvelously ludicrous moment is his spectacular suicide from the top mast after declaring that "the Age of Chivalry is over!" What was really over was Hitchcock's British period, which came crashing down to an inglorious end with the gigantic Laughton. (His only pleasant memory of the project was playing classical music for Laughton on his new hi-fi phonograph.) Hitchcock was already sailing into the more glamorous waters of Hollywood on a luxury liner financed by David Selznick. The sinking British film industry, which had condescended to him for fifteen years, could fend for itself. He was abandoning ship.

5

rebecca: music to raise the dead

A peculiar sound of unreality.

—Franz Waxman's description of the novachord in *Rebecca*

In *Rebecca,* Hitchcock's Hollywood debut, music has uncanny powers. It conjures the illusion of Rebecca de Winter's jealous ghost roaming the gigantic rooms of Manderley, watching her living love rival. It is a siren call tempting the new Mrs. de Winter to her doom as Hitchcock's claustrophobic camera locks her and her tormentor, the spectral Mrs. Danvers, in a double close-up framed by Rebecca's window. "You've nothing to live for," whispers Danny, urging Maxim de Winter's new wife to end her struggles with the old by leaping out the window. "Look down there, it's easy, isn't it? Go on, go on, don't be afraid." As Danny's mantra mingles with a crashing sea, a seductive two-note suspension sounds again and again, seeming to draw the despairing Joan Fontaine out the window—until suddenly, a real sound, a brilliant fireball exploding in the sky, startles her out of her trance, and agitated strings bring her back to the present. Here is a supreme example of what Hitchcock called "pure cinema," a treat to the eye and ear no matter how many times we experience it.

Rebecca marked the first time Hitchcock had access to a lush Hollywood score, and he used it to full advantage. Arthur Benjamin's *Storm Clouds Cantata,* Korngold's full-bodied orchestrations of Strauss in *Waltzes from Vienna,* and the lengthy quotation from *Tristan* in *Murder!* showed he was willing, in his British period, to experiment with big Romantic sounds, but only on a relatively restricted basis. Wagner on the radio was one thing, a Wagnerian score coursing through a two-hour picture something else alto-

Rebecca. **Music as siren call.**

gether. Part of Hitchcock's inhibition was undoubtedly budgetary: commissioning a long score with a full orchestra was difficult in the rickety British cinema industry in the 1930s. It was far easier in Golden Age Hollywood, which enjoyed a tradition stretching back to Max Steiner's *King Kong.* Part of Hitchcock's restraint was also aesthetic, a matter of choice: he was fundamentally a classicist, and his willingness to use a rich, extended symphonic score—the most radical instance being *Vertigo*—was reserved for projects that seemed to demand such music. Hitchcock's distinctive contribution was his ability to make music the center of the narrative even when its actual use was concise and spare. *Rebecca* marked the first time a symphonic composer was allowed full rein. Counting the Selznick "Trademark" overture by Alfred Newman, the dense three-and-a-half page cue sheet lists seventy-one items, most by Waxman but also six by Max Steiner and two by Johann Strauss. In *Suspicion* and *Shadow of a Doubt*, Hitchcock would distort classic waltzes for suspenseful purposes; here they provide a grandiloquent backdrop for the "whirlwind romance" between Max and the anonymous heroine. (The waltz playing during the "Hotel Lobby" cue is Waxman's own.)[1]

This symphonic lavishness is a startling contrast to the skimpy cues in British Hitchcock. More spare scores would follow, but subtlety was not the point of *Rebecca*. This is Hitchcock's Cinderella story, and music supplies enchantment. With few exceptions, Waxman's complex tapestry of moods and character sketches envelopes the movie from beginning to end: the haunted hero and heroine float through Monte Carlo and Manderley in a sonic dreamscape, carried along by anxieties and impulses powered by Waxman's sensual harmonies.

British Hitchcock relied heavily on source music, the sounds of real life, to make its dramatic points. This method worked admirably both as sonic realism and as a practical response to budget austerities of a film industry that by the onset of World War II was in depressing decline. *Rebecca*, Hitchcock's most dreamlike movie, deals in psychological realism only. "Last night I dreamt I went to Manderley again," begins Joan Fontaine's nocturnal voice-over, wrapped in harp glissandos; the movie records that dream, beginning with a wistful woodwind melody associated with the great house. Manderley is now "a desolate shell, with no whisper of the past about its staring walls. We can never go back to Manderley again; that much is certain."

But is it? An ascending brass chorale takes us back anyway, moving up a steep cliff to the top of the precipice from which Laurence Olivier's Max de Winter stares, contemplating suicide, the camera watching his feet move slowly to the edge until the young dreamer, powered by a redemptive love theme, intrudes to save his life. "Stop!" she cries, the first line in the scene. They meet and fall in love, then slowly into nightmare. Dissonant glissandos depict "I," the young heroine, dreaming uneasily of Rebecca after merely hearing her name; from there on, music becomes the sounding board for the subconscious.

Dreams this elegant are costly, but since the film was financed by David Selznick, Hitchcock was able to bring it to life with star power and glossy production values, including the high-Gothic cinematography of George Barnes. Selznick hired the best—not only Waxman, but Hitchcock himself. Indeed, Hitchcock came to America at Selznick's request. He put out the word that he wanted to relocate in Hollywood, and Selznick was shrewd enough to respond.[2]

It was an admirable arrangement: Selznick wanted stars for his four-year-old Selznick International Studio and knew Hitchcock was one of the few directors—in an era before auteurs were celebrities—who qualified as one. Hitchcock wanted more money for his projects, but he also wanted respect, something he would never get in a country that regarded movies as vulgar entertainment for the working class. For a European artist, Selznick represented an American ideal. America might be a philistine society, but Hollywood's tradition of blending high- and middle-brow culture into one glamorous product was Hitchcock's cup of tea.

In a happy coincidence, Franz Waxman, Dimitri Tiomkin, Miklos Rozsa, and other Hitchcock composers came to America during the same period. Max Steiner, who was working on *Gone With the Wind* with Selznick across the street from *Rebecca,* was already established, a role model for what could happen under the right circumstances. As Jews fleeing the Nazis, these composers had far more at stake than Hitchcock. They fit perfectly into his projects; thorough professionals and quick studies, they soon learned to combine European formalism with Hollywood glamour, exactly as Hitchcock would. Their scores provided the complex emotional undercurrent for Hitchcock's mixture of European sophistication and American brashness.

Rebecca's story line also fit the émigré pattern. Like Hitchcock and Waxman, its nameless heroine is an orphan, a stranger in a bizarre, glamorous new world. Manderley is a stand-in for Hollywood, a wondrous but artificial place full of seductive wealth and great peril. By marrying Maxim de Winter, "I" found herself hitched up with romantic excitement but also terrible trauma, as did Hitchcock-Waxman when they linked their fortunes with Selznick: as his studio began looking for a composer in August 1939, World War II erupted, leaving both men—along with Laurence Olivier and the rest of the British cast—shaken and worried about their loved ones back home. Hitchcock had chosen to come to America, but Waxman, after being attacked on a Berlin street by Nazis, left Germany for Paris and then America. He could never go back; for him, the Old World was lost forever.[3] It is not surprising that *Rebecca*'s music, despite its silken veneer, has a bleak, haunted undertone, nor that its most celebrated cues resurrect a dead past.

Like many of Hitchcock's composers, Waxman was well regarded, though not yet a heavy hitter. He had scored *The Bride of Frankenstein*—another Gothic thriller directed by a British auteur produced in Hollywood with a British cast—but James Whale was not yet a cult figure. (With its soaring "Bride" theme, its sustained pedal points, and its spectacular final inferno, *Bride* has eerie parallels to *Rebecca.*) On loan to Selznick International from Metro-Goldwyn-Mayer, Waxman had scored Selznick's 1938 *The Young in Heart,* receiving two Academy Award nominations. After *Rebecca,* he would make three other Hitchcock pictures: *Suspicion,* which has a Gothic splendor not unlike *Rebecca*'s; *The Paradine Case,* which is more experimental; and *Rear Window,* which maps out new territory altogether. Waxman was valuable to Hitchcock not only for his reliability and professionalism but for his remarkable versatility: a bearer of the Mahler-Strauss late-Romantic torch, he nonetheless got his start orchestrating Friedrich Hollander's *Blue Angel* and Jerome Kern and Oscar Hammerstein's *Music in the Air* and would go on to write scores ranging from the jazz in *Crime in the Streets* to the Rimsky-Korsakovian *Taras Bulba.*

Initially, Selznick wanted Hitchcock to direct a disaster movie about the *Titanic,* but prospects for that project suddenly sank when he discovered that the *Leviathan,* the World War I ship he wanted to use, was prohibitively expensive. Deeply skeptical of the project, Hitchcock was relieved and happy that *Rebecca,* Daphne du Maurier's best-selling Gothic, would be their first project. Both men had read the novel and sensed it could make a sensational picture.

But that was about all they agreed on. Hitchcock and Selznick had very different ideas about moviemaking, and both were powerful personalities obsessed with control. Each assumed from the beginning that he was the auteur. For Selznick, Hitchcock was a star hired to sell his product and submit to his authority; to Hitchcock, Selznick was a welcome entrée to America but also an interfering annoyance. His relationship with Selznick quickly became a struggle for control foreshadowing many others, including his crisis with Bernard Herrmann thirty years later.

From Hitchcock's point of view, the most revealing and critical fight was over *Rebecca*'s ending. The producer wanted a giant supernatural R to appear in the clouds as the final image, but Hitchcock found this idea unspeakable and managed to dissuade Selznick from perpetrating it; instead the R naturalistically goes up in flames on a pillowcase against a final orchestral blast of the Rebecca theme. As late as the 1970s, Hitchcock was still telling this story. He recounted it to John Williams during work on *Family Plot,* finding by then mischievous irony rather than scorn: "His point," says Williams "was that Selznick was not very talented, and had ideas that were not particularly good, but 'from bad ideas, good ones can come.'"[4]

Selznick won other struggles, however, and to this day, controversy continues over who is the real auteur. Selznick was determined to get all of Daphne du Maurier's popular, bleakly detailed novel up on the screen in linear narrative sequence, a method far more literal than Hitchcock's jagged, nonlinear eccentricities would allow. Selznick hated Hitchcock's "goddamn jigsaw cutting," even though he liked Hitchcock personally and admired his professionalism.[5]

Some argue that *Rebecca* was Hitchcock's picture for the simple reason that Selznick was preoccupied with principal photography for *Gone With the Wind,* his most famous production then, or ever: "Selznick just did not have time to interfere much," writes Hitchcock biographer John Russell Taylor, "beyond the usual barrage of memos."[6] According to John Waxman, *Gone With the Wind* was "the thousand-pound gorilla in the room" throughout the production of *Rebecca.*[7] Hitchcock's idiosyncratic method of "cutting in the camera," shooting only what was in the script rather than using lengthy master shots that allowed extensive reediting by the producer, was abhorrent to Selznick, who wanted control over the final picture. But he was too obsessed with *Gone With the Wind,* firing one director after another and ultimately directing it himself, to control *Rebecca* as well. He allowed Hitchcock to have his way, and *Rebecca* turned out to be such a hit, winning the Oscar for Best Picture, that conflicts on the set were forgotten. "Hitch was vindicated, and in after years Selznick would say that Hitch was the only director, absolutely the only director, whom he would completely trust with a picture."[8]

But others, especially highbrow Hitchcockians who love to sniff at *Rebecca* and Selznick, insist that Selznick won the battle. Since he had the power, they argue, he prevailed, resulting in an entertaining but non-Hitchcockian product.[9] This view extends to *Rebecca*'s music. According to Rudy Behlmer, "The musical decisions were made by Selznick, not Hitchcock. David was the guy who did the postproduction. He was responsible for *Rebecca*'s music."[10] (A third view holds that *Rebecca* is the product of a creative, mutually enriching tension between producer and director that forced each man to learn from the other: Selznick about visual composition and narrative suspense, Hitchcock about psychological nuance, good production values, and good taste.)[11]

The archives make it clear that Hitchcock was a strong force behind Waxman's music. Hitchcock did have a conference with Waxman in late November, after which the composer presented voluminous music notes to Selznick. This fascinating document, which Waxman calls "a rough outline on the musical score of *Rebecca,* with a few ideas of mine," is detailed and specific. It is one piece in the complex drama of a film composer caught between two powerful artists with conflicting agendas and demands. Some of the issues—the ethical appropriateness of a producer inserting other com-

posers' cues, the argument over whether the script should precede everything else—are contentious controversies to this day, in television as well as
film.

It all started with a hectic Selznick memo to the music department on
August 14, 1939, engaging Max Steiner to score *Gone With the Wind*—and
more: "If you can arrange for Max to start at once, please do so, and have
him report to me. The arrangement should include, if possible, our privi-
lege to use him in whatever capacity we want in connection with the final
scoring of 'Intermezzo.' . . . If you could arrange for him to stay here after
'Wind' to do the 'Rebecca' score, I would like this too."[12]

Max Steiner, then, was the original *Rebecca* composer. It is fascinating
to contemplate how his broad, sweeping style, so different from Waxman's
veiled impressionism, would have changed the tone of the picture. We'll
never know, for typically and impossibly, Selznick wanted everything, all at
once. Scoring *Gone With the Wind* at Selznick's breakneck pace almost did
Steiner in, as it did nearly everyone connected with the project; the notion
of creating three big scores simultaneously was unthinkable, even for the
prolific Steiner, even if such a thing was normal for the maniacally worka-
holic Selznick. Two months later, Selznick signed on Waxman in a loan-out
arrangement with MGM. "I am delighted," he wrote, "that you are going to
be doing another job for us, and a very important one."[13]

By November, Selznick was having doubts about Steiner's ability to
complete *Gone With the Wind,* so much so that he hired Waxman not only
for *Rebecca,* but also as an "insurance composer" for *Gone With the Wind*
against "the possibility that Max will not be ready by our deadline." In a frantic memo to Lou Forbes in the music department, Selznick demanded "a
daily report from you, without fail, telling me the exact progress of each
score." Adding to the freneticism was Selznick's determination to get *Rebecca*
out in time for Christmas, even in the tumult of completing his two other
projects: "This is an awful thing to bring up in the middle of our rush on
'Gone With the Wind,' and while Hal is still breaking his neck to get 'Intermezzo' out, but I regard it as of the most vital importance that we should get
'Rebecca' out with more speed than we have finished up any other picture."[14]

Selznick acknowledged that the December release date sounded ridiculous but insisted on pushing for it anyway. By early December, he had abandoned this fantasy, but not before subjecting everyone in the project to tremendous stress. The fall was flooded with Selznick memos denouncing the
"wretchedly organized" music department and demanding that Waxman
produce everything immediately. Despite Selznick's skepticism, Steiner pro-

SELZN K INTERNATIONAL PICTUR , INC.
CULVER CITY, CALIFORNIA

INTER-OFFICE COMMUNICATION

TO   Mr. Lou Forbes - cc: Mr. Ginsberg, Mr. Kern

SUBJECT:

OFFICE OF
DAVID O. SELZNICK
PRESIDENT

DATE   11/7/39 (Dict. 11/6/39)
                        copy

Commencing today, and daily until the score of "G.W.T.W." and the score
of "REBECCA" are completely finished, I should like a daily report from
you, without fail, telling me the exact progress of each score. In the
case of "Gone With the Wind," this should include exactly what Mr. Steiner
and his associates have accomplished, and exactly, also, what has been
accomplished by Mr. Waxman on the so-called insurance score that we are
having him write against the possibility that Max will not be ready by
our deadline date. Please be sure that this report does not include
hearsay information, but only facts that you yourself have checked.

Copies of this report should go to Mr. Ginsberg and Mr. Kern.

dos:bb   DOS

A demanding memo from David Selznick. Franz Waxman hired for *Rebecca* and as "insurance composer" for *Gone With the Wind*. (David Selznick Collection, Harry Ransom Humanities Research Center)

duced a score of sweeping grandeur and confidence, one of the most popular and enduring features of *Gone With the Wind*. Yet Selznick used the score as a template for disaster—he was convinced the score would flop and worried that the fiasco was about to be repeated: "Obviously," he warned on November 29, "we are about to be in for a repetition of our unfortunate Steiner occurrences, with Waxman."

Yet surprisingly, he submitted to an eccentric, time-consuming request by Hitchcock. Perhaps as a way of dealing with abandoning England for America, Hitchcock became obsessed with finding Norman O'Neill's music for a J. M. Barrie ghost drama he had seen in 1920 at London's Haymarket Theatre, a score he had never gotten out of his head. The play, *Mary Rose,* tells of a young woman who disappears while visiting an enchanted Hebrides island, reappearing unaltered twenty-five years later to find her young son gone; heartbroken, she dies and appears as a ghost in the family home. But she is too lost to remember who she is searching for when her son finally returns. The music in this production made a profound impression on the young Hitchcock; he was especially struck by "the Call" connected with the heroine's disappearance, an effect produced by bagpipes and "wordless voices" sounded from a musical saw. He remembered it as "celestial voices, like Debussy's 'Sirenes.'"[15] Desperate to recapture that lost moment, he engaged Selznick's management in a month-long search, hoping to fuse the *Mary Rose* music with Waxman's score.

On November 9, Selznick fired off a memo to his music department: "Can you dig up the music score which accompanied part of the J. M. Barrie play produced in New York fifteen or twenty years ago called 'Mary Rose' and starring, I believe, Ruth Chatterton. . . . Need this promptly if we can get it." The next day, he sent a follow-up to Daniel O'Shea, clarifying that the musical title was "The Call": "It is Waxman that I wanted to hear this music, and I want to hear it myself." We'll never know what Hitchcock said to tweak Selznick's interest, but it was obviously persuasive. (Selznick had heard the music himself but could not remember it.)

Unfortunately, no one ever got to hear *Mary Rose.* A series of futile searches by Selznick's searchers culminated in a bizarre November 15 memo describing a "most peculiar time trying to obtain Mary Rose music." The woman in charge of the estate was "slightly crackpot. . . . She does not feel well and it takes great energy to get into the files. We converse with her daily about her health." Apparently, they conversed with her for weeks, because Hitchcock did not abandon the search until late November, after *Rebecca* was officially in postproduction. The search itself may seem slightly crackpot, but Hitchcock somehow managed to communicate the lost, otherworldly tone of the *Mary Rose* score to Waxman early on. A memo to Lou Forbes on November 28 shows that Selznick encouraged Hitchcock to do precisely that: "Mr. Hitchcock agrees that the 'Mary Rose' music might be useful to Waxman in indicating what we are after for the 'Rebecca' theme." The same memo clarifies Selznick's own vision of *Rebecca's* motif: "Please make clear to Mr. Waxman that the 'Rebecca' theme should not be depressing. If anything, it ought to be on the sensuous side."

For Hitchcock, this was only the beginning. *Mary Rose* became a lifelong obsession, one not unlike those suffered by many of his characters who try in vain to resurrect lost loved ones. As Christopher Husted points out in a groundbreaking essay, the narrative as well as the tone of *Mary Rose* fit *Rebecca* with uncanny exactness: "Not entirely unlike Mary Rose, Rebecca 'returns' from the sea after a long absence."[16] And it fit other movies as well. As we shall see, Hitchcock instigated another futile search during *Vertigo*, again a film about an obsessive inability to bury the past. Again, he ended up with a sublimely ghostly score from his composer, Bernard Herrmann.

Immediately after the *Mary Rose* search, Hitchcock met with Waxman. Finally, he was able to deal with real rather than remembered music, with an artist in the present rather than an ephemeral, Proustian recollection. Produced through consultation with Hitchcock, Waxman's "Music Notes, Rebecca" are the earliest and one of the clearest revelations of how Hitchcock worked with a composer. Waxman sent them on December 2, along with his usual request to Selznick: "I hope you will have time to run the picture with me before you leave." In his memo, he expressed relief that Hitchcock agreed with his ideas; in the notes, he welcomed Selznick's input. Where Hitchcock and Waxman were undecided on whether or not to use music, or what kind, he left question marks and asked for Selznick's judgment (e.g., "Marriage Scene: Attention Mr. Selznick: Do you want music?").

Waxman's notes are similar in attitude and even style to those Hitchcock himself made, particularly in his later films, leading one to wonder whether Hitchcock was influenced by his association with Waxman in this, his first Hollywood picture. In the elaborate confession cue, Waxman stated that the music would be "very low in volume and register," building

> very slowly and very gradually, keeping the suspense higher and higher until after Maxim says "I hated her"—The Rebecca theme, which so far has been highly emotional and haunting, suddenly and very abruptly turns to an almost vicious character revealing the real character of Rebecca. We keep this mood through the following scene of his description of the life Rebecca was really living until he says: "She was alone." Only a faint tympani roll is heard, and at the moment the camera shows the close-up of the coffee table and couch, a new strain of melody starts ascending from a ghostly pianissimo, following the camera movement of Maxim's description of the accident. Together with Maxim's descrip-

tion of the boat capsizing and sinking the music comes to a tragic end, leaving the two people in silence. I am sure the following scene where "I" restores Maxim's confidence and encourages him not to give up, will be twice as effective without music, especially after the long and stirring dramatic sequence which has just ended.

The precision and accuracy of this description, realized in the final film almost exactly, reveals a composer in total charge of his craft, and thoroughly in tune with his director. Numerous details—the faint tympani roll, the subtle crescendo, the directive that the dramatic final moments should be shrouded in silence rather than concluding with a big cadence—were methods that had been part of Hitchcock's musical signature since *Blackmail*, as was Waxman's concept of music as a character marker and mood setter.

Many other scenes described in the notes emerged intact as well. An example is Beatrice's revelation about Mrs. Danvers's love for Rebecca during the dramatic profile shot of "I": "After Beatrice says 'she simply adored Rebecca,' we pick up the Rebecca theme with a chord as camera discovers profile closeup of 'I' turning around—music out as we dissolve to luncheon scene." The introduction of Mrs. Danvers and her dour woodwind theme is also clearly noted: "Music playing the Manderley theme during entrance changes with Mrs. Danvers' appearance—stops with dropping of gloves—a moment of embarrassing silence in the music—and with the picking up of the gloves the music slowly sneaks in reestablishing the former mood."

In these and other instances, Waxman was thus able to anticipate shifting moods and silences of the most minute sort. But other scenes were changed in postproduction. Selznick had his own music notes (apparently now lost), which, on November 28, he asked the music department to share with Hitchcock "in case he has any suggestions." Hitchcock's participation in the musical process, therefore, included consultations with both Selznick and Waxman, and he may well have concurred with some of Selznick's emendations. The most striking example of a scene changed after the Hitchcock-Waxman meeting is Max's explosive honeymoon slide viewing, an early instance of Hitchcock's fondness for movies within movies: "After 'I' says 'there would never be any gossip' music sneaks in under noise of camera—as a matter of fact, the first bars of music should mix with the camera noise so that when Max stops the camera the music will be there without having a noticeable entrance. Music will continue until the fadeout." Waxman's preference for music sneaking in without an entrance, blending subtly with other sound track noise, contradicts the myth that he was interested only in italicizing emotion. But his intentions were sabotaged, for there is no music in this scene at all. Its stark power, darkly shadowed except for Max's demonically lit face, is emphasized by deadly silence broken only by the clattering home-movie camera. Did Selznick make the decision to opt for grim silence or did Hitchcock, who had a penchant for quiet where we least expect it?

The notes reveal that Waxman shared Hitchcock's preference for counterpoint over imitation, as shown in the Manderley Ball scene: "As 'I' comes downstairs the orchestra strikes up some music of a neutral, rather conventional character which they would play at the beginning of the ball before the guests have arrived . . . music which should be in contrast to the excitement of 'I' and the nervous reaction of Maxim." This indeed turned out to be the scene with the greatest tension between music and the emotion shown on the screen. The note also clarifies what is implied but (because we never see an orchestra) not shown: the lengthy "conventional" waltz here is one of the few instances of source music. It is also—in contrast to the straightforward Strauss cues in the opening courtship scenes—another example of Hitchcock's use of waltzes as a veneer covering impending disaster.

Waxman made rough sketches of central themes early on. Like Hitchcock, he had an uncanny ability to see and hear things in advance. But because he had seen little of the picture, he could not, as executive manager Daniel O'Shea patiently pointed out in a memo to Selznick, work on the score in any sustained way "until he had complete sequences from us so he could accomplish his timing." While he was waiting, he was hard at work on *Florian* for his regular employer, MGM.

Selznick would have none of this. Furious, he sent out a barrage of the cranky memos for which he was notorious. The most extraordinary one, dated December 1, the day before Waxman sent over his music notes, blurts out a theory of film composing that had been implicit in his previous demands: "I have maintained for years, and still maintain, that the idea that music cannot be written until a picture is finally cut is so much nonsense. It is the equivalent of saying that the score for an opera or a musical comedy could not be written until the libretto was finally completed and cut." Like Hitchcock, Selznick saw film music as similar to opera. For composers, however, words to songs were not equivalent to images on a screen. Even in its early stages, film music was contracted to be written after edited scenes were available. Composers were put under tremendous time constraints but at least were able to see precisely what they had to do. Their talent consisted in being able to work quickly once they had what they needed; a genius like Korngold was capable of banging out the score on the piano as the scenes rolled by on a screen, much like a jazz improviser, but he needed to see and to measure.

This universally understood process was not fast enough for Selznick: "I think that scores have suffered tremendously because of this attitude, and that release dates have suffered also." As far as he was concerned, such expendables as melody, rhythm, and continuity could simply be adjusted after the fact. "There is no reason on earth why a score shouldn't be written from a rough assembly, even if it involves a certain amount of rewriting when the picture is finally cut. The exact timing of music has little or nothing to do with the composition of it, particularly as to the themes, and in fact all the music strains, regardless of whether a scene is ten feet or a hundred feet longer or shorter." Ultimately, Selznick wanted to take music out of postproduction altogether: "It is my conviction that as time goes on the score of a picture will be written from the script so that by the time a picture has finished shooting, the score is complete as far as composition goes, and only such rewriting and rearranging is necessary as editing indicates. . . . I think this ought to be hammered into Waxman."

The notion of music as an infinitely malleable piece of putty shaped in advance as the script was written may have been a Selznickian fantasy, but so determined was he to get his way that he came up with yet another plan for having the music when he wanted it: a corporate cannibalization (already in progress with a movie called *Raffles*). In a December 12 memo, he wrote O'Shea and the music department of his desire to experiment with a "Music Corporation scoring method" whereby MCA would cobble together a score based on the broad outlines of Waxman's themes. Typically, Selznick was simultaneously preoccupied with something huge and impending—the Atlanta premiere of *Gone With the Wind,* no less—and so delayed making a decision on this scheme until he came back: "I'd like to have all the information by the time I return, meanwhile letting Waxman proceed, without discouraging him with any knowledge that we are considering any other plan."

By January, when Selznick came back from Atlanta, some in the music department were having doubts, as indicated by a memo from R. A. Klune: "In order to have the Music Corporation estimate the cost of scoring *Rebecca,* using Waxman's compositions," Klune wrote on January 6, "it would be necessary for us to request Waxman to turn his compositions over to us for a period of a few days. In this event, we might be hard put as it would be difficult to employ subterfuge as a reason for this, and anything else would undoubtedly immediately make Waxman very recalcitrant."

Klune was not convinced that any subterfuges would actually save money: "Waxman has sworn to me that the cost of the Rebecca score, which would include arrangements, copying, and all musicians, would be kept within $12,000, including Waxman." Two days later, Selznick told Klune that he, too, was having doubts about making away with Waxman's manuscripts without his knowledge. Perhaps complete openness was the best policy, especially since Waxman was not costing the studio an inordinate amount of money: "Handle this matter any way you see fit, including possibly telling Waxman very frankly what we are doing. However, Waxman's estimate, if it can be accepted, seems reasonable enough. If you want to show the picture to the Music Corporation representatives, feel free to do so." Others in the music department, unaware of the plan, were urging Selznick to sit down with Waxman and hear his themes before storming through to completion with edited scenes. On January 15, Klune informed Selznick that the MCA "arrangement" of Waxman's sketches would still cost $12,000. Then there was the delicate problem of a maestro: "MCA feels that any arrangement calculated to use Waxman's compositions with somebody else conducting would not work out satisfactorily."

Here the paper trail ends, and so, apparently, did the proposed plan. By February 3, matters were back where they started, with Klune reminding Selznick that Waxman could not begin sustained work until he has completed sequences, and Selznick grumbling back: "I don't understand why it isn't possible for Waxman to go right ahead with the completion of his scoring. . . . The cutting is practically final on almost the entire picture and I think it is a pity that the music for the entire picture has not yet been even composed." There was no further mention of the proposed corporate scoring shortcut.

The good news was that the final cut was indeed nearly complete. Once edited scenes were available, Waxman worked intensively and completed over two hours of music, which he recorded in time for the New York premiere on March 28. Waxman was surely correct in insisting that he needed complete sequences to get right those pesky timings that Selznick deemed so insignificant.

The entire process had taken just over six months, with a big push at the end. Given the complexity and poetry of the score, this brief amount of composing time seems remarkable, but it was by no means unusual in the movie-music business. Hitchcock's contribution was scantier than Selznick's behind-the-scenes maneuverings, but more fruitful. His search for *Mary Rose* was a failure, but through it he communicated the haunted tone that Waxman got into the music; and his conference with Waxman certainly seemed more productive than Selznick's fretting.

John Waxman points out that his father and Hitchcock were together more than they were apart and speculates that they were "allies against Selznick's interference."[17] We can be grateful that Waxman was allowed to write his own score rather than having it snatched away and reconstituted by a corporate entity. But it was a close, scary call: "I think there is tremendous saving to be effected here," Selznick wrote in his memo of December 12, "and if the product doesn't suffer too greatly, I think we should go for it commencing with *Rebecca*." How greatly is too greatly? When music is seen as a product, one shudders to contemplate the answer. (This cannibalizing process was eventually unleashed on television, as we shall see, in *Alfred Hitchcock Presents*.)

Hollywood is as unreal as the movies made there; once *Rebecca* was released and became a hit, the tensions suddenly evaporated as if they had never existed. The score that had been so troublesome and the occasion of so much vitriol and manipulation became a hit, making lots of gravy both for the movie and for Waxman personally. Selznick's memos and Waxman's references to his producer became mutually benign and cheery.

On April 12, within a month of *Rebecca*'s release, Klune wrote his superiors that Waxman had been asked to arrange and conduct a twelve-minute *Rebecca* Suite for the *Standard Symphony Hour*, "as you know a very popular program," sponsored by Standard Oil on NBC. "Franz tells me," continued Klune, "that to the best of his knowledge this will be the first time" a film score would be used on the show. Sensing a golden publicity opportunity, Selznick encouraged Waxman to go ahead. He did, creating a suite consisting of variations on the *Rebecca* theme and conducting the Los Angeles Philharmonic in a performance that was recorded for Selznick by his music department. This was the first of many Waxman arrangements of his music for concert purposes, including another request by the Standard Oil program to use the *Rebecca* Suite in 1942. It was an early example of film scores used for concert purposes: Hollywood music would continue to cross over into classical, as it regularly does today. It was also an enterprising use of a score to promote a movie over a long period, a phenomenon that would continue with the next Hitchcock-Selznick production, *Spellbound*.

After the Standard Oil commission, Waxman was asked to deliver a talk to the Federation of Women's Clubs in Hollywood. His lecture, entitled

Rebecca Suite. An early instance of music enlisted to sell a movie. By Franz Waxman. (Courtesy of John Waxman. Copyright © 1940 by Bourne Co. Copyright Renewed. All Rights Reserved. International Copyright Secured.)

"History of Motion Picture Music," centered on *Rebecca*. As we shall see, it offered illuminating commentary, especially on the *Rebecca* theme. Waxman used the occasion to praise Selznick: "His interest and painstaking work for the minute detail in the production of a motion picture is stimulating to the creative artist." In addition, Waxman celebrated having become an American citizen, which he termed "the happiest day of my life." Klune, who encouraged Waxman to go forward with the lecture, attended and on

May 3 sent Selznick an ecstatic letter: "Approximately two hundred women were present. . . . Every one of them had seen *Rebecca* once and better than half of them had seen it twice."

For years, highbrow critics sniffed that *Rebecca* was a middlebrow women's picture, but the musical community was not so snooty. After the Los Angeles Philharmonic commission came a request by Gregor Piatigorsky, a lifelong friend of Waxman's and a great *Rebecca* admirer, for a symphonic poem for cello and orchestra based on *Rebecca*. In asking for permission from Selznick, Waxman stated that Piatigorsky "as you probably know is one of the two great living cello virtuosos [Casals, presumably, being the other]."[18] Selznick immediately responded to the music department regarding Waxman's query: "I think we should do this for him, and that we shouldn't try to make any money out of it."[19] Waxman, alas, never wrote the piece, but the incident illustrates that Selznick's behavior could be graceful as well as crass.

Crassness was nevertheless just around the corner, as was the need for control. Waxman could not have been happy (though he never said so publicly) that the music in the final cut of *Rebecca* was not entirely his. Fearing that the Waxman's score was insufficiently lush, Selznick had called on Steiner at the last minute to enrich several scenes, an ironic reversal given his hiring of Waxman as Steiner's "insurance composer." He inserted a Steiner cue from *Little Lord Fauntleroy* into *Rebecca,* and, much more bizarrely, stuck snippets from all sorts of things—Waxman's "Trouble for Two" from *He Goes to Court,* "Brink Is Back" from *On Borrowed Time,* "George Anne" from *The Young in Heart*—into the spare woodwind music for Mrs. Danvers. Out went Waxman's evocatively descending parallel chords; in went arbitrary tunes from other Waxman cues. He also yanked out Waxman's cool, elegant music for Beatrice, an incisive character portrait, again substituting a Steiner cue.[20] The conviction that a given score lacked Romanticism became a kind of obsession with Selznick: even *Spellbound* didn't meet his requirements, and at the end of postproduction he demanded that Miklos Rozsa add as many violins for the main title as Waxman had used in *Rebecca*. By this time, bolstered by the public's enthusiasm for the film, he had concluded that *Rebecca* was indeed lush enough a model for how souped up a movie score could be.

Even this eccentric tampering did not fundamentally alter Waxman's music. With more than seventy Waxman cues, Selznick had time to corrupt only a few of them. It was Hitchcock who gave *Rebecca* its distinctive flavor. According to John Waxman, Selznick had a "finger in the music," but the mood conjured by his father's music was "established by Hitchcock's vision. Hitchcock knew what he wanted."[21]

Selznick's influence was by no means all negative. It is hard to ignore his role in Hitchcock's initiation into Hollywood music, especially since some of the most striking Hitchcock scores were made in the Selznick Studio. Selznick was a lavish producer whose taste in music was, as with everything else, larger than life. Often in *Rebecca* one can sense the double imprint of producer and director, and Waxman's score reinforces the strengths of both. A stirring example of music playing out in both Selznick and Hitchcock styles is a cue called "Arrival at Manderley," which builds a crescendo on the courtship theme, continues in an impressionist wash of rain music, and culminates in a major-key explosion of the Manderley theme as Max, seeing the great house looming ahead, shouts "That's it! That's Manderley!" The majesty of the scene is Selznickian, like a black-and-white outtake from *Gone With the Wind*. But the camera closes on anxiety and awe in the close-up of Joan Fontaine, whose face precisely embodies Waxman's music, converting the scene into a Hitchcockian shot. This type of car scene, music coursing through rapid motion and close-ups, became a Hitchcock signature in *To Catch a Thief*, *Vertigo*, *Psycho*, and many other of his films.

The interaction among Selznick, Hitchcock, and Waxman, the New World and the Old, full of tension yet often complementary, parallels the *Rebecca* story line. The unnamed heroine played by Joan Fontaine—young, naïve, and clumsy, yet brave and spunky—is a stand-in for America, though not identified as an American, a breath of freshness and innocence, her identity unformed; her lover, Max, played by Laurence Olivier—brooding, burned out, given to sudden rages, obsessed by a dead past—is a European with lots of baggage, the Old World aristocrat reinvigorated and saved by the New. "You've blotted out the past for me more than all the bright lights of Monte Carlo," Max tells his "child" bride.

But keeping the past at bay is not easy. *Rebecca* is about the terrible struggle to break out of obsession with a deadly yesterday and to live for today, a conflict embedded in every phrase of the music. *Rebecca* was the beginning of a post-British Hitchcock sound that captured the suppressed obsessions of his characters more eloquently than words, even the torrent of them in this, the master's talkiest film. Waxman's music doesn't accompany the story so much as dramatize it, pitting the Rebecca melody, a siren call of the dead, against the music associated with the new Mrs. de Winter, including an airy courtship tune, an exotic car-driving melody (both part of a "Tennis Montage"), and a full-blown love song. This symphonic struggle is resolved only at the end, as the latter has the last word in the final cadence, after a climactic brass chorale of Rebecca's music and the omnipresent R on her pillowcase go up in flames.

Waxman's score provides inner momentum for a story line more languid than Hitchcock's usual. From the mysterious horn motif rising from dark string tremolos opening the title sequence through the secretive chords of the confession scene to the cathartic fire music, the score moves the drama, creating a meaning behind the images. Menacing variations on the *Rebecca* theme trouble the heroine's dreams even before she knows what the nightmares are about, suggesting what is behind the door as she moves trancelike toward Rebecca's bedroom to the strain of haunting string tremolos. These become more sinister as Mrs. Danvers, suddenly appearing like a ghost, opens the drapes to magical harp glissandos that fill the huge room with Rebecca's presence, the music enlarging its great space as it intones one of her many incantations: "Do you think the dead come back to haunt the living? Sometimes I wonder if she doesn't come back here to Manderley to watch you and Mr. de Winter." It is Mrs. Danvers, of course, Rebecca's emissary, who does the haunting and watching, her penetrating eyes (which Hitchcock "directed," Judith Anderson once said with admiration) moving about the enchanted room as it dissolves into the sea, its crashing waves mingling with the Rebecca theme.

Rebecca may be dead, but Waxman is the talisman who brings her back, much as Bernard Herrmann resurrected Carlotta in *Vertigo* and Norman Bates's mother in *Psycho*. In his speech to the Hollywood Federation of Women's Clubs, Waxman revealed that this was his most daunting challenge in the film: "The really dominant character in the story is dead. . . . Yet the entire drama revolves around her. Through the speech and action of others, and particularly through the use of music, her character, with all its powerful effects, had to be revealed to the audience." In its early stages, movie music was experienced by audiences as inherently mysterious and disturbing, so why not exploit its uncanny capabilities? "Whenever a scene involving Rebecca appeared on the screen, it was up to the music to give Rebecca's character life and presence."

This idea of music hovering about as a supernatural presence capable of revealing the character of someone living or dead was a Hitchcock signature, but it went against the academic notion, already hardening into cliché, that film music should be unnoticed and unnoticeable. Waxman was aware of his heresy: "I read a statement in one of the musical papers the other day where somebody said that a good motion picture score should be of such nature that you don't notice it. . . . It should be unobtrusive and so much in the background that on leaving the theater one wouldn't be sure that there was any music in the picture at all." Waxman thought this was silly: "If it is so subdued that its only virtue lies in the fact that it is not noticeable, it can hardly be effective. A motion picture score should be noticed just as much as you notice the other elements."

Waxman's vision of music as a palpable presence was precisely in line with Hitchcock's. From the opening timpani rolls and swirling string glissandos, *Rebecca*'s music is anything but subdued. Dramatizing James Joyce's dictum in *Dubliners* that "absence is the highest form of presence," Waxman evokes a character who is not there, yet always present, enabling Hitchcock to give us his most mysterious femme fatale, one never shown even in a flashback or photo. The *Rebecca* melody is omnipresent, though not always in full orchestral regalia. The lush orchestra of the title sequence is sometimes reduced to a smaller ensemble, a "ghost orchestra," in Waxman's words, colored by the unearthly sound of an electric organ and two electronic instruments called novachords, the predecessor of Miklos Rozsa's theremin in *Spellbound*. To Waxman, the novachord had "a peculiar sound of unreality—of something that you cannot define." Its "sinister purr," in Christopher Palmer's phrase, floats through the Gothic spaces of Manderley, appearing with the phantomlike Mrs. Danvers.[22]

Like a seductive disease, the Rebecca theme insinuates itself whenever the drowned femme fatale is mentioned or when the young bride blunders into one of her haunts, as in the discordant eruption of the tune in the boathouse scene. So potent is this idea that often only a fragment suffices, as in its brief return when the heroine's friend Beatrice dissolves and vanishes behind the anxious profile of "I" after revealing Mrs. Danvers's "adoration" of Manderley's former mistress (exactly as sketched in Waxman's notes).

But the love music is powerful as well and becomes a match for Rebecca's deadly siren call. The struggle between the two Mrs. de Winters, between life and the pull toward death, is dramatized symphonically. Stubbornly intervening during the haunted couple's worst crises, the love melody gradually solidifies the heroine's fragile identity, as when she summons her courage to demand that Mrs. Danvers throw out Rebecca's papers: "I am Mrs. de Winter now!" By the end, we know this is fully true as she leads Jasper, Rebecca's dog, from the flames of Manderley. Mrs. Danvers perishes in her own inferno as the love theme, rising from the ashes, does final, triumphant battle with the Rebecca motif.

Until recently, commentators tended to dismiss Waxman's *Rebecca* as gushy and overly italicized, but many cues tease the ear with irony and subtle counterpoint. Sometimes the score is comic, as when impish winds accompany Max's request, "Would you kindly ask Mrs. Van Hopper to come see me in my room?" or when collapsing strings draw "I" down into a chair at Max's exasperated marriage proposal: "I'm asking you to marry me, you little fool!" Sometimes it is whimsical, as in the delightful scenes where "I" sketches Alice in Wonderland and Joan of Arc for possible costumes. Sometimes it contradicts what is on the screen, as in the neutral waltz accompanying the disastrous masked-ball scene or the bland Monte Carlo restaurant music as the klutzy "I" has breakfast. Many cues have a rigorous classicism, including "Fireplace Tableaux," the creepy canon in Mrs. Danvers's penultimate scene, and the astringent waltz during her fiery immolation.

When the omnipresent music vanishes altogether, its sudden absence is shocking, as in the movie-within-a-movie honeymoon showing that the couple's happiness is "only a movie." The harrowing courtroom, blackmail, and medical-revelation scenes, in which Max must confront the legacy of his dead wife without the usual shields of wealth or charm, are shockingly bereft of music, making his isolation stark and painfully convincing. Although nearly every character has a Wagnerian motif, George Sanders's Jack, the "big bad wolf," has no music at all, allowing his scathing wit to come through unimpeded, keeping the movie from moving too far into Gothic otherworldliness.

The most original music in *Rebecca* consists of unresolved chord chains evoking anxiety and irresolution. These travel languidly around the mortified heroine after she smashes Rebecca's Cupid, drift through the dense fog as "I" searches for Max following her close call on the window ledge, surround the funereal close-ups of of men's feet in a barren room at the new inquest, give Rebecca's deserted boathouse a mysterious life, and ascend with morbid dissonance through the morning room of Manderley. Full of big Golden Age tunes, the score is most potent in its troubling evocation of ambivalence and mental instability: the hero with his mood swings and dark past, the young American heroine with her precarious identity. Commentators have given Bernard Herrmann credit for this modern musical style in cinema, but the seeds were in *Rebecca*.

The most extended example is in Max's confession scene, where Hitchcock, through music and circular close-ups of cigarette trays and other objects, manipulates the audience into visualizing Rebecca's death without resorting to flashback. As we have seen, Waxman and Hitchcock thoroughly mapped out this scene. It is long—indeed, its length feels risky—but the ever-shifting music brings it to life again and again when it seems to be faltering. This is a modern symphony of dread, repression, and final release based on color and wandering harmony. Scraps of motifs we have already heard—the sea theme, for example, crashing when Max reveals the secret of Rebecca's boat—weave through a haunted stream of tremolos, chimes, and novachords. This slow but strangely powerful sequence is suffused with secretive, anxious chords that speak painfully of Max's yearning for a peace and forgiveness not granted until the denouement.

In the climax of the scene, Max vents his rage at Rebecca, and "I" learns that her rival is a malignant fraud. As Waxman points out in his speech to the Federation of Women's Clubs (in language strikingly similar to his music notes), the revelation is musical: "At this moment, the theme, which so far has been given a haunting and almost lovely interpretation, turns suddenly vicious, revealing the true character of Rebecca, now played by the real orchestra in a dramatic and almost sinister form, ascending to the climax of the picture." The full orchestra takes over as Max sarcastically recounts Rebecca's ostensibly superior qualities—"breeding, brains, and beauty." It is the only full-blown melody in this lengthy musical narrative. The ghost orchestra never appears again; the real one plays Rebecca as she was, cool and vicious.

From here on, as Waxman notes, the real Rebecca is out in the open; the haunting is over. Knowing the true character of her rival, "I" rallies to save herself and her lover, confronting the fully orchestrated version of Rebecca's theme with her own music, which proves equally formidable. "Ascending to the climax of the picture" over the smoke and ruins of Manderley, this "almost sinister" music—a far more compelling embodiment of Rebecca than the supernatural "R" Selznick wanted etched in clouds—is vanquished by the soaring melody that belongs to "I."

Hitchcock was as ambivalent about *Rebecca* as he was about many of his films once they left his head and went into actual shooting. It made him famous in America and launched his Hollywood career, yet he made dismissive comments about it as a fairy tale and a "novellete" rather than a true Hitchcock picture. (His remark that it lacks Hitchcockian humor is odd given the hilarious Florence Bates in the Monte Carlo scenes and the scalding black humor of George Sanders and Gladys Cooper.) He did, however, agree with Truffaut's assertion that *Rebecca* always seemed undated, strangely modern—and confessed he had no idea why.

As we have seen, music is a key to the film's psychological modernity, for it consistently cues the characters' inner turmoil. *Rebecca* is indeed a fairy tale, a Cinderella story, but like du Maurier's gripping novel, is also a realistic depiction of guilt and anxiety. Dealing in psychology rather than physical confrontation, it is filled with suicides, both failed and successful: Max nearly plunges off the cliffs of Monte Carlo into the sea, saved at the last second by "I," who later nearly jumps out a window herself; Rebecca dies through a convoluted suicide designed to drag her husband down with her (a key change from the novel); she nearly succeeds a second time when Max almost surrenders his life to the hangman, again saved by the life-giving stubbornness of "I." In the only overtly physical sequence in the film, Mrs. Danvers consummates her passion for Rebecca by leaping into the flames of Manderley. These characters haunt themselves—they don't need Rebecca—and music unveils their obsessions. The use of a lavish, grandiose score to unveil a troubled inner world would continue in later Hitchcock movies, from *Spellbound* to *Vertigo*.

Waxman always regarded *Rebecca* as the masterpiece of his 144 Hollywood efforts. It was the score that gave him the most personal satisfaction and the most commercial cachet. The *Rebecca* Suite, the predecessor of his popular suites for *Sunset Boulevard* and *A Place in the Sun*, boosted his personal stock as well as that of the film; it also planted the seeds of Rozsa's *Spellbound* Suite five years later, which was used to plug the film in advance of its release. Waxman was convinced *Rebecca* would garner him an Oscar, so much so that he started to stand when he thought he saw Paramount's B. G. DeSylva looking straight at him before announcing Best Original Score, only to find the composers of *Pinocchio* rising behind him to get their award. As would be the case with later Hitchcock composers, Waxman's score represented a breakthrough in his career that other moviemakers asked him to emulate. Give us a *Rebecca* sound, they pleaded, even if the film had an urban setting. Christopher Husted notes that as late as the 1950s, Waxman films like *My Cousin Rachel* (another du Maurier treatment) and *Elephant Walk* "hoped to mimic the mystique of *Rebecca*."[23]

Hitchcockians distrust *Rebecca* because of its Selznickian linearity and lack of quirky eccentricity. The public, perhaps a better judge, has always loved it. Musically, it is one of Hitchcock's richest films, though for years commentators lambasted it for alleged hyperbole. Late in the twentieth century and early in the twenty-first, it got a significant boost with new recordings and reassessments. Robert Townson went so far as to declare it "arguably the best score for any Hitchcock picture."[24] Truffaut had it right in the 1960s when he commented that the music leaves a "haunting impression," one that lingers long after Rebecca's R has gone up in smoke.[25]

6

waltzing into danger

> Whatever you do, please don't hum that tune anymore.
>
> —Charlie, in *Shadow of a Doubt*

SCREWBALL ENCHANTMENT: *MR. AND MRS. SMITH*

Once Hitchcock landed in Hollywood, waltzes continued dancing through his movies. In a 1941 arrangement with David Selznick, he was loaned out to RKO, striking a two-movie deal. The first was a favor and tribute to his friend Carole Lombard, who had offered her house to the newly arrived Hitchcock family and who wanted him to direct her—not in a suspense picture but in a romantic screwball comedy, a film style whose name she had inspired.[1] The result, *Mr. and Mrs. Smith,* was Hitchcock's first attempt at an American genre with an American cast. It has brittle content but sensuous style, especially its music. Madcap comedy descends into acrimony, chaos, and a threat of violence, but the charming score whirls on unruffled.

Many commentators regard *Mr. and Mrs. Smith* as a bomb and an aberration—"not a Hitchcock picture," as the always damning phrase has it, especially when it is uttered by Hitchcock himself. (Its initial audience loved it, however.) This is a good time to assert that a Hitchcock picture is a picture made by Alfred Hitchcock. His signatures are astonishingly consistent, but no less remarkable is his variety. He experimented with practically every genre; it is simply not the case that suspense was his only game. Nor is it true, as some critics claim, that *Mr. and Mrs. Smith* is an anomaly.[2] The uncoupling—in this case, unmarrying—of a troubled couple through bitter fights, betrayals, and close calls before a grudging last-minute reconciliation is a common Hitchcock comedy trope developed early in *Rich and Strange* and *The Lady Vanishes,* and later in *North by Northwest.*

Indeed, the tense and humiliating dance-club scene in which David and Ann are filled with jealousy and regret when they see each other dating someone else is right out of *Rich and Strange.* In both films, vernacular dance music—in this case, 1940s swing—plays mocking counterpoint. (Mickey-mousing does occur, as in the blink from the orchestra when the camera shows Carole Lombard opening her slitty eyes from under the covers in the opening scene, but this is the exception rather than the rule.) The visual setup in the scene is also characteristic: as in *The Man Who Knew Too Much,* the camera moves with the characters into a restaurant, peeking back to reveal the orchestra, then following them through a crowd to a table. The band plays loudly through the scene, subtly influencing its outcome. David, whose real date is a grotesque tart, pretends to speak to an attractive blond to inflame Ann's jealousy. His empty words are covered by spitting brass and syrupy strings from the band behind him, the music helping him pull off the ruse. Ann responds to David's aggressively moving mouth and flirtatious eyes by dancing ever closer with her partner, moving into the music with a passionate, provocative clutch, though her pained expression reveals that David's mime is working beautifully. David literally says nothing yet makes a strong impact, a classic example of Hitchcock's dictum that sound and eye gestures trump dialogue, which "should simply be a sound among other sounds, just something that comes out of the mouths of people whose eyes tell the story in visual terms."[3] The tension between loud, cheerful dance music and quiet, subjective torture becomes so overwhelming that David fakes a nosebleed to get himself out of the club. When his real date— the blond having departed in disgust—puts a cold knife to his nose, he urges her to "just cut my throat with it," as the strings sigh into a schmaltzy cadence.

The film is full of light waltzes covering dark material. An especially sexy one appears in the title credits, an alluring introduction to the long fight-in-progress in the Smiths' bedroom. Another glides in as David, having been thrown out on the street by his wife, checks into the Beefeater's Club. Yet another caps the insult he hurls at her lawyer boyfriend. The most original instance is the waltz dancing in and out of the fateful scene in Momma Lucy's, a restaurant where David takes Ann after learning that because of an obscure town ordinance they were never legally married. Ann, who has just learned of her unmarried status, expects David, who doesn't know she knows, to propose to her again at the restaurant, the scene of their early courtship, now a dingy dive. David, played by a calculating but vulnerable Robert Montgomery, says nothing, his fatal passivity producing a rage in Ann that boils over through the movie until the final shot.

This superb scene opens with the camera panning through the restaurant, coming to rest on a dirty table where a cat slurps from a customer's plate. In counterpoint to the couple's mutually manipulative nonconversation at Momma Lucy's outdoor table, with the cat joining them but refusing to eat the food, and working-class kids staring at them as freaks from another planet, a ghostly street waltz drifts in and out of the sound track, apparently from a carousel across the street. After the waltz has wound down over empty streets, David becomes terrified by the cat's rejection of his soup: "That cat knows something!" Demanding a stomach pump, he doesn't realize that his relationship with Ann is what has been poisoned. It's a funny, charming, and unsettling scene. The fading waltz gives it an off-key feeling of impending danger.

Throughout this rather nasty but gorgeous-looking movie, enchanted music brightens black humor. David watches an "old goat" make an unsuccessful pass at Ann, his rage and frustration cushioned by a rising, romantic string phrase; as he bangs on her door with outrage, the strings rise again, like a benign chorus. When a tirelessly aggressive Carole Lombard threatens her nonhusband, throwing plates at him, kicking him out of their house, and telling him she will stab him and break every bone in his body, a recorder pipes an airy tune as David pounds on the door from outside; when she bloodies his nose by slamming a door in his face, woodwinds circle with Ravelian arpeggios. When David pours champagne, puts on elegant pajamas in front of a mirror, and tries to seduce his wife after learning that she really isn't, he whistles the recorder tune himself over zippy strings, an operatic experiment Hitchcock had just tried in the shower scene of *Foreign Correspondent*. When Ann discovers that David has been faking an illness, glittering harps roll through another furniture-throwing tirade. Even in the most rancorous scenes, the music dances with harps, chimes, sleigh bells, and wispy strings.

Whether these ultimately sweeten the film or make it more mockingly ironic depends on the viewer's sensibility and mood; the advantage of counterpoint is its openness and multidimensionality. Indeed, it was Hitchcock's achievement to show that comedy and suspense can be two sides of the same thin coin. The score goes more with the glamorous lighting and silken cinematography than with the hard-screwball narrative. As always, Hitchcock knew when to kick the score out: In the *Vertigo*-like Ferris wheel adventure, where Ann and her new beau are trapped high above a fairground for hours through a thunderstorm, the carnival-like music introducing the scene suddenly vanishes, a somber silence similar to the music-free shipwreck scene near the end of *Rich and Strange*. Only at then very end, when David sinks into Ann's arms from behind, does the music unite with the action, a caressing cadence for Ann's seductive entreaties and the sexy crossed-ski design that ends the picture. Even here, Ann's cooing is laced with physical threats.

So who wrote this crafty, bewitching score? The main title credits Edward Ward, as does the score in the RKO archive. According to Christopher Palmer, a highly reliable source, the real composer is Roy Webb, in his unacknowledged debut as a Hitchcock composer.[4] Palmer's one-time associate Warren Sherk, a film-music scholar and librarian at the Margaret Herrick Library, says that Palmer (who is no longer alive to verify the story) would not have made this up; he explains the discrepancy by pointing out that if a composer were ill or otherwise unable to complete an assignment, an uncredited assistant would do the job for him. Although directed by Hitchcock, *Mr. and Mrs. Smith* was a studio quickie; certainly no one lost any sleep over who wrote the score. With his early career in musicals and his demonstrated ability to write the kind of sinuous harmonies that distinguish *Mr. and Mrs. Smith*, Webb is a plausible candidate, but for now, the authorship of Hitchcock's wispiest score remains a mystery.

CARY GRANT'S DANGEROUS DANCING: *SUSPICION*

Hitchcock's second project for RKO during the loan-out, *Suspicion,* made an even more daring and extensive use of waltzes than the first. In the most celebrated scene, Cary Grant, in his Hitchcock debut, dances up a shadowy staircase with a brightly lit glass of milk that may or may not be poison for his ailing wife, accompanied by a dark spin on Strauss's "Wiener Blut" by Franz Waxman, in his second Hitchcock picture. Grant's character Johnnie—a womanizer, spendthrift, liar, and gambling addict who may also be trying to murder his wife—is continually associated with this waltz. Usually it plays with straightforward elegance; in this scene, however, it is weirdly distorted, a distant, bleak woodwind fragment colored by a fateful gong. The suspicions of Johnnie's wife, Lina, played with eloquent vulnerability by Joan Fontaine, appear to be justified.

"Wiener Blut" is heard six times in the film, debuting as a stylish contrast to the staid "Dance with Reggie," where "Lina the Spinster" (as cue number 7 calls her) dances with a dully respectable suitor before being

Suspicion. Cary Grant, a glass of milk, and sinister Strauss.

swept away on the dance floor by the attractive, mysterious Johnnie. Reggie's music is a pallid version of 1940s swing; Johnnie's is Strauss, seductively arranged by Waxman. Later, in Lina's bedroom, the waltz wafts in from a distance, again from a real band, an effect from *Waltzes from Vienna.* "Let's dance," offers Johnnie, "before we . . ." Yes," Lina interrupts, "let's dance."[5]

"Wiener Blut" represents Johnnie's allure and glamour, often seconds before Lina wonders whether he is a fraud. The couple's "Honeymoon Montage" includes waltz fragments (written by Waxman) from Italy, Paris, and London; in the final shot, the waltz, now "Wiener Blut," continues as the newlyweds dance privately, then is subverted by dissonance as Johnnie suddenly asks her for one hundred pounds. In later scenes, the meaning behind the waltz shifts with Lina's growing doubts. An anxious cue called "Looking for Johnnie" reflects her worry that Johnnie has pushed his old pal Beaky off a cliff for his money; when she finds the two together and realizes she was wrong, the waltz erupts for full orchestra. As Beaky recounts his near death on the cliff, her fears are revived; but when he points out that Johnnie saved his life, she is flooded yet again with relief. Through these huge mood swings, the waltz plays on, its significance continually changing.

In *Rebecca*, Waxman used conflicting themes to enact struggles between characters; here, the conflict is entirely in Lina's psyche and is evoked by a single, ever-changing cue called "Suspicion." Marked "Molto Appassionata" in the main title, this cue sounds seductive and dangerous, its line dropping as it attempts to soar, its exotic harmonies shadowed by chromaticism. This tight, monothematic structure is revealed immediately in the cue sheet, which lists twenty-five "Suspicion" cues, nearly half the score. The opening variations suggest over-the-edge sexuality as Lina falls suddenly and obsessively in love. Johnnie meets Lina on a train, a prime location for significant Hitchcockian encounters, to the teasing strains of a countermelody (similar to the courtship cue in *Rebecca*) associated with Johnnie's flirtatious charm, often before the main melody creeps in with a suggestion of something darker.

Hitchcock hated the film's title, forced on him by RKO after audience tests; he thought it unspeakably tacky and instead wanted the film to be called *Johnnie*. The central cue could be called "Johnnie" or "Suspicion," since the melody suggests both the charm of the male protagonist and a secret side. As the film progresses, "Suspicion" seems more apt; its colors and harmonies become increasingly uncertain as the heroine's doubts grow. (The original score preserved by RKO is called *Before the Fact*, the working title based on Frances Iles's novel.)[6]

The opening scenes immediately establish Hitchcock's growing mastery of sound. Clock chimes, church bells, barking dogs, and motor horns—all indelible parts of his sound tracks by the early 1940s—blend seductively with hunting horns in a surreal cacophony as Johnnie begins his hunt, obviously chasing after more than foxes.[7] Pretending to take Lina to church, he makes an aggressive pass at her on top of a hill over shrill tremolos: "Did you think I was trying to kill you?" he asks, setting up the suspense. Lina declines the advance, snapping her purse shut and declaring she would have no trouble "handling" Johnnie any more than she would one of her horses. When she grabs and violently kisses him at the bottom of the hill, boldly taking the initiative after hearing her father describe her as an old maid with "intellect and a fine, solid character," the strings tremble with dangerous passion.

From this point on, Waxman subjects the "Suspicion" tune to a variety of variations cuing Lina's tumultuously shifting inner state. She suspects that glamour-boy Johnnie is planning to kill her for her money but cannot be sure; all the evidence validates her growing panic, though her amorous feelings say the opposite. Drifting in and out of chronic suspicion, she exists in a state of exquisite ambivalence, a turn-on with constant cycles of tension and shuddering release fueled by variations that are sometimes lush, sometimes sinister—and often both at once. The "Suspicion Theme" thus parallels "Wiener Blut" as a psychological barometer, though it continually changes. Because we really don't know whether Johnnie is guilty, we are as uncertain as Lina, from whose point of view we see the action, and whose fantasies are sounded by Waxman's ambiguous music. (Hitchcock kept an unhappy version of the ending on reserve, in case the censors who insisted on Johnnie's final innocence relented; except for the final cue, Waxman's double-edged score would have worked for that version too.) When Lina becomes too suspicious to sleep with Johnnie, "Suspicion" sinks into despair; when he makes charmingly contrite resolutions to mend his spendthrift ways, the music becomes lush and consoling. Rarely does it do the expected: when Lina peeks at a letter from the insurance company revealing that Johnnie gets her money in the event of her death, it whispers with eerie delicacy rather than exploding into a conventional stinger chord. When she refuses to let Johnnie take off her clothes prior to the scene of his carrying the milk up the stairs, she nonetheless falls into his arms and fantasizes about the first time he tried to undo her blouse, as the score reprises the passionate "Suspicion" cue on the hilltop. At a certain point (as in the novel), Lina seems to accept Johnnie's guilt and give in to it: when she looks knowingly at the glass of milk Johnnie has brought to her bedside in exchange for a goodnight kiss, the melody has a wispy resignation.

This intense irresolution characterizes other cues as well. As in *Vertigo*, the music enacts the title. (Given the number of Hitchcock villains who whistle, even Cary Grant's happy "Whistling Improvisation" sounds suspicious.) At "Isobel's Dinner Party," a writer of murder mysteries who claims she can determine if someone is a killer by his or her face takes a look at Johnnie's: a back-and-forth dissonance forms a question mark—it could easily go either way. "Car Ride" begins with silken strings as the lovers exchange endearments, degenerates into ugly discords when Lina reveals her knowledge of Johnnie's job termination, then lurches back to romance when Johnnie turns on the charm. As he declares his intention to develop a spectacular sea vista, a horn plays a lyrical but anxious solo.

In its darkest moments—the fateful waves of sound following Lina's interrogation by police, the revelations of Johnnie's employer—Waxman's score signals pure terror, something far beyond suspicion. "Anagrams," the most shivery example, begins with a Mussorgskian chord when Lina sees "Murder" on the game board, evoking a subjective montage of Beaky being thrown off a cliff, his screams mingling with garish brass clusters. When Lina opens Johnnie's drawer and discovers *The Trial of Richard Palmer,* the story of a notorious poisoning case, a massive wave of sound resembling the ocean music in *Rebecca* crashes through the scene. When Johnnie locks the door following Isobel's dinner party and leads Lina up shadowy stairs to the bedroom, a long bass pedal provides shuddery commentary.

Suspicion has striking musical correspondences with other Hitchcock movies. Lina writes an "I'm leaving you" letter to Johnnie over the hum of a pedal point, then tears it up, a forecast of Judy's letter and its music in *Vertigo.* In haunting echoes of R*ebecca,* a novachord quivers through Lina's panic, and mysterious glissandos sweep upward as she opens bedroom curtains. Waxman's score also anticipates later films: the foreboding woodwinds introducing "Inspector Hobson" and the wandering harmonies as Lina is introduced to Johnnie's employer foretell similar sounds during the Herrmann era.

The most dramatic parallel is literal: "Too Fast," a crescendo of speed and panic, later lifted by Selznick for the ski sequence in *Spellbound.* This double-duty cue comes at the controversial end, where Johnnie turns out to be not a killer but a Hitchcock wrong man, the object of Lina's fearful projections. Many have complained that this is a false happy ending, but it is consistent with Hitchcock's preoccupation with obsession. He is always more interested in how people perceive reality and deal with troubling epiphanies than in who-done-it.[8] In the end, Johnnie is absolved by music, and Lina is liberated from her mental torture. Whether we fully believe the happy outcome depends to a great extent on how convincing we find Waxman's harmonies. The near-fatal car scene, in which Johnnie saves Lina's life as she thinks he is ending it, is energized by an ostinato that collects all the

anxiety the movie has generated, bringing it to a point of no return. Released by Lina's cathartic scream, the bottled-up terror of "Too Fast" turns
into a new version of the main theme, which appears in minor-key fragments surrounded by breathless tremolos as Lina realizes that Johnnie
planned to poison himself rather than her and that he is guilty only of financial improprieties: "If only I had understood," she cries, accusing herself
of self-absorption, vowing to start the relationship over, and demanding an
equal openness from Johnnie. He declares himself "no good. . . . You can't
change people overnight." But the metamorphosis in the score, the ascending patterns moving painfully toward resolution, suggest change is possible;
the music slowly takes a U-turn with the car and with the newly hopeful
characters as the fragments come together, now ringing with chimes in consonance and closure, a satisfying symphonic resolution after so much
disharmony and paranoia. This major-key peroration of "Suspicion," which
might now be called "Trust," tells the final story: the concluding shot catches
the reunited couple as they drive away so that we cannot see the expressions
that have replaced their anguished close-ups. The credibility of the ending
is tightly linked with that of the music.

The fatal threat turns out to have all been in the heroine's head, a stream
of fantasy cued by lusciously fearful music. Hitchcock's next exploration of
a young woman's dire suspicion about a charismatic man would again use
waltzes as a psychological keynote, but this time the threat would turn out
to be real, indeed far worse than imagined.

WALTZING FROM HEAD TO HEAD: *SHADOW OF A DOUBT*

Teresa Wright, star of *Shadow of a Doubt,* remembered Hitchcock taking her
aside just before filming and telling her every sight and sound in the movie.
So vivid and precise was his narrative that she had the eerie feeling during
the first screening she "had seen the movie already"—as indeed, she had.[9]

Her character, young Charlie, is haunted by the sound we hear most, a
waltz. "I can't get that tune out of my head," she says, obsessed by a melody
whose origin and title she can't place. At first a nuisance, like Mr. Memory's
tune in *The 39 Steps,* this mysterious tune becomes a clue to a crime and a
deep part of Charlie's subconscious that she hums even as she falls asleep. It
dances through the sound track in a startling variety of guises, first as a
dream, then as a thickening nightmare.

According to Olivia Tiomkin, Hitchcock got the idea for using "The
Merry Widow" waltz from her husband, Dimitri, who composed the score.
In the 1920s, Tiomkin was the piano accompanist for his first wife, Al-

bertina, a ballerina and vaudeville dancer who choreographed the movie version of *The Merry Widow.* This film ingrained the waltz in Tiomkin's imagination. To him, it was perfect not only for the villain but also for the movie's mood and even the sound of the performers' voices. "Dimitri always composed for voices," Olivia recalls, in this case the sonorous instruments of Joseph Cotten and Teresa Wright. He, like Hitchcock, envisioned movies as choreographed movement, a form of ballet.[10]

In *Shadow of a Doubt,* the basic montage rhythm during moments of crisis consists of mysterious cuts to imagined dancers from long ago whirling to "The Merry Widow." The mystery is how the waltz gets into Charlie's head. She theorizes that it somehow came from her family's guest, her handsome and charismatic Uncle Charlie, through a kind of musical telepathy. "Whenever I think about how I feel," she says, "I always come back to my Uncle Charlie." He's her "twin," her secret sharer and soul mate. Indeed, as Charlie puts it, this is a story "*about* souls"; any important music in Uncle Charlie's head will eventually get into hers.

"I think tunes jump from head to head," she tells him at the dinner table, after humming the tune and wondering aloud which waltz it is. But Uncle Charlie doesn't want to hear it or its title: in a superb sample of Hitchcockian "negative acting," Joseph Cotten's charming smile suddenly collapses into a scary snarl. In anxious close-up, he blurts out that Charlie's tune is "The Blue Danube," an awkward feint unworthy of his customary suavity. Hitchcock's most attractive villains always have memorable music, often a waltz: Uncle Charlie is the heir to Cary Grant's Johnnie in *Suspicion* (it's only a technicality that he turns out to be innocent) and the precursor of Bruno in *Strangers on a Train.* Charlie suddenly recalls the waltz's real name: "I know what it is, it's the "Mer—," but Uncle Charlie knocks over a glass of wine, cutting off her line. A keen observer, Charlie knows something is amiss; a musical shadow has been cast that continually darkens.

The idea of music jumping from head to head wasn't new for Hitchcock. Here, however, the idea has a touch of the supernatural. Although commentators call *Shadow of a Doubt* Hitchcock's exercise in realism, a documentary of small-town America, it is something more interesting and seductive, a fantasia on musical memory where evil is a psychically implanted waltz, where the central clues are the unseen and the unspoken.[11]

These and other subtle exchanges between the dueling soul mates in *Shadow of a Doubt* take place at the family dinner table, where Hitchcock's theme of terror in the ordinary could be enacted with great subtlety. Food, wine, and dramatic dinners were a central part of his world, both on and off camera. Tiomkin's bewildering initiation into the Hitchcock world centered on food as well. "When I knew Hitchcock first he was ponderous and rotund. Then, when I saw him again, he was thin. Next he was fat again. . . . He could take off or put on 75 pounds with the greatest facility. . . . He told me: 'Some people eat, and some dine, I dine.'" At the studio preview of *Shadow of a Doubt,* everyone "tried to follow the Hitchcock maxim of not eating but dining." This was the most "excruciating" preview Tiomkin "ever suffered through. With a gripping thriller on the screen, most of the studio executives, having wined and dined in sumptuous Hitchcock style, went to sleep. One, sitting next to me, snored in two notes. Even my ear-torturing versions of 'The Merry Widow Waltz' didn't wake him up." The rest of the audience was worse: "They laughed. They giggled through my sinister waltz harmonies and laughed loudly in moments of terror."[12]

Utterly depressed that the audience had snoozed through his provocative music, Tiomkin slinked over to the bar afterward, where Hitchcock sat sipping a brandy with his wife and his screenwriter. Expecting Hitchcock to be "in the depths of woe after such a flop," Tiomkin went over to console him, but Hitchcock was smiling. Tiomkin declared the audience's laughter to be a calamity; Hitchcock assured him that "it was quite all right." "But Hitch," Tiomkin protested in his broken Russian-English, "when should be fear, terror, they going ha-ha." Hitchcock was serenely confident: "The laughs were a sign the picture had them on edge. . . . American audiences will break into nervous laughter when they are overwrought, a good sign for a suspense picture." Tiomkin was astonished. A Russian audience "would have been in tears" during the "shuddering apprehension" in *Shadow of a Doubt.* But this was America: "Hitch was right about it. *Shadow of a Doubt* did big business in the theaters."[13]

The Russian intensity of Tiomkin's musical style proved right for a picture that presented America from an émigré perspective, as alluring but dangerous. In contrast to the English ambiance of *Rebecca* and *Suspicion,* Hitchcock wanted a contemporary American setting, but one that would exchange the clichés of American realism for the enraptured perspective of a foreigner. Sleepy Santa Rosa, with its perfectly manicured lawns, its benevolent policeman directing ordinary folk across the street to music of Coplandesque tranquility, is so impeccably pastoral—at least until Hitchcock peels off the veneer—that it seems exotic.

The scenario feels like an outsider's reimagining of *Our Town,* rapturous with sinister overtones—exactly so, since Thornton Wilder wrote most of the screenplay. The "Til Two" bar, its jukebox blaring, is the town's shadowy counterpart, paralleling the doubling of Charlie and her evil uncle. "I've never been to a place like this," she protests, as Charles drags her in to tell her about the derangement of the world.

Tiomkin composed an American movie score with a foreigner's tonality, Franz Lehar superimposed on Copland. A Russian émigré and virtuoso pianist who gave the European premiere of George Gershwin's Concerto in F, Tiomkin was adept at mixing European and American motifs. Like many Hitchcock composers, he favored chimes, whistles, bluesy piano chords, and colorful percussion effects. The sound of *Shadow of a Doubt* was a forerunner of numerous American suspense films that combined outward amiability with a hidden threat.

"I gave 'The Merry Widow' the atonal treatment and worse," Tiomkin quipped. This is the most dramatic example in Hitchcock of waltzes deviously distorted to produce irony and anxiety. The manipulation begins immediately in the main title, a misty vision of couples dancing to Lehar in formal evening gowns, turning, smiling benevolently as the credits flash onto the screen, an image associated with the male lead's memories of an innocent era. But something is off: the harmonies are slightly dissonant, the colors a bit garish; the effect is hallucinatory rather than nostalgic. From the beginning, the waltz hits a subtle sour note, not quite atonal, but far from reassuring.

With the dancers superimposed on the screen, ominous brass growl as the camera pans through an urban landscape of litter and abandoned cars, sweeping across the Hudson, down a street with children at play, and into the window of a shabby hotel (a premonition of the opening of *Psycho*), finally landing on Joseph Cotten lying in bed. A creepy, chiming variation on the "Merry Widow" tells us he is up to no good. Cut to a languorous melody evoking sleepy, innocent Santa Rosa. Charlie is introduced by a schmaltzy violin tune, a disguised version of the waltz, as she lies on her bed in exactly the same posture as her Uncle Charlie. Again, something is awry: the music should be comforting, but the twin image makes it oddly disturbing.

Hitchcock transfers the "Merry Widow" from one psyche to another with consummate subtlety. A distant chorus, one of his favorite effects, hums it as the dancers spin, superimposed on Charles's head. A sound montage passes it from the singers to young Charlie, who hums it while setting the table before delivering her eccentric but accurate theory of musical telepathy. Once in her head, it's akin to a supernatural presence, a dark energy connected to the black smoke belching from Uncle Charlie's train as he arrives in town. In a haunting piece of editing, Charlie hums it while she falls asleep as the camera cuts to Uncle Charlie lying in his bed, the smoke from his cigarette mingling with a distant train whistle. By the middle of the narrative, Charlie's mother has picked up the waltz and is mouthing it too, but by now Charlie hates the tune, which marks her initiation into evil, an end of innocence: "Whatever you do, please don't hum that tune anymore. I just got it out of my head, and I don't want to get it started again."

The library discovery scene marking Charlie's abrupt maturation is a musical tour de force. As the camera follows her anxious stride to the library, a crescendo rises in the strings mixed with the detectives' piano theme and Uncle Charlie's fateful chimes. Charlie is now the investigator, hoping to establish her uncle's innocence. As she reaches the library, real chimes announce its closing, and the music stops, a lonely, empty moment, but Charlie frantically pushes her way in. Another crescendo fuels her nerve-wracking search for the right newspaper, followed by a high pedal in the winds as she looks for the story. The moment, registered by a sudden silence, could not be more tense.

According to Hitchcock's assistant director, the camera is supposed to "gasp" at the shocking headline of the "Merry Widow Murderer."[14] What really gasps is the music, a shocking dissonance that rips through the silence, ending Charlie's consonant life. As in a trance, she slowly takes off Uncle Charlie's ring, her adoration for him snuffed out along with everything else familiar and comforting. The "Merry Widow waltz sounds with grim triumph as the camera looks on from an aerial view, the scene dissolving to dancers spinning over Uncle Charlie reading his own paper as the chimes and waltzes fade.

"Charlie doesn't look quite herself," says mother the next day. Indeed she isn't. From this point on, the music depicts her isolation and dark secret, often in stark contradiction to images and dialogue. When Charlie looks through the front-door window to an elegant scrim of her uncle and mother in loving conversation, the music is a torturous, Bergian string line. In the turning point of the film, Herbie and Charlie's father, both detective-story nuts, prattle on about the Merry Widow murders. "I guess that closes that case," says Herbie in the foreground of the screen after repeating the radio news that the likely suspect was killed trying to escape police. But ominous woodwinds suggest a far more troubling outcome, and when Jack the detective bounds in with a smile to tell Charlie her uncle is off the hook— "Charlie, I've got great news for you!"—the camera peeps down from an aerial shot at Charlie struggling for words. "Oh, I *am* relieved," she finally stammers, but unsettled strings say the opposite.

The tension between sound and image continues along with a battle between score and source music. In the powerful "Til Two" scene, Uncle Charlie articulates his horrendous vision of life, completing the rape of young Charlie's innocence as suave pop music from the jukebox competes with, then is invaded by, mordant piano-percussion riffs, a nightmare version of 1940s jazz. "You've gone through your ordinary life dreaming stupid, peaceful dreams," snarls Joseph Cotten, his façade of charm suddenly gone, "and I brought you nightmares. You're a sleepwalker, blind. How do you know what the world is like?"

By the end of this wrenching scene, Charlie's sleepwalking has ended. For the remainder of the film, the music is twisted with irony, sounding out Uncle Charlie's nightmare like an evil omen. The orchestra shudders and collapses as Charlie falls down suspiciously broken stairs; when she investigates them at night with a flashlight, the waltz creeps through the shadows in a minor key. Radio dance music stifles her screams from a carbon monoxide–engulfed garage as Uncle Charlie turns up the volume; the detectives' piano theme accompanies his "rescue" of his own victim following Herbie's discovery. As Charlie tries in vain to phone the real detective and frantically searches for Uncle Charlie's incriminating ring, the orchestra roams from one dissonant pattern to another, searching for closure.

By now, the waltz has come to represent the loneliness and futility of Charlie's position. As her deadly nemesis contemptuously reminds her, it offers no legal remedy: "Who would believe you? A waltz runs through your head!" Nonetheless, if the content of souls could be offered as evidence, Charles would be caught. The waltz is the key to his character, his obsession with the good old days, his terrible need to kill off useless widows who enjoy living in the present. To him, the past is paradise: "Everybody was sweet and pretty then, Charlie, the whole world, wonderful world, not like the world today." As in a Nathaniel Hawthorne story, the railer against the contemporary world, the champion of innocent bygone days, is himself the evil he fulminates against. A stand-in for nostalgia, Lehar's waltz becomes a warning against fetishizing the past, a theme Hitchcock would continue to develop, often through music.

In the traumatic train finale, all the music—waltzes, chimes, jazz riffs, train sounds, sinister percussion—come together in a surreal montage. Uncle Charlie boards the fateful train with his niece to continuous hisses and chuggings, which gradually give way to a final, frantic crescendo of "The Merry Widow" as young Charlie becomes the unwitting minister of justice. The chorus hums the tune, and the long-ago dancers spin one more time as

Uncle Charlie dies, a far more appropriate elegy than the official one. Hitch-cock's typically swift denouement turns the clang of the engine into funeral bells. The rackety train noises that brought him to Santa Rosa sound out his violent death.

Shadow of a Doubt, which Hitchcock often described as the favorite of his fifty-three feature films, has one of his most disquieting endings. Santa Rosa is as oblivious now as it was when Charles threatened it. The American small town, tenaciously invested in protecting its innocent image, comes through untainted. Pious religious music and memorials to Uncle Charlie, a lost "son . . . brave, generous, kind," show that the community will continue to "sleepwalk." Charlie, now in a state of terrible wakefulness, will hide the truth forever, ensuring that her family will continue to snooze; her boyfriend, Jack, the force of law and order, will apparently hide it too, institutionalizing the cover-up.

Meanwhile, Hitchcock's music, its dark overtones still ringing in our imaginations, reminds us, as Uncle Charlie puts it, "what the world is really like."

7

sounds of war

I can see intangible things.

—The blind pianist in *Saboteur*

In the early 1940s, Hitchcock directed a series of unusual war-propaganda films. Three of these—*Foreign Correspondent, Saboteur,* and *Lifeboat,* all loan-outs from the Selznick Studio—were full-length features; two, "Bon Voyage" and "Aventure Malgache," were shorts for the British Ministry of Information that were meant as salutes to the French Resistance. All were thrillers with a strong antifascist message. Hitchcock loathed the Nazis and was eager to demonstrate his patriotism both to his American colleagues and to his fellow Britons. In spite of being uncharacteristically didactic, these films are superb specimens of their genre, though only recently have their merits been grudgingly recognized. One way Hitchcock enlivened the war-espionage thriller was through music. With the exception of the ending to *Foreign Correspondent,* he avoided bombastic patriotic songs and marches, opting instead for subtlety and spareness. Particularly impressive is the use of source music, both classical and pop, to make political and psychological points—rarely the ones we expect.

UMBRELLA BALLETS AND TORTUROUS JAZZ:
FOREIGN CORRESPONDENT

Hitchcock once called the chase "the final expression of the motion picture medium." He did not view it merely as a feature of thrillers but as a classical element in drama, the depiction of a character under duress running toward a goal, often "with the antiphonal motion" of someone fleeing a pursuer. He considered *Hamlet* a chase, its hero a detective.[1] (In the late 1940s, Hitchcock toyed with making a film of *Hamlet* starring Cary Grant but, alas, never did.)

According to Hitchcock, music was fundamental in creating the tempo of a chase (indeed of any scene), its underlying rhythm and design. The composer was a choreographer in a cinematic ballet. Hitchcock's use of words like *antiphonal* make it clear that he viewed the chase in musical terms. The basic structure was antiphony and call-response: one voice pursuing a goal evokes another pursuing him or her. The only thing better than a chase was two of them—or more: "In the best chase plots there are usually several chases going on at once . . . which eventually run into and influence each other."[2] One kind of double chase occurs when the hero, mistaking evil for good, is pursued by the character he thought he was pursuing; another involves the falsely accused being hunted by police while he goes after the villain to clear his name. Like a fugue, each strand in a chase has a life of its own, yet each influences and crisscrosses the others, producing a seductive paradox: exciting action in a unified, static design.

When a chase reaches its maximum precision, as it does in *Foreign Correspondent,* Hitchcock's first American movie independent of Selznick, it moves beyond action into character and psychology. "The good chase will also reveal character and use psychology to build up tension. . . . The tempo and complexity of the chase will be an accurate reflection of the intensity of the relations between the characters."[3] George Sanders's character, for example, is revealed almost entirely through a deadly car chase, the tempo of which is set by bouncing and exploding fragments of the score's main theme.

Truffaut and others disdained *Foreign Correspondent* as a B movie, but it enjoyed superlative reviews when it appeared in 1940. "This, literally, is a sensational picture," said the critic for *Variety,* "told in a reportorial manner with the factual semblance of a newsreel."[4] *Hollywood Reporter* gave Hitchcock credit for raising the stock of the motion picture business, including the producer and studio: "Alfred Hitchcock has delivered to Walter Wanger, for his distribution through United Artists, the best picture that has ever carried the Wanger name and a great piece of screen entertainment for the whole picture business . . . a standout hit, and an individual triumph for Mr. Hitchcock." Only the title, worried the critic, would be a "burden" that might keep audiences away.[5]

Even the music was touted. *Variety* praised Alfred Newman's score and direction as "of a caliber with the rest of the technical contributions." Newman, a renowned arranger and maestro as well as composer, had written the Selznick Trademark fanfare used in *Rebecca* (as well as the more celebrated one for 20th Century Fox); indeed, he would have been a plausible composer for *Rebecca* given his ghostly music for *Wuthering Heights,* which premiered a year earlier. (The latter even has a spooky offstage female chorus, an effect Hitchcock sought during his search for the *Mary Rose* music.) For *Foreign Correspondent,* Newman contributed a tightly organized work. The composer of *Song of Bernadette, All About Eve,* and *How Green Was My Valley,* he became known for silken lyricism. In cues like "Carol's Love Theme" and "Van Meer's Theme," the most conventionally lush Hollywood melodies in *Foreign Correspondent,* this quality was already on display, but as usual with Hitchcock's composers, he went beyond his normal boundaries. Set against his signature delicacy is a brusque, Beethovenesque architecture of tiny motifs, unusual for a composer who favored rich, extended chord patterns. Stressing economy over variety, Newman's score has ninety-four cues, more than in most Hitchcock films, but they are predominantly variations and reprises. Source music includes Strauss waltzes (by now a Hitchcock staple), the "Star-Spangled Banner," and jazz that is literally torture. Otherwise, the music blossoms from a three-note motif, "Johnny's Theme," which bangs through practically every scene and undergoes as many transformations as Johnny himself.[6]

This theme, announced immediately in the main title and rising in ascending scales as titles dedicate the film "to those forthright ones who early saw the clouds of war while many of us at home were seeing only rainbows," has an innocence that defines Johnny Jones, an American journalist played by a boyish Joel McCrea. A stand-in for America on the cusp of war—which was declared within months of the film's release—Johnny is a sincere, laidback, rather dim guy who is hopelessly out of his element in a crisis-torn Europe. His girlfriend, Carol, played by Laraine Day, tells him that his "childish mind is as out of place in Europe as it is in my bedroom." In a harrowing series of chases, assassinations, and disasters, Johnny gradually finds his voice, renounces his indifference, and as Rick would do in *Casablanca,* becomes a reluctant hero in the fight against fascism.

A constant metamorphosis of moods and textures, "Johnny's Theme" develops with the character. In Johnny's introductory shot, where he is busy cutting paper designs, a saucy saxophone version for swing band plays as he announces his intention to resign from the New York *Morning Globe.* Here is Hitchcock's first use of swing, a genre he would insert cunningly a year later in *Mr. and Mrs. Smith* and would continue favoring throughout the

1940s. It aptly introduces Johnny, one of those deplored in the title for seeing only rainbows, who nonchalantly tells his boss he "hasn't given much
thought" to the European crisis. In *Saboteur,* Hitchcock would use swing for
a similar purpose in a party scene where the heroine denounces the dancers
for partying as the fascist threat gathers around them. The steady rhythm
and unperturbable bubbliness of swing gave Hitchcock an American version of music-hall ditties and Strauss waltzes; here it plays on, unruffled
over Johnny's paper cutting and his boss's angry shouting, and continues
during his farewell to his bantering family, who are apparently as oblivious
of the threat facing him as he is. Later, as Johnny types his "biggest story of
century" telegram to his editor, as if it's merely a journalistic coup, the cocktail version of his theme fizzes back, still signifying his innocence and Amer-
icanness; he is only beginning to grasp the gravity of his big story.

"Rule Britannia" acts as a transition to Old World music as Johnny
boards the *Queen Mary* to London. When he enters a large reception for
diplomats, Strauss's "Artists' Life" and "Pizzicato Polka" pick up where
swing left off, playing with dignified indifference as Van Meer, Holland's
"strong man," avoids Johnny's questions about impending war and as
Johnny flirts with Carol, the daughter of Stephen Fisher, head of the Universal Peace Party. Johnny gets Van Meer to say one ominous thing about
what is to come: "I am old and tired and powerless."

"Scenes of Holland," a folkloric piece full of drones and modal harmonies, is a deceptive overture to the umbrella-assassination sequence, one
of Hitchcock's most spectacular ballets. A frenetic fugal variation on
"Johnny's Theme" combines with a series of angry clusters called "Menace"
as Johnny pursues the killer first through a thicket of umbrellas, then in an
explosive car chase that veers unexpectedly into comedy as a villager attempting to cross the street is interrupted several times by speeding cars before giving up and going home. As usual, Hitchcock uses counterpoint in
comic moments—brutal "Menace" chords punctuate the villager's hilarious back-and-forths—to balance laughs and thrills. A scene that begins
with a shocking eruption of blood as a politician is shot in the face concludes with slapstick antics and George Sanders's witty banter.

As the celebrated windmill sequence commences, the killer and the
score vanish simultaneously. Eerie silence is broken only by noise effects:
blasting wind, creaking windmills, and motor sounds from cars and planes.
(The circling airplane on a lonely road is a forerunner of the crop-duster
scene in *North by Northwest.*) Inside the claustrophobic windmill, birdsong
accompanies the revelation of a Nazi conspiracy as a drugged and trauma-

tized Van Meer tells Johnny he is chasing a double. Not sure who he is, Van Meer anticipates being flown away "like a bird" by his kidnappers as his theme floats through the scene in a disoriented version full of ghostly percussion, its harmonies brightening as he looks up longingly at a bird. Pointillist dots from the "Johnny" and "Menace" cues mix with birds and the endlessly turning windmill.

Avoiding the "big tune" approach, Hitchcock works with musical shards that race through the narrative, infusing objects, psyches, and source music. Like a character in an opera, Johnny sings his theme in the bathroom just before his balcony escape, an experiment Hitchcock would repeat in *Mr. and Mrs. Smith*. Dixieland clarinets blare on the radio for Van Meer's interrogation, apparently the preferred form of torture for Herbert Marshall's Nazi thugs. (Twin cues, composed by Gene Rose, are called "Torture in A Flat" and "More Torture in C.") The medieval chant "Dies Irae" floats through Westminster Cathedral during an assassin's attempt to push Johnny off the tower and continues as the killer's body falls through space, accompanied by screams from below. Following the fall, the chant continues as nuns cross themselves, still a Mass for the Dead but now for a different corpse.

The most powerful musical moment is the lifeboat scene following a harrowing plane crash (a warm-up for *Lifeboat*), where Johnny's motif takes on a stark grandeur very different from its earlier, innocent incarnations. In these final moments, Johnny emerges as an authentic hero, a bearer of the Allied torch, his new activism defined by sinewy music. The disaster itself is free of music, with only the frightening sounds of screams, bombs, and faltering engines. Hollywood movies conventionally use big music to imitate the dramatic scenes and tell us how to feel, but Hitchcock denies us this easy correspondence; music should establish a design, not imitate it, reveal the underlying emotion, not italicize the one already obvious.

The exception, not easily forgiven by critics, is the blasting of the "Star-Spangled Banner" as Johnny delivers his stirring speech at the end, urging solidarity against the Nazis. Hitchcock blamed his producer, Walter Wanger, claiming that he was forced into this flag-waving finale as a necessary inclusion in a war-propaganda picture. Hitchcock's biographers counter that he was personally more invested in this overt patriotism than he liked to admit; mischievous irony was his public persona, not patriotic fervor, which he kept largely to himself.[7] Whatever one believes, *Foreign Correspondent*'s coda is satisfying because it is earned: the music to this point has been taut and sophisticated; a broad, familiar anthem enhancing Joel

McCrea's sonorous voice is a refreshing contrast and release. As news from Europe turned unspeakably grim, the audience apparently went away from *Foreign Correspondent* feeling proud to be Americans. Hitchcock would have wanted no less.

THE CALM OF DELIUS IN THE CHAOS OF THE CHASE: *SABOTEUR*

Two years later, Hitchcock created a classic wrong-man double chase in *Saboteur,* sending a bedraggled Robert Cummings, in flight from the police as he pursues Norman Lloyd and his Nazi colleagues, who have framed him for a fire in an aircraft factory. Again, stark motifs, composed this time by Frank Skinner, propel an ordinary-guy American hero through treacherous scenarios. On the road across America, the handcuffed Barry runs from the law as a hitchhiker, swims treacherous currents, speeds through hair-raising car chases, and, in Hitchcock's homage to the American Western, steals a horse and tries to hoof it through the prairie.

Hitchcock's first American road movie opens with a stabbing nine-note title theme that blazes up in a terrifying fugue for winds during the Stewart Aircraft inferno, swirls through the kidnapping and horse-race sequence, and broadens heroically during Barry's leap off a bridge into dangerous currents. In the climax, the heroine chases the villain to the top of the Statue of Liberty, where the motif becomes distorted, veers out of control, and collapses into silence—the terrible void into which Norman Lloyd falls, his scream a long decrescendo. During the end credits, the theme finally assumes a properly patriotic posture, a march with blazing fanfares and major-key harmony, belatedly reminding us that this picture is supposed to be a war effort, not just a road thriller.

The lyrical moments in the score are ironic, including the highway courtship scenes between Barry and Pat, his annoyingly distrustful girlfriend; the carnival scene where the bearded lady praises Pat for sticking with Barry when in fact she is constantly betraying him; and Barry's deceptively pastoral arrival at Tobin's ranch. As in *The 39 Steps* and *Notorious,* wicked people have lovely homes, sweet families, and tony musical taste. Tobin, who turns out to be the leader of a Nazi cell, plays idyllic string-quartet music on the radio, a ballet for a beautiful baby girl who toddles about on the edge of a swimming pool as a letter montage reveals his villainy. Later, Barry rolls his eyes at Nazis in a car as they sing a love duet based on Tchaikovsky's Piano Concerto.

In Hitchcock, music can be distracting and treacherous. In the big-band party scene, Pat deplores everyone's enjoyment of swing music as the forces of evil prepare to attack: "It's so unreal, all these people dancing and having a good time." This indictment of fiddling-while-Rome-burns is given additional force by the band tune, which subtly morphs into a swing version of the sinister main title. Pat's speech on unreal dance music gives voice to the theme Hitchcock had developed in *Secret Agent* and *Foreign Correspondent;* the difference is that she gets it while the oblivious characters in those films do not.

Originally an Illinois band arranger, Skinner was an ideal composer for the latter scene. His score for *Saboteur* is full of variety, drama, harmonic subtlety, and melodic invention; the music should have been a breakthrough for him, as other Hitchcock scores were for their composers, but such was not the case. This neglect comes partly because *Saboteur* has never been rated highly in the Hitchcock canon and partly because Skinner was typed as a horror composer (along with his collaborator Hans J. Salter) for his work during the long run of Universal's monster series. Franz Waxman also wrote for Universal in the late 1930s, but *Bride of Frankenstein* was far more celebrated than anything Skinner scored, and *Rebecca,* unlike *Saboteur,* was a major hit.

As he so often did, Hitchcock mixes the score with references to classical music. A wanted man hitchhiking in a truck, Barry whistles the opening of the Beethoven Fifth, a symbol of victory over the Nazis. "Catchy," says the truck driver, suddenly singing the theme himself. When Barry admits he didn't realize he was whistling, the driver says, "Then you must be happy; easy to see what's on your mind." A close-up of Barry's anxious face shows us he isn't happy at all, but the Fifth Symphony, a deeper signifier, conveys the truth of his character: his unconscious whistling of Beethoven's motif, conceived when its composer realized the severity of his growing deafness, reveals Barry's goodness and stubborn determination to overcome adversity.

The most extensive musical sequence invokes the British composer Frederick Delius, a figure rarely referenced in cinema (a happy exception is Ken Russell's BBC film *A Song for Sunrise.*). Philip Martin, the blind pianist who welcomes Barry into his house and instinctively befriends him, plays Delius's "Summer Night on the River," commenting that the composer was blind like himself. As languid arpeggios drift through the scene, the starving Barry grabs for food, contributing what Philip calls "an interesting effect: an obbligato on an apple." Divining that Barry is an innocent man who has been framed, Philip articulates the main idea of the film, the need for trust in the struggle against evil. Hitchcock's pervasive theme, the battle against guilt, comes to the fore as well, assuming a patriotic dimension. In Hitchcock, guilt can be psychological, as in *Notorious* or *Vertigo*, or part of a wrong-man scenario, as it is here. "It is my duty as an American citizen," Philip tells his niece, the skeptical Pat, "to assume a man is innocent until proven guilty." It is also one's duty, he continues, to sometimes resist the police. Like the patriotic truck driver, Philip is willing to help Barry hide from the law. Typically, a musical performance defines a character; Philip can't see, but his intimate connection to the piano enables him to play beautifully; the instrument, he says, "pays him the compliment" of trusting him. Like Delius, he sees with a vision deeper than sight: "I can see intangible things—for example, innocence."

Just before thrusting himself back into a hostile world with Philip's distrustful niece, Barry tells Philip he played triangle in the high school band; Philip suggests that he "get back in practice on that triangle." As in many Hitchcock films, music is a metaphysical energy, a path into healing and truth. Supplementing "Summer Night on the River" is a Skinner cue for strings and harp full of Delian rapture, climaxing during Philip's speech on innocence and trust, halting only during the sight of the inept, profoundly unmusical police. (Only on second hearing do we realize that this ecstatic music is a variant on the grim main title.)

This homage to Delius, an oasis in the midst of the film's chaos, is touchingly apt: like Hitchcock, Delius was an Old World artist sparked with New World energy, an Englishman who came to America and drew inspiration from its vernacular culture; and like the creator of *Vertigo*, Delius devoted his most profound musings to loss and recaptured memory. There is nothing in Hitchcock's propaganda films quite like this plunge from the world of violent action into hypnotic spirituality. The kinetic music in *Foreign Correspondent* and *Saboteur* is deftly in touch with the dynamics of the chase. This contemplative moment was Hitchcock's way of commenting, with Philip as his stand-in, on the meaning of an art he understood deeply but only intuitively.

The intensely interior score in Hitchcock's next feature film involving espionage, *Notorious*, would collapse the chase into a claustrophobic world of cellars and staircases. In the latter, Hitchcock left propaganda behind to create one of his most sophisticated films. But even in *Saboteur*, continually dismissed as superficial, he struck unexpected depths.

WATER MUSIC: *LIFEBOAT*

There are no chases, of course, in *Lifeboat*, where the cast is confined to a boat adrift on a claustrophobic, Poe-like sea. Hitchcock, who enjoyed working with self-imposed restrictions, told Truffaut that *Lifeboat* was an exceptionally "rigorous" film because it had only one set and no music. Yet the film opens with Hugo Friedhofer's apocalyptic main title, an explosion of dissonance that evokes with terrifying precision the torpedoing of an Allied ship. (This shuddery piece is far removed from Friedhofer's celebrated, Coplandesque *Best Years of Our Lives*.) After the fortissimo dies down, discords continue quivering like aftershocks as the camera pans the ocean for debris and survivors. Once the camera finds Tallulah Bankhead wittily manning the lifeboat, the score disappears. Hitchcock jokingly explained this absence by asking his production crew, "Where would the music come from?" again revealing his idiosyncratic notion of music as physical presence akin to a character. The famous retort was "Where does the camera come from?" The former gets an answer but not the latter. Music does appear, all of it bleakly ironic, and all with a highly visible source inside the lifeboat. Joe, one of the survivors, plays cheery recorder music as the deadly sun bakes down on them, then again during a harrowing emergency amputation. The German sailor, Willie, the stand-in for Nazi Evil, sings lovely German songs as he rows his unwitting captors toward a German ship. Willie is like the Nazis in *Saboteur* and *Notorious,* all musically sophisticated villains who invert Shakespeare's dictum that the man with no music is the one who is untrustworthy.

The remainder of *Lifeboat*'s "music" consists of an alternately gentle and crashing sea, the terrifying emptiness of which is continually captured by the camera. Sometimes hypnotic, sometimes frightening, the ocean rises in crescendo during squalls and fades during periods of calm, providing (like the sea in *Jamaica Inn*) its own sonic drama and atmosphere. At the end, when an Allied rescue ship appears on the horizon, Friedhofer has the last word: a majestic cadence. None of the survivors in the lifeboat seems to mind that his orchestra comes from nowhere.

MUSIC NOIR: "BON VOYAGE"

Lifeboat wasn't the end of Hitchcock's war against the Nazis. Under the auspices of the British Ministry and with the help of exiled French actors, he made "Aventure Malgache" and "Bon Voyage," two short, twisty espionage films. Again, these were meant as contributions to the war effort, to be released the same year as *Lifeboat,* but this time Hitchcock could not rein in his antididactic impulses. (Ironically, *Lifeboat* is now downgraded as too propagandistic, even though it was panned as insufficiently so in 1944.)

Both shorts were judged far too eccentric and "inflammatory" to be useful to the Allied cause and were not shown.[8]

"Aventure Malgache" has no music, but "Bon Voyage" is a small musical masterpiece, with a provocative score by Benjamin Frankel incorporating fragments of "La Marseillaise" and "Deutschland Über Alles." In its thirty-five-minute running time, this stark film, which feels more like gangster noir than war-effort allegory (a not uncommon combination for the time), projects numerous Hitchcockian effects, including dramatic chimes, long pedal points, dissonant wind choirs, whispered string tremolos, and austere timpani solos. The narrative juxtaposes two conflicting flashbacks of the same convoluted spy story about Gestapo double agents. The somberness of the film is counterpointed by bittersweet restaurant piano music that subtly weaves its way into the score, even into a disturbingly dissonant cue during the murder of one German agent by another to cover his tracks.

An apt complement to the French narrative, Frankel's transparent orchestration and floating seventh chords often sound like Poulenc or late Debussy. On the other hand, the gruffness of the nontonal sections (the train tunnel scene, for example) harks back to the Weillian expressionism of *Blackmail,* amplifying the shadowy lighting of the famed cinematographer Günther Krampf. The climax of this incisive score is a heart-stopping string glissando during the murder of Jeanne, a young female Resistance fighter, by one of her own colleagues.

In "Bon Voyage," Hitchcock managed to communicate the twisted grimness of war in a way that *Foreign Correspondent, Saboteur,* and *Lifeboat* do not attempt. Those who seem most trustworthy turn out to be Gestapo agents; Resistance heroes are as ruthless as the fascist enemy. This dark relativity alienated the film's sponsors; it was not a message the British Ministry of Information wanted to air. Years later, Hitchcock told Truffaut that he made these films because he felt an intense need to help the Allied cause; unfortunately for him, though not for us, his creative impulses got out of hand.

8

spellbound: theremins
and phallic frescoes

You need that music to give Gregory Peck some emotion.

—Jules Feiffer

Wouldn't it be nice if psychotherapy were like *Spellbound*? The leading man is so beset by neurotic guilt that he doesn't know his own name and is worried he may be a murderer. Not to worry, says his beautiful psychiatrist (Ingrid Bergman, no less); just tell me a dream. He does, whereupon she unveils his identity, cures his illness, solves the murder, nails the villain, rescues him from jail, and goes away with him on a train.

We aren't meant to take any of this seriously, of course. As Michael Wood puts it, "Hitchcock is showing us the utter impossibility of such things: you want a solution, he says, I'll give you a solution."[1] *Spellbound* is as much a fairy tale as *Rebecca,* though with gender roles reversed, and with psychoanalysis standing in for magic. A consummate professional, Hitchcock knew that the best way to put over such stuff was to play it straight. The story is mined for maximum thrills and romance, with music to match, the most romantic score in any Hitchcock picture, and also, thanks to the theremin, the spookiest. The theremin quivers through *Spellbound* like a sorcerer, giving the characters' anxieties and identity crises an otherworldly aura.

Hitchcock called the movie standard mystery fare "wrapped up in pseudo-psychoanalysis," but for its time, *Spellbound* was quite daring.[2] Analysis, pseudo or not, was new to motion picture entertainment (though in 1941 Kurt Weill had paved the way on Broadway with *Lady in the Dark*). To increase the novelty, Hitchcock hired Salvador Dalí to give the movie a new surrealist look and Miklos Rozsa to give it a new sound. Rozsa's theremin and Dalí's "phallic frescoes" (as a Selznick flack called his sets) added greatly to the film's exotic allure.[3]

As usual, Hitchcock was culturally prescient: a rash of psychiatric movies followed *Spellbound,* just as the theremin became the instrument of choice for spooky characters or transnormal scenarios.[4] David Selznick was deeply worried that audiences would stay away from such untested material, but curious moviegoers on both sides of the Atlantic flocked to *Spellbound.* To this day, it is more popular with the common viewer than with critics. (It also continues to be popular with Rozsa and theremin cultists, two intensely loyal constituencies.) Rozsa's score was a significant factor in the film's success, both before and after its release, so much so that it is a milestone in the history of cinema music. For many, *Spellbound* is the quintessential Hitchcock score. Michael Dirda, the Pulitzer Prize–winning literary editor at the *Washington Post,* told me that when he thinks of Hitchcock and music, "the first movie that comes to mind is *Spellbound.* Rozsa's score makes a deeper impression than the music in any other Hitchcock film."[5]

Yet Rozsa was not the first choice. Selznick wanted Bernard Herrmann, who would later become Hitchcock's longest-standing musical collaborator. "I still can't see anyone to compare with Herrmann," he wrote in a memo, a sign of a musical astuteness at odds with his reputation for crassness.[6] Herrmann's music for Orson Welles's *Citizen Kane* was celebrated, but the film was not, to put it mildly, a commercial success. That Selznick would rate Herrmann the premiere Hollywood composer is admirable, though he apparently did not know of Herrmann's reputation for irascibility.

Once Herrmann made it clear that he was unavailable, the choice of Rozsa was mutual between producer and director. Hired for four thousand dollars, Rozsa was first approached by Hitchcock, who admired the score for Billy Wilder's *Double Indemnity;* Hitchcock thought Rozsa's style had the "right kind of tension" for *Spellbound,* Rozsa recalled.[7] But the critical player in his hiring was apparently Lionel Barrymore, who wrote Selznick an enthusiastic letter of recommendation, to which Selznick replied with a warm thank-you note.[8] Rozsa's moody, noirish style seemed right for *Spellbound,* and indeed it was—though one would never know it from what went on behind the scenes. Rozsa's relationship with both Hitchcock and Selznick deteriorated to the point of near-total alienation. It is remarkable that the *Spellbound* score got written at all, or that it was used.

Hitchcock's attraction to Rozsa illustrates his willingness to try innovative music. Although fetishized by fans now, *Double Indemnity* was a controversial score for its time. As Royal S. Brown points out, its refreshingly nonmelodic style broke away from standard Hollywood melodic lushness. Rozsa's signature sound, unabashedly sensuous yet curiously stark in its preference for octaves, parallel fifths, and other open sounds, suited *Spellbound*'s narrative, one that combines high dementia with high romance.

Spellbound was an extreme example of Hitchcock's obsessive theme: a character with identity problems struggling to break out of a terrible past; here he had two, for the heroine must break through repressions of her own. Hitchcock needed music both claustrophobic and soaring, sinister and transcendent. His openness to experimentation was a welcome change for Rozsa, who was eager to try out the theremin, which the producer of *Sundown* had rejected four years previously. He had also wanted to use the ondes Martenot, a keyboard instrument resembling the theremin, in the 1940 *Thief of Bagdad;* that exotic instrument was vetoed as well when it was discovered that no one was available who could play it. "Hitchcock and Selznick hadn't heard of the theremin," Rozsa recalled, "and weren't quite sure whether you ate it or took it for headaches, but they agreed to try it out."[9]

According to Rozsa, whose debunking of Golden Age music is more entertaining than the current adulation, it was unusual to find any filmmaker open to innovation:

> The general idiom was conservative and meretricious in the extreme— diluted Rachmaninoff and Broadway. In *Double Indemnity,* I introduced certain asperities of rhythm and harmony which wouldn't have caused anyone familiar with the serious scene to bat an eyelid, but which did cause consternation in certain musical quarters in Hollywood. The musical director couldn't stand the score from the beginning. . . . Did I really have to have a G sharp in the second fiddles clashing with a G natural in the violas an octave below? . . . The place for such eccentricities was Carnegie Hall, not a movie studio. I refused to change a note and thanked him for the compliment; he assured me it wasn't meant as such. . . . The story gives one some idea of how difficult it was to maintain any decent level of musical integrity in the Hollywood of those days.[10]

Ironically, it was the lushness of *Spellbound*'s music, passionately projected by the Hollywood Bowl orchestra and recorded at a high-decibel level, that attracted audiences—and that eventually irritated Hitchcock. It doesn't sound like Rachmaninoff, but any "asperities" have gone largely unnoticed. They certainly exist: the G against G sharp that dismayed the music director is nothing compared to the sustained discords in the Dalí dream scene. Still, what Hitchcock regarded as the "terrible" schmaltz of the love theme is what audiences go away with.[11]

Selznick is partly to blame. After Rozsa had scored the main title, he called his secretary and asked how many violins were in the score, wanting to make sure it had at least as many as Franz Waxman had used in *Rebecca*. When it turned out *Rebecca* had more, Selznick demanded that Rozsa make up the difference and re-record the title with the additional complement. The composer "happily did" (it was Selznick's money, after all) but doubted that Selznick could tell the difference.[12]

Throughout the early stages of composing, Rozsa claimed he "was bombarded by the famous Selznick memos, which "virtually told me how to compose and orchestrate the music scene by scene." There may be a bit of hyperbole here. The *Spellbound* memos that survive in the archives consist mainly of a seven-page document from Selznick called "Spellbound Music Notes," dated October 6–19, 1944. Unlike Hitchcock's nuanced, detailed musical notes (alas, he apparently did not make any for *Spellbound*), Selznick's are sketchy and curt, essentially a dubbing sheet indicating where the score should be laid in. Selznick does indulge in a few brief characterizations of the type of music he wanted: "JB's arrival" in reel 2 should "pick up with a sympathetic Murchinson theme"; the dining scene should be perked up with "gay music," which should become "slower" during JB's "forgive me" following his first breakdown; the love theme cuing "Constance in bed seeing light under JB door" should have a "warm" version of the love theme, with a sound "like Debussy." Selznick also requested "actual hot dance music from radio" during "Constance packing," his one request for source music.[13] *Spellbound* could have used more hot dance music to rev up its stately tempo, but *Notorious* would compensate for this lack the following year, with Hitchcock rather than his producer overseeing the dubbing of the film. (In the final release, the radio music occurs during JB's packing scene, not Constance's.)

One Selznick directive filled Rozsa with rage: after the "Debussy" moment, Selznick wanted Rozsa to use "cymbals etc." to "sell . . . her emotion when she sees the light under his door." Rozsa thereafter "completely disregarded all [Selznick's] musical ideas. I 'sold' Ingrid's love in my own way and with my own theme."[14] As we shall see, Selznick wound up denouncing Rozsa's music even though it was critically acclaimed and adored by audiences. The sourness and personal animosity of his remarks seem to issue from something other than just the music. Something went badly wrong in the relationship between the two; the flap over cymbals seems to have been the beginning.

On the face of it, "cymbals etc." seems another example of Selznick's crassness. But though Rozsa and his admirers ridicule Selznick for wanting cymbals during the love epiphany, Rozsa does "sell Constance's emotion," not with cymbals but with a huge crescendo when Constance sees the light seeping under JB's door. The orchestration is so heavy it doesn't need cymbals. Furthermore, the preceding music, with its soulful cello solo and shimmering percussion, is indeed a warm version of the theme and does carry a hint of Debussy. Selznick was not a musical ignoramus, as sometimes depicted. Rozsa followed the spirit if not the letter of his ideas, producing an unforgettable scene.

Nor is it clear that Selznick was rigid in these minimal demands or that he told Rozsa how to write the music scene by scene. According to his secretary's addendum to the musical notes, "Mr. Selznick wants you to feel very free to suggest any ideas you may have that are different from his notes on the picture concerning his scoring." The sentence may squint, but its message is clear: the creative freedom Rozsa insisted on having was granted, at least after October 6, 1944, when this postscript was attached.

Rozsa arrived at the *Spellbound* theme quickly. He saw an early preview of the movie in Pasadena, with images accompanied by stock music from other films (an odd but common practice). Emerging from the theater, he "immediately jotted down the love theme—it came to me, as it were, straight from the picture."[15] (This was the deliberate method of Rozsa's émigré colleague Erich Korngold, who would sit in the projection room and bang themes on the piano as scenes unrolled.)

Another cue composed early on was "Razor," the fearful nocturne for Gregory Peck and his shiny blade, a marvelous specimen of "silent" Hitchcock in a talkie. This exercise in sustained anxiety was Rozsa's test for the film. Hitchcock and Selznick both liked the double theme of love and paranoia when Rozsa played it for them but were still dubious about the theremin. Selznick finally suggested that Rozsa write the razor scene and include the controversial instrument. They liked what they heard. The contrast between shadowy darkness and clinical whiteness in George Barnes's photography, crucial to the solution of the film's puzzle, finds an exact counterpoint in Rozsa's bleakly colorful sounds: the theremin sliding into the foreground, frenetic snare ostinatos in back, and a plunging motif that captures JB's descent into madness. Hitchcock and Selznick approved the tryout recording, encouraging Rozsa to continue using the theremin throughout the score.

Despite having had only two conferences with Hitchcock, Rozsa precisely understood the director's concept—the thin line between passion and anxiety, love and terror. The resplendent love theme and the creepy theremin motif are variants of each other: in the romantic version, the melody's four-note nucleus soars up and down with plush harmonies, igniting the romance between JB and Constance; in the "paranoia theme," the four notes slither up and down chromatically, shadowed by the theremin. The two versions of the same idea, one lyrical, the other sinister, reflect Hitchcock's preoccupation with doubles. This is a story about sexual ambivalence: the first big kiss, with Salvador Dalí's doors flying open into infinity, features "The Awakening," the most dramatic statement of the love music, followed immediately by the theremin paranoia variation as JB sees parallel lines on Constance's robe. In the second kiss scene, during the couple's honeymoon in Alex's house, Rozsa's music repeats precisely the same attraction-repulsion pattern, as JB notices the straight lines on Constance's bed covering.

Spellbound was the most luscious and atmospheric Hitchcock score since *Rebecca*. Its dark sensuality is the sonic equivalent of George Barnes's seductive shadings and shadows. Unlike Roy Webb's surgical, spare music for Hitchcock's next film, *Notorious,* it surges through the movie practically from beginning to end. Only the opening scenes of mental cases, the documentary exposition, leave music out. (Selznick's notes specify "no score as Harry enters and goes toward nurse" and ask for continued silence until JB's arrival.)

But it was the theremin that made the score a sensation. Here was an instrument that seemed magic, in both its sound and the way that sound was created. One plays the theremin without ever touching it: the performer moves his or her hands above the object exactly like a magician, producing otherworldly sonorities that theremin lovers call ether music. (The magician in *Spellbound* is Stanley Hoffmann, the reigning wizard of the instrument, who went on to play it in *The Lost Weekend* and many other films.) It isn't really magic, of course, but an electronic field that produces the sounds. The theremin was heard as a "primal scream," the first "coming together of science and music."[16] It was therefore perfect for *Spellbound,* where it invokes the science of psychiatry in the guise of what seems like supernatural spookery (or, depending on one's point of view, the reverse). It is impossible to understate the PR value of the theremin: in the twenties and thirties, it was regarded as a revolution, a phenomenon that might well replace pianos and records. And here it was for the first time in a movie, reaching a bigger audience than ever.[17]

The beneficiaries were Selznick and Hitchcock. The former referred to Rozsa's theremin idea as the "white theme," tapping into an identification of terror with whiteness that goes back in American culture to Edgar Allan Poe and Herman Melville. Melville's "Whiteness of the Whale," a chapter in *Moby-Dick,* links whiteness with blank, nameless terror, a primal fear of annihilation—very much like the symptoms of *Spellbound*'s crazed, clueless hero. Snow, white gowns, shaving cream, and bathroom porcelain send JB into his worst spins, with the theremin following him down into madness. In an addendum to his music note, Selznick asked Rozsa to "use 'white' theme whenever JB has a breakdown—a mixture of romance and psychiatry with build and excitement in tempo." He specified JB's anxious observations of "fork lines on tablecloth in dining room scene," "lines on Constance's robe," "surgery," and "other spots in later reels." Rozsa followed these directives precisely, with all the "build and excitement" one could ask, delivering the "mixture of romance and psychiatry" that defines the film.

The celebrated love-terror music was only one of numerous themes evoking a disturbed subconscious. The ugly brass dissonance following JB's outburst—"Edwards is dead. . . . I killed him!"—is one of the most ghoulish stinger chords from the period, and the dream sequence is a masterpiece of Schoenbergian chord coloring. This is not the first Hitchcock film in which music represents the alternate world of the psyche, but it is the first to make that world the movie's theme. Never before had there been a sustained music of mental disintegration like this in the movies.

The score, however, does not always correspond with the images. Again, Hitchcock used music to depict feelings at odds with what characters say on the screen. This is especially important in a movie about how the subconscious speaks the truth: when Constance, who has almost as many repressions as her patient, claims her feelings about the latter have "nothing to do with love, nothing," the juicy crescendo tells us the opposite; when she debunks falling-in-love myths during the picnic pastoral, the seductive wind music wafting through the trees makes one wonder if she really means it; when JB snarls hatefully at Constance on the train that she is a "smug woman . . . babbling like Solomon," mellow horns reveal that the psychoanalytic healing process is gradually winning the day. In *Spellbound,* people tell lies, especially to themselves; the music shows what they really mean.

The most celebrated depiction of the subconscious is the famous nightmare sequence. Selznick was puzzled by Hitchcock's insistence on hiring Dalí, but the director knew that Dalí's theatrical surrealism would help deflect attention from Ben Hecht's didactic script. Like Rozsa's music, Dalí's sets were a far more compelling evocation of the inner life than psychiatric jargon. They also matched Hitchcock's double aesthetic: the classicist who preferred Romantic material and the meticulously logical craftsman who depicted the chaos of the subconscious. Hitchcock admired Dalí's hard literalness, his rejection of vagueness and atmosphere when evoking dreams.[18] Thanks to music, Hitchcock was able to have it both ways. Rozsa provided all the atmosphere one could desire, and his sounds are not vague; the icy clusters, plummeting scales, slashing chords, and swooping glissandos provide a sharp parallel universe to Dalí's staring eyeballs, free-falling men, giant scissors, oversized playing cards, and monstrous Hitchcockian birds.

The conductor John Mauceri argues that composers like Korngold and Rozsa kept the Romantic flame alive in the movies even as it was being snuffed out by serialists in the concert halls. Rozsa's "Awakening" cue makes his point, but the nightmare music, where the sounds are nontonal, reveal that Hollywood émigrés did modern music a favor as well. Rozsa's dreamy discords also saved the sequence from the clunkier effects of voice-over. Selznick insisted on having Gregory Peck's voice explain Dalí's images. Hitchcock's compromise on September 11, 1944, was to have Rozsa "score [the] entire sequence"; if music could not eradicate the scene's didacticism, it could at least mitigate it. Selznick apparently agreed: his own notes say "score all illustrations."[19]

Rozsa was forced to write the dream scene near the end of postproduction: terrified of alienating audiences, Selznick cut a large chunk of Dalí's surreal images (to the sadness of many, including Ingrid Bergman, who in the excluded footage dramatically exploded from a statue wearing a death mask). Rozsa had to wait until the end of 1944 for a leaner dream sequence to get his timings. This was the first of many delays. After a February preview, Selznick tried to fix everything the audience found wrong; this tinkering, plus a string of summer hits, forced him to delay the release until November 1. On May 4, Selznick expressed regrets to Rozsa and his lawyer about the delays but gruffly threatened to "hire another music director and scorer to take over Dr. Rozsa's music" if Rozsa did not agree to stick around. He did, recording the "Gambling Dream" and "Rooftop Dream" in September (apparently, with difficulty: the latter went through seven takes).

An instructive contrast to the overly explanatory narration during the dream is Leo G. Carroll's voice-over in the murder-mystery revelation, an example of this Hitchcockian device at its best. This is one of the great frissons in the film: Carroll's voice is a mysterious fragment "explained" only by Rozsa's goose-pimply music, Ingrid Bergman's trembling body language, and a powerful crescendo of repetition ("knew him slightly . . . knew him slightly . . . knew him slightly!") that allows us to piece together the voice's meaning ourselves. The vocal sonority becomes a grim bass instrument; as in the voice-overs in *I Confess* and *Psycho,* it becomes part of the music.

Spellbound's images of a downhill mental plunge find their dizzying climax in the skiing scene. A Selznick memo from October 30, a few weeks after his unwelcome music notes, requested that Rozsa create a "distorted treatment of whatever theme you are using throughout the picture for each psychoanalytical reference to childhood causes, which should be used here very strongly as a counterscore to the suspense of the scene. Please note that the last part of the childhood illustration will have no narrative—just music scored." This is exactly the kind of memo telling him his business that Rozsa resented; to make matters worse, Selznick substituted Franz Waxman's "Too Fast," the out-of-control driving scene from *Suspicion,* also a dizzying sequence involving dangerous speed and the heroine's anxiety over whether the leading man will murder her.

It's one thing to expand a cue, as Selznick had done to "Mrs. Danvers" in *Rebecca,* and quite another to lay in someone else's entirely, especially in an extended, climactic scene. Yet Waxman's cue does work: against the white mise-en-scène with parallel lines, the design of the movie, the lovers plunge downward as the music moves inward, beginning with Constance's anxiety and resting deeply within JB's repressed memories. Propelled by a relentless ostinato, the snow peak becomes a child's sliding board leading toward the fatal spikes from JB's childhood—the subconscious finally erupting. When Edwards, now Ballantine, cathartically shouts, "I didn't kill my brother. It was an accident, an accident!" the music winds down: the terrible dissonance of repressed guilt is gone.

Again, Selznick's crudity and high-handedness are balanced by shrewd musical judgment. This is not a case of Selznick simply throwing in one of his favorite tunes. Although intended for frenetic car driving rather than skiing, Waxman's breathless cue provides the distorted sound he wanted. For the gruesome spiked-fence image, he requested "no narrative, just music": Waxman's piercing discords provided that as well.

Once JB is cured, there would seem to be no more need for nightmare music. Not quite. Freed from his inner prison, he is hauled off to a real one by Hitchcock's typically wrong-headed police, in one of the master's most concise jail montages. (Alas, with John Ballantine cured, there is no more need for a theremin, and we never hear that magnificently creepy sound again.) With Gregory Peck in jail offscreen, Rozsa needed to provide new music for Constance's confrontation with Dr. Murchinson. This he apparently failed to do, at least to Selznick's satisfaction. Again, the producer went to another composer, this time Roy Webb, soon to be the composer for *Notorious,* and got what he wanted.[20]

Light seeps under Murchinson's door—an exact parallel to the first door image when Constance approaches JB for the big love scene, now guided by a sinister crescendo rather than a romantic one. Once Constance is in Murchinson's room, at the mercy of his gun, we get Webb's shivery cue, full of grim tremolos. This is Contance's moment and hers alone, without her lover or mentor—the Hitchcock heroine taking command. Once she is back out the door, we are left with Murchinson's suicidal despair, again, fearlessly captured by Webb's music, the most disturbing in the film. In the famous revolving gun scene, Murchinson blows his brains out—and ours—as the score explodes into madness and death, an aural equivalent of the red gore Hitchcock splashed across the black-and-white screen. Again, the artistic and ethical issues are murky and complex: the effectiveness of Webb's cue makes it harder to deplore Selznick's high-handedness, one more blow to the integrity of the film composer.

In any case, Rozsa had the last word. He won the Academy Award for Best Score, and the theremin became a stock device for scary music in both film and television. (Where would *The Thing, The Twilight Zone, Alcoa Presents, The Outer Limits,* and *When Worlds Collide* be without its slithery sound?)[21] Hitchcock himself returned to it in the rooftop finale of *To Catch a Thief* and in the flashback of "Mrs. Blanchard's Secret."[22]

On the surface, everything seemed to go relatively well with this score, but behind the scenes were dark rumblings. Indeed, just before the film's release, Rozsa found himself embroiled in an odd and ugly controversy. Hitchcock complained to Audray Granville, head of the music department, that Rozsa's music for *The Lost Weekend,* shot after *Spellbound* but released just before it, had a duplication of the *Spellbound* theme. On October 8, Selznick made the same discovery on his own, sending a scorched-earth memo to Granville before she got to him: "Unless I am very much mistaken, one of the few measly melodic themes that Dr. Rozsa gave us in *Spellbound*, and the most important of these, has been used by him again in *The Lost Weekend,* with even the exact instrumentation and orchestration. . . . I would be interested to know how Dr. Rozsa explains this." Granville responded with an equally tart letter: she had questioned Rozsa "about this similarity. He admitted using the theremin as the alcoholic motivation in the same manner as it is used in our amnesia sequences, but that the melody was not the same. He evidently wrote three different notes. Am sorry about this, but if Dr. Rozsa chooses to repeat himself, we of necessity must suffer along with him."[23]

Furious, Selznick called Rozsa's office and demanded that he explain himself. Rozsa's unrattled rejoinder became the best line in *Spellbound* lore: yes, I did use the theremin, "and I used the violin, the oboe, and the clarinet as well. Goodbye."[24]

Good-bye, indeed. Rozsa never saw Selznick again. It is just as well. Selznick's memo, copied to everyone but Rozsa, reveals a more far-reaching bitterness than his annoyance over the composer's alleged self-plagiarism. He was clearly disappointed with the score, judging it to have only a "few measly melodic themes." If Hitchcock found the music overwrought, Selznick found it under. In a memo of September 11, he warned Granville that he was "deeply concerned" that the film would have an "unsatisfactory score." In addition to demanding more strings from Rozsa for the main title and substituting cues by Webb and Waxman taken from other movies, he asked Granville to make whatever changes she could in the remaining three weeks before the opening to improve the music. Granville was the editor, not the composer, and it is not clear how far Selznick wanted her to go. She apparently did tinker with the score, but declared she was "not satisfied. . . . I don't believe there are over 20 bars of original music in the score, and the repetition is maddening. Under these circumstances, I found what melody was there and tried to use it to advantage."[25]

Apparently then, the producer, director, and music editor all disliked a score that the public, critics, and Academy Award judges adored. Selznick's objections are particularly odd: for anyone with two ears, it is simply not true that *Spellbound* has only a few measly themes that are recycled in *The Lost Weekend.* (The "Nightmare" cue in the latter, the one most similar, resembles *Spellbound* only in the theremin coloring and Rozsa's signature chords.) The power of the music resides precisely in its unity, its uncanny ability to generate a variety of powerful ideas from the small nucleus that registers both love and terror.

Rozsa never complained about Granville's "improvements" or Selznick's string doublings, but his contempt for Selznick spilled out into his memoirs. The story of *Spellbound*'s music inverts what happened with *Rebecca*, where tensions bristled throughout postproduction but resolved into a happy ending and amicable words all around. Here, the snubs and blowups occurred at the end, apparently costing Rozsa a significant commission. As late as August 8, Selznick pondered using Rozsa for *Duel in the Sun;* on September 15, he wrote his associates that he was "awaiting impatiently the score of *Spellbound* so I can decide about Webb or Rozsa."[26] (He also briefly considered using Korngold.) Ultimately, he hired Dimitri Tiomkin and never used Rozsa again.

Neither did Hitchcock. Indeed, Hitchcock's treatment of Rozsa was as incomprehensible and unmannerly as Selznick's. He never thanked him for the score, even after it won the Academy Award. One wonders if this rebuff—even allowing for Hitchcock's distaste for the gushy string sonorities and the Constance theme—had to do with Rozsa's success. Hitchcock regarded himself as the auteur and may have resented the composer's winning an Academy Award when he didn't. His relationship with Rozsa was a portent of his connections with his other star composers. For Hitchcock, complex issues of authorship were always bound up with how he treated them.

Spellbound's music endured long after the grumblings of Hitchcock and Selznick. Indeed it has enjoyed a curiously long cinematic afterlife. The first spin-off, however, was a spectacular flop, and a fascinating example of how the lure of a hit song could skew the judgments of normally sensible people. The convoluted twists in the story help explain Hitchcock's exasperation and short temper during his battles with Herrmann over a popular song in *Torn Curtain*. The *Spellbound* incident reveals that these contentious issues were not new with the rock-and-roll period but had been brewing for a long time.

On the face of it, the idea of someone bursting into romantic song in the middle of *Spellbound* seems ludicrous, yet in October 1944, J. J. Robbins submitted a song called "Spellbound" to Selznick for use in the film. No record of a rejection exists, but Selznick apparently (mercifully) rejected it. In March of the following year, Decca approached Rozsa for permission to record an album of *Spellbound* music, the beginning of a far more fruitful idea; Rozsa had enjoyed spectacular success with albums for *The Jungle Book* (the first recording of an American movie score). On March 22, during postproduction editing, Granville wrote Selznick suggesting a *Spell-*

bound Suite. (Waxman had paved the way with *Rebecca*.) Granville proposed that Rozsa's suite come out before the picture's release rather than after, as was customary. This novel idea would work out smashingly.

In the same memo, she brought up the notion of a pop song, an idea she attributed to Rozsa: "He says that the love theme would lend itself to a popular ballad, using the title 'Spellbound,' but that he is unfamiliar with this field of music and would require a popular songwriter. . . . Would you be interested in proceeding along this line?" The same day, Selznick fired back a memo declaring himself "heartily in favor" of all "exploitation possibilities on the music of 'Spellbound,' including the production of a 'popular ballad.'" As usual, he wanted it immediately—the deal would be conditional "upon his getting it out earlier than is normally the case"—and he wanted it cheaply, declaring he didn't "see why we should invest any money."

Thus began an interminable flurry of memos, permission requests, proposed lyrics, diatribes, and personal denunciations. Contacted by Selznick's advertising director, Don King, the lyricist Ned Washington expressed interest in writing lyrics but pointed out that he would not do it for free; Granville reminded Selznick that the orchestrator, copyist, and musicians would have to be paid as well. On April 5, King praised Washington's lyric but expressed dismay that he had asked for eight hundred dollars ("too high"), then had gone ahead and written the lyric "without any authorization from me." He was also chagrined that King had recorded it "on film with Rhonda Fleming [who plays the viciously flirtatious psychiatric patient] doing the vocal."

Meanwhile, editor Hal Kern, sensing disaster, complained to Selznick that Granville could not possibly handle these dense *Spellbound* tangles while simultaneously doing tracking for *Duel in the Son*, Selznick's already out-of-control vehicle for Jennifer Jones. Firing back that he could easily juggle two complex projects at once (his usual practice), Selznick commanded everyone to shut up.

Not surprisingly, Washington was dropped as lyricist, and by May 21 Granville had selected another for Selznick's approval, Buddy Morris, who "thoroughly believed in the song" and was "the only publisher on the coast," a man who had immediate access to Decca and "all the name bands." In an ecstatic telegram, Don King urged Selznick to grant Morris immediate approval, claiming that "five publishers are clamoring for Spellbound song" and that everyone was "raving about it . . . really, it's a swell song."[27]

The next day, Selznick wrote Robert Dann, in the music department, unleashing one of the lengthiest, most bitter denunciations in the history of Selznick splutterings. It attacked the song as "utterly inane" and "unutterably bad," but that was the least of it. Selznick, who had never heard of the allegedly famed songwriter, was particularly incensed because he had already rejected the song and already issued instructions to hire a "first-class writer—preferably Johnny Mercer, who did so brilliantly with the 'Laura' music. . . . I want you to send for both King and Audray and tell them I deeply resent this high-pressuring on a song which I turned down cold." As was often the case, the attack turned personal, with Selznick declaring King incapable of being "the judge of 'a swell song'" and impugning Granville's motives: "I resent and suspect Audray's plugging of the work of this song writer. . . . There is a personal connection, I believe a romantic one, which I think accounts for all our song problems being routed through this one song writer, which on the face of it is ridiculous." As far as Selznick was concerned, the messages were trumped up: "I don't believe 'five publishers are clamoring for this song.' . . . In any case, publication doesn't mean a thing. Thousands of songs are published, but very few get anywhere."[28]

For the next six months, numerous songwriters bid for the song, including such major artists as Mercer and Oscar Hammerstein, and many minor ones as well.[29] Adding to the tangle was the music department's discovery that twenty-two songs entitled "Spellbound" already existed in copyright. Hitchcock became involved in the back-and-forths as well. He preferred the lyrics by Allie Wrubel:

> *I see the stars tip-toe . . . there they go two by two*
> *Am I seeing things?*
> *Or am I spellbound when I'm with you*

This preference "disturbed" Selznick's editors, and disturbing it is: if this was Hitchcock's prize lyric, it's hard to imagine the clinkers. But many other lyrics were equally unimaginable, including this typical one from Al Stewart:

> *You sigh, and I'm spellbound*
> *I can hear angels sing*
> *And in my heart*
> *I know the thrill of Eternal Spring.*

To his credit, Selznick denounced all this appalling stuff and demanded that the music department start over again. He also declared he didn't have more time to devote to the endless mess. That he had bothered for this long indicates that he was deeply worried about *Spellbound*'s reception, increasingly distrustful of Rozsa's score, and desperate for a hit song.

After a new round of commissions and rejections, a song was finally chosen and published by Chappell, with lyrics by Mack David and an arrangement by André Kostelanetz, along with promised recordings on RCA Victor, Columbia, and Decca. (The latter two apparently never materialized.) Chappell wanted to use a choral version of the song for the main and end titles, but Selznick torpedoed the idea in a single-sentence memo. Clearly, he was tired of the whole business.

And in the end, it was all for nothing. Recorded on RCA Victor, the song was promoted and played on Al Goodman's Prudential Hour, but it never caught on with the public. According to John Waxman, there were "high hopes for the song which never materialized."[30] Selznick's outburst proved prescient: "Thousands of songs are published, but very few get anywhere."

The futile search for a hit song was a forerunner of many other such cases, the most striking being *Vertigo*. As would be the case with that film, which also centers on obsession and breakdown, the failure to find a hit song was fortunate. It is as painful to contemplate Rozsa's sensuous Largamente main title and Herrmann's haunted Prelude being replaced by a pop tune. Moreover, the dreamlike atmosphere of this film, as in *Vertigo*, is created to a large extent by its omnipresent score; for a Hitchcock picture, there is remarkably little vernacular music of any kind (even less than in *Rebecca*) to compromise *Spellbound*'s surreal ambiance.

Moviegoers had no problem with this aspect of the film. Indeed, this is a case of the public's being smarter than condescending studios. Audiences wanted more of the real thing—the full-throated symphonic *Spellbound* concert piece—not a pop-song spin-off. Don King, Robert Dann, and Chappell's Jean Aberbach all tried to bring out an album of Rozsa's complete music, but the breakthrough came when Jerome Kern, part owner of Chappell, asked Rozsa to publish the music under the title "Spellbound Concerto." Concertos culled from movie music constituted an odd new 1940s crossover genre, exemplified by the enormously popular "Warsaw Concerto" by Richard Addinsell (who scored Hitchcock's *Under Capricorn*), and Kern wanted to cash in on this vogue. When Rozsa, who was frequently dismayed by Hollywood gaucheness, protested that "it's not a concerto," Kern said, "Oh, never mind that!"[31] The word *concerto* had sex appeal, and that's what he intended to call "Spellbound."

Rozsa let Kern have his way and call his piece a concerto. As Kern predicted, the public didn't care, but the distortion bothered Rozsa so much that later he revised the orchestration to justify the label, transforming the score into two concertos, one for piano, another for orchestra. The latter became a popular favorite, brighter and brassier than the movie version, but retaining Rozsa's dark modal harmonies. That it stands on its own in more than one concert version is a testament to the richness of this music.

Indeed, it was popular in this form even before the movie's release or Rozsa's completion of the score. Leopold Stokowski approved the premiere of the "Suite," as Rozsa preferred to call it, for a performance on July 28. Again, Audray Granville demonstrated her shrewdness. "I believe," she wrote Selznick on July 16, "this is of greater advantage to us than having it performed on motion picture night, as it is being performed not just because it is a motion picture score but as an outstanding concert contribution." On the 21st, Rozsa personally invited Selznick to the concert, which he conducted, and sent him two tickets, adding that he would be honored if Selznick would attend. Vanguard Films informed Selznick that they were inviting Gregory Peck, the Hitchcocks, Ben Hecht, Michael Chekov, Rhonda Fleming, and "all critics in the Los Angeles area." The letter asked Selznick for additional names, but a brusque handwritten note responded, "DOS said you handle—he brushed it off—he's in a hurry."[32]

Selznick was no fan of Stokowski's. When early in the project someone suggested Stokowski to do *Spellbound*'s score, Selznick rejected him with the comment that "on the last job he did he drove everyone out of their minds as regards time and expense."[33] Fortunately, Selznick's snubbing of the concert was not a harbinger of things to come: following the Hollywood Bowl premiere, the Suite and Concerto continued to enjoy success both in performance and as recordings.[34] (Selznick did send Rozsa a note of "sincere thanks and appreciation" on July 30.) Most important, a transcription, sent to one thousand radio stations, was broadcast nationwide so that by the time the film was released, audiences already knew the music. Here was an early example of how a strong synergy between a movie and its score could propel the fortunes of both. The *Rebecca* score helped the movie only after its premiere; Rozsa's music, a forerunner of contemporary practices, started the marketing process earlier.

The popularity of the score follows a pattern we see repeatedly in this book. Like other composers, Rozsa received early acclaim for his Hitchcock score, and Hitchcock's cachet gave him a launching pad for later important works, from *Ben-Hur,* whose major motif is anticipated in Gregory Peck's breakdown music, to *Providence,* a surreal dreamscape that picks up where *Spellbound*'s nightmare scene leaves off. Troubled dreams and a theremin

Spellbound on vinyl. A score promoting a movie before its release. (Courtesy of George Chastain)

evoking mental disintegration also figured in Rozsa's score for Billy Wilder's *Lost Weekend* (the subject of Selznick's temper tantrum), also an instant hit. The "Awakening" cue became a template for a style of unabashed lyricism that would crop up not only in later Rozsa love themes but in the gloriously schmaltzy second movement of his Violin Concerto. For better or worse, Rozsa's name became attached to the theremin, so much so that the makers of *The Red House* demanded he use it, even though he thought it did not suit the movie. Rozsa was Mr. Theremin, said Edward G. Robinson; audiences expected its now familiar sound, and that was that.

In the long run, the theremin played a significant role in keeping *Spellbound* and its music not only alive (being a Hitchcock movie, it would be that in any case) but continually seductive. By the 1970s, the instrument had practically dropped out of sight, replaced by the more practical ondes Martinot, which delivered a less exquisite shiver but had a proper keyboard that made it much easier to play. (Not many musicians, it turned out, were resourceful at producing music out of thin air.) In 1974, Rozsa himself declared the theremin passé, a "lost instrument," no doubt increasing its romantic cachet. The theremin appeared to be one of those fads that flare up brilliantly for a considerable time, then sputter into extinction.

But wait! In the final years of the twentieth century, mysteriously and unexpectedly, it came slithering back; by 2000, it was all the rage again, not only in concert music but in pop and performance art, with thousands of new theremins being made each year. It even had a poetics: Albert Glinsky's wonderfully titled *The Theremin: Ether Music and Espionage* (1994). Whenever the phenomenon was mentioned in the press, *Spellbound* was as well, for that was where the theremin first emerged in popular culture. National Public Radio's piece on the theremin, aired in 2002, began with the spellbinding music from *Spellbound*, followed by Sara Fishko asking, "How could you not want to play the theremin after hearing that sound?" Indeed. And how could you not want to play *Spellbound* on one of its various DVD releases? Suddenly the movie was back in vogue, propelled by its music and bringing a new generation under its spell. By now, the sound of *Spellbound* is nearly in the same class of audience recognition as *Vertigo* and *Psycho*. It has stood the test of time longer than either.

9

notorious: bright sambas, dark secrets

An imperceptible suspension in the syncopation, a nonchalant respiration, a light pause that I found very difficult to grasp.

—Darius Milhaud, on Brazilian dance rhythm

Notorious is the least celebrated of the major Hitchcock scores, one few scholars or fans talk about. Deeply interior, lacking an easy-to-hum big tune, and projecting only a hint of romantic feeling, it has not enjoyed popular recordings or spin-offs.

The neglect is unfortunate, for Roy Webb composed one of the most deftly designed scores of any Hitchcock film. It weaves a unique spell, one Hitchcock had not conjured before, and the hip, swingy source music is novel as well. After the thickness and warmth of *Rebecca, Suspicion,* and *Spellbound,* the *Notorious* music is like a cool, stinging shower, ideal for the movie, which has a formalist precision resembling musical composition. As François Truffaut put it, *Notorious* "gets a maximum of effect from a minimum of elements. . . . Of all your pictures, this is the one in which one feels the most perfect correlation between what you are aiming at and what appears on the screen. . . . To the eye, the ensemble is as perfect as an animated cartoon."[1]

To the ear, the ensemble is perfect as well. According to the film historian Rudy Behlmer, we are lucky to have this self-effacing score: Hitchcock did not intend for Roy Webb to write it, even though he was the house composer for RKO, which released the film in a loan-out arrangement with the Selznick Studio.[2] (Webb *was* favored by Selznick, who recycled his cues in *Spellbound* and *The Paradine Case*—at least he wouldn't have to do so this time.) Max Steiner's assistant until 1935, Webb was regarded as reliable but unglamorous, not yet a recognized force in his own right. Hitchcock wanted a star like *Citizen Kane*'s Bernard Herrmann, who was again unavailable.[3]

In some respects—an unflinching use of dissonance, a favoring of spare motifs and ostinatos—Webb's style resembles Herrmann's. Generous and self-abnegating, Webb regarded Herrmann as the master: "Benny writes the best music in Hollywood, with the fewest notes."[4] But Herrmann's quick temper and easily bruised ego made his relationship with Webb an uneasy one. Three years before *Notorious*, his finale to Welles's *Magnificent Ambersons* had been replaced by RKO with a hastily composed cue by Webb meant to fit a last-minute happy ending. Flying into a rage, Herrmann demanded his name be removed from the credits and threatened a lawsuit, resulting in a film with no composer credit.

Although *Notorious* was originally a Selznick International Studio production, David Selznick was involved only in the beginning stages and was blissfully absent during postproduction. His unsolicited mentoring and bitter quarrels with Hitchcock on the sets of *Rebecca* and *Spellbound* are part of film lore. But in the case of *Notorious*, Selznick's guiding—to Hitchcock, strangling—hand was missing. Selznick's messy affair with his new star Jennifer Jones coupled with the overseeing and financing of her starring role in *Duel in the Sun* necessitated his selling the rights to *Notorious*. He did not have the time, money, or emotional energy to get through another complicated project with Hitchcock. Selznick's buyer, RKO, was delighted to acquire this tony picture with its famous director and glamorous stars, and Hitchcock was free to be his own producer.

Only at the last minute did Hitchcock give Webb the okay, but as Behlmer points out, he was "perfect for the subject and treatment"; once Webb began composing, Hitchcock became "very involved with the music, as he usually did."[5] As we have seen, Selznick deplored Hitchcock's "goddamn jigsaw cutting," the dreamlike, jagged images that create his signature subjectivity. But Webb didn't mind jigsaw cutting at all. It complemented his fragmented musical architecture, just as the blocked passions of the film's characters reflected his unresolved harmonies. As Behlmer puts it, Webb's music was "more subtle, less bombastic, less melodically defined" than the usual Hollywood product.[6] Like Hitchcock, Webb favored atmosphere and tonal nuance over broad gestures. Both men were classicists dealing in darkness and chaos. Like Hitchcock, Webb pulled his punches, saving the knockout for the big scenes, as in the spectacular Gothic finale of Robert Wise's *The Body Snatcher*. In everything from *Bringing Up Baby* to *I Walked with a Zombie*, he emphasized structural refinement.

Rozsa's *Spellbound* is memorable precisely because its robust Romanticism works against Hitchcock's cool sensibility, producing a special tension. Webb's slithery bitonal chords and complex love theme, on the other hand, are exactly in tune with Hitchcock's own aesthetic. At Columbia University, Webb had cultivated a love of Bach and Beethoven and was especially entranced with Bachian geometries. He was admirably suited to providing the emotional life for Hitchcock's elaborate designs: the inversions and retrogressions of scenes, the transformation of physical objects such as keys and wine bottles into design elements that resemble musical motifs. Webb was also a fast-working professional who got the job done with a minimum of fuss, a quality Hitchcock always valued. As his own producer, Hitchcock was able to spot the score himself and get the symmetries exactly right, without Selznick's interference—no more sudsy violins in big love scenes, no more recycling of Selznick's favorite cues from past movies.[7]

Another liberating aspect of *Notorious* was Hitchcock's authority to choose his own source music. The latter, of course, was something he could control more fully than the score, and he made sure there were no south-of-the-border clichés in his manipulation of Brazilian tunes. After the absence of vernacular songs in the heavily symphonic *Rebecca* and *Spellbound,* he wanted something lighter and fizzier. Selznick gave him the green light in an April 16, 1945, memo to the head of his music department, Audray Granville: "I am most eager to have a good deal of representative Brazilian music in *Notorious.* Suggest you have a meeting with Mr. Hitchcock . . . list all various numbers and get Mr. Hitchcock's ideas on what type of music he thinks we should use."[8]

There was one close call. Having failed to get a popular song for *Spellbound,* Selznick made another pass in *Notorious.* A series of memos from Barbara Keon and others in the music department reveal a search for "gooey-sentimental" songs (in Keon's alarming phrase): "something Alicia would have liked as a young girl before she's become disillusioned with life and with her father: something getting over perhaps that she's looking for a Prince Charming or a little love nest with some nice guy." Among the eighteen gooey-sentimental tunes considered were "Love Nest," "Don't Give Any More Beer to My Father," and "In a Little Love Nest Way Up on a Hill."[9] Selznick also received a letter from the music publisher Nat Winecoff, who claimed to "control most of the Brazilian music made in that country," promising material that "we can turn into American song hits." [10]

None of this, fortunately, made it into the film. Instead, Hitchcock chose a colorful variety of folk material. In the Rio scenes, tambourines, guitars, drums, and Brazilian trumpets swing into Brazilian dance music, providing sensuous foreplay for the tumultuous love affair between Ingrid Bergman and Cary Grant. These include "Carnaval no Rio," "Meu Barco," Aloysia Oliveira's "Guanabara," and two sambas, "Ya Ya Me Leva" and an arrangement of "Bright Samba" by Rene Garriguenc, with Brazilian trumpet, tom-tom, tambourine, and guitar.[11] The sexy syncopation of these dances provides a backdrop all the more alluring because Hitchcock keeps the volume turned down. *Notorious* rocks, but its beat is discreet, getting into our bloodstream rather than assaulting our eardrums. In addition to sambas, we get racy American dance tunes, formal waltzes ("The Emperor Waltz," "The Terry Waltz," "The Birthday Waltz"), Schumann piano music, and much else. The opening party tune, "Lovely Way to Spend an Evening" (after Ingrid Bergman's sardonic line), suggests Alicia's "notorious" looseness and drunkenness. (The original cut, before the censors intervened, had her much looser and drunker.)

In the famous wine cellar scene where Grant's character, T. R. Devlin, discovers Nazi uranium, Bergman's Alicia, his undercover coconspirator, asks the band to stop playing stuffy waltzes and liven up the music with Brazilian music, hoping the volume will cover their dangerous search operation. During the party, waltzes provide counterpoint to the jealous suspicions of Alicia's husband, Alex Sebastian, and the spying couple's anxious plotting. Once the latter are in the cellar, Hitchcock takes the risk of relying entirely on Latin dance tunes rather than on a suspense cue. Brazilian syncopation snakes through Ted Tetzloff's shadowy lighting and the explosion of a smashing wine bottle, giving the scene a unique tension.

Just why this relatively reticent pre–bossa nova works so brilliantly is somewhat of a mystery, but a partial answer is provided by Darius Milhaud, whose "Le Boeuf sur le Toit" and "Saudades do Brasil" are two of the great Brazilian-inspired classics from the early jazz era. Brazilian dance music was endlessly alluring, but "there was an imperceptible suspension in the syncopation, a nonchalant respiration, a light pause that I found very difficult to grasp."[12] These imperceptible suspensions were precisely what Hitchcock exploited: a subtle space in the syncopation that gives the camera freedom and allows the suspense to gradually bubble up.

Source music plays an important part in Hitchcock's depiction of evil. When Alicia enters the Sebastians' sumptuous house, the Nazis' hideout, she is greeted by Schumann piano music, the delicate sighs of the Chopin section from *Carnival.* Wicked they may be, but these terrorists have artistic sensibilities and impeccable taste, as do those in *The 39 Steps, Saboteur,* and

Notorious. Cary Grant on piano, Ingrid Bergman on the bottle.

both versions of *The Man Who Knew Too Much.* Hitchcock telescopes the debate over art versus virtue, especially the fascist fondness for great music, making the point that aesthetic refinement by no means connotes morality. Like Poe, Hitchcock found art and morality, beauty and truth, to have little to do with each other. *Rope,* his next film, would widen the chasm even further.

Hitchcock's daughter, Patricia, rates *Notorious* highest among her father's works because of its impeccable casting, and indeed one could hardly find an ensemble with more glamour and chemistry than the triangle of

Cary Grant, Ingrid Bergman, and Claude Rains. But it is the dangerous atmosphere of *Notorious,* the exquisite buildup of doom, that gives the performances their special frisson. With the exception of the traumatic "Alicia Collapses" cue and the guillotinelike final cadence, the score is never loud or brutal. Neither is the film itself: other than Cary Grant smacking Ingrid Bergman after the drunk-driving scene, *Notorious* has no on-screen violence, yet it manages to communicate a unique aura of suppressed menace. Unlike a typical Hollywood score in a 1940s war-espionage movie with over-the-top music, Webb's lies under the film, caressing and insinuating.

The narrative is simplicity itself: two men love the same woman, one of whom employs her to spy on the other. As in a Poe story, the design moves inexorably inward. The story opens with broad, colorful locations and exteriors, settles into the stark interiors of the briefing room and the Sebastians' bedrooms, and closes claustrophobically into the psyches of its three principals. It follows the aesthetic advanced by the narrator of "The Fall of the House of Usher," who argues that strictly self-imposed limits create opportunities for the limitless. The music is clear in its outlines but secretive and suggestive in its harmonies and variations—again, a Poe effect. Webb's score sounds submerged, bottled up, like the relationship between Devlin and Alicia, but capable of exploding like Sebastian's jealousy, building inexorably toward the dark minor chords that crash down on him at the end.

This is not to suggest that *Notorious* is merely a technical exercise. Despite its elaborate artifice, this film connects in a disquieting way with reality, like a dream that makes us see the waking world in a new light. As Michael Wood points out, Hitchcock always leaves an emotional residue, causing us to view the modern world differently. In *Notorious,* it is partly the shrewd depiction of romantic relationships; the spy story may be far-fetched, but the rendering of sexual fear and betrayal has powerful credibility. Also disturbingly real is the deadly secret announced by the film's somber trumpet fanfare: the lethal powder that Claude Rains and his colleagues are using to make the ultimate terrorist bomb. It was certainly credible to the FBI, which wondered how Hitchcock could have come up with the concept of the atomic bomb before it was dropped on the Japanese and accordingly had him watched for four weeks.

The unobtrusiveness of the music fits the strategy, creating an aura of conspiracy and repression. In *Notorious,* music mediates between Hitchcock's audience and characters. In one of the few appreciations of Webb's art, Christopher Palmer pinpoints how the score enhances the early, critical scene where the heroine is "rendered defenceless" by Devlin playing a recording of her denouncing her Nazi father: "It is the music that, entering unobtrusively at this moment, helps us feel its significance and her emotion—as so often, it acts as the 'communicating link' between screen and audience. Were we actually in the same room with Alicia, we would have no need of any music to experience the emotion. As we are not, we need the music to help us, to create the missing dimension of reality."[13] Hitchcock, of course, *was* in the room, and he instinctively knew that music was needed at that moment, though the film's opening scenes have little. In Palmer's reading, and contrary to the conventional notion of a score providing a cushion against realism, music makes the scene more real. The "missing dimension of reality" is an emotional truth Alicia is trying to deny; Webb's score enacts what Alicia is feeling: the painful and bitter rebuke of her father's legacy, which is the whole point of the scene.

The idea of music as mediation rather than leading player was central to Webb's aesthetic. He had a modest ego, a handy trait when working for a control addict like Hitchcock. In an article for *Film Music Notes* published four years before *Notorious,* he wrote that the film composer's art is one of self-effacement: "The composer must subserve his music to the requirements of the scene. . . . He has to be careful not to be carried away with the development of the musical qualities of his composition. A long, sweeping melody may suddenly have to be interrupted by a comic theme or an equally foreign element of some kind, which, from the standpoint of composition, is very awkward. A man must be willing to forget any temperamental notions."[14] This is a modernist position not unlike that of Eliot and Joyce: the artist stands aloof from his product, submerging his ego, subserving the larger requirements of form. Romantic, temperamental notions only get in the way.

Restraint and submission were useful traits for surviving in the film-music business. Indeed, RKO blamed Herrmann's temperament for the fiasco over the music in *The Magnificent Ambersons.*[15] Webb's philosophy of composition gave his career stability and built him a reputation for professionalism, enabling him to remain with a single employer, RKO, through the mid-1950s. Ironically, Hitchcock, who put a premium on restraint and top-down control, favored composers like Herrmann and Tiomkin, whose forward, highly visible music reflected their iconoclastic personalities. Even Waxman, an artist not known for emotional volatility, explicitly rejected the notion of film music's invisibility, as he made clear following *Rebecca.* Hitchcock valued subtlety, but also operatic intensity. There was room in his musical universe for *Mr. and Mrs. Smith* and *Notorious,* but also for *Rebecca, Strangers on a Train,* and *Vertigo.*

Webb's ideas clearly fit the widespread notion of movie music being invisible and unobtrusive. A practitioner of the mosaic style that is the visual hallmark of *Notorious,* Webb was perfectly willing to interrupt a "long, sweeping melody" for a "foreign element" necessary in a scene, or to forgo it altogether. In a love scene, he admitted, "a jazz tune on the radio might point up the scene better than anything": no need for a broad, romantic tune. A striking example is the flight from Florida to Rio, where the camera subtly reveals Devlin's attraction to Alicia as she looks out the window in profile: Webb's sensuous melody, which captures the romantic moment admirably, is interrupted by jazzy Brazilian tunes following a cut to a Rio restaurant, source music that indeed points up the sexual repartee "better than anything."

Some of Webb's effects are so subtle—attenuated even further by Hitchcock's economical spotting—that a second viewing is required to appreciate them. The first sound we hear over the Selznick logo is a whirring trumpet alarm, followed by the seductive main-title melody, marked Dramatico. Together, the two deliver the double theme of so much Hitchcock: love and terror. But what do the alarms portend? We don't find out until near the end, during the second scene in the wine cellar, when Alex scans wine labels and discovers the fatal bottle tampered with by Devlin. So much hangs on this moment: the heroine's identity and endangerment, the villain's sexual betrayal and vulnerability, not to mention the exposure of a deadly uranium bomb, all brought to a head by those riveting trumpets, once enigmatic, now terribly clear, heard only in these two moments. This is the kind of powerful restraint and avoidance of obvious repetition that make *Notorious* pleasurable the second, third, or tenth time around.

The love music is also developed with striking economy that often seems to subvert its purpose. Sexy and full of danger, it is a typical Hitchcock romance theme, though it is rarely used romantically. Even when Alicia and Devlin ascend a hill with a spectacular view and embrace during the initial courtship scenes—surely the cue for a fortissimo eruption of love music, à la *Spellbound*—the theme sounds only for a teasing instant. For the most part, it appears at unpredictable times, in increasingly troubled harmonies, to capture the couple's shifting sexual subcurrents: Alicia's hurt and suppressed longing, Devlin's fear, jealousy, and hesitation. Hitchcock's spotting removes any hint of sentimentality from this elegantly hard-boiled movie.

Often, the love scenes have no music at all; the famous embrace on the veranda—a series of short, passionate pecks rather than the "prolonged, lustful" kisses that the censors would have forbidden—begins with distant music on the balcony, but the music disappears as the lovers move inside to their private world, imparting an austere eroticism as the camera glides with them from the veranda to the phone. Devlin is cool to a fault, and the denial of music won't allow us to forget it; his brittleness keeps love from flowering. Even the bedroom climax at the end of the film is bathed in silence: the hero and heroine speak almost inaudibly to each other as they finally reveal their mutual passion. The whispered sensuality is part of the austere atmosphere of *Notorious,* but it is also plot-driven: Devlin must be quiet to avoid detection in Alicia's room. Voices needing to release passion even as they must stifle it create a strange and powerful tension, one Hitchcock would continue to exploit during the nervous whispers in *Stage Fright, Rear Window, Psycho,* and other of his films.

The film's title refers to a typical Hitchcockian struggle with a guilt-ridden past. Alicia Huberman is "notorious" for a drunken promiscuity that blots out her guilt over being the daughter of an unrepentant Nazi criminal who commits suicide rather than reveal state secrets. She tries to break out of this legacy through a dangerous spying assignment for American intelligence commandeered by Devlin, the "copper" she initially hates, then passionately loves. Devlin responds first with passion of his own but is soon suffering from his suppressed agony over the triangle he has helped create.

These conflicted emotions are cued by music, which enacts the characters' inner lives rather than imitating what is on the screen. Seductive and sinister, the music has a teasing ambivalence that reflects the advance-retreat love test between Alicia and Devlin. It helps us sort out emotional entanglements that are complex even for Hitchcock: Devlin setting up Alicia as sexual bait, refusing to take any responsibility for his role, then feeling devastated when she does a superb job; Alicia finding herself coldly manipulated by the man she loves, seeing her notorious behavior exploited for political purposes, then fearing desertion by the lover who has put her in the excruciating predicament of spying on her late father's Nazi colleague by sleeping with him—a man who genuinely loves her, perhaps more than Devlin. Hitchcock's most painfully sympathetic villain, Alex, is driven by his profound jealousy and rage—not to mention his enthrallment to an emasculating mother—culminating in an abrupt, absolute imperative to kill the love of his life.

These convolutions are enacted with the sparest musical fragments.

The main title is an ingenious chromatic paragraph, easily recognizable yet sufficiently complex to permit all manner of sly variations, which Hitchcock exploits to the maximum. When a dangerously ill Alicia tells Devlin good-bye after his announced departure from the assignment, the music is a tortured miniature of the love melody, dramatizing her fear of desertion. It also cues the audience's apprehension: Devlin thinks Alicia is "still tight," drifting back to the bottle, but we know she is being slowly poisoned. When Alicia lies dying in bed, looked after only by her killers, another variation on the melody drifts ghostlike through the scene, indicating she has not given up hope.

As Robin Wood points out in *Hitchcock's Films Revisited,* Hitchcockian suspense is fundamentally sexual, and Hitchcock uses Webb to bring it out. In "The Key," a nail-biting moment, the love melody is spooked by a celesta as Alex comes into the bedroom when Alicia is stealing his key for Devlin: with a breathless montage of close-ups, the camera shows Alicia throwing her arms around his neck in an embrace so he won't see the key, then kicking it under a table as the love music slithers downward into a grotesque self-parody. To love Devlin, Alicia must prostitute herself for Alex; the camera registers the suspense, the music the bitter irony.

Gil Grau's orchestration contributes to the elegant symmetry: celestes and chimes continually ring out in scenes involving keys, impending danger, and sexual deceit. Throughout his career, Hitchcock favored bell-like keyboard and percussion, and this film is no exception. In the most sustained sequence of musical subjectivity, a suspicious Alex awakens to somber chimes ringing through a low pedal and dissonant chords. Originating from a clock, a real object, these transform into pitched percussion—a Hitchcockian instance of source music invading the score. Collapsing basses register Alex's dismay at finding his missing key mysteriously returned. Moving into the wine cellar, he grimly ponders rows of bottles. Quizzical woodwinds give way to the fateful trumpets, then the entire orchestra shudders and collapses as Alex stoops to see the no-longer-secret powder. His anxiety transformed to despair, he marches upstairs, shown in an aerial shot, a dead man walking, his realization of doom sounded by horns, timpani, and a pounding ostinato. Entitled "Troubled Mind," this cue surges through a long scene bereft of dialogue, a classic specimen of pure cinema.

Hitchcock then shows his mastery at fusing music with dialogue, as Alex confides in his mother, played by Leopoldine Constantin (whose imperious wickedness nearly steals the show). "I knew!" she gloats, over cool

PIANO CONDUCTOR

ALICIA COLLAPSES
_(M):95_

ROY WEBB

"Alicia Collapses." The traumatic climax of Roy Webb's *Notorious*. (Copyright
© 1946 by Bourne Co. Copyright Renewed. All Rights Reserved. International
Copyright Secured.)

vibraphones. But it's much worse than even she thinks. Surrounded by shimmering pedals and atonal winds, the camera peers down at Alex as he quietly utters his unforgettable line: "I am married to an American agent." The sinister delicacy of this music reaches its apex in a harp ascent as Mrs. Sebastian, pondering the next deadly move, tensely lights a cigarette, her malevolent eyes staring threateningly at the camera.

Another devastating discovery cue, "Alicia Collapses," dramatizes the heroine's realization that she is being poisoned. As Alicia's anxious gaze focuses on the lethal coffee cup, churning strings reveal that she finally comprehends what is in it. First heard in the "You're still tight!" farewell scene with Devlin, this spinning dissonance (which resembles *Vertigo*'s rooftop chase cue) combines with a deathlike ostinato as her poisoners' disembodied voices kindly inquire about her health. Near collapse, she faces the blurred outlines of her assassins as fragments of the love tune tell us that Devlin is still in her head. These survive over a vibrating pedal point building to a shuddery discord and crashing, as Alicia falls to the floor. The bass vibrations capturing Alicia's nausea and terror are so intense that we suspect Hitchcock is experimenting with electronic instruments, as he did with *Spellbound* and would do with *The Birds*. But there are no electronic devices in the score; it's all done with strings, vibraphones, and uncanny harmonies.[16]

The staircase rescue reprises the whirring strings from "Alicia Collapses" in one of the least climactic and most subtle Hitchcock finales. Entitled "Saved," this cue is marked "Molto Misterioso"; it is nearly subliminal, just potent enough to pull us into Devlin's deadly manipulation of Alex and his mother. As with the bedroom scene, the narrative provides a rationale for the weirdly suppressed atmosphere, the sense that dialogue and music are sinking into a decrescendo precisely when the dramatic temperature is rising: the strings whisper to avoid covering the necessarily quiet dialogue, a complex game in which Devlin, without allowing those downstairs to hear him, threatens to expose the Sebastians to their murderous cronies as he maneuvers Alicia out the door. The languid, multisubjective camera descent down the stairs, like Alex's slow death march up them in "Troubled Mind," is as mesmerizing as a ballet.

Psycho is generally regarded as the score that broke away completely from Hollywood lushness for a modern astringency. *Notorious* was already moving decisively in that direction, though it is more subjective, revealing emotional secrets the characters themselves don't know, though they are shared with the audience in a subtle intimacy. In *Notorious*, Hitchcock avoided the Wagnerian method of film scoring—dark motifs representing the evil characters, bright tunes the good ones—for a fluid, shifting interior music that is unerringly in touch with Hitchcock's world of moral ambiguity and sexual tension.

Ironically, Roy Webb gets little credit for a masterful score precisely because it has the same high level of sophistication as everything else in the film: rather than standing out, it is content to be, in the best sense, invisible.[17] Webb insisted that the composer was subservient, and both this score and its reception are consistent with his philosophy. Nonetheless, he couldn't help being proud of this music; as with Waxman, Rozsa, and Herrmann, Webb created something special for Hitchcock, a standout in his composing career.

The last word in *Notorious* is his, a deadly cadence as Alex ascends the final staircase to meet his doom. Any expected reprise of love music with Alicia and Devlin driving into the sunset does not materialize. Instead, "The End" appears on a dark screen, the staircase suggesting gallows. Hitchcock is known for swift, concentrated endings that bring all the elements in the picture together, but nowhere else do we get a more terrible sense of termination. Sound and image unite to provide an unforgettable final impression. Again, Christopher Palmer gets it just right: "When Sebastian mounts the steps of his house to meet his nemesis at the hands of his ruthless compatriots, the music swings eloquently to a close—like the huge front door—with an air of black and terrible finality."[18]

10

the paradine case: the unhappy finale
of hitchcock and selznick

We know that Hitchcock is having a wonderful time in Old Bailey, and will stay there forever if we don't do something about it.

—David Selznick

Hitchcock's final collaboration with David Selznick was as ill-fated as its doomed heroine and her love-smitten lawyer. Everyone groused about it: Hitchcock, who resented being stuck with the interfering Selznick, for whom he had to make one more picture and whose bondage he could not wait to terminate; Selznick, who continued to find Hitchcock's camera claustrophobic and "excessively cutty"; Gregory Peck, who pronounced it his worst moment, a judgment with which Hitchcock concurred; and Louis Jordan (in his movie debut), who was even more hopelessly miscast, Hitchcock believed, than Peck.[1] (In fact, both deliver robustly self-tortured performances, as their characters require.) Selznick struggled strenuously to promote this melodramatic story of a respected English barrister who falls in love with his beautiful, guilty-as-hell client, but the verdict at the box office was the same as hers. Unusual for a Hitchcock picture, the judgment has stood up. A hanging by public and critics is one thing, but *The Paradine Case* has not enjoyed the retrial and vindication of *Rich and Strange, Vertigo, Marnie,* and other of his films that were once deemed dismal failures. The continued neglect of *The Paradine Case* is perversely notable.

Yet with its high-tone suspense, dark romance, and exploration of moral ambiguity, this is a distinctly Hitchcockian picture. Romantic obsession and the struggle between personal feelings and public obligations were two of his central themes, especially when they involved representatives of the law or the medical profession falling in love with patients or suspected criminals. But this picture was considerably more downbeat than *Murder!*, *Spellbound*, even *Notorious*, all of which explored similar psychological terrain; the public was not accustomed to suffering through the leading man's humiliating personal and professional defeat (especially with a popular star like Gregory Peck), his adoring wife's sustained betrayal, and the leading lady's imprisonment and death sentence. Anthony Keane risks everything and loses much of it by falling morbidly in love with his manifestly guilty client. Tony's wife, Gay, does everything a long-suffering wife can to remain loyal to her husband, but the outcome is so grim that it is hard to imagine audiences taking to the film—or why Selznick thought they might. Except for Charles Laughton's trademark blustering and ranting (laced with cruelty and lechery), Hitchcock's usual humor is absent, and the film lacks that ineffable quality that audiences always count on, even in his darkest movies: charm.

Yet the somberness of the film, its consistent aura of doom, is precisely what is compelling for those willing to put up with the narcissism, self-destructiveness, and sadism of the characters. (Robert Hichens, on whose book the film is based, projects a similar downcast atmosphere in his prose style.) The tense tracking shots through Old Bailey during the trial and the funereal cinematography by Lee Garmes have an unrelieved starkness, an eloquent morbidity.

The film was almost scored by a composer with a style darker than Waxman's. A letter from Ted Wick in the music department recommends that Selznick consider hiring a radio composer: "The radio industry has many topnotch composers who are worth looking into as possibilities for our future films. A great number of half-hour dramatic programs demand full original scores and many of these men write a complete score every week and get it all rehearsed and ready for airing in a few short hours. Conceivably, if we could get a radio composer who is used to working against split second timing, and with a small budget, we could turn out some very creditable scores at a much lower cost than is customary."[2] Along with Leith Stevens ("excellent taste") and Bernard Katz ("rich and extremely melodic"), Wick recommends "Bernard Herman [*sic*]: Mr. Herman has composed for motion pictures previously, and though somewhat of an individualist is one of the really top radio composers."[3] Once again, Herrmann was considered for a Hitchcock picture.

"Somewhat of an individualist" is a wonderful understatement. It's hard to imagine the control-obsessed Selznick putting up with Herrmann,

Franz Waxman. (Copyright © John W. Waxman Collection. All Rights Reserved.)

though he would have welcomed the lower cost and Herrmann's extraordinary speed. Selznick admired Herrmann's work and had wanted him aboard the *Spellbound* project. Herrmann certainly could have written a score sufficiently dark; *The Paradine Case* would have probably had an even more oppressive atmosphere. But James Stewart, the sound engineer, added to Selznick's concern by warning of Herrmann's "musical independence," and thus ended Herrmann's chance to score the film.[4] Waxman was again Selznick's man; he had delivered a hit with *Rebecca*, and his *Suspicion* was a score Selznick enjoyed enough to keep cannibalizing in later films, including this one. Waxman's dusky colors, mesmerizing pedal points, and chromatic lyricism would again color a Hitchcock-Selznick picture.

By this point, music in a Hitchcock film was a rich network of echoes and correspondences. *Rebecca* rings through several scenes (as it does in *Suspicion*): Gregory Peck's novachord-tinted "Second Interview" with Maddalena Paradine echoes mysterious chords from *Rebecca*'s confession scene;

his entrance into "Mrs. Paradine's Room" (richly orchestrated by Paul Dessau) recapitulates the haunted sound from *Rebecca*'s "West Wing."

Sometimes we get quotations rather than correspondences. As usual, Selznick pilfered from previous films. The musical timing sheet instructs that "a cue from *Suspicion*" be used with a shot "from a very high angle" as "Keane Leaves the Court," the devastating overhead shot after Gregory Peck breaks down in public defeat and humiliation. *Suspicion*'s mournful, plaintive string theme gives the shot a tragic dignity after icy quiet in the courtroom.

Most memorable of all is Franz Waxman's music, his most noirish score for Hitchcock, and his most undervalued. (With some fanfare, Alco made a recording for Selznick's Vanguard Films in March 1948, but the score has languished and other recordings have not materialized.) Waxman, who was known for his patience and good temper, enthusiastically fulfilled his obligations in a project everyone else seemed to grudgingly struggle through. Waxman's neoclassical "Old Bailey" fanfares for brass and organ and the obsessive dissonance during the "Interview" and "Consulting Cell" cues have an unusual tartness and severity. Others are poetic and haunting, most notably "Matron's Room," where a ground bass growls through the prison corridor over a drunk woman's keening of "Annie Laurie" as the heroine's cell is slammed shut, a premonition of Henry Fonda locked up to despairing music in *The Wrong Man*.[5] Imprisonment scenes had a special, personal resonance for Hitchcock, and he took great care when filming them; this gripping sequence is no exception.

Roy Webb is also plundered, as he was in *Spellbound*. The Misterioso atonal snarls and Molto Crescendo tremolos blending with gusts of wind when Louis Jordan's Latour confronts Keane at the Station Inn are from Webb's "Poet's Sequence" cue in *The Seventh Victim* and "Jealous Husband" in *Experiment Perilous*. The delicious irony of the latter, given that Mrs. Paradine murdered her jealous husband for Latour's affections, will be lost on all but the few Roy Webb admirers who recognize the music, but the dramatic power is undeniable. "If ever there was an evil woman, she is one," warns Latour, and Webb's ominous sounds tell us that the stubborn, love-smitten Keane should listen carefully. On a lighter note is Webb's "Salon Music" from *The Locket,* plundered the previous year for *Notorious* and now again, this time as restaurant counterpoint for the troubled thoughts of Gay, Keane's wife (played exquisitely by Ann Todd), as she ruminates on his passion for Maddalena. Entitled "The Terry Waltz," this number continues Hitchcock's tradition of using light waltzes for dark moments.

For Hitchcock, music was a basic component of identity, a point he makes elegantly in the opening scene. Maddalena, played with stony stoicism by Alida Valli, performs Waxman's chromatic main-title melody on the piano as she waits for the police to arrest her for murder, a tune the audience has just heard, and that exactly fits her chilly, seductive beauty. Entitled "Appassionata," this cue suggests a passion that smolders dangerously; its musical line and unstable harmonies form a melody that is lyrical but unsentimental. In varying forms, it dominates the film, both visually and aurally, even when Maddalena is not present. In "Mrs. Paradine's Bedroom," it becomes a ghostly piano concerto (one that became a self-contained work on its own, the *Paradine Rhapsody*) as the camera pans from Maddalena's portrait on the bed stand to a close-up of the "Appassionata" score on her piano. Rather than put the music in the background to accompany Mrs. Paradine, Hitchcock has her play it as her signature: the performance defines her character. After playing this haunted nocturne twice, she calmly lets the police into her house, where they arrest her; she then leaves forever, telling the servants she won't be home for dinner.

The Paradine Case may be problem Hitchcock, but scenes like this have a hypnotic mixture of opera and cinema that draws us in: little dialogue occurs, just sound and image, pure cinema at its most rigorous. Throughout his career, Hitchcock blurred the boundary between the artificial score and music from real life; here he obliterates it. The music has somehow gone from its invisible source behind the credits to Maddalena's fingers, following the logic of opera more than narrative cinema.

Set against Mrs. Paradine's coolly passionate theme is a warm melody associated with Gay, Tony's relentlessly selfless, ever supportive wife. A beacon of light in this gloomy picture, she is surrounded by music of Straussian plushness, with soaring solos for violin, cello, and horn. In "Frustrated Lover," Gay suspects the worst as she observes her husband's fanatical devotion to Mrs. Paradine; nonetheless she proclaims, "I want her to live! . . . If she dies, you're lost to me forever." This painful but noble speech is carried aloft by a serene horn solo. As the camera pans back to Keane, Maddalena's theme suddenly intrudes, changing the aural point of view: he's hopelessly lost to Gay, thoroughly under Maddalena's spell. At the end, in the Keanes' final scene together, Gay's solo horn once more appears in counterpoint to the melody of her nemesis, leaving the audience to decide whether her chastised husband's obsession will heal. She delivers another dignified, self-abnegating pep talk, but the music leaves us suspended in poignant irresolution.

Dour and downbeat as most of the music is, it is never unfeeling. In *Rebecca,* Waxman's score made romantic situations more sinister; in *The Paradine Case,* melodies like Gay's and the effulgent travel cues ("Ride to Hindley Hall" and "Journey to Cumberland") humanize a movie that might otherwise seem cold.[6] The bleak lighting, claustrophobic camera, and grim narrative become less alienating, a bit easier to sit through.

Truffaut argued that the best thing about *The Paradine Case* is the eccentric dinner couple, the merciless hanging judge Horfield, scathingly portrayed by Charles Laughton, and his compassionate wife, Sophie, played with compelling sensitivity by Ethel Barrymore. This couple liven things up whenever they appear, and Waxman contributes his quirkiest, most unpredictable music to enhance their unending debate over punishment versus mercy. An elaborate cue called "Justice and Horfield after Trial" begins pensively as Sophie questions the judge about his sentencing intentions, melts into compassion when she pleads for mercy on Maddalena's behalf—"Doesn't life punish us enough?"—then snarls with pitiless discords as Horfield declares, "The Paradine woman will be hanged," before calmly finishing his dinner. (The sheet lists this cue twice, implying there were to be two such scenes, but one, alas, was apparently cut.)

Selznick provided definite ideas about how Waxman's music should be used; unlike *Notorious,* this was a project where Hitchcock did not have free rein. As in the case of *Spellbound,* Selznick, despite his reputation for total control, sometimes deferred to the composer. A telling example is the "Trial Transition" scene noted in the handwritten timing sheet: "Exterior Old Bailey . . . Dissolve to L. S. Thames River (Night) Selznick's note on this shot is as follows: 'Change the music on Thames River—some kind of 'city' music. Or no music over the river shot. Let Waxman decide.'" Waxman opted for no music: Big Ben, the first sound we hear in the film, rings out the city atmosphere alone.

The most powerful instance where silence reigns is the lengthy, riveting courtroom scene in which the obsessed lawyer, his guilty client, and her secret lover are all undone. The myth that Hitchcock resented everything about this movie, and really didn't care what happened, is belied by Arthur Rosenheimer, citing no less impressive a source than John Houseman. Rosenheimer reports in a letter that Hitchcock was actually more deeply involved with *The Paradine Case* than usual, which may explain his bitterness over the movie's failure: "Twenty-three pages of script—about a half hour of film—were shot in five takes with four cameras recording simultaneously. . . . What he felt was so important was to get the relations between the people in the court at their peak moments, not picking up each one with isolated shots. With these four master strips he has, of course, one master sound track, and this he uses like a playback in a musical patterning his shots against this sound. . . . I was impressed by how certain he was of what he wanted. . . . Houseman tells us he is more interested in this picture than in any he has done since he came over here, and that is perhaps why he watches over everything with an eagle eye."[7]

As always, it is relations between people that interest Hitchcock, what the participants are feeling and subtly communicating at their peak moments. Conventions of courtroom drama—which invariably result in "photographs of people talking"—were of little interest. Even more revealing is the comparison of Hitchcock's master sound track to "a playback in a musical," presenting a paradox similar to Truffaut's description of the crop-duster scene in *North by Northwest* as being "like music," even though music vanishes.[8] Hitchcock liked his courtroom to be bereft of the comfort of a score. Here, he patterned his shots "against this sound" so that the four camera setups would have a musical unity. Especially striking is Louis Jordan's complex ballet as the camera sweeps him around and behind Alida Valli against the tense murmuring in the courtroom as he sees the back of her head rather than her steely face. As Rosenheimer's analogy implies, Hitchcock used all sound, including dialogue, like a composer creating a musical.

The Paradine Case has Hitchcock's first musical cameo. Carrying a cello case, he follows Gregory Peck out of the Cumberland train, a broad grin on his face, perhaps indicating relief that this was the end of his contract with Selznick.[9] Whatever the achievements and frustrations of these often contentious collaborations, *Rebecca, Spellbound, Notorious,* and *The Paradine Case* have some of Hitchcock's most powerful Golden Age scores, partly a legacy of Selznick's lavish musical taste, partly a result of Hitchcock's increasing sophistication with spotting and ability to inspire the needed mood or design. The music soars even when other elements flounder. Now on his own, Hitchcock was about to rein in Hollywood lushness with *Rope.*

11

hitchcock in a different key: the post-selznick experiments

> The only murderer is the orchestra leader.
>
> —Marlene Dietrich, in *Stage Fright*

POULENC AND THE RHYTHM OF GUILT: *ROPE*

Having liberated himself from David Selznick's demands and diatribes, Hitchcock sailed into dangerous—some would say stagnant—waters. His next three films were an indulgence in experimentation; in them he tried out everything Selznick would not have permitted, especially the manipulation of music, and many things he himself would not have countenanced, including the sabotaging of montage and suspense.

In *Rope,* the iciest and most fascinating of these experiments, music went the way of montage. The camera roaming through a single claustrophobic apartment in unrelieved long takes has no score to cushion its anxious movements or humanize the chilly partiers speaking Arthur Laurents's cynical lines. Franz Waxman's moody score for his unhappy finale with Hitchcock and Selznick, *The Paradine Case,* gave the audience something to latch onto, even with unsympathetic characters, but Hitchcock was determined to move as far as possible from *Paradine* and the Selznick universe of omni-music.

This is not to say that *Rope* has no music, just that it is exceptionally spare and incisive. This is a modernist film, cool and ruthlessly objective, with music by a renowned modern composer, Francis Poulenc, who, like Hitchcock, created enduring art from popular culture (in his case, tunes from music halls). As with his use of Walter Benjamin, Johann Strauss, and

Cole Porter, Hitchcock veered toward classical composers who based their art on popular motifs. Their definition of modernism, like his, fit Baudelaire's: a conjunction of the ephemeral and the eternal. Laurents thought Poulenc was a good match for his script, and Hitchcock ratcheted up its effectiveness by making it part of the narrative.[1] Virtually every Laurents line is spiced with irony or double entendre, and the music works the same way; both the language and the score are turned against themselves.

The warm "Pastorale" that opens the main title is a deviously deceptive overture to the shocking killing in the first scene. What follows in the title, Poulenc's "Mouvement Perpétual No. 1," is not what it appears to be either. This is a fully orchestrated Hollywood bloating of an early-minimalist piano solo from 1918.[2] Poulenc's relentless circling and recapitulation of a single idea parallels the mesmeric repetitiveness of *Rope*'s four- to ten-minute takes and obsessive dollying through one small apartment. At the beginning of the film, however, the tune's cool insouciance is slowed down and drenched in syrup, making the original all the more piquant when the tune reappears in the nervous piano performance of Farley Granger's Phillip.

A tense, sixteen-second cue called "Mood," a suspenseful buildup to the victim's scream, is an abrupt mood swing indeed. The scream silences the music; a brief, terrifying image of David's face a split second after death is silent as well. Suddenly, we are in the Hitchcock sound world of musical irony and pure cinema.

Poulenc appears again under Phillip's fingers as a piano fanfare announcing the entrance into the party of Rupert, their amoral mentor in the art of murder. Played against type by James Stewart, ruthless Rupert uncovers the crime he unwittingly helped them conceive. "Your touch has improved," he tells Phillip, who has just been told by a palm reader at the party that he will have "famous hands." Rupert thinks he has merely made a witty remark; he can't yet see the grim irony. But later, he begins to suspect something is seriously awry, and Phillip's increasingly agitated and perpetual playing of the "Mouvement Perpétual" melody helps plant his suspicion. Like the music, Phillip's guilt-ridden mind is traveling in futile circles, falling back on itself; Rupert, speaking in code (as does everyone in Laurents's insidious script), tells him, "You're very fond of that little tune, aren't you?" This is only the beginning. Again in a Hitchcock picture, an out-of-control performance reveals more than words possibly could. But we get words as well, a convoluted, Jamesian interaction between two characters who imply more than they say as the music adds the crucial meanings.

Rupert's initial assessment that Phillip's playing has improved is soon reversed, and the revision is the catalyst for his suspicions.

Hitchcock required Farley Granger to learn the musical piece his character performs, as he did Henry Fonda in *The Wrong Man* and Tippi Hedren in *The Birds*. Granger plays it just well enough at the beginning to make its collapse convincing. Rupert suspects something is out of kilter when Janet says nervously that the missing David is "never this late" and when Mrs. Wilson, the maid, comments on the oddity of serving the party food on a chest. Phillip harshly chastises her for stepping out of her servant's role—"Don't lecture!"—then begins playing to cover up his anxiety. When Rupert leans over the keyboard and sharply asks, "What's going on, Phillip?" he just keeps playing.

As Rupert persists in his interrogation, Phillip performs over his questions, as if he hasn't heard them, but his stop-go phrasing and jerky rubato betray his nervousness as distant police sirens blend with Poulenc's bittersweet chords. Unable to deal with the anxiety, Phillip jolts to a complete stop, but Rupert brings him a drink, asks him to continue, and turns on a lamp, seeking enlightenment on what Mrs. Wilson has called a "peculiar party." After Phillip demands that he turn off the lamp, Rupert turns on a metronome to control Phillip's increasingly frantic fingers.

To no avail. Indeed, the clacking metronome increases the extraordinary tension of the scene. Rupert doesn't quite know which questions to ask to get Phillip to blurt out what's happening; "I wish I could come straight out . . . I merely suspect," he says in frustration, but Phillip's botched performance tells Rupert his suspicions are well founded. At one point, the music collapses under Phillip's nervous, relieved laughter as Rupert seems to go off track, but he quickly gets back on, demanding to know why Phillip lied about his adroitness at strangling chickens, a question too close to the mark. Phillip has played his last perpetual motion; the piece crashes to a halt.

This is a superb example of a Hitchcockian musical performance acting as a barometer of guilt and anxiety.[3] The other party music in *Rope* also bristles with irony and unintended resonance: Mack David's "Candlelight Café" playing warmly on the radio as Janet and Kenneth, the estranged couple, bitterly discuss "that grim day at Harvard" when they broke up; and "I'm Looking over a Four Leaf Clover" as they become increasingly nervous about the whereabouts of David and demand that Brandon, Phillip's co-conspirator, explain why he lied to them. This conversation plants more

Rope. Farley Granger plays Poulenc: the "Perpetual Movement" of guilt.

dark seeds in Rupert's mind that "something's gone wrong," or as the song has it, there's something "I've overlooked before."

What he's overlooked is the possibility of his young mentees enacting his own heartless theory, a debauched distortion of Nietzsche, of murder as a fine art to be practiced by superior beings on the inferior. This aesthetic version of fascism is his own creation: the strangled chickens have come home to roost. In the unforgettable final scene, the three principal players sit down wearily as darkness gathers and New York street sounds—crowds, sirens, agitated conversations—pour in the window in a haunting crescendo, an eerie premonition of the sonic landscape in *Rear Window.* "They're coming," is the final line. It's the end of the party, and the end of the young men's experiment in violence as the ultimate thrill.

Perfect for a Hitchcock movie, Poulenc's early piano music is all about charm turning sour, or, as Poulenc's inscription for another piano work, "Badinage," puts it, "orangeade growing warm in glasses." In the final shot, Brandon pours himself a last drink as Phillip plays bleak, drooping intervals on the piano, the dying remains of "Perpetual Movement." The police are on the way; the conspirators' lives are about to end. As the pianist

Paul Crossley points out, Poulenc's music is "redolent of parties, festivals, carnivals," but the real message is, "The party's over."[4]

ADDINSELL AND ANTI-SUSPENSE: *UNDER CAPRICORN*

In *Under Capricorn*, Hithcock continued his antimontage experiments but inverted the musical strategy of *Rope*. In this nineteenth-century period piece set in Australia, music moves in languid rhythm with an endlessly tracking camera, filling in the spaces of Jack Cardiff's deep-focus photography. In *Rope*, the lack of music emphasizes the claustrophobia of the single set; here, it amplifies the expansiveness of the Australian New World and the vast interiors of sumptuous houses.

Richard Addinsell's score has an eloquence no one in the cast was quite able to summon, not even Joseph Cotten and Ingrid Bergman, two quintessential Hitchcock actors.[5] Ably conducted by Louis Levy, Hitchcock's main composer during his British period, the music distracts one from the picture's talkiness and dodgy costumes to create a rich alternate universe. This is a classic instance of the music being better than the picture, as some of the reviews pointed out. *Trade Show*, for example, panned *Under Capricorn* as unsubtle and overly long but praised Addinsell's contribution.

Still, in this unlucky project, even the music proved troublesome, at least from a legal standpoint. *Under Capricorn* was filmed and scored in England, presenting formidable artistic ownership problems. Victor Peers, who had the daunting job of securing musical copyright transfer from the Composer's Guild of Great Britain to Warner Brothers, negotiated strenuously but fruitlessly, as documented in the Warner Brothers music file. At the end, he threw up his hands: "We are consequently forced to accept the situation. . . . We do not propose to have much music in the picture in any case, and none of it is likely, I think, to be of the 'popular' variety with any sort of commercial value."[6] In fact, Hitchcock did use a great deal of this stately music, and it turned out to have considerable cachet. Addinsell turned out to be one of the film's strongest assets, artistically if not commercially.

Eschewing the noirish colors and minor-key harmonies of his celebrated "Warsaw Concerto," Addinsell opted for a modal lyricism and fanfare folksiness similar to the style of the Australian composer Percy Grainger, with additional Celtic touches to emphasize the Irish ancestry of the principal players. Like Grainger, Addinsell contrasts lush harmony and melody with moments of queasy bitonality, as illustrated by the music that seeps in during the runny-eggs "Breakfast" cue. The score is predominately lyrical, accentuating the film's lavish color and expansive takes. Sam's lengthy story about his criminal past and adoring wife is carried aloft on a ravishing string melody culminating in a Delian cadence as the camera pans slowly up in the night air for a shot of Ingrid Bergman swaying despairingly on the balcony; this cadence is reprised in a gorgeous shot of her coming down the staircase in a cue called "Henrietta Downstairs," and it brings the curtain down as Charles goes back to Ireland. Henrietta's troubled story to Charles involving her crumbling marriage and her husband's imprisonment for murdering her brother is darkened by a haunted, restless version of the same material. The most passionate unfolding of Addinsell's main themes occurs during Henrietta's revelation that she is guilty of the crime for which her husband was imprisoned. Scored for full orchestra, punctuated by ravishing string and wind solos, this lengthy cue makes Henrietta's soliloquy sound like a scene from an opera; indeed, the cue sheet calls it "Henrietta's Aria."[7]

Hitchcock used source music to evoke British sounds of Empire, including "God Save the Queen" and "The British Grenadiers." His most characteristic touch is a sumptuous "Valse" during the lavish, disastrous, doubly crashed party, one of several instances where music brings this stagy movie to life.

In *Under Capricorn*, the "master of suspense" drained suspense away. Let's see how slow and static we can be, the movie seems to say; let's show that a Hitchcock picture can violate expectations and produce a kind of anti-suspense. The unrelenting stateliness of Addinsell's score in tandem with the talky script and slowly panning camera produces an aestheticized sleepiness that may have pleased Hitchcock during this restless, rebellious period in his career but that alienated audiences and critics. (Later, he renounced the project as an unfortunate symptom of his obsession with Ingrid Bergman; nonetheless, the French New Wave championed it, as they did *I Confess* and other Hitchcock failures.)

The one powerful suspense sequence unfolds without music: the lightning-filled, high-Gothic climax in Henrietta's bedroom in which a jealous Milly, a second-rate Mrs. Danvers, is revealed as the malignant enabler of Henrietta's alcoholism. Rain, thunder, garish red lighting, and a camera that for once pans to something shocking—all conspire to momentarily turn *Under Capricorn* into a "Hitchcock picture." I can still do it when I want to, the master seems to be saying, but I'm only going to do it once. In *Stage Fright,* his next fascinating flop, he decided to trample conventions once again, with equally grim results at the box office, but with fresh and surprising rewards for those who come to the movie without preconceptions.

MARLENE DIETRICH'S CABARET CINEMA: *STAGE FRIGHT*

"In Alfred Hitchcock's book, she is still top temptress for the screen."[8] That's how Carlisle Jones described Marlene Dietrich, who in *Stage Fright* sings Cole Porter and turns in a stunningly sultry performance as Charlotte Inwood, a steely, desperate cabaret singer. She was too tempting, apparently, for Joseph Breen, a censor who found "The Laziest Girl in Town," her keynote song, "quite offensive" and made a long list of demands: wear a proper slip when she removes a blood-stained dress, remain "out of scene when she changes her costume," avoid "lustful, prolonged, or open-mouthed kissing," and "put a robe on her before she and Jonathan embrace."

Breen's two-page list of demands in separate memos concludes with "delete the underlined word in the following speech by Dietrich: 'Go blow *yourself*.'"[9] No one blows himself in *Stage Fright*, but Charlotte does blow her big song. Like *Young and Innocent* and *Rope*, this is a narrative in which a disastrous performance causes justice to prevail. Music is the doorway to truth. The camera tracks a Boy Scout bringing a bloodstained doll to Charlotte's attention during her performance of Edith Piaf's "La Vie en rose," rattling her so much she can't finish the song. This is one of Hitchcock's most theatrical musical sequences, a further development of the movie-opera hybrid that began with *Blackmail*, *Waltzes from Vienna*, and *The Man Who Knew Too Much*.

Stage Fright marked Hitchcock's return to England and the world of British musical theater, the enchanted obsession of his youth, which he had exploited so winningly in *The 39 Steps* and *Murder!* The narrative twists the usual Hitchcock formula: the wrong man, Jonathan, turns out to be the right one; the diva turns out to be a villain, not an instrument of justice; the heroine, Eve, played by Jane Wyman, betrays her lover-fugitive rather than saving him.

As with *Under Capricorn*, Hitchcock was determined to break out of suspense clichés and go after something different. In Dietrich's unhappy cabaret scene, he experiments with musical space: Charlotte's number is first heard from a distance outside the tent as the boy approaches the entrance. Inside, Eve's father cues her that the child is drawing near; the camera follows him in a series of point-of-view shots—Eve's, her father's, finally Smith's—then closes on Charlotte's singing, the boy's startled face, and a bloodstained doll that is (as in *Murder!*) part of a theatrical strategy to get a killer to confess. Her sultry voice falters and the prompter tries to intervene, but the song collapses, followed by the orchestra. The scene is significant

Stage Fright. Hitchcock directs Marlene Dietrich.

less in its thriller-suspense effects than in illustrating how a song can flower, crumble, and, in its demise, reveal something significant.

Stage Fright is usually regarded as a run-for-cover project after the disaster of *Under Capricorn,* a lightweight trifle marking time. To Hitchcock, however, it was a daunting, complex experiment in the merging of cinema with musical theater. In a nervous letter to Jack Warner, he spoke of the challenges, which included "background of the stage, with musical comedy going on; a garden party with all kinds of singing and other sounds. . . . Unless this is handled directly by myself or someone who knows exactly what is wanted, the completion of this picture would drag on for months."[10] Drag on it did, with Hitchcock worrying about Jane Wyman's maid disguise (too pretty, he thought) and Alastair Sim's eccentric performance as her father. But he apparently got what he wanted from Marlene Dietrich, and the musical experiments came off impressively, though Dietrich complained that he never indicated his satisfaction or disapproval with what she was doing.

She certainly succeeded in inspiring the camera. Hitchcock blends cinema with musical theater in Dietrich's musical numbers, panning offstage and onstage to fuse the songs with the murder mystery. She is filmed in a dazzling long shot during "When You Whisper Sweet Nothings," declaring that "the only murderer is the orchestra leader." In delicious close-up during "Laziest Gal in Town," she perches and writhes catlike on a divan against a decadent backdrop of floating clouds, the camera swirling up and jerking back. The chorus is part of the action, shown in a left-side offstage shot as the camera swivels onstage toward Charlotte; it also floats into the dressing room where Charlotte and Jonathan trade threats. The prelude to "La Vie en rose" is background to the police search for the suspected killer, and for Eve in her fainting scene. As Bob Fosse did twenty-two years later in *Cabaret*, Hitchcock turns cabaret numbers into a fluid "score" that parallels and comments on the story.

Dietrich was ideal for the role of Charlotte. Alma Reville, in her meticulous screen treatment, describes the character as the embodiment of the Dietrich persona, "a strikingly attractive woman with many sides to her nature. She is a very successful musical comedy star, who, on the stage, can make her audience roll in the aisles with a comic song. Off stage, her sultry sort of beauty and slightly flashy manner keep us guessing about her true personality. . . . Is she scullery maid or princess, kitten or tiger behind those startlingly fashionable clothes? Whatever she is revealed to be, she is consistently fascinating, dynamic, and like a magnet where men are concerned. Incidentally, the magnet is in constant use."[11]

The magnet did not, alas, attract audiences or critics. Like *Under Capricorn*, *Stage Fright* was a commercial and critical flop on both sides of the Atlantic, even with the star power of Dietrich and Jane Wyman, who plays the fickle heroine. Unless one assumes the film was ahead of its time, the reasons for this disappointment are hard to fathom. This is one of Hitchcock's most inventive looks at backstage theater life, with a murder-mystery counterplot and a stunning final epiphany. But once again, Hitchcock was hurt by not coming through with a suspense picture. As revealed in numerous interviews, he was all too aware that whenever he stepped out of his role as master of suspense, he frustrated those who expected his usual formula. That he chose to step out so frequently indicates he had larger ambitions than his critics or audiences were willing to grant.

Stage Fright is about listening and reinterpreting what we hear. A memorable piano performance tells Eve she is in love with the wrong man; Charlotte's botched song tells the detective something is amiss in his case; the resonant sound system in the theater during the finale tells what has really been happening throughout the twisted narrative, something neither we nor Eve wants to hear; the ensuing silence tells Jonathan, the wrong man turned sympathetic villain, that he can trust Eve when she tells him they are alone

and promises to help him escape. Eve is lying—the film's final whopper—
and the loudspeakers don't tell the truth either. This is a treacherous world
in which we can't always trust what we hear. The most reliable sounds are of
music: Charlotte's disastrous performance and Smith's sublime one.

Musically, *Stage Fright* is a remarkable film, mingling a haunting score
by the British composer Leighton Lucas, who had orchestrated *Under Capricorn* a year earlier, with sensational songs by Cole Porter, Edith Piaf, and
the great émigré cabaret composer Mischa Spolliansky. Watching Dietrich
sing these through Hitchcock's dramatic camera angles is alone worth the
price of admission. As we would expect in a story about musical theater,
Stage Fright has other clever source music as well, including Alastair Sim's
accordion rendition of Mendelssohn and the boisterous band music during
the garden party.

Lucas came through with one of the most lyrical melodies in a Hitchcock movie. It begins as source music, a piano tune played by "Ordinary"
Smith for Eve (published as "Eve's Rhapsody"). Its six-note phrase, looping
back on itself in melancholy harmonies, suggests unattainable longing, but
Eve, like many of Hitchcock's heroines, has a determination that precludes
giving up. She dumps the wrong man, Jonathan, for Smith, the detective
pursuing him, even before discovering that the former is guilty after all; in
the coda, after watching in horror as the curtain literally comes down on
Jonathan, she promenades down a theater corridor with her new lover in a
graceful long shot made more so by a final eruption of Smith's melody,
scored for full orchestra, its harmonies now upbeat rather than bittersweet.

Just as a catastrophic performance wrecks one character, a strong one
empowers another. The seductiveness of Smith's signature theme inspires
Eve to fall in love with him and ditch Jonathan; at the piano, "Ordinary"
Smith is anything but. To Eve, the important thing about Smith is not his
police credentials, but his presence at the keyboard, as she makes clear when
she introduces him to her mother: "Mr. Smith is a pianist," she says; her
mother immediately compares Smith to Sherlock Holmes and his fiddle.

The next time Eve embraces Jonathan, she looks away from his eyes to
gaze at the piano. The camera suddenly deserts Jonathan, panning to a
close-up of the keyboard, and the luscious piano melody wafts into the
scene, a musical memory in Eve's head. The aphrodisiac for one lover is a
turnoff with the other. This is Hitchcockian counterpoint at its slyest: the
heroine kisses one man while thinking of another, whose music evokes her
fantasy. Like Shakespeare in *Twelfth Night*, Hitchcock uses music as the
"food of love."

In the cab scene, the theme returns as a lush, 1940s-style piano concerto as Eve slowly turns her erotic allegiance over to Smith, concluding on a perfect cadence as they finally kiss.[12] But rather than give in to gushiness, Hitchcock again provides shrewd counterpoint. Eve's agenda is making Smith suspicious of Charlotte: the warmer the music gets, the more she accuses Charlotte of being cold, ruthless, capable of homicide. Eve's love for Smith erupts at the precise moment she expresses her hatred for Charlotte, yet the music suggests that her attraction to him is real, not a just a manipulation, like the wine cellar kiss in *Notorious*. A consummate actress, she nonetheless "wasn't acting in the taxi. . . . I felt I was on a great golden cloud."

By the end of this romantic but strangely caustic scene, that cloud has begun to envelop the movie. Smith's piano melody becomes part of Lucas's symphonic rhetoric, moving from the piano in Eve's memory to woodwinds in the invisible score, climaxing in a passionate outburst during Eve's revelation to Smith about her role in helping Jonathan elude the police. Entitled "Piano Solo" in the cue sheet, the tune is initially associated only with Smith but eventually becomes a larger signifier of love's fickleness.

The operatic quality of Hitchcock's musical treatment is similar to the innovations in *The Paradine Case*. Again, the most luscious melody is played on the piano by the character whose personality it comes to represent, becoming a leitmotif only after that person actually performs it. Hitchcock used this device again a year later in *Strangers on a Train*, when Bruno sings "The Band Played On" during the carousel scene, making it his grim motto. In Hitchcock's world, music is a fundamental part of the human makeup.

Lucas's score has other deft touches as well. The tense chords in the main title move immediately into "Bloodstained Dress," a cue that mysteriously counterpoints a violent crime with soaring melody. The contradiction makes sense only after we realize that Jonathan's story is a lie to get Eve on his side. Hitchcock's resort to a bogus flashback has been frequently criticized, but the device is consistent with a movie about performances and performers; everyone in *Stage Fright* is acting, covering up, re-creating reality onstage and off. "You must call the theater," Charlotte tells Jonathan during her crisis. "I can't play tonight." In fact, she is always playing, as are the other actors. Indeed, this statement itself turns out to be a hoax.

The fake flashback is controversial precisely because it is so effective. Since the lie is dramatized, we feel *we* are being lied to. The music is as meticulously organized as the camera, conferring a strong authenticity.

"Bloodstained Dress" segues to an untuned piano during Jonathan's discovery of the body, returns with a harp glissando following the maid's scream, loops back in his fearful fantasy of the maid talking with the police, and is finally jolted into oblivion by a loudly ringing phone. Who would think this superb sequence is a fraud?

Much of Lucas's score is pleasantly melodic, largely avoiding suspense-movie dissonance. Eve's journey to London and introduction to Smith are cued by pastoral winds, which take on a comic inflection, thin out into obsessive pizzicato, and melt into a wistful melody when she dresses up as Doris the maid. The establishing shot of London is bathed in a rapturous, broad theme. Along with *Under Capricorn*, this is Hitchcock's most distinctively British score since the Gaumont–Louis Levy era. (Levy assisted with the musical arrangements for *Stage Fright.*)

Like everyone, Hitchcock undervalued *Stage Fright*. During shooting, he couldn't wait for the project to conclude. The musical difficulties were a "big headache," he wrote Jack Warner, made more so by the coarsened musical sensibilities of his former British colleagues. This letter is drenched in disillusionment. In Hitchcock's now pro-Hollywood view, the stereotypes were reversed: the Americans were musically refined, the Brits crude beyond compare. "Although they have nice, new, shining instruments to work with this, there is a slight question of taste involved, of which there is exactly none here whatsoever. . . . Believe me, they have some pretty crude people. . . . I don't want to bother you with the sordid details. . . . They are my affair, really, and all I have to do is deliver you a picture."

The sordid details must have been grim indeed. Until *Frenzy* twenty-two years later, there would be (with the exception of scenes from *The Man Who Knew Too Much*) no more nostalgic returns to England. "Well, Jack, that's about all. . . . As soon as I'm finished shooting and I have the picture rough cut, I'm going to pack all the dubbing tracks into tins and get the hell out of here." That he did, bringing back with him what he regarded as the biggest asset from the project, a savvy young production assistant named Peggy Singer, later Peggy Robertson. Robertson had worked on *Under Capricorn;* impressed with her professionalism, Hitchcock indicated his desire to have her be part of his regular production staff. Her work with other producers separated her from Hitchcock for seven years, but beginning with *Vertigo,* she permanently joined the Hitchcock film family. As we shall see, Robertson turned out to be a significant force behind the musical maneuverings for the rest of his career.

12

the band played on: a tiomkin trio

If Dimitri hadn't become a composer, he would have been a maître d'hôtel.

—Olivia Tiomkin

MUSICAL CRISSCROSS: *STRANGERS ON A TRAIN*

In *Strangers on a Train,* Hitchcock struggles aboard a train with a double bass, an instrument nearly as big as he is. The last film in which he had used a string instrument for a cameo was *The Paradine Case,* the first in a series of fascinating flops that had continued right up to this picture. Now he was back in form, with a tight, sensational thriller that reconnected him with his audience.

Strangers on a Train was the first of three consecutive collaborations with Dimitri Tiomkin, who had not worked with Hitchcock since *Shadow of a Doubt.* With eerie exactitude, Tiomkin picked up where he'd left off a decade earlier, finding a new design for Hitchcock's continuing obsession with doubles and identity transferences. Tiomkin's vivid colors, brassy sonorities, and preference for brashness over refinement fit the tone of the film, a crack of emotional thunder after the cerebral attenuations of *Rope, Under Capricorn,* and *Stage Fright.* Like Stephen Sondheim, who also invested a popular genre with classical rigors, Hitchcock suffered numerous crushing setbacks, yet he always picked himself up and moved on to the next project, even as the current one was metastasizing.

Right from the beginning, Tiomkin's lavish main title gives *Strangers on a Train* a special seductiveness. The piece is scored for a large orchestra, including alto, tenor, and baritone sax; three clarinets, four horns, three pi-

Strangers on a Train. Musical cameo.

anos, and a novachord. (Although the arranger is listed as George Parrish, the instruments are penciled into the score by the composer.)[1] The title music vividly introduces several of the numerous themes we are to enjoy throughout the movie, including queasy motifs associated with Bruno and an elaborate, swooning violin tune for Guy and Ann, the beleaguered couple whose romance is spoiled first by Guy's emasculating wife, Miriam, who refuses a divorce, then by Robert Walker's Bruno, the most formidable Hitchcock villain since Joseph Cotten's Uncle Charlie, who handily solves the divorce problem with a murderous Faustian bargain to which Guy unknowingly (subconsciously?) assents.

Throughout the film, Tiomkin sounds the theme of "crisscross," the term used by Bruno to describe his insidious homicide-exchange. In *Shadow of a Doubt,* Hitchcock contented himself with a single waltz subjected to Tiomkin's ingenious transformations. A far richer score, *Strangers* uses crisscrossing motifs organized into nine medleys, some packed with as many as six ideas.

As with *Psycho* a decade later, Hitchcock poured more music into the film than he originally intended. Some of the most powerful cues—the careening carousel, the unwrapping of Guy's gun, the awesomely quiet demise of Bruno—do not appear on the cue sheet. The first shot—two sets of male shoes, loud versus conservative, moving toward a train—carries a gruff bass motif set against Gershwin-like riffs, a two-part medley called "Strangers" and "Walking" that (typifying the profligacy of the score) is never heard again.[2] Hitchcock strikes a note of comedy: vulgar versus fashionably formal shoes are a witty synecdoche representing two worlds. As in *Frenzy,* he does not tip us off that this will be one of his darker films; instead he uses music to deceive us.

For "Guy's Theme," Tiomkin created a hesitant, passive idea, made-to-order music for Farley Granger's performance, about which Hitchcock famously complained in his interview with Truffaut. (William Holden, the director said, would have made a stronger Guy.) Tiomkin apparently assumed that Granger's acting style was in sync with the shaky ambivalence that defines his character. "Had Hitchcock expressed to Tiomkin his reservations about Granger's performance," writes Christopher Palmer, "the composer could have strengthened the actor musically."[3] Despite this lack of communication, the score precisely follows Guy's development. In the exposition, he is blocked, frustrated, passively furious; in the heart-stopping tennis and carnival scenes where Guy jettisons his ambivalence and becomes a proper hero, the tempo of the theme quickens, its harmony and orchestration become brighter and more decisive. Guy's motto often carries a mocking irony, as when Ann first notices the "Bruno" tie, implying Bruno's charming effect on women, and when Guy slugs Bruno in the jaw, a kind of lover's spat to please the many viewers who find homoerotic subcurrents in their decidedly peculiar relationship.

Harmonic complexity defines the motifs associated with Bruno: rumbling bass, shocking clusters, and glassy string harmonics. These disturbing sounds, heard to superb effect in cues such as "The Meeting," "Senator's Office," and "Jefferson Memorial," are not just about Bruno but about how he is perceived by those whose lives he crosses—first Guy, then everyone in Guy's entourage. When Guy takes out a gun and prepares to enter Bruno's house, Bruno's creepy harmonics crisscross over to him; suddenly he has become the scary one. Hitchcock's tilted camera watches him ascend an expressionist staircase complete with a great, snarling dog at the top—Hitchcock's highest Gothicism since *Rebecca.* Entitled "Menace," this malevolent cue follows all the suspense rules until Guy is standing at the door of Bruno's father; suddenly, dissonant fragments broaden into a fateful brass chorale, the moment of truth signaling Bruno's decision to regard Guy's fake crisscross as a fatal double cross. The most horrific sounding of Bruno's music is a cluster exploding in "Mother and Bruno" and "St. Francis" (the kind of uncompromising modernism Tiomkin delivers in Howard Hawks's *Thing from Another World*). Again, the music is not just about Bruno but about his larger reality, in this case, his malignant family.

Most memorable is the simplest of Hitchcock's many waltzes, a carnival organ blaring "The Band Played On," sometimes alternating with other carnival tunes like "Carolina in the Morning," "Oh, You Beautiful Doll," and "Baby Face" (songs chosen by Tiomkin). This strangely unsettling melody sets up the movie's most elaborate transferences. I'll commit your murder if you'll commit mine, Bruno tells Guy on the train, flattering him as an adoring tennis fan; I'll do in your heinous wife if you'll do the same for my hateful father: "some people," he says matter-of-factly, echoing the amoral young men in *Rope*, "are better off dead." An interesting nut, thinks Guy, blandly agreeing with the scheme to get Bruno off his back. But in Hitchcock, the fantastical has a way of becoming real; Bruno's reality as Guy's alter ego who enacts his darkest fantasies is established by real music, "The Band Played On" wafting eerily from across the pond when he emerges from the carnival shadows to kill Guy's wife.

This is an early sounding of an American Gothic trope, one borrowed from the German expressionist tradition in which Hitchcock was immersed: the amusement park as nightmare. (A decade later, *The Alfred Hitchcock Hour* would present Ray Bradbury's carnival story "The Jar"; this time the creepy carousel music would be by Bernard Herrmann.) In one of Hitchcock's most explicit operatic gestures, the characters at the fateful carnival sing the score, giving it full dimension as part of the drama. In a conventional movie, the tune would play in the background as a clever ironic backdrop. But Hitchcock takes music to another level. Miriam and the two boyfriends in her odd ménage à trois bring "The Band Played On" to life by singing it on the merry-go-round, lustily and loudly. (This was the only time that Laura Eliot, who played Miriam, ever sang in a movie.) Grinning balefully on the horse behind them, Bruno then sings it himself, making it his motto. The band plays on through Bruno's stalking of his victim and during the murder itself, blaring from the front of the screen, then receding into the darkness as an eerie obbligato when the doomed Miriam enters the Tunnel of Love. Although it becomes Bruno's leitmotif, Miriam sings it first, telegraphing her fate in the lyric "the poor girl would shake with alarm," the film's most unsettling crisscross. Unlike his distortion of "The Merry Widow," Hitchcock allows this waltz to play on unembellished, with terrifying indifference, as we watch Bruno strangle Miriam in a reflection through her glasses.

The most elaborate crisscross involves the subconscious. In a pair of surreal scenes, Barbara, played with blunt charm by Hitchcock's daughter Pat, peers deeply into Bruno's eyes, which glower malevolently at her glasses; these mysteriously beam forth a flame from the nocturnal strangling, accompanied by "The Band Played On." The script reveals scrupulous planning:

> From Bruno's viewpoint, as Barbara speaks, CAMERA MOVES IN CLOSER until the faintest impression of the merry-go-round fills the screen with the effect of whirling around Barbara's head. Her glasses seem to glint until her eyes are obliterated by the glare. All talk dies out as all eyes turn to Bruno, who is staring at Barbara. Except Ann's who is saying quietly to Bruno: This is my sister Barbara. Barbara, this is Mr. Anthony.
>
> CLOSEUP BRUNO He does not acknowledge the introduction immediately. He is still staring at Barbara. Then he nods abstractedly.
> CLOSEUP ANN She is looking at Bruno, wondering what mystery lies behind this strange individual and why he and Guy have disclaimed any previous acquaintance.

Once the music was laid in, the mystery was elucidated, at least for the audience. "The Band Played On" creates the effect of whirling that binds the murder with Bruno and Barbara's trancelike communication.

In another doubling, those who are delightfully mortified by this scene get to experience it again. This time Barbara watches Bruno nearly strangle a spoiled society lady at a party:

> Her glasses glint in the light. . . . [Bruno] is now transfixed. His breathing becomes heavy. A strange expression comes over his face. He still stares off at Barbara. Medium shot Barbara: we see the whirling merry-go-round spinning around her head. . . . [Bruno] now seems to have almost gone into a trance. Over the shot we begin to hear a strangled cry.

This time Barbara gets it: "His hands were on her throat, and he was strangling me," she tells Ann. "He went into sort of a trance." At this chilling moment, "The Band Plays On" crisscrosses from the carousel organ into Tiomkin's full orchestra, now part of the underscore. This musical telepathy recalls *Shadow of a Doubt,* though here the psychic transfer involves a vision as well as a waltz. The scene is not actually supernatural, of course. Like Poe, Hitchcock favored the illusion of the supernatural: the music and cigarette lighter emerge from Bruno's weird mind, not from Barbara's glasses. As in

Rebecca and *Family Plot,* music suggests the paranormal, though the scene is psychological.

Throughout the film, the crisscross design becomes more ornate. Rapid pizzicato, a Tchaikovskian variation on "Guy and Ann," follows Guy through his nerve-wracking tennis match, the outcome of which determines his guilt or innocence; a more dizzying variation leads into a dance-like race through a train station, always one of Hitchcock's favorite ballet stages. Intercut with these delicate sounds is "Cigarette Case," a cue whose growling Bartókian brass slides depict Bruno's frantic attempts to extricate Guy's incriminating cigarette lighter from a street grate. "The intercutting," says Olivia Tiomkin, "switches from one man's theme to another," resulting in "the balancing of the two characters."[4] Here is one of the most dynamic examples in a Hitchcock film of music not only depicting an idea but standing in for characters.

Some cues are so swift and witty that they make sense only on a second viewing. The scene in Miller's Music Store is a complex medley of piano tunings, the Scherzo from Mendelssohn's *Midsummer Night's Dream,* and pop songs like "Keep Cool Fool" and "Don't Cry Baby," all a sardonic foil for Guy's bitter fight with Miriam: played for a fool, Guy fails to keep cool, and Miriam unleashes sarcasm without tears. Another dynamic musical contest consists of a medley in which Guy's frantic "Train" cue alternates with "Ain't She Sweet," "Baby Face," "Ain't We Got Fun," and, of course, "The Band Played On." The cacophony continues as Bruno waits for darkness, then spins out of control as the merry-go-round collapses in flying metal and gunfire, a carny Götterdämmerung crushing the score's themes into its wreckage.

At the end, "Bruno's Death" is dignified by somber Mussorgskian chimes, a quiet forecast of *Dial M for Murder,* as the tireless Bruno tries in his last gasp to transfer his guilt to Guy. In the coda, the love theme loses its ambiguity, rising in splendor for a proper cadence as Guy and Ann flee from a priest on a train who utters Bruno's opening lines—a final, wicked transference. In the last variation on the love theme, the coming together of the troubled couple is graced by a waltz, for once a romantic one.

The multiplicity of musical ideas resulted in part from Tiomkin's smooth working relationship with Hitchcock. As Olivia Tiomkin recalls, Hitchcock "allowed him to do his own thing" after the director communicated what he wanted. There was also a personal dimension to Tiomkin's fondness for this picture: "He liked families," says Olivia, "and he liked that

Pat was in it." Everything went well for this project, including the ticket sales, yet like Tiomkin's other Hitchcock scores, *Strangers on a Train* goes largely uncelebrated. Tiomkin has always been sniffed at by critics, who hold his broad hyperbole against him. According to Olivia, he never lost any sleep over this. "We don't need glory," he would say. "We're just like Liberace. We cry all the way to the bank."[5]

If the score remains obscure on its own, it nonetheless lives on as an inextricable part of one of Hitchcock's most popular movies. Indeed, so seamlessly and inevitably does it fit the picture's design that it seems like an element of Hitchcock's storyboards. According to Joseph Stefano, the screenwriter for *Psycho*, the music was like the script: Hitchcock was so certain of what he wanted that he "almost heard it before it was written."[6]

MUSICAL SECRETS: *I CONFESS*

I Confess is an uncompromising specimen of three Hitchcock signatures: negative acting, transfer of guilt, and music that speaks the unspoken. Montgomery Clift, as Father Michael Logan, hears a murderer confess a crime that the criminal manages to transfer to him; he can't reveal the truth that would save him from the gallows without violating the confidentiality of the confessional, and he can't reveal his love affair with Ruth, played by a sultry Anne Baxter, who could supply his alibi. Indeed, he can't say much about anything, only contort his face and radiate pain, something Montgomery Clift always does well, though Hitchcock deplored his Method eccentricities.

Father Logan isn't the only one who can't speak. This is a movie where everybody has secrets, and once again Hitchcock entrusted them to Dimitri Tiomkin, whose score suggests everything they can't say. Indeed, the composer tips off the audience before anyone in the movie realizes what's happening. Whoever listens attentively to the music knows the truth. We know the émigré penitent, played by a furtive Otto Keller, must be someone with a dark side, not just a victim of circumstance, because Tiomkin gives him an extraordinarily sinister theme, a muted string motto in irregular (5/4) meter similar to the one he created for Bruno in *Strangers on a Train;* we know that Ruth still loves Father Logan before she says so because of a sexy melody during their terse phone conversation and a sensuous mini-violin concerto during their ferry meeting; and we know that Father Logan plans to pay the ultimate price for the confessional's secrecy because of a tragic *marcia funebre* accompanying him in his long walk to the police station, an unmistakable allusion to Calvary. The confession scene itself has no music, only stark silence, but in the scenes connected with it, the score has a whispered suppression, the film's most powerful metaphor.

The most striking instance of music revealing buried emotion comes during a seemingly innocuous breakfast scene in which the guilty penitent's wife, Alma, bringing coffee to a group of priests, paces behind Father Logan. The dialogue between the priests, as François Truffaut points out, "is completely innocuous. It's only through the image that one understands that the essential of the scene is happening between the woman and Montgomery Clift. I don't know any director who successfully conveys that, or even tries to." Hitchcock's reply reveals that the contrapuntal relationship between sound and image is the heart of his aesthetic: "You mean the sound track says one thing, while the image says something else? That's a fundamental of film direction. Isn't it exactly the way it is in real life? People don't always express their inner thoughts to one another; a conversation may be quite trivial, but often the eyes will reveal what a person really thinks or feels."[7] This is a cinematic version of Joycean epiphany: accidental gestures or verbal slips betray what someone really feels even as he or she says something different. Tiomkin's cue, a series of icy chords called "Worried," allies with Alma's nervous glances at the back of Father Logan's head. The priests' prattle exists in another, less significant world.[8]

The most memorable example of revelatory music is the distant song that expresses Ruth's hopeless, doubly forbidden love for Michael. Her status as a married woman and Michael's as a priest are expressed by a soprano singing distant vocalese, Tiomkin's most sensuous nocturne:

Music of the night
One can hear its lonely beat
On each dark deserted street
The dreams and hopes of yesterday
Sigh and slowly drift away: All the sounds of earth unite
Secretly in the night.

I Confess is defined by "dark deserted streets" (those of Quebec, the film's oddly anonymous location) and fateful confidences whispered in the night; the singer is recorded at such a distance that her lyrics seem yet another secret.

This is Hitchcock's Catholic version of a Hawthorne story, where everyone harbors corrosive guilt. The movie's ambiance is enshrouded in this desolate song. (The initial title in the archives is "Love, What Have You Done to My Heart?," broadened in a revision to "Love, What Have You Done to Me?") The first sound we hear, it establishes a haunted mood in the main title that, thanks to Tiomkin's veiled harmonies and Robert Burks's dark cinematography, never dissipates. Later, the song floats through Anne Baxter's dusky voice-over during her long flashback about her affair with her bad-luck priest, quickening into a delicate "Scherzo" and wedding "Congratulations," exploding into a "Storm," and sinking into a foreboding cue called "Discovered," which sets up the blackmail at the center of the mystery plot. The song gives the montage continuity while also suggesting its substance. Abandoning his customary musical irony, Hitchcock allows Tiomkin to deliver an unapologetic passion and longing as the enraptured couple dance into each other's arms in slow motion.

Hitchcock uses another fateful theme as well, one much older than Tiomkin's song: "Dies Irae" rings ominously through the film, sometimes in heavy fragments, as in the interrogation montage, sometimes with dizzying contrapuntal lines, as in the opening scenes. Like Liszt, Berlioz, and Rachmaninoff, Tiomkin uses the seventeen-note chant to evoke a relentless doom, re-creating it with subtle variations and reinforcing it with liturgical source music, including his arrangement of "Veni Creator Spiritus."

I Confess was Tiomkin's favorite score for Hitchcock, and indeed it is hard to think of anything more artful in his prolific output.[9] (The Delian chorus and impressionist nocturnes in *Red River* perhaps come closest.) "The Chase" in the finale and the "Quebec" cadence at the end are typically colorful, robust Tiomkin moments, but otherwise the music has a veiled austerity—the muted strings in "The Ballroom," for example, when the villain confronts his own evil.

When the film was released, this singularity did not go unnoticed. "The entire story is strengthened dramatically by Tiomkin's powerful music," wrote the *Hollywood Reporter*, "which achieves a hauntingly lovely quality. . . . A single soprano voice is used . . . with beautiful, mood-inspiring effect."[10] But as with *Under Capricorn, Stage Fright,* and *Topaz,* the music could not save the film, which was an especially painful bomb after the triumph of *Strangers on a Train. I Confess* frustrated and bewildered non-Catholics, who couldn't comprehend why Montgomery Clift didn't just *tell* the police. But it offended Catholics as well; some reviewers called it a vicious attack on the Church. The film has never quite recovered, although the French New Wave always championed it and some regard it as another instance of a Hitchcock failure simply being ahead of its time.

Whatever one makes of this controversial work, it is another example of Hitchcock's bringing out the best in his composer. Hitchcock told Truffaut that *I Confess* was a fundamental mistake, a movie that should never have been made. One cannot say the same of Tiomkin's lonely score.

DIAL M FOR MUSSORGSKY

Dimitri Tiomkin made a contribution to *Dial M for Murder* that Hitchcock undoubtedly prized more than the composer's music: Grace Kelly. According to Olivia Tiomkin, it was her husband who suggested Kelly to Hitchcock after working with her on *High Noon*.[11] Tiomkin's fourth and final collaboration with Hitchcock marked the first time Kelly appeared in a Hitchcock picture; like Tiomkin, she would work with him three times consecutively, becoming (besides Ingrid Bergman) his favorite diva.

Kelly was the most significant outgrowth of Tiomkin's amiable relationship with Hitchcock. One reason they got along was because both loved to eat, drink, and throw big parties. A Hitchcock-Tiomkin project was like a lavish food and wine festival. (Oddly, Frank Capra had fought bitterly with Tiomkin on the set of *It's a Wonderful Life,* finding his music downbeat and suicidal.) A virtuoso pianist in the twenties and thirties, whose many achievements include teaching himself the art of composition, Tiomkin switched to composing for film largely because he hated the isolation of the practice room and loved collaborating. He enjoyed meeting people, entertaining them, and sharing ideas. The motion picture medium suited his gregariousness; unlike his émigré colleagues, who led two lives, he never considered writing concert music. "If Dimitri hadn't become a composer," says Olivia Tiomkin, "he would have been a maître d'hôtel."

As with many Hitchcock films, cocktails and restaurants figure significantly in *Dial M for Murder*. Like *Rope,* this is an experiment in how to remake a play into cinema; the setting is mostly a single room where foul play is covered as long as possible by good manners and witty repartee. "Martinis," a cocktail waltz, fizzes innocuously through the exposition as the mystery writer Mark Halliday, played by Robert Cummings, discusses the perfect murder with Tony Wendice, played by an elegant Ray Milland (alas, his only Hitchcock picture). What Mark doesn't know—a secret whose details are revealed to the audience through a sly cue called "Deceit" as Tony furtively exchanges a set of keys to his flat—is that Tony is planning a perfect murder his own: that of his wife, Margot, with whom Mark is having an affair.[12]

"Martinis" is a silken variation on the title cue, "Dial M," a waltz that plays through the main title after the "Grandioso" opening fanfare and continues in the opening double kiss scene with Margot and the two men, setting up what would appear to be a love story or comedy of manners spiked by adultery, not a mystery thriller. But the tone changes quickly. The unexpectedly shocking murder, made more so by an onslaught of dissonance ("Lesgate's Death"), is intercut with an elaborate, formal restaurant scene where Tony, while dining with friends, waits for Margot to be strangled by Swann, his reluctant hired assassin. His problem is that the wrong person ends up dead: Grace Kelly, as Margot, wields a pair of scissors with deadly dexterity, foiling one perfect murder but setting herself up as the "wrong woman" for another.

All this is set in motion by Tony's watch accidentally stopping, throwing off his meticulously timed homicide. As Tony and his hired killer nervously check their watches, Tiomkin unleashes one of his most harrowing cues, a variation on Mussorgsky's coronation scene from *Boris Godunov,* its relentless chimes suggesting a huge clock rather than the Russian cathedral bells in the opera. This theme, a hypnotic repetition of darkly colored chords, is part of a larger stream of sinister harmony called "The Plan," a cue that commences when Swann enters the apartment to murder Margo; it rings dolefully through the rest of the film, giving talky detective scenes a subtle frisson. It sweeps aside the martini waltzes and divertissements, making them seem part of a deceptively superficial overture. A balancing of Old World gravitas with Hollywood glamour had been part of Hitchcock's aesthetic since *Foreign Correspondent.* Tiomkin, who spent his career Americanizing Tchaikovsky and Ukrainian folk tunes for Westerns, was ideal for this kind of juggling act.

For the most part, "The Plan" plays, like a ritornello, at a constant volume, providing somber counterpoint. In two scenes, it rises in terrifying crescendo: one, a surreal close-up of Tony's delayed call traveling across telephone wires during the killing, and another, when an ashen Grace Kelly appears against a blue backdrop changing to black and garish red as she is tried and sentenced to death. (The coarsening musical textures as Robert Burks's imagery blackens and reddens are a striking piece of tone painting.) Obsessive repetition of a song or chord pattern combined with a ticking clock was a technique Tiomkin had used to powerful effect in *High Noon,* though there the tune begins as a quiet ballad in the main title and builds to a shattering crescendo. In *Dial M,* a sinister fragment of the theme appears after the Warner fanfare (with a dramatic close-up of a telephone) but it is buried so quickly under cascading harps that we register its alarm only subliminally. When Tony phones the man he is about to blackmail into killing his wife and seals the deal, the motif appears again, then vanishes just as quickly, a teasing warning whose meaning we cannot yet grasp except to associate it with telephones. An idée fixe like this was at the center of other Hitchcock-Tiomkin collaborations: a recurring waltz linked to train whistles dances through *Shadow of a Doubt;* "Dies Irae" pounds through *I Confess.* Only in *Strangers on a Train,* the Hitchcock-Tiomkin film with the greatest range of moods and scenarios, does Tiomkin deliver variety and multiplicity.

An unusual feature of *Dial M for Murder* is a sympathetic detective, Inspector Hubbard, played with supreme urbanity by John Williams. Most of Hitchcock's detectives are bumbling incompetents; as in Poe's detective stories, the villain is brought to justice by amateurs (Grace Kelly herself in Hitchcock's next picture). Hubbard icily disdains the latter and staunchly defends police professionals, but he solves the crime only by stepping outside legal boundaries and improvising the kind of outlandish scheme favored by amateur sleuths. The layers in Williams's civilized and sardonic performance are enhanced by a searching string melody called "Hubbard," implying cerebral superiority and hidden depths, and a jaunty cue called "The Key" (the pun surely intended), as Inspector Hubbard bursts into uncontainable glee at his own cleverness in solving the crime, acting for a second more like a bubbly schoolboy than an officer of the law. As Hubbard sets in motion his plan to entrap Tony, his bright music increasingly shines down on the grim shadows of "The Plan." When he combs his mustache while making the phone call that saves Margot's life, a warm string version of the "Dial M" waltz dances in as Tony (like Brandon in *Rope*) pours a final cocktail before being taken to his doom.

Unlike *Rope,* this talky but gripping picture paid off at the box office. Being released in 3-D may have helped. (Hitchcock regarded this as an irritating and redundant gimmick, but I remember sinking in my seat in delighted terror as Grace Kelly grabbed behind her for those three-dimensional gleaming scissors.) In addition, *Dial M* had the star power of Grace Kelly—and also Tiomkin, who was more of a celebrity than is commonly recognized: advance newspaper stories on the movie stressed his Academy Award–winning stature. (Westerns were enormously popular in the 1950s, and Tiomkin, the recognized master of the genre, was well known.) Once again, Hitchcock tried and failed to get what might have enhanced his profits: a hit song. Tiomkin tried something called "My Favorite Memory," with lyrics by Jack Lawrence, but this music never made it into the film.

Tiomkin began his Hitchcock collaborations with a fragmented waltz (his distorted "Merry Widow") and concluded with a smooth one. For the

THE BAND PLAYED ON   168

most part, his dealings with Hitchcock resembled the latter. Hitchcock had clear ideas about what a picture should sound like and entrusted Tiomkin to enact them. Joseph Stefano's statement about Hitchcock almost hearing the score before it was composed presupposes trust: "Tiomkin was one of the top composers in Hollywood. Hitch's feeling was that by the time you get to sit in his office and talk with him, you know what you're doing, so I'll trust you. This is a wonderful way for a director to be. We don't have that anymore."[13]

The downside, according to Stefano, is that when the music does not measure up to Hitchcock's preconceptions, "out goes the score."[14] We know from *Spellbound* that this was not always true, though Hitchcock did oust Herrmann and Mancini with startling abruptness. With Tiomkin, he was able to reach compromises when the two quarreled over changes that he wanted but that Tiomkin was loath to make once orchestration was complete. (It must have added to his irritation that Tiomkin, despite taking this stance, often fiddled with the orchestration himself on the sound stage during recording sessions.) The relationship between the two was positive enough to keep them together through four films stretching over ten years. According to his wife, Tiomkin dealt with conflict openly, venting his anger quickly, then forgetting its source. Hitchcock's last repeat composer, Bernard Herrmann, would nurse grudges rather than forgetting them; the ride would be rougher but full of glory.

13

rear window: the redemptive power
of popular music

Where is that wonderful music coming from?

—Lisa, in *Rear Window*

Rear Window is Hitchcock's most daring experiment in popular music. Its pop-song surrealism is the forerunner of *American Graffiti, Mona Lisa, After Hours,* and many other films, but the way tunes and street sounds drift through the sound track, in and out of windows and the protagonist's dreams, is unique.

Indeed, *Rear Window* feels like such a radical experiment, unlike anything in a movie before, that we need to remind ourselves that its roots go back to British Hitchcock—to *The 39 Steps, Rich and Strange,* even *Blackmail.* Although *Rear Window* seems thoroughly American, especially in its celebration of American popular song, it marks a return to Hitchcock's fondness for crisscrossing vernacular tunes. These films pushed vernacular movie music to the limit, before powerful Hollywood scores à la Franz Waxman and Miklos Rozsa (the legacy of David Selznick) buried their delicate zing under what Hitchcock called those "terrible" strings.[1]

It is not just the swingy ambiance of these brave British experiments that *Rear Window* reinvokes: it is also the strategy of having popular music shape the narrative. This would become a curse as much as a blessing, as studios began pressuring moviemakers to stuff their products with arbitrary popular songs to sell sound tracks and reap profits. In *Rear Window,* the songs are understated and organic, interpenetrating every aspect of the movie rather than appearing in isolated segments as they do in *The Lady*

Vanishes and *Young and Innocent;* yet they are never gratuitous, as in so many rock-infused movies from the 1980s and 1990s.

Rear Window's cue sheet instantly reveals an astonishing diversity and richness.[2] It lists thirty-nine songs, ballets, "improvisations," boogies, and "jukeboxes" by a dizzying variety of songwriters. The official composer is Franz Waxman, on his fourth Hitchcock film; the list also includes Leonard Bernstein, Richard Rodgers, Jay Livingston, Johnny Burke, Walter Gross, Schubert, and Mendelssohn. The final cut of the film has a cue not listed on the sheet: an excerpt from Waxman's 1951 *A Place in the Sun,* an early Hollywood jazz score, which is played as the dog is lowered to the courtyard in a basket.[3] Clearly, Hitchcock wanted to grab anything jazzy and spicy that he could for this musical gumbo; that Paramount had so many ingredients to throw in the soup made it all the better.

Aided by Lewis Lipstone and Sid Herman at Paramount, Hitchcock made meticulous and exacting choices.[4] The fusion of these songs with the action is graphed in a densely detailed six-page "description of the manner in which the music is used." Dated July 6, 1954, the same date as the cue sheet, this reel-by-reel account reveals Hitchcock's scrupulous attention to musical detail, indicating precisely what tunes are playing, often many simultaneously, as Jeff, Hitchcock's voyeuristic hero, spies on his neighbors.[5] The first item, "Rear Window Prelude and Radio," shows that we are to read Waxman's main title as source music, a subtlety not necessarily apparent on first viewing.[6] With its squealing clarinet, bluesy strings, and celesta-timpani duet playing at full volume, the Prelude seems to be a standard invisible main title establishing the movie's tone, in this case a cool urbanity. (The feline elegance is made definitive by an omniscient shot of a sleek black cat meowing in counterpoint as it scampers up the courtyard stairs.) But the annotation shows that the title tune isn't conventional at all: "From screening credits—camera pans from window to courtyard buildings. Cut to James Stewart (Jeff) at window and thermometer. . . . Cut to composer shaving, as composer changes station on radio." The Prelude is thus coming from a real source, the composer's radio, and it concludes when he switches stations to drown out an obnoxious commercial aimed at "listless" men over forty. What plays on the radio next are the sexy trumpets and thumping basses of Waxman's Rhumba for Miss Torso's "ballet exercises" so admired by Jeff. So it goes throughout the picture: in *Jamaica Inn, Lifeboat,* and *Rope,* Hitchcock experimented with minimizing the symphonic underscore; here he eliminates it altogether.

For those who have always been struck, as I have, by the startling simi-

Rear Window Prelude. A main title from a radio. By Franz Waxman. (Courtesy of John Waxman. Copyright © 1954 (renewed 1982) by Famous Music LLC. International Copyright Secured. All Rights Reserved.)

larity of the music following the Rhumba to Leonard Bernstein's *Fancy Free,* this document provides the reason: it *is Fancy Free,* Bernstein's jazzy ballet. Its big-band sound is "superimposed over composer piano no. 1, consisting of Lisa and Piano Improvisation." Here we see the skeletal beginnings of "Lisa," the song at the heart of the narrative. We also have the first in-stance of simultaneous musical layers played over one another, as they often are in modern life. The sustained blasting of *Fancy Free* from the composer's radio as he bangs improvisations and "Lisa" motifs on the piano—all blending with trucks, chattering neighbors, and clattery street noises—is a piece of musical surrealism worthy of John Cage, whose "radio music" period coincided with that of *Rear Window*. Hitchcock had experimented with radio music in *Foreign Correspondent, Saboteur,* and other films, but never with this complexity.

Even with multiple counterpoint, Hitchcock maintains the musical focus as precisely as he does the camera's: as Thelma Ritter's Stella enters, warning of voyeurism and "red hot pokers," all the sonic layers vanish except for the "Lisa" nucleus. Throughout the sound track, "Lisa" manages to grab our attention, even in the noisiest, most complex moments. At the "Rear Window Finale," the multiple superimpositions thin down to this crucial song, in its resplendent final form. The precise volume of each tune and noise is cued by Hitchcock's nineteen pages of dubbing notes for Waxman and George Tomasini, his film editor, indicating crescendos, decrescendos, and silences, all in relation to where a noise is coming from.[7]

Critics, especially those who accuse Hitchcock of anti-intellectualism, assert that he privileges popular over classical music in his films, the former representing the earthy and the ordinary, the latter the stuffy and hypocritical.[8] But Hitchcock loved all types of music and used each genre positively, negatively, ironically, or objectively, depending on the context. For every example of a negative use of classical or a positive use of pop, there are striking exceptions. Mozart and Johann Christian Bach take on claustrophobic connotations in *Vertigo,* but Beethoven, Delius, Wagner, and Tchaikovsky provide life-saving motifs in *Saboteur, Murder!,* and *Torn Curtain;* popular song is redemptive in the 1956 *Man Who Knew Too Much* and also in *Rear Window,* but darkly ironic in *Blackmail, Rich and Strange,* and *Strangers on a Train;* folk song saves the day in *The Lady Vanishes,* but sinks it in *Topaz.*

Rear Window is Hitchcock's ultimate paean to popular music, so much so that he really had nowhere to go with the genre afterward. *The Trouble with Harry* has John Forsythe briefly bursting into song, but in *North by Northwest, Psycho,* and *Marnie,* Hitchcock decreased the use of pop material, until it practically vanished in *Frenzy.* Hitchcock's music notes show that in *Vertigo,* he went so far as to spurn several specific suggestions in the script for pop-source music, giving Herrmann's exquisitely complex score full rein. After *Rear Window,* only the remake of *The Man Who Knew Too Much* would make significant use of a popular song.

In *Rear Window,* the songs are active and liberating, opening Hitchcock's often cramped view of human relationships, constantly transform-ing and interacting with each other and with the characters. They are an an-tidote to Jeff's stubbornly rationalized refusal to connect with Lisa, a neuro-sis scathingly diagnosed by Stella, as well as to the national illness of Peeping Tomism she also identifies. As we shall see, Lisa embraces the power of song while Jeff sarcastically dismisses it; the dismissal is a symptom of his emo-tional uptightness, though as compensation he gets some of the funniest lines: "Where do you think he gets his inspiration?" Lisa wonders aloud about the songwriter. "From the landlady, once a month," Jeff retorts.

The music for *Rear Window* also explicates a complex process, some-thing that always interested Hitchcock. "I wanted to show," he said, "how a popular song is composed by gradually developing it throughout the film until, in the final scene, it is played on a recording with a full orchestral ac-companiment."[9] We see Waxman's "Lisa," composed for the film (lyrics by Harold Rome), go through a full metamorphosis, from tentative piano noodlings through gradual instrumentation and voice-piano tryouts and improvisations—a drama of creation that occurs independently of the ac-tion even as it profoundly influences it—until the finished, recorded prod-uct sails into play behind the concluding image of Lisa reposing in serene control as her musical ID concludes the movie.

The song in progress drifts through windows, in and out of the multiple story lines, commenting on them, contradicting them, moving them for-ward, ultimately saving the life of Miss Lonely Hearts, Grace Kelly's sad alter ego. It begins in skeletal form as single piano notes when Stella enters, smelling "trouble" and discoursing on Peeping Tomism. The composer plays a slightly fuller but still faltering version with Hitchcock looking over his shoulder in one of his wittiest cameos. When Lisa comments rhapsodi-cally that this "enchanting" song seems "written especially for us," Jeff dryly comments, "No wonder he's having so much trouble with it." The com-poser's creative block thus parallels Jeff's difficulties with love. The trouble is really his, not Lisa's, as Stella ruefully tells him.

"Lisa" continues to take shape as Jeff takes out his telephoto lens to watch Thorwald unpacking knives and saws. It is embellished with Lisztian cadenzas as Raymond Burr's Thorwald empties jewelry from his wife's purse, and it goes through tentative orchestration in what the notes call a "rehearsal jam session" as Lisa and Stella dig in the courtyard garden for ev-idence, and as Lisa bravely breaks into Thorwald's apartment. During these tense scenes, fragments from "Lisa" blend and collide with Walter Gross im-provisations and other unidentified songs in a mysterious collage. When the song reaches penultimate form, the composer says, "All right fellas, let's start from the beginning." They do, and "Lisa," suavely orchestrated and nearly complete, sweeps down into Miss Lonely Hearts's apartment with a rapture that keeps her from ending her life. Jeff and Stella watch her renounce her suicide pills; Miss Lonely Hearts stares upward beatifically, searching for the source of her deliverance.

The way a song reaches out to save a lonely middle-aged woman from despair and death constitutes the film's most moving musical drama, a powerful counter to the charge that Hitchcock was cold and unfeeling and a useful reminder of his belief in the therapeutic power of art. Throughout *Rear Window*, Jeff watches the desperate creature he has dubbed Miss Lonely Hearts struggle with anxiety and isolation, pantomiming fantasy dates, drinking alone, picking up a young man who makes a drunken pass, and finally deciding to kill herself—until "Lisa" drifts in her window from above, making the world seem, for that crucial moment, a benevolent place. Suddenly she stands in ecstasy facing her window, much as Lisa does when she hears the tune, both dressed in Edith Head's resplendent outfits. The musical life force proves stronger than the death wish. Captured in a long shot, tastefully avoiding sentimentality, this scene is Hitchcock's most beautifully realized musical epiphany. Yet it also has a fragile evanescence, making it a modern revelation in the strictest sense: a second later, the scene vanishes as Thorwald enters his apartment to find Lisa inside, jerking us back into the messy crime narrative. Only at the end, after Miss Lonely Hearts has paired up with the songwriter does she make a statement about the meaning of the music, and she still can't put it into words: "I can't tell you what this music has meant to me."[10]

Miss Lonely Hearts is like anyone whose life is made meaningful by music: none of us can adequately explain the strange power of musical emotion. Like the camera, music allowed Hitchcock, who distrusted language, to convey a meaning beyond words. Nonetheless, his characters, like all of us, can't help using language. Lisa tries adjectives: "There's that song again," she says, calling it at various times "enchanting," "wonderful," and "utterly beautiful."

As with Poe, Hitchcock's literary muse, beauty and truth are usually separate; vicious terrorists have impeccable musical taste; an exuberant cantata is the medium of an assassination. But in *Rear Window*, a Shakespearean comedy disguised as a suspense thriller, beauty and truth come together; the utterly beautiful saves a life. The final communion of the composer and Miss Lonely Hearts has a poignant symmetry: the songwriter struggles with his song in lonely, frustrated, drunken isolation, not unlike that of Miss Lonely Hearts, as shown when Jeff observes him hurling his score about the room.[11] The songwriter needs Miss Lonely Hearts, his best audience, as much as she needs him.

Whatever his problems, the songwriter is engaged in an affirmative alternative to the Peeping Tom passivity and inertia diagnosed and denounced by the one-woman Greek chorus, Stella. Gathering with his noisy friends to piece together the song in progress, he invokes an era when people informally sang and played instruments, a period that, with the coming of television, was nearing its end. (Hitchcock would contribute to the new passivity himself two years later with *Alfred Hitchcock Presents*, making introductory jokes about being trapped in a television box.) Rather than looking outside into others' lives, says Stella, we should get beyond ourselves and look in. That is what the songwriter does, getting out of his ego and looking into his imagination, finding a song that changes a life.

The manner of its creation and its integration into the drama are, to use Lisa's term, as "enchanting" as the song itself. Yet Hitchcock grumbled about Waxman's contribution, telling Truffaut he was disappointed with the music, saying that "it didn't work out the way I wanted."[12] What could he mean? "Lisa," is indeed shown "gradually developing" with "full orchestral accompaniment," at the end completing an organic process depicted with great cinematic subtlety. Hitchcock sounds a bit like Jeff, a man who doesn't know what a good thing he has.

Fourteen years later, he elaborated: "I was a little disappointed at the lack of structure in the title song. I had a motion picture songwriter when I should have chosen a popular songwriter."[13] John Waxman recalls amiable meetings between his father and Hitchcock but adds: "Hitchcock knew what he wanted—he always did—and he wasn't getting it from my father. He wanted a hit song, and my father was after something else."[14]

But what was it he was after? The structure of "Lisa" is as firm as many other popular songs Hitchcock appropriated. "Miss Up to Date" (in *Blackmail*) and "Que Sera Sera" (in the remake of *The Man Who Knew Too Much*) are more complex in structure and offer a more detailed correspondence between lyrics and story, but "Lisa" is richer in its meanings and uses. It mounts a subtle crescendo, bringing together the murder mystery and romance, blending with other tunes in a beautiful and mysterious cacophony. Its very simplicity and easy-to-recall musical line make it amenable to all sorts of fusions and fragmentations: we can always pick it out in the dense skein of music and street noise. The gradual accretion of this song's musical and dramatic layers constitutes one of the film's wonders.

There was apparently a platonic *Rear Window* in Hitchcock's head, an ideal musical storyboard that Franz Waxman could not manage. This was the beginning of Hitchcock's increasingly debilitating obsession with hit tunes, something that came largely from studio pressure and that was very much at odds with his deeper instincts about music. In *Rebecca, Spellbound,* and *Notorious,* this pressure was only a minor distraction; the numerous songs submitted for these films were so ghastly and embarrassing that Selznick (who had better musical taste than is commonly supposed) rejected them all; by the 1960s, however, Lew Wasserman and others were relentlessly demanding hit tunes, one of the pressures that poisoned Hitchcock's relationship with Bernard Herrmann.

Hitchcock often grumbled that music was an element over which he had limited control, even though he regarded his role as similar to a composer's. His cameo commiserating with the songwriter at the piano is perhaps a comment on the director as a kind of composer, someone who manipulates audiences through miraculous sights and sounds. Hitchcock used musical metaphors to describe his creative process; he compared himself to a conductor, organist, and orchestrator, and likened film to opera.[15] In the cameo he identifies himself with the musical process, at the same time commenting on his frustratingly scant control over the actual composer: standing over a clock, he looks down at the songwriter with a touch of apprehension. Give me what I want this time, that look says.

Rear Window is the most musically allusive of Hitchcock's films, not only in the songs it quotes but in its reference to larger structures. Like *Stage Fright,* it mimics many musical forms, especially the Broadway musical, a genre suggested at the very beginning by the excerpt from a Bernstein show. Backstage (or back-window) performers sing, whistle, hum, or turn on radios and LPs, sometimes commenting on the music. The ghostly pileup of distant songs yields almost as much music as a Broadway score. In the lengthy composer's party, guests arrive to a boisterous piano fanfare, where they sing and play into the night. A pulsing piano boogie-woogie by Walter Gross provides a bass for their raucous nocturne; Lisa's hums her theme song as it snakes in Jeff's window, a haunting vocalese against a distant chorus of partyers. In the morning, after all the experiments and improvisations, after all the night revelers have staggered home, the songwriter plays the show's theme song in bright sunlight for Miss Lonely Hearts, summarizing the drama in a grand reprise before the curtain comes down.

The party fanfare suggests another musical form, the serenade. In its Mozartian format, this consisted of a march or fanfare introducing a noc-

Rear Window. Hitchcock directing his songwriter.

turnal musical entertainment in several sections, juggling comedy, romance, excitement, and a touch of melancholy. The remarkable scene involving the courtyard digging, the break-in, the composition of "Lisa," and
the salvation of Miss Lonely Hearts not only parallels the eighteenth-century serenade but harks back to its beginnings, when it was the outpouring
of a would-be lover wooing his beloved under her window. Here, the songwriter woos Miss Lonely Hearts unintentionally, above her window rather

than below it, but these are merely technicalities. The important thing is that the composer's song, serenaded into the night, brings her to him.[16]

Thanks to Miss Torso, the film also takes on elements of ballet, a form that acts as a metaphor in dancelike movies such as *Foreign Correspondent, North by Northwest,* and *Topaz,* but here becomes more literal. Under Jeff's happy gaze, she dances to Waxman's Rhumba and his bustling, neoclassical "New Ballet," to Bernstein's *Fancy Free,* and to Schubert's *Rosamunde.* These are some of the wittiest moments in the film, foils for Stella's and Doyle's withering commentary on Jeff's voyeurism. Miss Torso's funniest turn is saved for the end, when she whirls to the door, opens it, and joyfully leaps on Stanley, her soldier boyfriend, a nerdy little guy with glasses, about half her height, who has returned at last.

Often, *Rear Window* feels less like a single musical than an anthology. Songs by many composers glide through Jeff's window, each making its contribution to the action and atmosphere. Critics assert that the songs, unlike those in realist cinema, correspond with what is shown on the screen. Sometimes this is indeed the case, as in the playful version of "That's Amore" jangling loudly as Jeff watches a new bride being carried across the threshold (Hitchcock ruled out using a wedding march); or when Lisa's song appears during the revelatory moment when she sees Thorwald putting a heavy rope on a trunk (the beginning of her transformation from Fashion Queen into Girl Friday); or when the piano boogie concludes at exactly the moment Doyle declares, "Lars Thorwald is no more a murderer than I am," seeming to shut down Jeff and Lisa's detective-voyeurism game.[17] The most precise synchronization is the drooping of "Lisa" into a minor-key cadence when Lisa's face caves in following Jeff's sarcastic remark about her lobster dinner: "It's perfect, Lisa, as always."

The most dramatic correspondence between music and action occurs when Miss Lonely Hearts puts "To See You Is to Love You" on the phonograph, poignantly constructing a dinner date with a fantasy partner. This Johnny Burke–James Van Heusen ballad plays on with wistful string accompaniment as she raises her drink to toast an invisible love: "I see you everywhere," continues the song, "in the same old dream tonight." Movies are a controlled dream, but this is the same old dream, an unending melodrama of unfulfilled fantasy blurred by alcohol. In one of the film's most touching moments, Jeff twice toasts her from across the way as she toasts her fantasy date. A similarly sad motto for Miss Lonely Hearts is Waxman's "Many Dreams Ago," which plays during her pickup journey to the restaurant across the street.

Sometimes the correspondences seem clear, then suddenly blur. "To See You Is To Love You" aptly enhances Miss Lonely Hearts's imaginary date, but when a string variation continues as Miss Torso performs what Lisa calls "a woman's hardest job, juggling wolves," the tune seems suddenly ironic; playing on as Thorwald enters his wife's bedroom, it becomes bitterly so. Schubert's stately *Rosamunde* accompanies Miss Torso's most lyrical ballet but continues to pour in the window during the caustic argument between Jeff and Doyle. Waxman's "Many Dreams Ago," the background to Miss Lonely Hearts's anxious pickup scene, is about "waiting for my true love to appear." But the shot of Miss Lonely Hearts's seating herself at a table in the back of the frame is suddenly displaced by a shocking close-up of Thorwald returning to his apartment, a far more sinister portrayal of someone who has given up waiting. By the time Miss Lonely Hearts has succeeded in finding a romantic partner, "Mona Lisa," a Livingston-Evans standard, is belted out loudly and out of tune by partyers in the composer's apartment, covering the young pickup's near assault (a "tussle," according to the description sheet). The drunken, off-key lyricism is at once out of sync and sadly appropriate.

Often the tunes do not complement the action at all or move in sharp counterpoint to it. Rodgers and Hart's "Lover" plays through the thunderstorm as the older couple camping out on the fire escape scramble for cover and continues arbitrarily as Thorwald leaves his apartment with a suitcase. The upbeat jazz clarinet during Lisa's delivery of the letter to Thorwald's apartment and the fizzy violin during his hasty exit after Jeff's threatening phone call are in "tempo" with the scene, to use Hitchcock's term, but out of sync emotionally.

As in the Salvation Army marching band in *The 39 Steps* or the schoolyard song in *The Birds,* the cheery counterpoint mysteriously increases the suspense in a way that a conventionally anxious score would not. Waxman's "Street Music No. 1," a bubbly arrangement of Thomas Moore's "Carnival of Venice," carries a similar electrical charge during the ominous scene where Thorwald chases the dog from the garden. Street music and other urban sounds ratchet up the excitement while seeming to function only as sonic realism. The very inappropriateness of the music heightens the nastiness of what Jeff and Lisa believe they are observing in Thorwald's apartment.

We feel this tension throughout the film. Tunes such as Waxman's "Jukebox No. 6," a chic clarinet-vibraphone duet, squeals happily as Lisa slips the note under Thorwald's door and as Miss Lonely Hearts takes out her fatal pills; "Red Garters" plays breezily as Jeff gets Thorwald out the door with a fake phone call. Seeming to cry out for heavy suspense music, these oddly exciting moments cut against every Hollywood musical norm. Even "Lisa" often plays against the emotion of a scene. The smoothest moment during the jazz-combo version of "Lisa," after the musicians have worked out its kinks—shown in a quick shot of the composer's apartment with guitarist, pianist, harmonica, and brass players confidently performing—occurs during the film's most disturbing moment, when Lisa screams "Jeff, Jeff!" as he helplessly watches Thorwald attack her.

Sometimes the songs are just mischievous Hitchcockian jokes, as when Livingston-Evans's "Lady Killer" plays while Doyle presents ostensibly definitive proof that Thorwald didn't kill his lady. Occasionally, the irony is cruel, as when Thorwald kills the dog, to the hysterical wails of its owner, an indictment of her uncaring neighbors—set to the loud, indifferent strains of a Livingston-Evans swing tune, "Bad News." For a moment, in one of the few omniscient shots in the film, the many minor characters peer anxiously and empathetically out all those windows, touched by the woman's distress, but just as quickly they return to their insular routines and revelries.

Coming in an endless stream, the musical connections and ironies are not easy to sort out. The whistling of Mendelssohn's "Spring Song" through the courtyard ("Whistler No. 1") occurs during Lisa and Jeff's second kissing scene; the kiss is more inert than springlike, with Jeff preoccupied with what has happened to Thorwald's wife rather than with the exquisite woman in his arms. "I want all of you," says Lisa, full of repressed passion, though she gets little. Everywhere, the sound track upsets conventions. Lisa's floating entrance into the movie and into Jeff's dreams—one of the most ravishing shots in all Hitchcock—is announced not by a lush nocturne but by a faraway singer warming up on the piano, blending with the cries of children playing in the last glow of sunset, a touch of realism that imparts sublime poetry.

Fascinating as the referential songs are—and they clearly appealed to Hitchcock's love of designs and correspondences—it is these the moments of pure poetry that make *Rear Window* such a haunting and original work of art: the piano boogie-woogie pinging into Lisa's subconscious as she hums what is to be her theme song; the distant waltz incongruously supporting the doomed dog's courtyard digging; the Ivesian blending of all the music in a dissonant fabric of crisscrossing songs and city noises.

Hitchcock was a grudging Romantic with the methods of a painstaking classicist. The ambivalence is dramatized in the conflict between the two main characters, one denouncing intuition, especially women's, the other affirming it at every point. Unlike Jeff, Lisa believes in music, imagination, and enchantment. Her intuition about jewelry, makeup, and travel bags, and her willingness to takes risks and improvise, even daring to burglarize Thorwald's apartment, solve the crime. Jeff's intelligent, mature way of approaching life and love—a stance ridiculed by Thelma Ritter as the world's greatest cause of trouble—is as inadequate for romance as it is for catching the bad guy.

In the use of music, however, the film is profoundly modern. Indeed, *Rear Window* is a return to the modernity Hitchcock pioneered in *Rich and Strange* almost exactly twenty years earlier. In both, he eschewed symphonic tradition for pop source music, giving these dark comedies a sharp contemporary edge. Later movies like *American Graffiti, Diner, The Big Chill,* and *Avalon* would use hit songs from the past for instant nostalgia. But the songs in *Rear Window* have a freshness, a sense of being in the moment, especially when they sound together in rowdy dissonance. As we see in the good-old-days soliloquies of Uncle Charlie in *Shadow of a Doubt,* a serial killer whose motto is a nineteenth-century waltz, and in the denunciation of modern jazz by Drayton in the 1956 *Man Who Knew Too Much,* an assassin whose fetish is old-fashioned love songs, Hitchcock distrusted nostalgia: those who can't bury the past, from Scottie Ferguson to Norman Bates, are either bad guys or good ones headed for tragedy.

We can tell tales about the good old days, says Doyle to Jeff, but we know they are lies. Music is a force that keeps the film's heroes and heroines in the present. Lisa is empowered by her song in progress, recognizing its potency even in its earliest fragments; the same song saves Miss Lonely Hearts the minute these fragments come together in completion. All the songs are sung or played out the windows of people who need them to maintain their connection with life or simply to get through the night. Robin Wood points out that every character is isolated, each imprisoned in a small apartment, but music provides a mysterious connectedness that Lisa, the composer, and Miss Lonely Hearts reach out to embrace.[18]

At the end, popular song affirms the comic vision: the loose ends are tied together, the correct couples coupled. Miss Lonely Hearts is united with her life-saving composer. "Love Is Just Around the Corner," gruesomely ironic when it played after she threw out her drunken pickup and prepared her suicide pills, is now revealed as prophetic. Lisa has mastered her romance with Jeff, her theme song overpowering the "Rear Window Finale." "Lisa" plays triumphantly through the courtyard and in all the windows, a coda for the various reunions and romances—even for the heartbroken dog mourners, who have a new pet.

Music can provide a closure even more concise than the camera's. Despite a few discordant notes, *Rear Window* ends resolutely and happily in the home key, as does all comedy. "It's great to be home," says Stanley in the final line, just before Waxman strikes the major chord in the swift, perky final cadence. For once, the music does not seem to have a source—the first and only instance of an invisible score. Following scene after scene of real music, the omniscient composer has the last word, proving that *Rear Window* is, as Hitchcock would say, only a movie after all.

14

lethal laughter:
hitchcock's fifties comedies

Many directors can make one or two good movies, but how many can make fifty great ones like Hitchcock?

—Bernard Herrmann

For Hitchcock, comedy was essential.[1] The movies he grumbled about as not being authentic Hitchcock pictures were invariably the ones he judged insufficiently comedic. Comedy permeated his tone, dialogue, and narrative structure, which was frequently Shakespearean: from *The 39 Steps* on, he loved to set up a quarrelsome romantic couple, beset them with elaborate obstacles, take them on a dangerous adventure far removed from their ordinary lives (in the case of *Rear Window*, a journey voyeuristic rather than geographical), and unite them in a finale full of sparkling music. Often the threats to the couple are deadly, moving the genre toward tragicomedy, but everything ends on a major chord, even if the cadence sounds only at the last minute.

The early 1950s were a fertile period for Hitchcock's comic muse. Here he used music in a Shakespearean manner, as a signifier of harmony and order. *Rear Window*'s rich layering of themes and musical motifs culminates in a restoration of harmony and a unification of lovers as previously fragmented sounds play on the phonograph as an orchestrated song. Hitchcock's next two comedies were less complex but equally sharp and original, especially in their handling of music. Again, the narratives veer close to tragicomedy, the anticipated sweet harmonies and wedding bells threatened by everything from a formidable mother to an insufficiently buried corpse.

MUSICAL COCKTAIL, 100 PROOF: *TO CATCH A THIEF*

To Catch a Thief, which immediately followed *Rear Window,* is an airy di-
vertissement. Shot on location on the French Riviera, it serves up music as
elegant as its setting. Breeziness undergirded by menace, Hitchcock's favorite double mood, is established right away when Lyn Murray's fizzy main
title—a mini-piano concerto in the style popular in the 1940s, the period of
the story—is suddenly jolted by a scream from octave strings and a jewel-
heist victim. This jarring juxtaposition is followed by mysterious atonal
winds, "Le Chat," cuing both the Cat Burglar and an actual cat. The audience is charmed but unsettled.

   To Catch a Thief marks another instance where Hitchcock wanted
Bernard Herrmann—who this time had a conflict with Fox—and got another composer who worked out splendidly. Lyn Murray, recommended to
Hitchcock by the producer William Perlberg, took three weeks to mix a
complex musical cocktail. Like John Michael Hayes's script, the score is
stinging and duplicitous, its precision aided by Hitchcock's three-page,
single-spaced music notes. Part of its originality had to do with censorship
issues. When a seemingly icy Grace Kelly suddenly kisses Cary Grant in the
doorway of her hotel room, a sultry saxophone highlights the sensual surprise. But as the affair progresses, the score moves away from sexuality, a
subtle strategy for fooling the censor. When Hitchcock shot John and Francie entwining passionately on a couch, using the fireworks outside as a glorious accompaniment to their building climax, he knew he might not get
away with it. According to Hitchcock's granddaughter, he left the shot intact
but instructed Murray to compose a comedic rather than sexy cue, desexing
the scene and throwing the censors off.[2]

   The cues also veer away from overt comedy. Clearly, Hitchcock was after new musical moods and effects to cut against norms and clichés. Above
all, he was determined to avoid comic mickey-mousing (the chortling
winds during his bus cameo are an exception). Instead, he used musical abstraction: neoclassical wind chords during the spectacular Riviera vista
shots with Grant and Kelly, creating a subliminal unease; whole-tone scales
as John Robie, Grant's character, looks up at towering castles and ruins, providing a peek into his anxieties as he struggles to prove his innocence to the
police. Throughout, witty lines are underlaid with mysterious sonorities,
suggesting anxiety under surface banter. A wispy harp plays against a
somber pedal as Francie Stevens offers to be John's chauffeur, making a
throwaway scene mysteriously suspenseful. Francie admits her sexual fetish

for criminals—she finds John stimulating precisely because she thinks him guilty—against scary woodwinds. For her as well as Hitchcock's audience, danger is a turn-on; indeed, she declares her love to John against a backdrop of sinister octaves sung by a distant funeral choir. Even their languid embrace in a car overlooking a stunning Mediterranean vista after a discussion conflating sexual foreplay with chicken (right out of *Notorious*) is spiced with dissonance: "Which would you prefer," Francie asks, "a leg or a breast?" "You make the choice," John replies.

The beauty of the Riviera setting, photographed by Robert Burks in daring, innovative helicopter shots, is allowed to speak for itself rather than be apostrophized by the score. Similarly, in the car chases, which have a spark and momentum that anticipate *North by Northwest* and *Family Plot*, Hitchcock shuts off the music when the road game gets dangerous, allowing the roar of engines and car horns to produce their own music.

Throughout, we get sly versions of Hitchcock's signature effects: pealing bells at the beginning and end, tense pizzicato in the first "Rooftop" cue, growling ostinatos in the second, sinister pedal points at dramatic moments, a funeral with shuddery organ chords, terse motifs during action scenes, and woozy sounds for Jesse Royce Landis's "Bourbon" cue (Herrmann would compose another one for her son, played by Cary Grant, in *North by Northwest*). As John prepares to unmask the villain in the finale, a theremin, echoing *Spellbound*, becomes a marker for hidden identity as it slithers with organ sonorities along the rooftop.

Score and storyline conspire to produce the peculiar sharpness and quirkiness of Hitchcock comedy. The sonic tour de force is the elaborately decadent costume ball at the end. Murray composed what the cue sheet calls "The Big Waltz," a grandiose version of one of Hitchcock's favorite forms, along with 1940s jazz and a fiery swing tune. These counterpoint the party's complex maneuverings and disguises; they also remind us that this movie is set in the late 1940s, though vivid color and VistaVision make it look like the 1950s.

At the end, music delivers a final ironic bite. The rocky road of love is smoothed, as it must be in comedy, and we find John and Francie together in a sumptuous villa. All the knots seem untied, but suddenly a new one twists into being. Steamy saxophone jazz returns from the first kiss scene as John ruefully admits, "I needed the help of a woman"; the piano concerto bubbles back from the main title, accompanied by wedding bells. But we also see a final, terrified glance by Cary Grant as Grace Kelly tells him, "Mother will love it up here!" As with his previous picture, Hitchcock delivers an ambivalently comic ending. A peppy wind cadence, much like the one in *Rear Window,* ends the picture, with Grace Kelly again smiling with lofty self-satisfaction. All's well that ends well—at least for Hitchcock's heroine.

A PORTRAIT OF HITCH: *THE TROUBLE WITH HARRY*

Although Lyn Murray delivered a zestful score for *To Catch a Thief,* his most significant contribution was recommending Bernard Herrmann as the composer for Hitchcock's next comedy, *The Trouble with Harry.* Murray, who was unavailable for the project, guessed that the two would work well together, and he was right; what he didn't know was that they would team up for more than a decade to become the most brilliant director-composer collaboration of the era—indeed, the most celebrated in the history of cinema.

The personal and artistic bond between the two men was deep and complex. Hitchcock, a Catholic Cockney, and Herrmann, a Russian Jew, were both stubbornly independent outsiders who abhorred mediocrity and spurned the establishment even as they sought its approval; neither artist ever received an Academy Award, yet both craved respect and recognition. According to Steven Smith, Herrmann's biographer, "Both men desired social mobility, Hitchcock aspiring to join the English upper class, Herrmann seeking a place among top rank conductors in his own country and abroad." The temperaments of the two were opposite—Herrmann infamously raw and explosive, Hitchcock cool and detached—yet that seems to have benefited their collaboration. Herrmann's passion was "the perfect complement to Hitchcock's often detached images," writes Smith, "giving them an emotional center and reinforcing thematic purpose." The two were "destined to come together," states Royal S. Brown, "because of the age-old principle 'opposites attract.' . . . [Hitchcock] was forever the calm, rational being, the very prototype of British unflappability. At the opposite extreme, the American-born, Jewish Herrmann was possessed of an almost legendary irascibility. . . . Herrmann's musical translations of raw effect seemed to be waiting for the counterbalancing effect of a Hitchcock-style cinema, with its carefully elaborated visual structures." Beneath the counterbalancing personae was a deep emotional correspondence. The two shared "a dark, tragic sense of life," says Donald Spoto, "a brooding view of human relationships, and a compulsion to explore aesthetically the private world of the romantic fantasy."[3]

Spoto recently reminded me that there were also practical reasons for the collaboration, and that luck played a role as well. A "distinctly commercial purpose" lurked behind Hitchcock's hiring of Herrmann and, indeed, Waxman as well. These were "the very best in the business during the golden age," and Hitchcock knew it. In a happy accident, Herrmann became available at the moment Hitchcock became his own producer: "Remember that Hitchcock had no choice of composer until he also produced his films—and even then he had mostly to use studio personnel. His clout enabled him to have Herrmann, who was not attached to a studio in any case."[4]

In *The Trouble with Harry,* Hitchcock got not only his first but his favorite Herrmann score, and Herrmann got something he had always wanted, the opportunity to write a comedy. The two hit it off so well and Hitchcock admired the score so unreservedly that Herrmann quickly became a friend of Hitchcock's family, partaking of Alma's cooking and helping Hitchcock wash dishes. According to Norma Shepherd, Herrmann's third wife, these occasions gave the two men an opportunity to share their aspirations and mordant humor: "They'd talk about what they would do if they weren't in the film business. Benny wanted to run an English pub until someone told him you actually had to open and close at certain hours. Benny asked Hitch what he would be. There was a silence. Hitchcock then turned to Benny, his apron folded on his head, and said solemnly, 'A hanging judge.'"[5]

The Trouble with Harry created a bond between the two men that went far beyond kitchen banter. Their mutual trust resulted in Hitchcock's inviting Herrmann to the set before shooting, asking in advance which scenes should have music and altering their timing accordingly. The continuity of the collaboration reinforced future successes, for Herrmann craved dependability in a business that he viewed, like life itself, as chaotic and treacherous. Indeed, he responded positively to Hitchcock because of his staying power, praising the director for making one distinguished film after another since the silent era. The good feelings even allowed Herrmann to sometimes ignore Hitchcock's instructions and get away with it—at least until their final confrontation.

Despite the importance of the *Harry* music, it is far less celebrated than that composed for *Vertigo, North by Northwest,* or *Psycho,* even though it is as original and inventive as any of these. Here is another instance of Hitchcock's easy label as the master of suspense causing false expectations. For this slow-motion comedy, almost entirely bereft of suspense, Herrmann created the most genial of his Hitchcock works, perhaps the most tuneful of all his cinematic scores, the kind that often becomes a hit on its own as a recording.

Bernard Herrmann asleep on the job.

That it never has says a great deal about the movie's reception. *The Trouble with Harry* was simply too bizarre for the American public, which was not accustomed to its alienating style of black comedy. A corpse pops up in a gorgeous Vermont woods, puzzling the little boy who discovers it, then throwing into chaos the pastoral, genteel adults, including the unlikely romantic couple, Sam Marlowe and Jennifer Rogers, played by John Forsythe and Shirley MacLaine (in her film debut); the body is then rediscovered by the boy and buried by the proper authorities one more time so that order can be restored and the couples coupled.

Because this is comedy, chaos is only temporary: everyone treats Harry's corpse as a vulgar nuisance that must be continually dug up and reburied. The cool detachment of Hitchcock's characters is carried to such a deliberately ludicrous extreme that the tone veers way beyond normal deadpan. American audiences didn't get the joke, though the film, like *I Confess* and other audacious Hitchcock flops, was a hit in Paris. Even in the DVD era, *The Trouble with Harry* has received scant attention, despite its provocative idea and its luscious cinematography and score. Hitchcock and his fans blame its failure on its "English humor," but Americans always loved *The 39 Steps* and *The Lady Vanishes*. The humor in *Harry* is actually something less parochial and more original, closer to theater of the absurd than anything specifically English. Here again Hitchcock's Old World sophistication interacts with a Hollywood cast and a New World setting—in this case, a pristine New England that doesn't remotely resemble Britain—to produce something daring and unclassifiable. Only the score sounds English (in part like Elgar, whom Herrmann admired), but its lyricism is another layer of irony in the narrative.

The music does have its admirers. Royal S. Brown sees the tight four-note motif opening the film as the genesis of Herrmann-Hitchcock, a paradigm of the recurring statement Herrmann would continually use to bolt together the pieces of what David Selznick called Hitchcock's "jigsaw cutting." Spoto regards the score as nothing less than an exorcism of sex and death, "as fresh and hummable as a country tune. Like the gorgeous color, it urges an exorcism of precisely the fear and trembling that surround the two traditional American obscenities. . . . Sex and death are thus accepted like the seasons."[6] Freshness and hummability are not often associated with Herrmann, but in Spoto's reading they brighten what Puritanical Americans view as dark, a reversal of the usual Hitchcockian pattern of having music reveal concealed darkness within something deceptively cheery.

At the very beginning, in the captivating main title, Herrmann sets the ominous-merry mood: an imperious woodwind motif is contradicted by an impish tune; banal oompahs compete with somber ostinatos, the kind later used in *North by Northwest,* another comedy full of double moods and entendres. The duplicity continues through the main title into the discovery scene, where to ravishingly lyrical music, the boy discovers the body. Here, in its purest form, is Hitchcock counterpoint, the score contradicting what is on the screen. The double mood became the director's signature: Gounod's "Funeral March of a Marionette," his choice for *Alfred Hitchcock Presents* a year after *Harry* appeared in theaters, again projected jocularity with a hint of the sinister. *Harry* is a sonic version of the persona he presented in interviews, television introductions, and trailers.

Herrmann's lyricism is everywhere: in the bucolic woodwind tune during the discovery of the corpse, the beautiful horn theme during the scene displaying Sam Marlowe's paintings, and the Romantic idea floating through the finger-teacup and art-sale scenes. Equally engaging are a series of mock-formal waltzes (a form always welcomed by Hitchcock) and a courtship melody for Captain Wiles and Miss Gravely during their genial argument over who hit Harry on the head, who finished him off, and who had the right to dig him up again. At the end, Sam proposes to Jennifer with a love melody that, in its passionate longing, prefigures *Vertigo,* and all the themes suddenly come together in a comedic coda. This is elegant stuff for an off-beat comedy, as is Robert Burks's painterly photography, shimmering against the corpse-as-nuisance storyline. To remind us that this is supposed to be funny, Herrmann delivers merrily tooting woodwinds—but these take on a bizarre quirkiness since they play during the endless burying and reburying of poor Harry, the central character, who has the bad taste to be dead.

In his introductory scene, Forsythe's Sam sings "Flaggin' the Train to Tuscaloosa," a ballade with lyrics by Mack David and music by Raymond Scott. Captured in a long shot, Sam belts this tune as he approaches the camera, his voice soaring over the pastoral countryside and a montage of the film's eccentric characters, gradually drifting into vocalise colored by church chimes. It's a lovely moment, a prelude to the film's ensuing drama of disappearing love mates ("Gotta get back to Tuscaloosa, back to the girl I left behind") and a commentary on Hitchcock's love of trains ("Oh, do I love that choo-choo sound"). Defying realism, Hitchcock again embraced opera.

So quintessentially Hitchcockian is this music that Herrmann converted it into a charming suite, "A Portrait of Hitch." Dedicated to the director, the suite is a deft specimen of musical portraiture capturing Hitchcock's mischievous personality. This was apparently the way Herrmann viewed Hitchcock, as jokey and fun to be around, not as the cold authoritarian with whom he later struggled for control. Hitchcock was so benignly engaged with this project—he always maintained it was one of his favorites—that others on the set experienced him this way as well. John Forsythe called him a "glorious guy" with a "wonderful sense of humor."[7] If the humor was a little weird, no one seemed to mind.

The Trouble with Harry was indeed a portrait of its director, just as Herrmann envisioned. Breaking one of his cardinal rules, Hitchcock made it for himself, not for his audience, calling its half-million-dollar box office loss "an expensive self-indulgence." He was especially fond of the high contrast between the grotesque and the humorous, which elevated, he said, "the commonplace in life to a higher level."[8]

The score, full of exposed solos, requires delicate playing. Herrmann was not happy with the performance of Paramount's orchestra, especially the oboist, whom he berated for sloppiness. This was the beginning of the turbulent Herrmann-Hitch collaboration: the composer and director clicked marvelously on this project, but Herrmann's bitter fights with the oboe player were a warm-up for his quarrels with others, ultimately with Hitchcock himself.

One reason the rift did not happen sooner is that Herrmann's infamous tantrums were usually directed at those he felt were frauds or incompetents; he had enormous professional respect for Hitchcock, a feeling amply returned when the latter stood up for him against criticism from studio heads.

As Steven Smith points out, *The Trouble with Harry* was "Hitchcock's favorite Herrmann score for him. He thought Herrmann had done a superb job capturing the macabre humor in this subject. He knew how important music would be in carrying the delicate tone of this unusual film." This comment illustrates again that Hitchcock's music carries the film rather than accompanying it. "Herrmann knew exactly what Hitchcock was trying to achieve," Smith concludes. "He didn't just decorate the film with his music." For Hitchcock, music was never decoration, but a central part of the design.[9]

Five years later, again with Herrmann's music, he would attain the summit of comedy in *North by Northwest*, again mixing wit with mayhem, but also with suspense, sexual titillation, chases, and everything else audiences had come to love in his work. *Harry*'s failure compared to this success parallels a contrast twenty years earlier between *Rich and Strange* and *The 39 Steps*, the former a strangely static but brazenly original black comedy, the latter an audience-friendly comedy-suspenser, both rich in innovative music.

15

the man who knew too much:
doris day versus the london symphony

Doris surprised a lot of people with her acting in *The Man Who Knew Too Much*, but she didn't surprise Hitch.

—James Stewart, on Doris Day

"I'm not hearing the London Symphony!" That was Hitchcock's complaint to James Stewart during the Royal Albert Hall sequence in the 1956 remake of *The Man Who Knew Too Much*. "You're talking far too much." Never one for talk, Hitchcock was particularly irritated with it here, for it was covering Arthur Benjamin's gorgeous and gripping *Storm Clouds* Cantata, which he had commissioned twenty-two years earlier for the assassination montage in the first *Man Who Knew Too Much*, one of the most spellbinding specimens of "pure cinema."[1]

The original *Man Who Knew Too Much* united a cantata by one of Hitchcock's favorite composers with the climax of a kidnap-assassination plot in a dramatic blending of action and music. It was a marvelous idea, but Hitchcock felt the execution could have been more elegant. Twenty years later, more experienced as a movie maestro, he decided to try again, this time with considerably more technical flashiness—too much, some critics maintain. He owed Paramount a picture, and he saw his chance. This time, the movie would have a symphonic scope and richness: the cantata would play in Technicolor, not grainy black and white, in a more complex montage; the symphonic centerpiece would again be a concert at Royal Albert Hall (though what appears in the film is an astonishingly convincing mime of a prerecorded session), but in a more elaborate version featuring Hitchcock's favored composer as a character; the orchestra would be the London Symphony at its peak.

This movie would be about music, not just a brief depiction of it in a single scene. The conductor would appear on camera as a major part of the visual design. And who better to fulfill that role than Bernard Herrmann, Hitchcock's new house composer?[2] Leopold Stokowski, who had appeared in *Fantasia* with no less august a star than Mickey Mouse, was considered, but he was rumored to be impossible to work with. Herrmann, who was rapidly becoming what critics called Hitchcock's alter ego, the person giving voice to the emotions behind the images, seemed the perfect choice.

Hitchcock and his screenwriter, John Michael Hayes, greatly expanded the film's musical dimension. In addition to classical music, this *Man Who Knew Too Much* would feature pop—indeed, a pop-star heroine, Doris Day, whose work Hitchcock had seen and admired so much that he had promised her a role someday. Herrmann's formidable concert music would be set against vernacular song: high culture versus middlebrow, one of Hitchcock's favorite juxtapositions.

Hitchcock was lucky with both genres. The issue of whether to commission a new song was vexing; he was sensitive to the charge of exploiting a new tune to make money, and songs for *Spellbound* and *Notorious* had bombed. Fiercely loyal to Hitchcock, Herrmann insisted that the architecture of the finale, not commercial considerations, necessitated a song. In any case, Paramount had already hired Jay Livingston and Ray Evans to write the songs, so any ambivalence on Hitchcock's side was rendered moot. The team created "We'll Love Again" and "Golly Gee" for the movie, then decided, after being asked to come up with something "international," to use "Que Sera Sera," which they had written after viewing Joseph L. Mankiewicz's *The Barefoot Contessa*. (The title was changed to "Whatever Will Be" following the discovery that another song called "Que Sera Sera" already existed.)[3] According to Livingston, Hitchcock was in a grumpy mood about the whole matter but resolved everything swiftly: "'I need a song. I don't know what kind of song I want.' When we played 'Que Sera, Sera' for him, he said, 'Gentlemen, I told you I didn't know what kind of song I wanted.' He hesitated, then pointed a finger at us and said, 'That's the kind of song I want.' Then he got up and walked out."[4] The song proved perfect for the movie and became an Academy Award–winning hit.

Resolution of the classical piece was equally fast and felicitous. Hitchcock gave Herrmann the choice of writing a new work if he liked, but Herrmann had the judgment and taste to realize that nothing could outdo Arthur Benjamin's *Storm Clouds* Cantata from the 1934 original. Hitchcock agreed. On January 5, 1955, he sent Sidney Bernstein an inquiry about Alma's glasses, three suits made for him by Hawes and Curtis—and the rights to Benjamin's Cantata: "The musical piece that was used in the Albert Hall sequence . . . written by a composer named Arthur Benjamin. . . . Whether Gaumont British have any record of this I haven't the faintest idea, but in case we want to use this in the present version, I am sure that Paramount will require some clearance. Of course, it is quite possible that all the actual material has been destroyed." On February 11, the music director Roy Fjastad contacted Benjamin for the rights, though he was not altogether sure what the piece was about. "I believe," he wrote Benjamin, "it was composed in such a manner as to reach a climax involving a cymbal crash at the very instant that a murder was being committed."[5]

At first it appeared the request would present troubles. Bernstein reminded Hitchcock of the snafu over Addinsell's *Under Capricorn:* "It is impossible for us to get the rights to the original sound track of 'The Man Who Knew Too Much' or the music used on the track. This contains licensed music which, in England, is licensed for one film only, and it is impossible to transfer the copyright to anybody. You probably remember when we were negotiating with Richard Adenfel (sp?) for 'Under Capricorn.' Victor (Peers) went to endless trouble to try and get the rights to music in perpetuity, and although he met with the Composers' Association he was unable to get anything different from what is usual here. When the film comes to 'an end,' the rights of music expire."

But matters took a quick, positive turn. On February 25, Benjamin wrote, "I have located, at long last, the Full Score. . . . The Orchestral Material, Chorus Parts have been destroyed but you may be interested to have the orchestration for the 'Oratorio Section': 3 flutes, 2 oboes, 2 bassoons, 4 horns, 3 trumpets, 2 tenor trombones, 1 bass trombone, tuba, 3 timpani, bass drum, cymbal, harp, large gong, triangle, organ, strings mixed chorus." On March 11, Fjastad wrote Benjamin: "Hitch has decided to use it, congratulations. Can we reconstruct the score 'by extracting the individual parts from the master orchestra score?' Hitch wants to 'elongate the playing time of this composition by about 1 and a half minutes.' Can you do this?" In a March 24 night wire, Benjamin accepted, agreeing to "rewrite additional music." Finally, on May 15, Gainsborough Pictures, the successor to Gaumont, gave the rights for the Cantata to Paramount for five hundred pounds.

Herrmann enhanced Benjamin's orchestration with new colors for harp, organ, and brass.[6] Herrmann's experience with the London Symphony Orchestra was decidedly happier than his quarrelsome (and more typical) one with the studio orchestra in *The Trouble with Harry.* He worked well with the LSO, leading a performance that was colorful and exciting in the Cantata, lean and incisive in his underscore. After the shooting, the LSO players presented Herrmann with a book on the symphony, inscribed "The Man Who Knows So Much." (Later, he would fight bitterly with the orchestra, especially over the hiring of the "jazz boy" André Previn as musical director.)

Benjamin recommended Muir Mathieson, who would later conduct *Vertigo,* as maestro, but Hitchcock was set on Herrmann himself. In addition, he got from Herrmann an exceptionally moody score for the suspense scenes leading up to the Royal Albert Hall montage: this was the first Herrmann-Hitchcock thriller (*The Trouble with Harry* being something else entirely), with music that was compelling on its own and the nucleus of masterpieces to come. The confluence of Benjamin's Cantata, Doris Day's songs, and Herrmann's score again demolished the myth of cinematic music being invisible. As Murray Pomerance put it, "Here Hitchcock advances a step further than any other filmmaker has done, dramaturgically shifting the music on occasion to a foreground role as important as any other roles in the film. No longer a merely visual form decorated by music, the film is here transferred into visual music itself, even opera, in which the director's profound contemplation of our dramatic condition finds release."[7] Hitchcock had actually begun this shift much earlier, using music as foreground and opera in *Blackmail, Waltzes from Vienna, Stage Fright,* and other films; but *The Man Who Knew Too Much* raised the ante. Herrmann conducts on camera; far from being the composer of invisible music, he is a commanding presence, his name emblazoned in close-up on the program outside Royal Albert Hall before Jo goes in.

Completing a happy picture was a setting that cried out for vivid music: filming on location in Morocco provided a spectacular market sequence, and a restaurant with hopelessly tiny seats for an oversized James Stewart was a made-to-order setting for the requisite Hitchcock food-foible scene. The North African ambiance gave Hitchcock the opportunity to experiment with chants and drumming in a way he hadn't tried since *Rich and Strange.* This music would be richer and stranger than ever.

Music defines the movie from the beginning. A shiver of percussion announces Bernard Herrmann's majestically sinister main title, played on-screen by the London Symphony as the camera in a medium shot watches the brass and timpani, gradually closing on the cymbals as the player spreads his arms for the final crash. The seven-note fanfare—a dark variation on the original *Man Who Knew Too Much* main title, itself a riff on the *Storm Clouds* fanfare—is interrupted by an anguished string line suggesting tortured ambivalence.[8] This double mood, opulence undermined by anxiety, telegraphs the *Storm Clouds* montage.

That Hitchcock would use a symphony orchestra playing on camera as a galvanizing opening typifies his trust in music. It also speaks volumes about that era. Such a prelude would not, alas, be possible now, except in an art film. In the age of Stokowski and Bernstein, the image of a symphony still had commercial cachet; the music could sell the movie. (Now, the inverse is true: Bernard Herrmann is a cult figure only because he worked for celebrity auteurs like Hitchcock and Scorsese. His career as a concert composer is known only to his most devoted admirers.)

The symphonic opening sets the tone and lays out the substance: a sentence appears on the screen during the deafening crash of cymbals, declaring the movie's theme: "a single crash of cymbals and how it rocked the lives of an American family." The cymbals continue to resonate in the first scene, segueing into the sound of the tour bus. Soon to rock their lives, it is for now a subliminal shimmer. As Hitchcock put it in his exacting sound note for the opening reel, "At the very outset, the ring of the cymbals should carry over into the whine of the tires on the roadway." Through this subtlest of sound montages, the audience is subconsciously prepared for what is to come.

The Man Who Knew Too Much pits the messy ambivalence of life against the perfection and closure of music. Music is first corrupted by evil conspirators into an instrument of violence, then re-created by the heroine as a force of healing and transfiguration. The classical piece is shattered by a scream; the popular song, as in *Rear Window,* brings everything together. Music tames the wild beasts, Doris Day playing an unlikely Orpheus, but only after it has aided them in a near-lethal attack.

In both cases, it is the heroine who faces the music. Traveling with her family in Morocco, Josephine McKenna suspects that they are being spied upon; her husband, Ben, a prominent Midwest doctor, dismisses her suspicions as nonsense. Jo also thinks her husband has unwisely divulged private family information to a too-slick, self-appointed Arab mentor named Louis Bernard. Ben rejects that warning too. Indeed, at every point he ridicules her intuitions about the conspiracy gathering around them. Jo turns out to be right in every instance, just as she is correct about later details such as

"Chapell" being a place rather than a name. When the McKennas' son, Hank, is kidnapped and they find themselves enmeshed in an assassination plot hatched by the couple Jo has suspected of watching them, Ben continues to suppress her, refusing to tell her their son has been kidnapped until he has pumped her with drugs. Fortunately, Jo's instincts prove as sure in solving the crisis as in seeing it coming. Through music, she saves everyone: the Prime Minister, her son, and the family trust that has been unraveling since the opening scene. She is like Iris in *The Lady Vanishes*, another so-called hysterical woman who turns out to be correct about everything, in another movie where music saves the day. Equally striking is her resemblance to Lisa in *Rear Window*, who is also ridiculed by a contemptuous Jimmy Stewart for (correctly) relying on woman's intuition.

Jo first saves the day by anticipating a cymbal cue timed to cover the gunshot that kills the Prime Minister—a musical touch the composer "would have appreciated," says Drayton, the chief plotter, echoing Abbott's line in the original *Man Who Knew Too Much*. This perversion of art by an assassin is a rare Hitchcock variation; music can be a vehicle for exposing an evildoer, as in *Young and Innocent;* it can be a secret code to fight fascism, as in *The Lady Vanishes;* it can signify the unpleasant truth that bad people can have good taste, as in *Notorious* and many other of his films; or it can be ineffectual in bringing light to darkness, as in *Vertigo*. But it is not often manipulated as a direct means of doing harm.

The famous Albert Hall scene is a thrilling interaction between music and movement, an elaborate version of two favored Hitchcock designs: the chase and ballet. As Bill Krohn puts it, the many pieces in the montage are "partners in a great dance."[9] Even the tuning of the orchestra generates eerie suspense as the assassin floats ghostlike down the lobby stairs from long shot to creepy close-up, warning Jo to keep her mouth shut. From here, Jo begins her attempts to piece together the conspiracy; like other Hitchcock heroines—Constance, Lisa, and her predecessor in the first *Man Who Knew Too Much*—she must become the detective and protagonist, searching for the right decision in the midst of moral chaos.

Like the title sequence, Herrmann's onscreen appearance draws an implicit parallel between maestro and director: Herrmann is the director of the complex score, just as Hitchcock is the manipulator of a 126-shot montage of instruments, singers, assassin, victim, heroine, hero, audience, and score, each image in rhythm with music building in real time. The montage slashes and fragments what we see, but the music sustains what we hear in an unbroken line, the chorus singing of "whispered terror," "nameless fear," and "finding release" in the breaking storm clouds. As usual in Hitchcock, light exists only in relation to extreme darkness and breaks through only after a great struggle.

The remake of the movie has a small but telling change in the Wyndham Lewis libretto that makes it less literal, more poetic than the original:

Solo
All save the child—all save the child
Around whose heads screaming
The night birds wheeled and shot away

In the new version, "All save the child" is changed to "Yet stood the trees," a less specific line. The emotional resonance is no longer limited to a kidnapped-child scenario. Hitchcockians have long assumed that Herrmann made the change, just as he tinkered with Benjamin's orchestration, but the archives tell a different story.[10] The "child" line is crossed out by pen and the new one inserted in handwriting that is not Herrmann's. When I showed the edited libretto to Christopher Husted of Bernard Herrmann Music, he identified the handwriting as Benjamin's. Herrmann did make a quick final check of the libretto, as a memo of April 18 from Herbert Coleman indicates: "Herbie Coleman to Bernie: Will you please check the text of the enclosed for accuracy before we send it on for censorship approval." At the bottom, the libretto is okayed in a hand different from the one that made the text alteration.

The new emphasis on abstract anxiety is ironically appropriate, for it is difficult to hear the words in either version of the film. The counterpoint between sound and image is what rivets our attention. The tempo of both music and action is Allegro Agitato rising in steady crescendo, the Covent Garden Chorus singing with full force; the assassin preparing for the kill; Ben rushing about breaking into boxes; the police bumbling around with their usual incompetence; the cymbal player readying his instrument for the final crash, each cymbal viewed from opposite sides of the screen as the camera looks between them at Herrmann conducting; the score in close-up leading with rests to the fatal cymbal crash; Jo's face contorting as she struggles to decide between saving her son and the ambassador; the latter thrusting his considerable stomach out, as if asking for it; the killer eyeing him seductively from the box. "Look lovingly at him," Hitchcock told Reggie Nalder, "as if you're glancing at a beautiful woman."[11]

Anyone who has been to Albert Hall knows its diabolical suitability for this montage. It is a grand dome, rather like the Roman Colosseum, with

The Man Who Knew Too Much. **A cymbal crash rocks an American family.**

huge circles stretching around the hall to the orchestra, guaranteed to in-
duce anxiety in anyone attempting to locate a specific person in one of its
many boxes. The design reflects Jo's suffering, an endless circle of searching
and entrapment; she is alone in her dilemma, facing the huge space, caught
in the desolation of losing a child, and at the same time seeing an adult life
about to be snuffed out. Embodying her terror, the hall becomes a sounding
board for her catharsis—her shattering, life-saving scream, the release
telegraphed in the libretto.

When Ben and Jo find each other, they talk excitedly—but we hear
nothing: all speech is obliterated by music, which refuses to recede to the
background. Hitchcock's sound notes for this reel are emphatic: "The main
sound will remain exactly as the existing music track from beginning to
end." The original script had elaborate dialogue; the audience was to hear
Ben and Jo's abrasive exchange, as well as other dialogue in the lobby. But
during shooting, Hitchcock asked everyone to stop talking: "Why don't you
cut the dialogue and let us hear the music?" Everyone on the set thought he
had lost his judgment, if not his marbles, but once the talk was eliminated
the sequence became strangely compelling.

Here is Hitchcock's ultimate rejection of "photographs of people talking." We don't need to hear what Jo and Ben are saying; music and imagery
tell the story far more effectively. *Storm Clouds* blankets everything, blast-

ing at full volume even in the lobby and hallways. In real life, the orchestra would be muted by the time it traveled that far. "We have taken dramatic license," Hitchcock explains in his sound note, "to preserve the same volume of sound whether we are in the hall, the lobby or the corridor and this should remain so in order not to disturb the music unity of the cantata." Benjamin's score, shown in giant close-up as Herrmann flips the pages, is all-important. At all costs, music unity must be preserved.

For Hitchcock, who favored counterpoint over synchronization, music existed in its own abstract space and time. The band plays on in *Strangers on a Train* during the most traumatic scenes; the waltz continues in *Rebecca* during the excruciating Manderley masquerade ball. For Claudia Gorban, an astute critic of cinema sound tracks, the music's refusal to participate in the emotion of a scene carries its own strange emotional charge: "Musical time is abstract time. Once begun, a piece's musical logic demands to work itself through to the finish. This is what can put music at odds with human time, which is less logically predictable time, more subject to the aleatory experiences of 'real life.' The Hitchcock examples testify to the power of this music which blissfully lacks awareness or empathy; its very emotionlessness, juxtaposed with ensuing human catastrophe, is what provokes our emotional response."[12] Like the songs in *Rear Window* during suspenseful scenes, the Cantata increases tension by complicating or contradicting the narrative. The alternation between major and minor fanfares in the prelude suggests the glory of the music versus Jo's excruciating experience of it; Benjamin's echo of *Tristan* harmonies captures her ambivalence (as *Tristan* itself does in Herbert Marshall's moment of truth in *Murder!*); thunderous brass in the fanfare fires Ben's frantic searching and Jo's mounting crisis, even as its exultant mood ignores their anguish.

As the main title promises, a symphony orchestra in all its majesty becomes a formidable engine of drama and suspense, a force that can change everything. Hitchcock could have chosen a more modern score for the LSO to play, something overtly anxiety producing or terrifying; Herrmann, after all, was his composer. But as Irwin Bazelon points out, such a choice would have produced a very different effect, less credible and exciting: "Benjamin's cantata is exactly the kind of conservative, English concert piece one would expect to find on a subscription concert program. It was probably chosen because its climactic signpost, the cymbal clash, would be easy for the assassin to pinpoint. If, for example, the piece had been avant-garde, the complexity of the music could have made it difficult for the unmusical killer to spot his gun cue—although the strongly accented, discordant impacts of a contemporary work might have stimulated audience restlessness and given him more than one opportunity to fire his shot. On the other hand, the long cinematic and musical crescendo leading up to the explosive cymbal crash would have been destroyed, and with it all the mounting tension."[13]

This sensible analysis still begs the question of how, even with a conservative work, the killer can possibly time his shot for the exact second of the cymbal cue. Clearly, the viewer is not meant to ask this sort of question. Hitchcock teases us into thinking that this assassination plot is more realistic than the one in the original movie: he has Drayton put the phonograph needle on the cymbal cue twice, for example, not once, and places someone who can read a score next to the killer. In any case, the impact of the scene is meant to be aesthetic, as Hitchcock emphasized at every point. His memo to the sound department, for instance, asks the engineer to "sweeten the cymbal crash." Benjamin's cantata exists independently of the deadly drama in Royal Albert Hall, transcending it even as its crescendo provides the requisite mounting tension, a sublime example of cinematic counterpoint.

The only instrument allowed to compete with the London Symphony and Covent Garden Chorus is Doris Day's scream. The first real music we have heard in twelve minutes, it is a powerful moment, a release of unimaginable pent-up agony, strong enough to throw off the gunman's aim and save the ambassador's life. Jo is a singer finally using her voice again. Just why or when she decides to do so for the sake of a stranger rather than remain silent for her son (an issue much debated by critics) is a mystery. (It is also possible, as we have seen in our analysis of the first *Man Who Knew Too Much*, to interpret the scream as an eruption of anguish and confusion.) Benjamin's music replaces explanations and interior monologue: all we know is that the split second before the crash of those imposing cymbals, she has her moment of truth, whether or not she has already arrived at it subconsciously. Hitchcock scored the scream and its impact like a composer. "The hubbub of the crowd should start a bit as Doris has screamed," he instructs in the notes; "she screams and although there is an immediate response, it should grow until the assassin falls, then it should treble in intensity because of the new element that has come into the disturbance."

A concert normally delivers repose and closure rather than disturbance. Jo is allowed to perform that function as well, but only at the end of the movie, where the order of music finally displaces the uncertainty of life.

This finale combines Jo's saving her career, at least for the moment, with saving her son. "That's my mother's voice!" cries Hank, on the verge of deliverance.

The murder and kidnap plots are parallel crises, each featuring Doris Day in a dramatic concert. Jo's singing career has been interrupted by a repressive 1950s culture and an authoritarian husband. Ben treats Jo like a hysterical child, forcing her to take drugs when she reacts emotionally to the abduction of their son and attempting to shut her out of all attempts to recover him. That he has the right to crush her singing career is simply assumed by the zeitgeist the film so accurately depicts and subtly critiques.

The kidnap rescue is set up early in the film when Jo and Hank sing a duet of "Que Sera Sera," followed by Hank's whistling the tune. "Whatever Will Be Will Be" eases the threat of *Storm Clouds:* when Jo screams to save the Prime Minister, she relinquishes control over what happens to her son, something she cannot really control in any case; when she performs for the Prime Minister, her song seems to travel up the stairs with a life of its own, connecting with Hank's echoing whistle, providing, in the words of the Prime Minister, "a tranquil coda to conclude a dramatic evening." The musical symmetry is cemented by Mrs. Drayton's decision to save Hank by directing him to whistle with his mother in another duet—her own musical moment of truth.

It was critical for Hitchcock to avoid anticlimax after the powerful Royal Albert Hall scene, and therefore essential to hire a diva like Doris Day. As James Stewart pointed out, Day's singing voice was a fundamental part of her performance: "Doris surprised a lot of people with her acting in *The Man Who Knew Too Much*, but she didn't surprise Hitch, who knew what to expect from her. A singer's talent for phrasing, the ability to put heart in a piece of music, is not too far removed from acting, in which the aim is to give life and believability to what's on paper."[14]

Hitchcock made clear in his sound notes that he wanted Day's song to carry: "When Doris starts to sing we must make sure that she is deliberately projecting her voice and this is most essential when we come to voice loud over the exit door of the ballroom. And when we come into the hallway for our first pan shot we should still feel conscious she is singing loud deliberately. . . . After Drayton's entry, the background remains Doris's voice and during the descent of the stairs, increases in volume as it originally decreased as we went up the stairs." These finicky crescendos and decrescendos are like dynamic markings in a score. Unlike the montage in Albert Hall, where music maintains a consistent level, the sound track here is realistic. Jo's voice increases and recedes as the camera travels down and up the stairs.

The Man Who Knew Too Much. Hitchcock directs Doris Day.

(Originally, Hitchcock wanted Herrmann to write music that would mingle with Day's singing as the camera tracked up the stairs, but he finally decided to allow her vocals to carry the scene entirely.) The music unity of the cantata is the centerpiece of the earlier scene; Hitchcock wants us to hear everything leading up to the all-important cymbal crash. Here, the drama depends on how music would actually travel, with Hank hearing only a wisp of his mother's song at the top of the huge house, just enough to respond with his whistle. The mother-son duet interrupted in the hotel is now completed.

Jo's character is predicated on her being a star of her time, neither ours nor the perennially chic twenties and thirties. This is a 1950s movie, and its heroine is the avatar of a conservative Rodgers and Hammerstein style.[15] The year 1955 was still the prerock era; Jo is definitely not a rocker, nor even a bopper. "I'm not one for this terrible Bebop," says Drayton in the restaurant scene, trying to ingratiate himself to Jo, who is poignantly aware she would still be a star were it not for the sexist culture she represents. She acidly informs the Draytons that her career is only temporarily on hold, despite what Ben says; Broadway musicals "are not produced in Indianapolis, Indiana. Of course, we *could* live in New York. I hear the doctors aren't starving there, either." Ben's retort is typically brusque: "It would be hard for my patients to come from Indianapolis for treatment." Until the final scene, he has scant confidence in the voice that finally saves his son, even though the crowd of adoring fans awaiting her at the London airport indicates she is by no means incapable of generating income. Her duets with Hank represent the viability of raising her boy as she sustains her career.

We never know whether Jo ultimately saves her career along with the lives of the Prime Minister and her son, though it is hard to imagine her going back to things as they were with Ben. Hers will probably not be background music for much longer. As with *Rear Window,* where another 1950s heroine faces off against a stubborn and obsessive Jimmy Stewart, music suggests a cautiously hopeful standoff. "We'll Love Again," Jo's final song, suggests a new beginning.

But Doris Day doesn't quite get the final tune. Hitchcock's sound note gives it to his musical alter ego: "After Jimmy Stewart's line about going to pick up Hank, Mr. Herrmann will take over." This he does, booming away with brass-timpani flourishes reprising the main title, but now in a happy major key. Herrmann's contribution, aside from appearing as LSO maestro, has often been underestimated. He provides not just functional underscoring, as some have said, but significant and original music that is the nucleus for better-known scores. A floating premonition of the Carlotta theme in *Vertigo* gives the checkers scene with the kidnapped Hank a mysterious poignancy; low winds creeping around Jo as she ventures on her own to Ambrose Chapel forecast *North by Northwest.* Who but Herrmann could create the flitting, mothlike line (a speedup of the secondary theme in the main title) that bites Ben's ear in the grim phone call from the kidnappers?

(A Hitchcock memo calls for "sinister music" and asks that it play through the phone call until Ben speaks to Drayton.)

Herrmann's spareness is a satisfying balance to the saturation of Benjamin's music in the Royal Albert sequence. As usual, Hitchcock's music acts as a concise narrator. The tip-off to the audience that all is not right in the McKenna's hotel is entrusted to Herrmann, as Hitchcock indicated in another memo: "Benny to consider musical motif for the Assassin. In bedroom scene—Mamounia Hotel—Assassin coming to door of McKenna suite—we have deliberately left out any comment on him by the McKennas, so that musically we can make a point about the mysterious reaction of Louis Bernard to this intrusion."

One of the most exciting moments, the tumultuous market scene, features syncopated Arab drumming gradually blending with low, creepy suspensions during the fatal Louis Bernard chase—hip stuff for a 1955 Hollywood product. Suddenly, the drums disappear and a stabbing dissonance announces Bernard's killing. Hitchcock specified that Herrmann's music should pound through the entire scene, stopping only when the Arab "pulls Ben down to whisper to him." The marketplace sounds "should be kept pretty low so that we can hear very clearly the cry of pain"; ultimately, all noise was removed.

The music undercuts conventional wisdom that Hitchcock lacks a sense of wonder. What could be more wondrous than the Muslim chants under a crescent moon in the beautifully lit hotel scene, poetically described by Hitchcock in the sound notes as coming from a distance "as though floating over the night air"? What could be more slyly mysterious than Herrmann's creeping woodwind glissandos and slithering strings mutating into restaurant music? The score also provides a saving humanity. In *Hitchcock's Films Revisited,* Robin Wood asserts that "the shots of Doris Day's voice traveling up the stairs (so to speak) are among the most moving in the whole of Hitchcock" and offers a personal testimonial: "Middle-aged academics are not supposed to admit that they burst into tears every time Doris Day sings 'Che sera sera,' but in my case it is a fact."[16] Especially touching is Hitchcock's delivery of sentiment without sentimentality: when Hank rushes into the arms of his parents, the reunion is recorded for a second in the corner of the screen rather than with tearful close-ups and obvious reaction shots.

Music provides the Hitchcockian balance between suspense and humor. One of the funnier moments is the awful singing of a church hymn about dire premonitions (deftly composed for the film), cued with precise auditory emphases: "The choir singing should remain as is and make sure when Jimmy and Doris sing that his voice is pretty much the same volume as the rest. Or rather should I say the rest of the singing should be brought up to maintain the same level throughout. It is only when Doris sings that it should be brought up to the rest so it directs attention to her." The most memorable comic sounds come from Herrmann in the swirling string number during Ben's slapstick "tussle" (as Hitchcock called it) with taxidermists and tigers' teeth.

Hitchcock's final sound note is as droll as the scene it describes. After the numerous befuddlements of the McKennas' unlucky house guests, whose party has been interrupted with Buñuel-like frequency by Ben and Jo's frenetic comings and goings, the guests at this party-that-never-happens finally conk out and are snoozing away when the reunited McKennas come rushing back to the hotel: "Special note: when we get back to the apartment, a couple of ladylike snores might be permitted."

This *Man Who Knew Too Much* has undergone unusual twists and turns in its reception. Dismissed for years as slick and overwrought compared to the original, it made a comeback in the twenty-first century, spurred to a large extent by new attention to its unique music.[17] The strangest twist came much earlier: Doris Day hated "Que Sera Sera," denouncing it as silly and embarrassing, but it ended up being her most popular song, another indication of the mysterious durability of Hitchcock's music.

16

the wrong man: music from the dark side of the moon

> I want it very cold and very factual.
>
> —Bernard Herrmann's instructions to his orchestra

The Wrong Man is about a wrongly imprisoned bass player who has good reason to pluck the blues. According to Henry Fonda, who plays Manny Balestrero, the downbeat hero, this was a uniquely challenging assignment, but not for the lines he had to learn. "Memorizing the scripts is a cinch. Learning to thump a bass viol for the Warner film was something else again. . . . Hitchcock insisted I actually learn to play four numbers." Fonda had "tootled on the trumpet" at the University of Minnesota, the extent of his musical experience. He spent six weeks studying with Allen Stanley, learning the finger movements for numbers like "Mambo 5" and "Shi-Shi-Shi."[1]

Fonda's enforced bass lessons are an indication of Hitchcock's determination to make *The Wrong Man* look, feel, and sound authentic. The characters are singularly unglamorous, the black-and-white cinematography gritty and ungratifying. Hitchcock's films have a strong grounding in reality and often center on ordinary people, but they are generously overlaid with comedy, aesthetic playfulness, and dreamlike effects. Little of that is here, unless one counts the hallucinatory camera work inside Manny's cell or the ambiguously supernatural miracle near the end, a nice trick that still has critics guessing and interpreting.[2] Departing from his usual trademarks, Hitchcock made this film as a faithful telling of a true story, appearing on camera at the beginning to tell us what we are about to see is factual, a far cry from his witty cameos and sardonic television introductions. This is his only cameo that isn't fun.

The Wrong Man. **Henry Fonda plays Bernard Herrmann's jazz Prelude at the Stork Club.**

This film must have had a deep and personal meaning for Hitchcock, or he would not have violated his usual procedures and doggedly plunged ahead in a project for which he donated his services. A consummate audience pleaser, he must have known this desolate movie would not easily sell tickets, yet he made it anyway—then followed it with *Vertigo,* another dark, personal experiment, though replete with gorgeous colors and visual effects.

Ostensibly, what drew Hitchcock to the story was the childhood trauma, recounted throughout his career as a set piece, in which his father took a misbehaving young Alfred to the local constable and had him thrown in a cell for a dreadful twenty minutes or so, an eternity for a child. Whether this incident is true or whether his neurosis had to do with broader experiences—childhood abandonment, Catholic guilt—Hitchcock had an obsessive dread of being imprisoned by police, which he projects in film after film, this one the most literal and specific. The "wrong man" motif in so many of his movies here becomes the entire narrative: an innocent man is locked up for a crime someone else has committed, his life torn apart, his wife unhinged so badly she is imprisoned too—in an asylum. Then, just as arbitrarily, the right man is found and the wrong one released. End of story. No romantic interest, quirky minor characters, or subtexts.

Yet *The Wrong Man* is undeniably haunting. We emerge from it in a cranky mood, but we don't easily forget it. Like Flannery O'Connor, Hitch-cock was a Catholic immersed in Poe and Kafka, and the spirits of both per-meate this film: it has a dark Poesque claustrophobia and a Kafkaesque nightmarishness in its depiction of an innocent man suddenly imprisoned by an all-powerful authority for something he didn't do and doesn't know about. In another perverse jolt, one worthy of a Hawthorne short story, he is just as suddenly released. How he goes on from there, his life and family having been decimated, we are not shown.

This is another Hitchcock movie in which music is central to the narra-tive. Manny's career as a musician is a bond of humanity that holds his fam-ily together, at least for awhile. In *Waltzes from Vienna,* music is an occasion for bitter competition between father and son. Here, it is a manifestation of love and connectedness between Manny and his boys. Manny works hard for little money but passes on a valuable legacy to his children. While prac-ticing a Mozart piano Minuet, Manny's son Bob is joined by his younger brother, Greg, who attempts an uninvited harmonica duet. When Bob pounds the keys and shouts at Greg to desist, Manny gently intervenes, urg-ing Bob never to give up or "let anything throw you off the beat." He assures the boys they both have talent and promises to give them music lessons, a pledge that becomes an emblem of hope after disaster strikes. "He'll give us music lessons as soon as he can," one of his boys says, desperately trying to console his brother following their father's arrest. The promised lessons be-come the children's mantra to keep them sane, just as Manny's Stork Club performances, intercut into the story line during his bail, sustain him. As in *Saboteur,* music and performance are linked with trust and innocence in the face of injustice. Manny's speech to his sons about not allowing anything to throw them off the beat becomes key to both his survival·and his children's. His wife, Rose, the only member of the family who does not play an instru-ment, has a complete breakdown.

The authorities who imprison Manny view his job with suspicion and hostility. A family man should have a normal job. Being a professional mu-sician is bad enough; playing jazz is worse. In 1956, jazz (soon to be dis-placed by rock and roll as an object of demonization) was viewed by much of society as both a cause and a reflection of deviant behavior. The police use Manny's Stork Club gig as part of their case against him—all those "women, drinks, a pretty high old time there." The staid Manny—probably the only Hitchcock hero who *doesn't* drink—could actually use a high old time, but that doesn't matter. Jazz and related forms of dance music form a slippery slope; Manny is automatically a suspicious character.

Hitchcock reverses the usual moral equation, presenting the police as cold and unfeeling, men without music; when Manny is interrogated and put on trial, music ceases, a silence consistent with other Hitchcock police-station and courtroom scenes. Manny may be relentlessly ordinary, but once he is convicted and sent to prison, he becomes a musical martyr, canonized at the end by a cue called "Prayer" and a mysterious montage of a Christ figure looming over a superimposed image of a criminal double as he plays at the Stork Club before his resurrection from darkness.

Denying catharsis, the bleak score by Bernard Herrmann increases pity and terror rather than releasing it. After the genteel pastorale of *The Trouble with Harry* and the classical-pop of *The Man Who Knew Too Much,* Herrmann was entrusted to create something grittier, more urban and contemporary. This was not necessarily the original scenario. Hitchcock considered using jazz standards; he had Herbert Coleman order three sets of 78s that included "Brazil," "Jalousie," and "Begin the Beguine." The legal team was instructed to engage a "Latin male vocalist." But by the time the sparse cue sheet (twenty-nine cues) emerged in December 1956, Herrmann was listed as the only composer, the sole exception being Mozart, whose Minuet Herrmann arranged as the piano-harmonica duet for Manny's sons.[3] Hitchcock knew he would get something special; he had so much faith in Herrmann that he pressured Warner Brothers into raising the composer's fee. *The Wrong Man* suffered at the box office, but discerning critics praised Herrmann: *Variety* admired the "simple yet effective score"; the *New York Post* spoke of the "excellent musical score by that master of the medium."[4]

Hitchcock knew that his faux-documentary style in this picture could benefit from Herrmann's methods. The violinist Louis Kaufman once remarked that Herrmann "had his own conceptions of sound. We tried to please him and be as expressive as we possibly could—a lot of vibrato and so forth—and he immediately shut down on it. . . . 'Cool it down! I don't want a hot sound. . . . I want it very cold and very factual.'"[5] With his penchant for muted strings and trumpets, low woodwinds, and sinister clusters, Herrmann was able to create something very factual to complement *The Wrong Man*'s stark images.

This is an early "black and white score for a black and white movie" (Herrmann's famous description of *Psycho*). Indeed, it is even starker and more monochromatic. *Psycho* has the most sensational musical effects in film history, all the more so in that they are achieved by strings alone. There is nothing sensational about *The Wrong Man*. Even the Latin-jazz Prelude that Fonda plays in the Stork Club (a favorite Hitchcock hangout) in the main title has been criticized as limp and insufficiently jazzy—a misunderstanding of its function, since it accurately represents the dour Manny Balestrero, whose drearily regimented lower-middle-class existence in the 1950s is anything but jazzy.[6] At the end of the main title, Manny appears on the left of the screen standing rigidly, like a marionette, a striking contrast to the festive balloons floating above.

Hitchcock's use of jazz here is consistent with his other movies: an exuberant surface barely hides a feeling of danger. Hitchcock's vision of the form resembled that of his fellow European émigrés, notably Ernst Krenek, who called jazz "the new unknown world of freedom."[7] Jazz is risky—it marks Manny as a shady character in the eyes of the police—but also liberating, as the camera shows in an elegant close-up of Manny's bass next to a saxophone just before his dramatic exoneration. This complexity echoes the scene in *Rear Window* where the jazz ensemble in the composer's living room cues the menacing arrival of Thorwald at the precise moment it saves Miss Lonely Hearts's life.

Hitchcock got what he needed from Herrmann. Marked "Allegro Brillante," the Prelude has a lugubrious undercurrent, with a jaunty fanfare undercut by a pensive woodwind countertheme. Herrmann favored contrasting, widely spaced colors; here he sets Manny's bass pizzicato against high, snarling brass. This music is central to the picture. Uniting score, source music, and the hero's profession, it is unobtrusive but insistent; it gets under our skin and stays there, creating a claustrophobia matched by the confining bars that appear everywhere in the movie, even in the insurance office Manny allegedly robs, culminating in the camera's excruciatingly detailed inspection of Manny's cell as he paces in mounting panic. Everything grows from the ostensibly upbeat but strangely pensive Prelude; Manny's bass begins in the narrative as a real Latin American number played in a club, then stalks like an apprehensive ghost through the rest of the film: into his children's bedroom when he peeks in on them; into "The Car," following his apprehension by the police, who tell him the pickup is "just a routine matter. . . . There is nothing for an innocent man to worry about"; into "The Store" and "Second Store" where he is misidentified by the owners; into the precinct office where he is fingerprinted; and into the cell, where the bass sinks lower as the brass spit higher, then spin out of control, following the camera circling Manny's terrified face intercut with his anxious children as they wait for their father to come home. In the scenes preceding the imprisonment, the bass plucks repeating patterns of major seconds and minor thirds against low woodwinds, evoking an inevitable catastrophe that contradicts the police's insistence that Manny, if innocent, has nothing to fear: music speaks far more truthfully than words.

The music notes from August, four months before the film's release, have numerous parenthetical and speculative instructions, but the imprisonment scene, the most powerful in the film, was fully planned:

> Music starts at finger printing and continues through to Manny being led to front desk for booking by Lieutenant. Here it stops. Music starts again when cell door slams—sneaks in and very soft . . . from Manny pacing in cell TO Manny being led along catwalk at Long Island City Jail prior to being put in cell. . . . Full Stork Club band starts on Manny's turn to look at bed . . . continues through cell scene getting louder and louder and gradually losing instruments one by one until double bass is only instrument playing when cut of Manny's clenched fists is on the screen. Music increases rhythm with the picture and finally fades out. Music starts again and continues through all the tank scenes up to Warder: Let's go, men.[8]

The combination of intensity and emptiness—the music "getting louder and louder and gradually losing instruments"—was thus calculated early on. Simply called "Cell 1" and "Cell 2," this cue brilliantly dramatizes anxiety and isolation. Herrmann did make changes. The full Stork Club band called for in the notes became, in the final version, a grim percussion explosion spreading out, then thinning and vanishing. And though the notes stipulate that Manny's lonely bass is left as the only instrument playing when he clenches his fists, Herrmann did not eliminate the brass. This is an instance when he ignored the literal instruction while heightening its intent; far from covering the despairing emptiness of the double bass, the muted trumpets intensify it. From here, Herrmann followed the notes precisely: the music increases rhythm with a frantically circling fanfare, then fades out on an excruciating minor second for brass and low woodwinds.

Herrmann refuses to indulge in the kind of lyricism that any Hollywood composer writing for a dark film—John Williams in *Minority Report* (his own "black and white" score), Herrmann himself in *Taxi Driver*—usually offers as respite. But the score does have an understated compassion. Icy as it is, Herrmann's music humanizes what would otherwise be unbearable. A powerful example is Manny's brief reunion with his family after being released on bail. The orchestration is limited to winds, and the restraint pays off. Henry Fonda's "I never knew what my boys meant to me until now" is not sentimental but emotionally resonant; the gentle music has the same quality. This understated cue is like Henry Fonda's acting, which Hitchcock admired: it speaks softly, with eloquent authenticity.

Manny's wife, Rose, played with uncompromising ashenness by Vera Miles, is the other victim of law and order. In "Farmhouse," a piercing harp against a snowy landscape and Manny's relentlessly pacing bass evoke her despair over the family's inability to corroborate Manny's alibi. Unison winds depict her collapse into dementia, brilliantly dramatized in the casual details of Miles's performance: her empty eyes and distracted scratching. (The music notes describe her "vacant look" during scenes with Manny's lawyer.) In the ugliest cue, "The Mirror," her guilt delusions flash into rage as she strikes her husband with a hairbrush, smashing a mirror that reflects his shattered face; the madness is made more palpable by splintering glass, a chiming alarm clock, and a rumbling subway (a haunting noise throughout the film) counterpointing Herrmann's gloomy woodwinds and harp.

Summarizing the world of the film, Rose's psychiatrist describes her as trapped in "a maze of terror" and existing on "the dark side of the moon," a mental wasteland the music captures with spectral organ music called "The Parting" (precursor of the graveyard organ in *Vertigo*) as Manny takes her to the asylum. Beginning with *Secret Agent,* continuing with the novachord in the *Rebecca* era, and culminating in avant-garde sonorities in Herrmann and Williams, Hitchcock used the king of instruments to cue psychological states, in this case crushing depression. In a heartbreaking montage, what the music notes call a "boisterous" version of the Prelude blasts from the Stork Club as the right man is apprehended and Manny is cleared; all Rose can utter, to Herrmann's blackest music, is, "That's fine for you," as the camera slowly inspects her asylum corridor, much as it did Manny's prison (and exactly as it would Scottie's asylum hallway).

At the end, the clouds lift, the mutes disappear, and the full orchestra blooms into a desperately upbeat finale as titles explain that Manny was released from prison and Rose eventually restored to sanity. What they don't tell us is how to regard a justice system that has destroyed a family and is so incompetent that the newly arrested criminal could easily be as innocent as Manny. Never trust the teller, trust the tale, D. H. Lawrence once said; never trust the titles, we might add, trust the movie.

17

sing along with hitch:
music for television

We ought to put Hitch on the air.

—Lew Wasserman, president of MCA, in 1955

"Do you like Brahms?" Vincent Price asks his legal adversary in "The Perfect Crime," an episode of *Alfred Hitchcock Presents*. "Not when it's a death march" is the answer. One death march people did like was Gounod's "Funeral March of a Marionette," which introduced this and the 358 other teleplays in the series. Indeed, though Hitchcock is revered for his visual brilliance, he is identified most immediately in the public imagination by this jocular music, a tune that marched on for a decade through *Alfred Hitchcock Presents* and *The Alfred Hitchcock Hour*. When Hitchcock appeared at the beginning and end of each story with a wicked joke and a poke in the sponsor's eye, he supplied the verbal equivalent of Gounod's march.

Typically, Hitchcock chose Gounod's march himself (conducted the first season by Lyn Murray), having admired F. W. Murnau's use of it in *Sunrise*.[1] As always, Hitchcock's musical judgment was impeccable: the impish, lumbering swagger of the piece perfectly embodied his image, embellished by the silhouette self-portrait that appeared with it. The ensuing music in the opening credits, a sinister string pedal with timpani, quickly established the countermoods of mystery and suspense.

With the encouragement of his producer-confidant Lew Wasserman, who wanted to "put Hitch on the air," Hitchcock launched his television adventure in 1955, the year he received his American citizenship. This was entirely appropriate, for 1950s television was the beginning of an American obsession. Many of the show's episodes featured ordinary American settings and middle-class American families in what Hitchcock, introducing "Mr. Blanchard's Secret," an episode he himself directed, called tales of "suburban mystery and intrigue." Under the auspices of his new telefilm company Shamley Productions, Hitchcock acted as host, executive producer, and director of episodes that Joan Harrison, his associate producer and trusted collaborator from his British period, thought would most fully engage him. As usual, Hitchcock combined the Old World with the New. Besides playing Gounod's march, he introduced the show with a British dryness and formality; sometimes, as in "Banquo's Chair" and "The Crystal Trench," he used European settings and subjects.

Indeed, he regarded the basic tonality of the show as British, a "humor of the macabre," a "strictly British genre of humor."[2] The episode that comes closest to English wit is "Wet Saturday," directed by Hitchcock, in which Sir Cedric Hardwicke protects the family honor by covering up his doltish daughter's murder of a schoolmaster who had jilted her. With the aid of his idiotic son, Sir Cedric must drag the corpse about in the basement during teatime; though he resents the indignity, he obstructs justice with admirable British restraint and manners, even when he manipulates his friend (played with stylish befuddlement by John Williams) into being the fall guy. Rumbling bassoons, squealing clarinets, and wa-wa brass mock his predicament in a droll score that comes nearest to matching the tone of Gounod's march.

But "Wet Saturday" is no more typical than any other teleplay in this huge anthology, which is remarkable for its variety. Included are film noir, comedy, melodrama, costume drama, suspense, spook stories, and much else. Hitchcock may have originally meant the show to emulate the comic mood of *The Trouble with Harry,* but he greatly broadened its scope. Many of the stories are not funny at all, and some are actually darker than Hitchcock's films. Some stories have comedy only in the form of "snapper endings," sudden, O. Henry–like reversals and ironic surprises. These shows have an uncompromising malice that Hitchcock did not get into his feature pictures, at least until *Psycho,* which was also a product of the *Alfred Hitchcock Presents* television operation, Shamley Productions.

Throughout his television career, Hitchcock took gleeful pleasure in manipulating the audience with music, as indicated by the devilish musical references in his introductions. In one of these, "sing along with Hitch," he dons a ludicrous wig, leading the audience in song, a parody of Mitch Miller; in another, he plays timpani with a pair of gigantic bones. In the most delightfully shocking moment, he bursts from a fiddle case armed

Hitchcock on television: mischievous mayhem.

with a machine gun, pointing it at the audience. Anyone who had seen the nastier episodes knew it was wise to duck.

One disappointment of the series is that none of the eighteen shows Hitchcock directed—the ones discussed in this chapter—had Bernard Herrmann's music. Some of Herrmann's contributions—"The Jar," for example, with its creepy calliope waltz transforming into "Dies Irae"—are among his weirdest, most striking creations. But all seventeen Herrmann scores for the show came in the final two seasons, when Hitchcock's interest in the series was waning.[3]

Nonetheless, the shows Hitchcock directed feature his customary types of source music and counterpoint. Strauss waltzes play through the "The Crystal Trench" (made a year after *Vertigo*), a tragic meditation on the consequences of fixating on the past. Radio jazz plays in Ralph Meeker's car as he drives home to discover his wife raped, then later as he is on his way to avenge the crime; the radio in this otherwise music-free show connects two acts of violence, the second as random as the first. (Entitled "Revenge," this downbeat shocker was the premiere episode, serving fair warning to viewers in 1955.) Quotations from Beethoven's Fifth and "Someone to Watch Over Me" become a duet as the "Horse Player" priest, played by Claude

Rains, gazes toward heaven and decides that winning is preferable to piety. "Deck the Hall" heralds Laurence Harvey's perfect crime in "Arthur."

In its infancy, television music was in a chaotic state reminiscent of the silent film era; indeed, music wasn't scored at all, but tracked. As Norman Lloyd explained it: "Somebody goes off and does a bunch of suspense cues, happy cues, sad cues, waltzes . . . and comes up with a library of cues that were placed in a show at the appropriate moment. The musician's union stopped that, however, calling it 'runaway music.'" By 1955, the situation was slightly better but still problematic. Under an odd legal arrangement designed to save money while giving composers at least a modicum of integrity, original music was composed for the early episodes in an anthology, then chopped up or cannibalized at will for others. (The end credits sometimes list a musical supervisor rather than a composer.) After the initial episodes in a given season, it becomes difficult to determine who did what—one more blow against the honor and livelihood of the composer in the industry's march toward anonymity and synthesizers.[4] Composers complained bitterly about this arrangement. According to Lloyd, the loudest protests came from Herrmann: "Bennie, who was a good friend of mine, always objected to everything anyway. He was some character, a real wild man."[5] Yet Herrmann's objections were entirely consistent with a career spent fighting the corporatizing of film music.

Not surprisingly, the initial thirteen scores in a given season, those individually composed, were often the most distinctive, especially in the shows directed by Hitchcock: Frederick Herbert's Gershwin-like jazz for "Mrs. Bixby and the Colonel's Coat"; Stanley Wilson's spoof of scary music in "Mr. Blanchard's Secret" (complete with theremin); Joseph Romero's "Bang, You're Dead," in which a little boy exchanges his toy pistol for his father's real one and takes it to the mall. The latter, a quintessential drama of terror in the ordinary, has a score consisting of piano-bass octaves showered with cymbals—little else—as the boy loads the gun with increasing numbers of bullets, points it at unsuspecting shoppers, and slowly pulls the trigger in agonizingly slow close-ups. ("See you on television," a supermarket manager says to the boy.) Counterpointing Romero's score are shopping center sounds—car beeps, cash registers, toy mechanical horses—which take on nuances of dread. This is Hitchcockian suspense at the highest level and a superb example of his sly soundtrack.

These are some of the strongest scores in television, the result of Hitchcock's insistence that the series sustain high production values even within the severe constraints of the medium. Indeed, those limitations proved beneficial. Because the shows in the first seven seasons came in at just twenty-two minutes, the composer, or supervisor, was forced to maintain sharpness and unity. Every show directed by Hitchcock offers at least one great shot, thrown into sharp relief by the minimalism of everything else: the gradual close-up of the grinning, homicidal housewife at the end of "Lamb to the Slaughter"; the split-screen climaxing "The Case of Mr. Pelham"; the blurry point-of-view shot through the life-saving tear in "Breakdown"—these are memorable moments in a medium known for mechanical and ephemeral gratifications. If the music for these shows is not always of the highest caliber, it rarely sounds bland or corporate and is consistent with the taut visuals.

The most celebrated episode, "Lamb to the Slaughter," combines humor and mayhem. Opening with happy-housewife string music, it unleashes creepy brass clusters when Barbara Bel Geddes whacks her adulterous policeman-husband on the head with the frozen leg of lamb she was fixing for his supper. Never had the domestic tranquility of the fifties been so brutally shattered. At the end, woodwinds wink with her at the camera as the police hungrily devour the missing murder weapon she has lovingly cooked for them and for which they are tirelessly searching ("It's probably right under our noses"). Afterward, Hitchcock delivers a dry postlude: "Well, that's the way the old meatball bounces."

The musical jeer in "Lamb to the Slaughter" is a trademark, often appearing in the final scene as a sardonic coda, a perfect segue to Hitchcock's verbal one. Keenan Wynn's fatal "Dip in the Pool" is memorialized by a chortling bassoon; David Wayne's undoing in "One More Mile to Go" is announced by blaring open fifths; Vincent Price's "Perfect Crime" concludes with chirping winds blending deliciously with Price's signature devilish grin; a saxophone mocks the flaw in John Williams's almost-perfect crime in "Back for Christmas."

Occasionally, the music abandons irony and serves up straightforward chills: the snakelike dissonance in "Poison," the quivery electronic effects in "Banquo's Chair," the Schoenbergian wind chords in "Arthur." Some of the scariest stuff comes in "The Case of Mr. Pelham," one of the master's rare excursions into the supernatural; in this episode an ordinary businessman is gradually displaced by a body-snatching doppelganger who moves in on his office, his dinner, his secretary, his servant, his home, and finally his checking account. Here is the ultimate manifestation of Hitchcock's obsession with doubles—a real one this time, not a psychological metaphor, as revealed by the spectacular split screen—codified with a chilling two-note motif drifting through the sound track. Throughout *Alfred Hitchcock Presents* we get an expressionist musical language that harks back to *Blackmail* and looks forward to *Psycho*. However commonplace this may seem today, it was radical for mid-twentieth-century television.

Although the intense economy of the half-hour shows is generally rated more favorably than *The Alfred Hitchcock Hour,* which commenced in 1962, the longer version did give everyone, including the composer, more space to develop ideas. The architecture of "I Saw the Whole Thing," the fourth episode in the first season, is particularly impressive. This is the only *Hour* show directed by Hitchcock. He reengaged Lyn Murray, whose swirling main title provides the bristling energy he brought to *To Catch a Thief.* The episode opens with a terrible hit-and-run car accident heard but not seen by the audience, a screeching dissonance standing in for those who claim they "saw the whole thing." Here, Hitchcock used music as an important element in the narrative and a clue to the mystery. The driver, played by John Forsythe, claims that the witnesses heard but did not see the accident. During the trial, Murray provides revealing codas to the testimony of four witnesses. As in *The 39 Steps* and *Rear Window,* popular music saves the day; in this case, it is not a 1930s show tune or a 1950s love song but the twist, which the first witness was doing with a boyfriend who really saw the whole thing.

Two other hour-long shows directed by Hitchcock appeared on anthologies that have now vanished into oblivion. "Incident at a Corner," which aired on *Ford Showtime* in 1960, is a corrosive indictment of suburban repressiveness and hypocrisy. Frederick Herbert's energetic main title sweeps through three presentations of the incident from differing points of view. When the wrong-man hero, the kindly Mr. Medwick, is falsely slandered as a child molester by a vicious PTA bully, he is regaled with "Happy Birthday" by his family, who don't yet know what has happened. Intimidated by gossip, they try to hush up the lie and end up caving in to the slanderers, but Medwick's daughter, passionately played by Vera Miles, fights back, her battle carried forward by a dark, Messiaen-like brass chorale. Counterpoint rules: when the chief accuser tells her son, "I know you're on my side," troubled string tremolos during his close-up contradict her. This is the only Hitchcock television show filmed in color, which helps showcase the plush suburban homes of Mr. Medwick's nasty accusers.

The most original and tightly controlled Hitchcock television music is for "Four O'Clock," the premiere episode of NBC's *Suspicion,* which aired in fall 1957. The teleplay was based on a story by Cornell Woolrich, who also wrote the story that provides the basis for *Rear Window.* Here Hitchcock returned to the world of sound designs and noise effects. Indeed, there is no conventional score at all; as in *The Birds* five years later, these are real sounds that gradually distort and expand, taking on the properties of an avant-garde score. The "music" is the precisely calibrated sound of clocks—hundreds of them, ticking relentlessly, mercilessly toward the hour of doom.

Musical clocks were not entirely new: a time-bomb montage had gotten Hitchcock into hot water in the notorious *Sabotage,* and he had experimented with scoreless clock music in "Revenge," which opens with Ralph Meeker's alarm clock incessantly ticking through Vera Miles's very bad week, which includes a nervous breakdown, an ostensible rape by one stranger, and her husband's vengeful killing of another one—the wrong man. The bleakness of Vera Miles's depression—as if she has wandered from the *Wrong Man* set onto this one—is captured by terrible silence broken only by relentless ticking.

In "Four O'Clock," driving the protagonist mad by endless ticking is an insidious form of poetic justice. Paul the clockmaker, played by E. G. Marshall, decides to destroy his wife and her secret lover with a bomb we watch him build in real time. After Harry Dean Stanton and a fellow mugger whack him on the head, tie him up, gag him, and leave him in the basement directly across from his own lethal device, he must watch his own life tick away, slowly, terribly. In a relentless Poe-like design, "Four O'Clock" ticks inexorably toward a climax even more troubling than what we expect. At first, in Paul's shop, we hear a growing cacophony of real clocks, one small, then a bigger one, then many others as he constructs his bomb. In a test, he watches in horrid fascination as an ugly drilling noise leads to the expected explosion.

Later, a kitchen clock ticks as Paul interrogates his wife, interrupted by the sudden hiss of her pressure cooker. From then on, the sound track is flooded with ticks, hisses, telephone rings, doorbells, bus and car noises—ordinary sounds transformed into pure anxiety. Whenever Hitchcock cuts, usually twenty minutes toward the expected explosion, the bomb ticks a little louder across from Paul's gaze, a subjective barometer of his growing panic. When the camera moves upstairs to the kitchen to view Fran, Paul's wife, and her brother (not a lover, as it turns out), a denser ticking is heard as the camera frames the shot through a close-up of a great clock in the corner of the screen. When Fran calls Paul at his shop to find out his whereabouts, the camera cuts to that location and we again hear all his clocks—seemingly an infinite number now—all at once. The final real-time four minutes are a horrific crescendo; then comes the final drilling noise leading to the explosion cued by E. G. Marshall's despairing voice-over—"It's coming! It's coming! It's HERE!" It never comes; instead, madness does: a white light, a huge eyeball filling the screen, one of Hitchcock's most intense close-ups. Because the device was not plugged in, it never explodes. "Don't leave me," pleads Paul to Fran as he is straitjacketed. That's what the ticking is about: the terrible loneliness of panic and death. Rather than saying "I'm dead now" when Fran and her brother leave for the final time, Paul's voice-over says, "They're gone now, and I'm all alone."

It's the same cry we hear in Joseph Cotten's voice-over in "Breakdown," when, paralyzed and believed dead, he must spend the night in the morgue, a night "so long, so dark." Here, too, the noise of real life—cars, drills, squeaking wheels, singing birds—substitutes brilliantly for a score. Only at the end, when the protagonist's tears save him from being buried alive, does music flow in, a flood of strings during his saving breakdown. As in *Rear Window* and *The Man Who Knew Too Much*, music is tied to healing and salvation. There's not much of that in the chilly world of Hitchcock television, so we should savor it.

18

vertigo: the music of longing and loss

I don't think Mozart's going to help at all.

—Midge, in *Vertigo*

Vertigo opens with triplets spiraling in contrary motion, plunging the audience into the cinema's most beautiful nightmare. Obsession, the film's theme, receives its definitive sound in Bernard Herrmann's endless circlings, recirclings, and suspensions. By the time the haunted Prelude becomes the furious whirrings launching the terrifying rooftop chase, we are already hooked. For the next two hours, Scottie Ferguson's obsession becomes ours.[1]

The gigantic terrified eye from which Saul Bass's geometrical circles spin herald some of the cinema's most hypnotic images. Bass might have designed an ear as well. Unlike *Notorious, Rear Window,* and other films in which sound and silence exist in tense counterpoint, *Vertigo* is driven by music practically from beginning to end, with enough ideas for three or four movies. Herrmann's sounds constitute an independent force, a dangerous fever enveloping the audience as well as characters. Critics have used musical terminology to describe the film even when not discussing music. (In his excellent study, David Sterritt calls *Vertigo* "a symphony of attraction-repulsion feelings projected by Hitchcock onto his characters.")[2]

This is one movie that is impossible to imagine without its music. Martin Scorsese states that the "tragically beautiful score by Bernard Herrmann is absolutely essential to the spirit, the functioning, and the power of *Vertigo.*"[3] Indeed, it is hard to think of any movie more dependent upon the seductiveness of its score. The violent sections alone—the "vertigo" chord and its many dizzying offshoots, the nightmare dissonance hurling James Stewart's Scottie into an open grave—are sensational enough to give the score permanent notoriety. Were there nothing else, this score would be groundbreaking. But the melancholy elegance of the love music, if anything, is even more gripping and obsessive, repealing forever two conventions: the notion of movie music as background and the standard view of Bernard Herrmann as exclusively a manipulator of tiny motifs who assiduously avoided melody, a myth he himself helped perpetuate. In *Vertigo,* Herrmann's signature scraps and fragments do appear, but in counterpoint with a sensuous lyricism unique to film music—the "Scene d'Amour," the luscious "Beach" and "Park" cues, the "Dawn" and "Farewell" panoramas, and many other moments. This music is modern, to be sure, but it is also unabashedly Romantic, the most Wagnerian score in the movies.

Wagner's imprint exists not only in the *Tristan*-infused suspensions but in the basic structure of music and story. Scottie's crazed attempts to resurrect the memory of a dead beloved make this a Liebestod in every sense. Throughout, Herrmann uses leitmotifs, not only for Madeleine but for locations and psychological states: when Kim Novak as Madeleine says her morbid memories are located in Spain, we hear Carlotta's habanera; when she worries about a fantasy of an open grave, we get a chasmic discord that appears again during Scottie's nightmare of plunging into it.

But *Vertigo* looks further back, to the beginnings of Romanticism. If the explicit backdrop is Wagner and his exalted fantasy of a doomed love affair, *Vertigo*'s vision begins with Berlioz's *Symphonie fantastique.* Berlioz's idée fixe, the precursor of the leitmotif, invokes an idealized heroine who brings the hero ecstasy, but also murder, retribution, and self-torment. The resurrected femme fatale described in Berlioz's descriptive program is never meant to be real, but a ghostly obsession based on someone whose actuality is tenuous to begin with, her loss and resuscitation bound up with the hero's tormented psyche. Like Herrmann's, Berlioz's music is sensual but spare, dreamlike but nightmarish, with formal waltzes, pastorales, and love scenes suddenly darkening into terror. Herrmann's harmonies may be Wagnerian, but his overall aesthetic, leaner and more harrowing, is closer to Berlioz. If ever there was an idée fixe in the movies, Madeleine and her music are it.

The reputation of Herrmann's score has been steadily building. It was in *Vertigo,* said Donald Spoto in the 1970s, that the Herrmann-Hitchcock "emotional landscape was most perfectly realized."[4] The dreamlike haze of *Vertigo,* unique even for Hitchcock, was credited by Spoto and others as

Vertigo Prelude: the sound of obsession. (Vertigo Theme from *Vertigo*.
By Bernard Herrmann. Copyright © 1958 [Renewed 1986] by Famous Music
Corporation. International Copyright Secured. All Rights Reserved.)

largely Herrmann's. In *Vertigo*, as in *Psycho* two years later, the music was inextricably linked to the central idea of the movie. By the 1990s, the general-
izations were far broader. Joseph Horowitz, a writer for the *New York Times*,
told me that the *Vertigo* score was a greater achievement than that of many
composers seeking to write the Great American Symphony; Alex Ross com-

pared the petrified-forest sequence to the avant-garde dream scapes of Morton Feldman and categorized the "Scene d'Amour" as "among the most bewitching stretches of music ever put on film"; in reviewing the lavish Varèse Sarabande recording of the complete score, he called it "royal treatment indeed for a mere movie score—but there is none greater than *Vertigo*."[5]

An extreme generalization, perhaps, but one hard to counter, especially given the adulation this movie, initially a box office failure, has recently received. *Vertigo* is now not just a movie but a cult, an object of fetishism much like its subject, a status enhanced since its dramatic re-releases in 1983 and 1996 and fueled by its long absence from the movie scene. Vanishings and resurrections are exactly what *Vertigo* is about, and the strange permutations of its music since 1958—homages, pastiches, symphonic renderings, installations, and much else—are part of its Proustian allure. Academics have joined in the idolatry as well: there is now a bar-by-bar harmonic analysis of every scene in the movie, with charts, cues, recording sources, and reprints not only of Herrmann's score but of music in the film by Mozart and J. C. Bach.[6] The hype sounds too good to be true, yet all we need do is start the movie: the moment Herrmann's score begins spiraling, we are hooked again.

What finally emerged was very different from what was planned. Originally, the film was to be called *Among the Dead,* and Herrmann was to share the stage with Norman O'Neill's lost score for J. M. Barrie's 1920 ghost story *Mary Rose,* which Hitchcock again tried to unearth seventeen years after his failed attempt during the making of *Rebecca.* The latter, like *Vertigo,* is an out-of-the-past resurrection drama involving a ghostly female. An unsigned memo of May 9, 1957 (probably from Peggy Robertson), asks Kay Selby of Paramount British Productions to "find recording of *Mary Rose* by J. M. Barrie . . . background sound effect . . . off stage, of eerie music, angels singing and a low moaning wind." Shortly after, another letter was sent, with a more urgent tone; this time, Paramount did find a couple of old records, "scratchy and ghastly," containing two excerpts.[7] This was more than the *Rebecca* project had turned up but apparently not sufficient to convey what O'Neill's music was really like.

So Herrmann was hired to write the entire score, for $17,500. From the beginning, Hitchcock told him that this film needed an unprecedented amount of music, and he got his wish: Herrmann wrote *Vertigo* in a feverish one month, thirteen days, not unusual for the deadlines film composers routinely face, but a miracle given the length, richness, and complexity of the score. *Vertigo* obviously meant something deeply personal to Herrmann, who regarded it as his best Hitchcock score. From *Citizen Kane* through *Cape Fear* to *Taxi Driver,* he dealt in obsession, loss, and the treachery of nostalgia, but he was never given such latitude to plunge headlong into these themes.

For Hitchcock, *Vertigo* was uniquely personal as well (one reason he yanked it out of circulation, say many commentators), the ultimate manifestation of a lifelong fixation on characters with a haunted past struggling to overcome guilt fantasies, with precedents in *Murder!, Rebecca, Spellbound,* and *Notorious.* The narrative is based on the French novel *D'entre les morts* by Pierre Boileau and Thomas Narcejac and a screenplay by Samuel Taylor, who never read the novel but based everything on Hitchcock's obsessive telling and retelling of the story, which like so much of his work derives from his admiration for Poe.

Vertigo is Hitchcock's "Ligeia," the story of a man who tries to re-create the image of his first, lost love in his second love, but is doomed to watch her die twice. Scottie Ferguson loses his beloved Madeleine, blames himself for her loss, and meets another woman he tries to remake in her image, only to see the tragedy repeat itself. Poe's anonymous narrator is never in love with the Lady Rowena, his replacement lover, but with Ligeia's memory. Poe's doomed hero, like Scottie, is a man incapable of living and loving in the present. Hitchcock's reincarnations and doppelgangers, like Poe's elaborate Gothic tropes, keep the disturbing central issues at bay until the tragic cost of preferring the fantastic over the actual, the fetish over the person, finally comes due.[8]

Although shrouded in a Poe-like air of the fantastic evoked by hypnotic color filters and Herrmann's music, *Vertigo* ultimately breaks through to reality. Compared to Poe's tale, Hitchcock's is less despairing: in love with being haunted, Poe's protagonist is forever trapped in an endless circle of false resurrections; "tired of being haunted," Scottie at least knows when he finally makes it to the top of the tower that Madeleine is gone forever, that there is "no bringing her back." His vertigo symptoms are gone; it is up to us to decide whether he is also internally cured, or whether he will soon be jumping off the precipice himself.[9]

As usual in his collaborations with composers, Hitchcock expressed strong ideas about the musical design he wanted but stayed out of the way. *Obsession* and *longing* are the words Herrmann used to describe his sense of what Hitchcock desired, and every note evokes those emotions. The only problem was that Herrmann's Prelude was so powerful that it created false expectations. There had never been a main title like this, the deadliest of Hitchcock's waltzes, a freefall into darkness. Combined with the churning "Rooftop" and the traumatic "Vertigo" chord as Scottie hangs on the precipice, it caused viewers to expect a taut suspense picture, especially since the director was Hitchcock. What they got instead was a languid psychodrama full of daring experimentation, with no closure in its tragic ending. Now a legend, *Vertigo* was initially a failure.

Like the movie, the music's architecture is bisected by the two heroines. At least five memorable themes appear in the "Madeleine" section; these explode into chaos as she falls from the tower and Scottie plunges into breakdown, reappear in ghostly variations as he returns to his old haunts in the "Judy" segment, and darken into tragic grandeur as he seizes his second chance in the tower. Scene by scene, Scottie's longing is directly sounded in Herrmann's music, so much so that by the famous dressing scene, music has replaced words. Hitchcock's usual detachment and wit are absent. The outer world of banter and irony, a healing or at least comforting force, gradually vanishes, as does Midge, their embodiment, leaving us with increasingly lonely images and sounds.

Scottie inhabits the Wagnerian realm of romantic passion, self-enclosed and indifferent to reality. The love theme appears first in an introductory motif as Scottie sees Madeleine in Ernie's; the full melody has not emerged, yet this prelude, marked "Lento Amoroso," has a melancholy eroticism that tells us Scotty is already smitten. In *North by Northwest* a year later, Hitchcock had Herrmann's score displace restaurant music; here, muted strings emerge from silence. He wanted a minimum of real music in *Vertigo*'s dreamworld; even the 1950s pop Scottie was meant to listen to in his car as he trails Madeleine, an original part of Samuel Taylor's script, was eliminated.

Hitchcock's sound notes show Herrmann nudging him into using more and more score: "As Madeleine approaches Scottie and becomes a big head, we should take all the sounds of the restaurant away so that we get a silence, indicating Scottie's sole impression of her." In the finished film, silence was replaced by Herrmann's "Madeleine's Theme," so what happened? Hitchcock gave Herrmann the option: "I don't know what Mr. Herrmann has in mind for music here, but should he decide upon no music, for fear it might sound like restaurant music, it would be better to avoid it in order to get this moment of silence, when Scottie feels the proximity of Madeleine." Hitchcock preferred no music here, but the decision was left to Herrmann; in the music went, making the scene less stark, more sensual.

"Madeleine's Theme" resonates throughout the first half, including scenes in the flower shop and in Scottie's apartment following the rescue from San Francisco Bay. As Scottie begins his stakeout of Madeleine, a ghost-like version for organ and bass clarinets set against high strings floats through the graveyard at the Mission of San Juan Bautista; a nocturnal statement for strings counterpoints the desolate clang of the streetcar outside Scottie's apartment, an indication that Madeleine inhabits his subconscious. A full orchestration climaxes in the Molto Appassionato kiss over crashing waves, the gushiest Hitchcock music since *Spellbound,* and a potent rejoinder to the claim that Herrmann avoided Romantic hyperbole. "Madeleine's Theme" gradually swells into the full love melody, which makes its initial appearance as Scottie and Madeleine drive to the sequoia forest, then fragments into a gathering nightmare during the stable sequence.[10]

The most memorable appearance of the love music is the dressing sequence, which Herrmann called the recognition scene. In his dubbing notes, Hitchcock instructed that when Judy "emerges and we go into the love scene we should let all traffic noises fade because Mr. Herrmann may have something to say here." Indeed, he did. This is one of the most sustained and passionate interactions between music and imagery in any movie. Introducing the scene is a whispered harp-celesta fragment of the film's Prelude, spiraling into a close-up of Judy in the beauty parlor as she is being made up to look like Madeleine. From here on, dialogue vanishes; Scottie's compulsion to remake Judy is captured with Herrmann's exquisite tremolos and suspensions as he waits for her to appear in the hotel transformed into Madeleine.

This is a ghost scene with two apparitions: Judy's first appearance is invoked by austere woodwinds, her hairstyle lacking the bun that will complete Scottie's fetish; then, at his command, she comes back with it intact. Herrmann's music conspires with Robert Burks's dreamy colors to invoke Madeleine in a green halo, a uniquely carnal ghost. "We'll just have the camera and you," Hitchcock told Herrmann, allowing him ten minutes of trembling lyricism rising in a crescendo of longing, an erotic spasm unlike anything in cinema.[11] As Hitchcock put it in the Truffaut interview, the dressing scene is really about undressing: "What Stewart is really waiting for is for the woman to emerge totally naked . . . ready for love."[12] (In the unexpurgated, unpublished translation, he is more blunt: "Jimmy Stewart has an erection.")[13] As the camera spins in a circle, the love music continues in counterpoint against surreal images of the mission stable and other scenarios from Scottie's troubled subconscious.

In the final scene, where Scottie faces reality and determines at the risk of spiritual death to "stop being haunted," the love theme and the illusions it represents are ripped into ugly scraps. A desperate reprise during the last kiss crashes over Scottie as Madeleine pleads for a renewal of their relationship. "Too late," answers Scottie; "there's no bringing her back," a grimly apt line just before Madeleine falls from the tower a second time. As he steps to the edge and looks down with "only his humanity," as Martin Scorsese eloquently puts it, the love music has the last word, resolved by a thunderous, hard-earned cadence: Scottie is shattered again, this time by the truth rather than by morbid fantasy.

"Carlotta's Theme," a Ravelian habanera, is also an important interior narrator. It glides hypnotically during the first Legion of Honor museum scene, then undergoes numerous metamorphoses. This is actually a dance version of a suspense cue in *The Man Who Knew Too Much*, signifying something not only mysterious but totally unreal: the reincarnation scam perpetrated on Scottie by his college friend Gavin in a diabolical scheme to get rid of his wife. When Scottie revisits the museum after his breakdown as both haunter and haunted, the rhythm is clothed in some of Herrmann's most seductive harmonies, but as he falls into an open grave during a nightmare, it is a scream of terror. When he kisses Judy during the circling apparition of the tower in her bedroom, the rhythm twists into ambivalence. In the great mirror epiphany, its meaning reverses, representing not delusion but reality, the terrible truth Scotty apprehends when he recognizes the necklace. Again, no words are necessary; Herrmann has become the narrator.

Much of Herrmann's music is astonishingly visceral, especially the famous "Vertigo" chord, a dizzying dissonance spiked with harp glissandi as the camera pulls back and zooms in. Here is a powerful instance of Hitchcock's music existing in its own dimension, making its own commentary on the narrative rather than imitating images; the chord induces vertigo even without Hitchcock's disorienting camera. Similar discords erupt through the film, including the murky choking as Madeleine jumps into San Francisco Bay, the sonic explosion following each plummeting death, including Scottie's nightmare, and the goose-pimply cluster traveling up the tower stairs with the shadowy nun—an angel of death if ever there was one.

Never had moviegoers been subjected to such a musical roller coaster —brought up to romantic heights, then crashed into nightmare, hypnotized, then assaulted. The score speeds at breakneck tempos, only to lurch to painful slowness, as in the furious Moto Perpetuo "Rooftop" cue, Hitchcock's most violent chase music, followed by J. C. Bach on Midge's record player. "Mr. Hitchcock's Additional Music Notes" provide a meticulous description of the opening: "An important factor is the contrast between the dramatic music over the rooftops and the soft totally different quality of the background music in Midge's apartment. . . . The rooftop's music is background music and Midge's apartment music is coming from the phonograph . . . small, concentrated music coming out of a box." The vivid, pounding stereo sound of the restored *Vertigo* makes the rooftop music more dramatic than ever and its contrast with Midge's phonograph all the more striking.

For *Vertigo*, Herrmann gave Hitchcock some of his most unforgettable waltzes. The Prelude is the most powerful; another, the middle section of the love theme, dances through both tower scenes; a variation on the latter, in the tragic key of C minor, the stunning switch to Judy's point of view, gives way to an exquisite pedal point (a fragment of the habanera) as she writes her confessional letter: "The moment I have longed for and dreaded," the moment that humanizes her and makes her more than a femme fatale. The ineffable beauty of this pedal combined with despairing bass clarinets as she opens her closet create a moving musical portrait of a vulnerable woman who has become a victim of the plot she helped hatch. Since we never get her point of view again, this celestial music never returns.

Vertigo contains many other musical ideas that are, once heard, never forgotten: the spitting woodwinds that take Scottie into the first hotel; the hypnotic cha-cha chords as he circles through twisty San Francisco streets in pursuit of Madeleine; the dense clusters caressed by chimes and organ during the petrified-forest scene; the somber string fragment, a premonition of *Psycho*, in the establishing shot of the courtroom where Scottie's guilt complex is worsened by the judge who accuses him of letting Madeleine die.

As usual, source music unites with the score. The organ-tinted cue in the Mission Dolores graveyard seems to waft from the instrument playing inside the church (an organ prelude composed by Herrmann). In his notes on the Mission Dolores bells, Hitchcock states: "When Scottie looks at the headstone and reads 'Carlotta,' we should hear the bang of the big bell from the basilica next door. It should ring about three times as Scottie is taking down the name." Whether this fateful bang is a real bell or Herrmann's score is deliberately ambiguous; bell sonorities continue ringing throughout the movie—tolling at Carlotta's grave, clanging forlornly from the streetcar in the foggy San Francisco night, pealing from the tower at the end as Scottie looks fearlessly down into the final abyss.

Hitchcock did not always get exactly what he wanted, as shown in the notes for Scottie's driving scenes where he ends up at his own apartment: "This music should start off quite dramatically and, by degrees, get more comic—developing when Scottie starts to throw up his hands." Actually, Herrmann's restless chords die away in a breathless whisper, a counterpoint to Scottie's quizzical expression. If this is a comic effect, it is a subtle one. Along with *The Wrong Man, Vertigo* is Hitchcock's most humorless movie, and the music sustains its uncompromising seriousness.

Even music itself—a potent healing force in *Saboteur, Rear Window, The Man Who Knew Too Much,* and *The Wrong Man*—can't brighten *Vertigo*'s darkness. From the beginning, when Scottie grumpily tells Midge to turn off her eighteenth-century music, art fails to tame chaos. A force of clarity and consonance associated with classicism, Midge can't compete with Scottie's attraction to the mysterious darkness embodied by Madeleine. In the asylum scene, she puts Mozart's Symphony no. 34 on the phonograph, telling a depressed Scotty that she had a talk with a musical therapist who said that "Mozart is the boy for you. The broom that sweeps the cobwebs away." She doesn't believe it: "I don't think Mozart's going to help at all," she says before disappearing, never to return, down the asylum corridor accompanied by somber cellos and basses, her music vanishing with her.

According to Midge, the mental institution has music for every kind of disorder: "music for melancholiacs, and music for dipsomaniacs, and music for hypochondriacs. . . . I wonder what would happen if somebody mixed up their files?" Hitchcock-Herrmann certainly mixed theirs, establishing an elaborate system of cross-references. The sinister chords from tracking scenes in *The Man Who Knew Too Much* reemerge in *Vertigo,* as do ghostly organ sonorities from *The Wrong Man.* The traumatic spirals from Henry Fonda's prison scene spin through *Vertigo* as well. In turn, *Vertigo*'s love theme makes a poignant return in *North by Northwest,* as does the vertigo chord when Cary Grant and Eva Marie Saint have their turn clutching Hitchcock's precipice. Herrmann-Hitchcock resembles a single, epic symphony, though each project has a separate tone. Eventually, these self-echoes made Hitchcock sour on Herrmann, but for that time, the golden period for both artists, they constituted an exquisite intertextual harmony.

As usual, the studio wanted a pop hit and failed to get one. Jay Livingston and Ray Evans, who had written "Que Sera Sera" for *The Man Who Knew Too Much,* were hired again. "Gentlemen," Hitchcock told the team, "the studio thinks that no one knows what 'vertigo' means, but that's what my picture is about, and if you will write a song explaining what 'vertigo' means, it will help me a great deal." The studio's assumption may well have been correct: the singer at the demo session thought vertigo was an island in the West Indies. But Hitchcock rejected the song, even though Paramount accepted it and was already using it in its public relations campaign. We can only be thankful: the thought of a pop song opening *Vertigo* instead of Herrmann's magnificent Prelude is profoundly depressing.

But the search for a hit song wasn't over yet. This was one Holy Grail that never stopped beckoning. The studio tried one more time, hiring Jeff Alexander and Larry Orenstein to write a song called "Madeleine," set to the love theme. Released after the film, it flopped. The only hint of a pop song is an orchestration of Victor Young's "Poochie," from 1941, which appears briefly during the scene where Scottie and Judy are dancing in the Fairmont Hotel.

The *Vertigo* songs have vanished from the scene, but Herrmann's score has continued to inspire adulation and controversy of a kind rarely seen in film music. One of Herrmann's keenest disappointments in a career filled with acrimony was not getting to conduct *Vertigo* himself. Hitchcock wanted a hometown orchestra to do the score, but this was not to be. Because of a musicians' strike coupled with Hitchcock's determination to finish the project on time, the director was forced to go abroad, commissioning a London ensemble—probably the London Symphony, although this is unclear—to record the work, to be directed by the Scottish conductor Muir Mathieson.[14] (The contract forbade an American conductor.) After recording the main title and eleven other sequences, the London players walked out in support of their American colleagues, again throwing Hitchcock's team into disarray. This time they packed off for Vienna, where two hastily assembled orchestras, the Vienna Film Orchestra and the Vienna Symphony (the opera label for the Vienna Philharmonic, which also appears by name in the file) stood at the ready, pending resolution of legal issues. This came in a March 24, 1958, memo from Max Kimental to Herbert Coleman: "Can do if commission does not come from Hollywood."

By March 31, Coleman, "busy dubbing the picture," expressed happiness about the performance, including one aspect that had caused controversy. "Remember the commotion about the heavy bowing from the strings?" he wrote Kimental. "Well, Mr. Herrmann said this was the effect he was after and is difficult to get here or [in] England because of the different technique." The visceral strings fit the intensity of *Vertigo*, but they had caused apprehension. On April 5 Kimental responded, "Very much relieved that the bowing sound from the strings has not caused a problem. Guess luck was on our side, though on the spot I would not have given a nickel on a bet that this was the effect Mr. Herrmann wanted."

As it turned out, he would have lost the bet. Herrmann denounced the recordings as sloppy and error ridden; ever since, numerous others have emerged, both orchestral suites and complete versions, claiming to be improvements over the originals, each heralded with finicky exegeses and critical comparisons.[15]

Before we embrace the new-and-improved *Vertigo*s, including Herrmann's own, we should remember that Herrmann was understandably bitter over losing the opportunity to direct a score that meant more to him than any of his other Hitchcock works; it is hard to imagine his being happy about Mathieson's getting the job, whatever the results. Furthermore, the errors critics find in the original sound track—a sloppy entrance here, a flubbed horn there—are not greater than moments of sloppiness on many celebrated recordings from the 1950s: technical standards (if not musical ones) are simply higher now.

Vertigo's music would not have exerted such extraordinary power over several generations were the performance weak. Both in London and Vienna, Mathieson presided over passionate readings that are forever linked —tempos, emphases, heavy bowing, and all else—with the film. There is only one movie, and one *Vertigo* music. Unlike opera and symphony performances, potentially infinite in number, a movie is single, immutable, like sculpture. It is hard to argue with Page Cook's assertion that Mathieson's "remains one of the greatest pieces of film music conducting ever recorded. . . . Every tempo, every rhythmic nuance, every dynamic inhabits the film."[16] *Vertigo* fans love to compare the Vienna and London cues, but what is most striking is the unity of all three orchestras under Mathieson's baton.

An eloquent bridge between *Vertigo* as film score versus concert music is Herrmann's 1967 Clarinet Quintet, full of melancholy suspensions and sighs from *Vertigo*'s love music, which Herrmann develops into a cohesive chamber work. Herrmann was discouraged by the obscurity of his concert music compared to his film scores, and this underperformed Quintet, a final resurrection of the lost Madeleine (his somber string quartet "Echoes" had resuscitated her two years earlier), indicates he had every reason to be. This Quintet is concert music of the highest order, even as it evokes the film.

Vertigo is now a meta-score. The French director Chris Marker, a lifelong *Vertigo* admirer who made the *Vertigo*-inspired *La Jetée* in 1964 and *Sans soleil* in 1982, has created a CD ROM called "Immemory," with allusions to Proust, Hitchcock, and Madeleine: "It is through a digitized Novak the user will gain access to different layers of my Memory machine."[17] There is also Douglas Gordon's 1999 *Feature Film,* an elaborate "cinematic installation" of the maestro James Conlon on a huge screen conducting Herrmann's score. The most gorgeous reinvention is Herrmann's own *Obsession* for Brian De Palma's *Vertigo* homage set in New Orleans. *Obsession* allowed Herrmann to realize a fantasy he had always maintained about *Vertigo.* As he told Royal S. Brown, he wished Hitchcock had set the story in New Orleans with Charles Boyer rather than in San Francisco with James Stewart. De Palma cleverly exploited New Orleans's stand-up graves and the decadent elegance of its Garden District. But Cliff Robertson is no Charles Boyer (let alone James Stewart), New Orleans is not evoked with the stately detail that Hitchcock invested in San Francisco, and, of course, De Palma is not Hitchcock.

Ironically, *Obsession* demonstrated the truth of *Vertigo's* theme: you can't bring back the past, even something lovely. Still, Herrmann's music soars through the movie with such haunted majesty that *Obsession* does have a hint of *Vertigo's* frisson. In conjuring *Vertigo's* ghost, he created something new and uncannily familiar, a musical doppelganger eerily appropriate to the *Vertigo* myth. *Obsession* clearly meant something profound to Herrmann, perhaps a memorial to his glory years with Hitchcock, his artistic alter ego: during final playback sessions in the summer of 1975, Royal Brown saw him "breaking into tears and sobbing unashamedly."[18]

"It's just a movie," Hitchcock told a nervous Kim Novak, recapping one of his favorite lines. In this case, the master was wrong. *Vertigo* has become an icon in modern culture, especially its score. More than any cinema music, it enacts the despair and stubborn persistence of our attempts to re-create the past. It is close to the tragic vision of Delius, the British composer Hitchcock alluded to in *Saboteur,* who spent his entire career trying to bring back a single moment of his youth in the Florida marshlands; indeed, cues like "The Graveyard" and "The Park" have a Delian longing.

There is something fundamental about this score, inextricably linked to the whole idea of movie music. Douglas Gordon chose *Vertigo* for *Feature Film* because it was "the single most generic sound I could associate with the cinema. I tested it on people. . . . Everyone knew that it was not written by a classic composer, and that it was a cinema score. But no one could place it as *Vertigo.* It was what I was looking for. It was the sound of cinema for an entire generation."[19]

19

north by northwest:
fandango on the rocks

The crazy dance about to take place between Cary Grant and the world.

—Bernard Herrmann's description of his main title
for *North by Northwest*

North by Northwest races off the screen, outpacing all previous musical chases. As in *Foreign Correspondent* and *Saboteur,* the chase design is established immediately. The MGM lion roars, the lower brass growls, the timpani rumbles, and Bernard Herrmann's steely fandango takes off. Saul Bass's urban grids spike into Herrmann's dance, then transform into lines of crawling cars, a modernist design that propels the audience into the movie and keeps them jumping through Hitchcock's longest, most generous entertainment.

Herrmann called this fandango a prelude to "the crazy dance about to take place between Cary Grant and the world."[1] The dance and the chase, two fundamental Hitchcock rhythms, receive their apotheosis. Roger Thornhill is set upon by more hostile elements than any Hitchcockian wrong man; his deadly dance across the United States with spies, counterspies, a hot female double agent, played by Eva Marie Saint, and the presidents on Mount Rushmore—all because he stands up at the Plaza Hotel at the wrong moment and is mistaken for someone who doesn't exist—is a combination of Fred Astaire and James Bond. It's crazy all right, but also exquisitely graceful. The dancer, after all, is Cary Grant.

This larger-than-life slapstick suspense comedy was Herrmann's fifth Hitchcock picture; the composer and director were both at the top of their game. Although *North by Northwest* is a sleek, glistening machine—this

North by Northwest. Eva Marie Saint and James Mason serenade Cary Grant.

movie is *about* technique—it never seems mechanical or cold. It radiates the sheer joy of movie and music making. Hitchcock pulled out all the visual stops, quoting and enlarging upon major moments in his career, from *The 39 Steps* to *Vertigo*. Herrmann unleashed his specialties as well: barking ostinatos, circling arpeggios, mysterious modal harmonies, dazzling colors ("kaleidoscopic" was his term for this project), and something one does not associate with him: a full-throated love melody. Hitchcock manipulated these with his usual wit, along with one of his most stunning episodes of silence.

But *North by Northwest* is more than an anthology of past triumphs. Hitchcock's movies usually offer musical innovations, and this one is no exception. The manic energy of Herrmann's score, setting duple against triple meter in an urbane version of flamenco, was new, juxtaposing the longueurs of suspense with the speed of the chase. Herrmann accomplished this with a daring minimalism far ahead of its time. Critics didn't get it: "The principal motif is repeated ad infinitum," wrote one, "and the listener is saved from acute boredom only by the ever-changing orchestral colors."[2] When Herrmann's new recording was released in the early 1970s, it was guardedly praised with the caveat that, unlike *Vertigo,* it needed the film to really come to life.

With film music as with any other genres, perceptions drastically alter over time. The once-criticized main title has won praise and recordings by prominent maestros, including Esa-Pekka Salonen, who gets the Los Angeles Philharmonic to play it at a speed even riskier than Herrmann's, transforming it into a superb orchestral showpiece. Nonetheless, Herrmann's tempo is so indelibly etched in our heads that the Salonen and all other versions that depart from the original seem like a separate work, oddly detached from the film.

The music reinforces Ernest Lehman's urbane script, perhaps the wittiest Hitchcock ever got. Were it not for Herrmann, Lehman would not have written this picture. Two years before *North by Northwest,* Herrmann got Lehman and the master together over a meal, the place where significant Hitchcockian transactions were enacted. "It was Benny," Lehman recalled, "who, as my friend and acquaintance, once said to me, 'I've got to get you and Hitch together. I think you would hit it off very well.' Before too long, I found myself invited to lunch in Hitchcock's office at Paramount, with Benny joining us, and Hitch and I did hit it off well."[3]

From the beginning, Hitchcock envisioned *North by Northwest* in musical terms. Before shooting began, he had drinks with Lehman during another meal and told him that "the audience is like a giant organ that you and I are playing. At one moment we play *this* note on them and get *this* reaction, and then we get *that* chord and they react *that* way."[4] In *North by Northwest,* they played all the right chords.

Things keep crackling after the main title's thunderous cadence. Hitchcock misses his bus, Cary Grant rushes into someone else's cab, then strides down the lobby of the Plaza Hotel to the Muzak strains of "It's a Most Unusual Day"—the kind of musical irony endemic to Hitchcock by now. Kidnapped by gunmen in a classic wrong-man fiasco, Roger Thornhill is escorted to a car as the music suddenly turns sinister: dark wind chords undulate as a gun is thrust into Roger's rib cage; a stark waltz in octaves evolved from the first three notes of the fandango dances ominously as he is driven through elegant Technicolor trees on Long Island and continues in the introductory shot of the villain, Vandamm, played by a suave James Mason, as he and Roger warily circle each other, much as Hannay and the Professor do in *The 39 Steps.*

"Bernard Herrmann's Music Notes" indicate the generous amount of music in the film. A typical example is the Thornhill kidnapping scene:

"START Putting gun in Thornhill's back outside Oak Bar / STOP Ringing off front-door bell outside Vandamm House."[5] This is a lengthy stretch, and Herrmann filled every minute with comic menace. Throughout, comedy and suspense fuse uncannily. There is no funnier slapstick routine than Cary Grant's drunk-driving police interrogation, just as there is no more riveting suspense sequence than the Mount Rushmore finale. Yet both are fueled by Herrmann's exhilarating fandango, the rhythms and intervals of which provide the nucleus for the entire score. The laughs give the thrills more bite; the thrills give the laughs intensity and release. Eventually, laughter and apprehension become so mixed up they become impossible to sort out. Three gruff ascending chords are the chaser for the bottle of bourbon Martin Landau pours down Cary Grant's throat; these become terrifying when transformed into screeching strings at the precipice from which the kidnappers contrive to hurl Grant and his car. Should we laugh or shudder? Why choose?

A stabbing discord jolts us out of our seats as Lester Townsend is suddenly knifed in the back at the United Nations, followed by the ludicrous sight of Cary Grant protesting his innocence while wielding a bloody knife: "Listen, I didn't have anything to do with this. . . . Stand back!" A dark variation on the fandango sets up the delightful Plaza Hotel elevator stunt, in which Roger's mother gets everyone to erupt into laughter, including the killers. In none of these instances does Hitchcock resort to imitative comic devices. Of all his comedies, this one uses music most aggressively as counterpoint, the funniest moments colliding with the most severe music, an avoidance of easy whimsy that insists laughs be earned. Conversely, in the most tense moments—Roger's flight from the U.N., the beginning of Roger and Eve's treacherous descent down Mount Rushmore—the fandango dashes ahead undisturbed. This dance seems impervious to danger. Things may look bad, it suggests, but this is a comedy where all will end well.

Sometimes the music moves beyond irony to outright deception, cuing Hitchcock's preoccupation with doubles and facades in a world where nothing is what it seems. Herrmann delivers his creepiest chords during and following Eve's fake killing of Roger—an insidiously manipulative scene—making us cringe every time we view it, even though we know the trick, like the child extra who spontaneously stops up his ears in the background of the scene. As in *Stage Fright,* music becomes part of an elaborate lie; with chords that deadly, how could the bullets not be real?

Everywhere, the score sows doubt and confusion. A quotation from

Vertigo, the ultimate music of longing, caresses Eve's sultry eyes as she embraces Roger in her hotel following his harrowing encounter with the crop duster. This is both visual and musical counterpoint, with Roger looking sullen and Eve ecstatically relieved, the music seeming to take her side. What can it mean? We don't know yet that Eve is really a double agent for the Professor. Is her villainous resolve weakening because of her unplanned attraction to Roger (another echo of *Vertigo*), or is Hitchcock tricking us again?

The musical tricks performed during the romance would mean little if we did not care about Eve and Roger, as Hitchcock knew when he got Herrmann to write a lyrical tune to humanize their romance. This is Herrmann's most graceful love theme, a languorous oboe-clarinet duet that heats up an already sexy train pickup. The censors made Ernest Lehman change "make" in the line "I never make love on an empty stomach" to "discuss," but they failed to drain the eroticism from "Conversation Piece," Herrmann's sultry cue circling with the lovers in the claustrophobic train sleeper—a scene that, according to Eva Marie Saint, was so hot it caused a cameraman to come crashing down from his aerial shot. This melody emerges subliminally from André Previn's "Fashion Show," playing in the dining car as Roger slinks out of the bathroom where he is hiding from the porter.

Like the music for *The Trouble with Harry*, "Conversation Piece" belies the often stated claim that Herrmann wrote only fragments, never full-blown melodies. Herrmann liked terse statements because the rhythm of a scene often favored them and because "the audience only listens with half an ear."[6] But when called upon to produce something lyrical, he could do so with the best of them. There is a veneer of coolness—this is Hitchcock, after all—but the erotic intensity is palpable. The slowly spinning lovers and their romantic tune are interrupted by the ugly buzz of the porter, but when he leaves, they pick up exactly where they left off: "Where were we?" "Here . . ." The melody continues all the way to the moment when the censors dictated the scene cease (embracing bodies could not recline on beds), concluding with an unexpectedly menacing cadence, a prelude to the revelation of Eve's note to Vandamm revealing her (apparent) treachery.

North by Northwest has a modernist objectivity, its melodies refusing to attach themselves to specific characters or settings. The vibraphone chords hovering like a low-grade fever over the elaborate Grand Central phone-booth scene and over the sweeping establishing shot in the auction have little to do with Wagnerian leitmotifs or inner revelations; the mysterious modal chords floating through Lester Townsend's house just before Vandamm goes in to meet his kidnapped victim (strikingly similar to the fantastical chords in Herrmann's score for *Fahrenheit 451*) are not married to Roger or his nemesis. When Vandamm says that matters such as Eve's betrayal are best disposed of "at a great height, over water," the oscillating arpeggios are less a comment on the line than an omnipresent design to which it aspires, a stately demonstration of Walter Pater's claim that all art aspires to the condition of music.[7] Herrmann's score establishes an alternate world, the absurdist fantasy Truffaut so admired in this film.

The Philip Glass school owes much to Herrmann's design, especially in this scene. But the most minimal moment is when Hitchcock uses no music at all, the iconic image of Cary Grant running full speed ahead of a biplane. No music is needed here. The bleak spaces of the long crop-duster scene are emphasized through a silence all the more eerie and shocking because the score throughout the film is otherwise so omnipresent. "Music" is provided by cars roaring across the screen through empty space with startling stereophonic realism and by the terrifying buzz of the deadly airplane. Totally out of his urban element, unable to comprehend the language or read the clues of an alien rural environment—"They're dustin' for crops where there ain't no crops"—Cary Grant runs for his life in this, Hitchcock's most famous chase scene.

Even when Grant isn't running, his motions are those of a chase. Hitchcock was specific on this matter: "It's the time factor in movement that makes the chase, as against the time factor that is static which makes only suspense. That's the difference."[8] In the auction, where Roger masters "the art of survival," the chords from the phone-booth cue creep slowly over him as he plots his escape and makes fake bids; lively woodwinds propel the time factor in movement when he executes the plan, converting suspense into action. This is an escape of fits and starts, retreats and regroupings, with musical patterns alternating in a complex dance.

In the stunning Mount Rushmore finale, Eve, who has been found out and is therefore, in the Professor's words, "as good as dead," escapes from the stairs of another deadly airplane into Roger's car; the car chase turns into a run through the woods, which becomes a descent down Mount Rushmore, Vandamm's men in pursuit of Roger and Eve, the Professor's associates after Vandamm. Entitled "On the Rocks," this jolting ballet uses Herrmann's alternating triple-duple fandango meter to maximum advantage as the characters pursue one another on the great monument, some falling to spectacular deaths, others clinging to the precipice, *Vertigo*-style. The complex timpani solo is a true tour de force even for Hitchcock-Herrmann.

That romance is part of the chase complicates the rhythm even more:

Roger, who doesn't "believe in marriage," proposes to Eve over the abyss as they cling from the precipice during the most slowed-down suspense moment, explaining that his former wives thought his life "too dull." This romantic interlude interrupts the chase proper; a percussive version of the main title then implodes into the *Vertigo* chord at the supreme cliff-hanger moment.

The ending provides comedic restoration: the villains are subdued ("That wasn't very sporting, using real bullets," complains Vandamm), the loose ends are tied together, and Hitchcock's wittiest montage sends the romantic couple from near death on the precipice into the bed in Roger's train. "I'd invite you to my bedroom if I had a bedroom," Roger explained earlier; now he has one. *Vertigo's* dissonance melts into the love theme, and all is right with the world. Because the censors wouldn't let Roger and Eve recline on the bed, Hitchcock delivers the bluntly comic montage of the train penetrating a tunnel, and the movie concludes with an orgasmic cadence, the timpani whacking away in triumph.

If critics had trouble with Herrmann's music, certain segments of the public loved it. Eva Marie Saint sent Herrmann a breathless telegram shortly after the release: "PICTURE SMASHING SUCCESS AT FESTIVAL YOUR SCORE TREMENDOUS STOP WISH YOU COULD HAVE HEARD THE STAGGERING APPLAUSE. LOVE, EVA AND JEFF."[9] Herrmann's typically sardonic response: "I am not surprised they like the music in Spain since it is based on Fandango music."

Truffaut regarded *North by Northwest* as a musical exercise. "Cinema approached in this way," he said, "becomes a truly abstract art, like music."[10] Yet the scene he was admiring was the "totally gratuitous" crop duster—one with no music at all. Truffaut understood that in Hitchcock every moment was musical, even silence; a rest could be as significant as a note. Eva Marie Saint also understood this fundamental musicality. Hitchcock, she said, directed actors the way a conductor leads an orchestra, rehearsing every note, "inspiring great confidence." Every sound mattered, including the timbre of an actor's voice. "He told me to lower my voice; it's still low to this day."[11]

But he didn't tell Herrmann what to do. The mutually understood dynamic between these two artists was to let Hitchcock be Hitchcock, Herrmann be Herrmann. The director set the design, the mood, the tempo; the composer enacted them. As Royal S. Brown puts it, "Hitchcock either sought or was lucky enough to get music that expressed in its own aesthetic terms what the filmic style was expressing in its particular manner. The general lack of direct interference between film and music in Herrmann/

Hitchcock collaborations allows the full communication of the deepest strata each art has to offer."[12]

Herrmann and Hitchcock were both stubbornly independent, helping this dynamic sustain itself. Like Hitchcock, Herrmann resisted interference from the studios. "The studio wanted Herrmann to do the familiar Gershwin city thing," states Christopher Palmer. "Instead he built the roars of Leo the Lion into the opening of what he described as a 'kaleidoscopic orchestral fandango designed to kick off the exciting rout which follows.'"[13]

For Hitchcock-Herrmann, there would be no more exciting routs through comedy-suspense, only the terror and silence of *Psycho* and *The Birds*.

20

psycho: the music of terror

When I first heard it, I realized what he'd done. He'd taken everybody's
guts and used them for music.

—Joseph Stefano, on Bernard Herrmann's music for *Psycho*

The most famous cue in movie history, "The Knife" in *Psycho*'s shower
scene, has been ripping through our culture ever since Bernard Herrmann
secretly created it. This is the cinema's primal scream, deeply imbedded in
our moviegoing subconscious. Anyone who teaches film knows that it is the
one piece of movie music all students, even the most clueless, instantly recognize. (John Williams's *Jaws* might be a second, which Hitchcock shrewdly
divined when he hired Williams as his final composer just after the release
of Spielberg's film.) *Psycho*'s strings scream through everything from the
disco version in *Re-Animator* to kitschy parodies in *The Simpsons, Daddy
Day Care,* and *Inspector Gadget II.* Just as *Vertigo* is the definitive sound of
obsession, *Psycho* is the sound of primordial dread.

Herrmann's music is inseparably linked with the film in the popular
imagination; indeed, without it, *Psycho* would probably not exist. As we
shall see, Hitchcock came to dislike *Psycho* so much that he was about to
slice it up for television—until Herrmann's shower cue made him change
his mind. Herrmann, who was on the set frequently, believed in the project;
he instinctively knew *Psycho*'s potential and fought to get it released.

When someone asked Herrmann what the shower cue meant, he simply said "terror."[1] This is exactly correct. Edmund Burke, Ann Radcliffe,
and other eighteenth-century theorists of the high Gothic linked terror
with the Sublime, a force evoking not superficial shock but a terribleness

Psycho, the shower scene. The cinema's most famous cue.

deep and abiding, not only sudden catastrophe but a fundamental treachery in life, a sense that the world is infinitely dangerous. In the state of terror, no safe haven exists, even in a comfort zone such as a shower. Herrmann might have answered "horror," which is contained in terror, but that is a more physical, present-tense emotion, a temporary effect of terror. The dread we take away from *Psycho* is lasting and has continued to haunt our culture since its creation in 1960. Sometimes horror is all we can bear. Burke's advice is to enjoy it, at least in our imaginations, to "fill the mind with that sort of delightful horror, which is the most genuine effect and truest test of the sublime."[2]

The awesome dissonance of *Psycho* works independently even as it instantly evokes Norman Bates's stabbing knife and Marion Crane's helpless scream. Once again Hitchcock overturned the convention that music must remain subliminally in the background of a film: in the murder scenes it is a force of aggression as frightening as the flashing knife; in its quiet moments, it roams grimly wherever it pleases, investing the most banal images—a toy, a car on an empty highway, a suitcase on a bed, a tchotchke of folding hands—with dread.

Psycho has received so many complex exegeses and ideological spins that it is hard to reconstruct the original delightful horror that initially made it so special. Those of us who saw it in 1960 remember something very different from the critics' musings on phallocentrism, patriarchal hierarchies, and male gazes. Not that gender is irrelevant. Males remember falling out of their chairs when they saw Janet Leigh in a brassiere, then diving under them when "The Knife" cue commenced. Females, including Janet Leigh, remember not being able to take a shower for a very long time. It is easy to forget that Hitchcock conceived *Psycho* as a high-end variation on a low-end genre, a shocker that would enable him to "direct the audience" for maximum thrills and box office. Moviegoers were eager to be directed, lining up in record numbers, ignoring the pious outrage of critics who denounced both the movie and its director, many claiming he had harmed his reputation irreparably. With *Psycho,* Hitchcock again accurately took the pulse of the American public, which was imbibing the tacky thrills of American International double features and Roger Corman schlock, as well as the salacious scares of Britain's Hammer Productions.

Part of the magic was that audiences were not allowed into the theater after the movie started. Unlike today, when we pick apart and dissect any scene we want on video or DVD, *Psycho,* including its deftly structured score, had to be experienced from start to finish, in a dark theater on a big screen. (The critics had to see it that way too, a major reason they panned it.) The moment the music started, with its slashing dissonance and manic pulse, audiences knew they were in for a stomach-churning roller-coaster ride they could not get off unless they left the theater.

From the era of Poe and Hawthorne to that of Anne Rice and Stephen King, America has been entranced by horror. *Psycho* is the most artful cinematic specimen of the genre, the score its greatest music. Stephen Sondheim, whose *Sweeney Todd* is an homage to Herrmann, once pointed out that music is more important in horror than in any other type of cinema, cuing the scares and their buildup. (*Sweeney Todd's* opening chorus, with its indeterminate chords, functions the same way as *Psycho*'s Prelude.) There are other distinguished director-composer examples in the genre—James Whale and Franz Waxman, Val Lewton and Roy Webb, Jack Clayton and George Auric, Roman Polanski and Chick Corea, Ridley Scott and Jerry Goldsmith, David Cronenberg and Howard Shore, M. Night Shyamalan and James Newton Howard—but *Psycho* retains its power more than any of these. So eternally popular is this film that it is linked with Hitchcock in the popular imagination in ways that are not always accurate. When my students write that Hitchcock is the master of horror, for example, they are thinking of *Psycho,*

Psycho Prelude: Hitchcock's highway to nowhere. (*Psycho* [Prelude]. Theme from the Paramount Picture *Psycho*. Music by Bernard Herrmann. Copyright © 1960, 1961 [Renewed 1987, 1988] by Ensign Music Corporation. International Copyright Secured. All Rights Reserved.)

often the one Hitchcock film they have either seen or heard about. In fact, Hitchcock made fifty-three films, and only two (the other, *The Birds*) are horror movies.

Part of *Psycho's* allure is its curious contemporaneity and hipness. Gothic creakiness, normally an inseparable part of the genre, does not exist on this film's lost highway, where going nowhere is signified by Herrmann's wandering ostinatos. Like other aspects of Hitchcock's cinema, this music simply doesn't date. Its icy modernity warmed by a single, restless melody from the main title seems always up-to-date. (When Gus Van Sant made the ill-considered decision to remake *Psycho*, he simply reused Herrmann's score and let the famous strings scream again. What else could he do?) Hitchcock himself spoke of the "despair and solitude" established in the first scene, a profound disquiet emerging as a basic condition of modern life.[3] His forlorn characters seem driven through the movie by Herrmann's restless music, trying, in Norman Bates's phrase, to claw their way out of their cages.

Psycho almost didn't happen. This is a unique case of music literally saving a film. Despite an initial burst of enthusiasm, after watching a rough cut of the film Hitchcock became so depressed and dissatisfied that he pondered cutting the movie and using it for television. The devastating score made him rethink this decision after Herrmann wrote the murder cue against his wishes. Like everything else in this daredevil project, the music was shrouded in secrecy.

The story behind the film's near demise and last-minute resurrection illustrates again the centrality of music in Hitchcock's cinema. He originally approached *Psycho* with a malicious glee and bravado, keeping the sensationalism of the narrative under wraps as long as possible, not breathing a word to the Hollywood community. "We could get a star!" he told the screenwriter, Joseph Stefano, before shooting, launching a secret plan to have Janet Leigh killed halfway through the film.[4] He was also full of mischievous delight with his other casting coup: Anthony Perkins, a teenage heartthrob, as the transvestite murderer. But near the end of the project, he was afflicted with terrible doubts: it was one thing for a respectable picture like *The Paradine Case* or *Stage Fright* to flop, but a failed shocker would be embarrassing. Yet something was missing, Hitchcock felt, something fundamental was keeping the picture from delivering its punch.

The problem was that Hitchcock hadn't heard the music. Herrmann, part of his trusted inner circle, talked him into listening to it before making any final decisions. At first, things did not look good. To Brian De Palma, Herrmann recalled the scene in his typically gruff, vivid way: "I remember sitting in a screening room after seeing the rough cut of *Psycho*. Hitch was nervously pacing back and forth, saying it was awful and that he was going to cut it down for his television show. He was crazy. He didn't know what he had. 'Wait a minute,' I said. 'I have some ideas. How about a score completely for strings? I used to be a violin player, you know.'"[5]

Herrmann shrewdly advised Hitchcock to "'go away for your Christmas holidays, and when you come back we'll record the score and see what you think.' . . . 'Well,' he said, 'do what you like, but only one thing I ask of you: please write nothing for the murder in the shower. That must be without music.'"[6] Herrmann was dumbfounded. Was Hitchcock losing his judgment? He knew that Hitchcock feared the picture "was going to be a flop" and worried he wasn't thinking clearly. "He didn't even want any music in the shower scene. Can you imagine that?"[7]

Indeed, the entire Bates Motel sequence was meant to unfold without music. "Mr. Hitchcock's Suggestions for Placement of Music," dated January 8, 1960, are explicit: "Start music the moment Marion drives away from the Highway Patrolman and continue when she arrives at the Used Car Lot. Music all through the Used Car Lot continuing until she arrives at the Motel. Stop music when she blows her horn. There should be no music at all through the next sequence (the first Motel sequence). Start music in the

January 8th 1960

"PSYCHO"

MR. HITCHCOCK'S SUGGESTIONS FOR PLACEMENT OF MUSIC

Music in opening of picture.

Music through first sequence.

No music in the Real Estate Office.

Music should start the moment we see the money on the bed and continue through Marion's drive up to the night when she is blinded by headlights.

There should be no music when the empty car is discovered.

Start music the moment Marion drives away from the Highway Patrolman and continue when she arrives at the Used Car Lot. Music all through the Used Car Lot continuing until she arrives at the Motel. Stop music when she blows her horn.

There should be no music at all through the next sequence (the first Motel sequence).

Start music in the Hardware Store and continue music all the way through the Hardware Store and through Arbogast's search. Stop the music when we see Norman on the porch just before Arbogast enters because we must hear the sound of the approaching car.

Start music as soon as Arbogast leaves Norman on the porch steps and play it through the telephone conversation. Continue music for Arbogast's return, his approach to the house -- and continue the music until Mother emerges with the raised knife and shut music off when Arbogast's face is slashed.

Start music back at the Hardware Store until Sam and Lila come outside the Sheriff's house when the music should stop.

Start music after Sheriff says: "If the woman up there is Mrs. Bates -- who's the woman who's buried out at Green Lawn Cemetery?"

Start music when Norman goes into house and carries Mother down. Stop music when we come outside the church.

Start music as the truck drives off after the church scene. Continue music during the drive right until Norman comes down and joins them at the Motel.

No music until Lila starts to go up to the house on her own. Continue music until the skeletal head turns so music segues into the scream of Lila and Norman.

The rest of the picture is silent even up to the End Title.

- - - - -

Psycho. Hitchcock's original vision: no music in the shower scene. (Margaret Herrick Library)

Hardware Store."[8] Thus, in Hitchcock's original conception, there was to be no music during Marion's suggestion to Norman that he institutionalize his mother—the famous "Madhouse" cue—and none during the Peeping Tom scene, which in its final form ("The Peephole") turns out to be one of the most disturbing musical moments in the film. *Psycho* was to evoke a bleak world without music.

According to Hollywood rumors—emphatically denied by Stefano—Hitchcock wanted no music at all and had to be persuaded by Herrmann to use a score. But Hitchcock gradually allowed Herrmann's music to seep in. At the beginning of January, for example, he wanted music to "start the moment we see money on the bed" and continue throughout Marion's nightmarish drive, with the exception of the patrolman scene. A set of music notes dated January 12 is more precise: the score was to jump in with two startling jerks: the first as Marion "reacts to Lawery" [*sic*] and "quickly starts off" on her journey, the second as she drives away from the patrolman. By January 25, Hitchcock was asking for music during Marion's unpacking scene in the motel, but none during her conversation with Norman in his office—and still none during the shower scene.

Hitchcock's decision to use the shower cue apparently came after January 25, not immediately on his return from Christmas vacation, as Herrmann's interviews imply. (Indeed, Joseph Stefano, who was on the set through December, does not recall Hitchcock's actually taking a vacation; Stefano and his wife had their own Christmas party for the Hitchcocks.) Until very late in the game, *Psycho* was to have no music at all in the initial Bates Motel scenes. Hitchcock's insistence on silence for the shower murder may seem odd—it is now impossible to imagine this excruciating montage without it—but he had always defied conventions about musical spotting even before they existed: the knife murders in *Blackmail* and *Sabotage* were without music, as was Norman Lloyd's fall from the Statue of Liberty in *Saboteur*. Silence, the master knew, could be more sinister than any music. Hitchcock undoubtedly felt he was on solid aesthetic ground in making this call. In any case, for Herrmann to ignore his instructions was something that, on a Hitchcock set, was simply not done.

But ignore them Herrmann did, with unforgettable results. Here is one instance of Herrmann's legendary stubbornness paying off. The cat-and-mouse game he played with Hitchcock climaxed at their post-December meeting, though what happened is not entirely clear: some say Hitchcock himself finally asked Herrmann for a shower cue, others that Herrmann made the proposal. Herrmann was emphatic about what happened: "We played the score for him in his mixing and dubbing studio. . . . We dubbed the composite without any musical effects behind the murder scene, and let him watch it. Then I said, 'I really do have something composed for it, and now that you've seen it your way, let's try mine.' We played him my version with the music. He said, 'Of course, that's the one we'll use.' I said, 'But you requested that we not add any music.' 'Improper suggestion, my boy, improper suggestion,' he replied."[9]

Herrmann's ignoring of this improper suggestion saved the shower murder, and he prevailed in other scoreless scenes as well. Hitchcock hadn't wanted any music in the opening hotel sequence, which now seems inseparable from Herrmann's sultry chords.[10] And he wanted to cut altogether the early scene in which Marion nervously dresses as the camera peeks at the money on her bed. Thanks to Herrmann's anxious violas, this became a superb specimen of cinematic tension, the music and camera telling the story. Some cues went through complicated cuts and restorations. Originally, the agonizing ascent of the detective, Milton Arbogast, up the stairs was to have music, but a music note of February 2 instructed that it be cut. Finally, it was restored as whispered tremolos and harmonics, an extraordinarily suspenseful prelude to "The Knife," a variation on the shower cue that startles no matter how many times we experience it. The final attack in the basement was originally silent, but Hitchcock changed his mind and asked Herrmann to bring back the slashing again. Following this bloodcurdling climax, all music was to vanish, "even up to the End Title"; by February 4, we get a very different instruction: "Start music on cut to Norman in Interior of Police Station jail. Continue as camera dollies in and cover last speech. Music ends on fade End title." With formerly silent scenes now spooked by Herrmann's score, the entire movie took on a new tone, an electrifying charge.

Nonetheless, the silences kept are extraordinarily haunting. After the lengthy music during Norman's ghastly cleanup scene, the quiet during the sinking of Marion's car—broken only by the quiet sucking sounds of the swamp—creates unnerving suspense. But as late as January 25, Hitchcock wanted the score to "cover the scene of Norman pushing the car into the swamp and watching it disappear." When mother's mummified head turns slowly around under a naked bulb to stare at Lila and the audience, it is accompanied not by a scary stinger chord but by terrible quiet, which is finally shattered by Lila's scream. Originally, Hitchcock wanted music to continue "until the skeletal head turns so music segues into the scream of Lila and Norman"; later he asked for the moment of silence that makes the scene so deliciously shocking: "End music on [Lila's] line, 'Mrs. Bates!' Music starts after Lila's reaction and second scream at finding the body." The most unforgettable silence follows the shower murder. Shuddering basses collapse with Marion, a deathlike silence splashed by the running shower, suggesting the tragedy of a young life down the drain.

Herrmann was convinced Hitchcock was crazy to consider demoting *Psycho* to a short television piece; he was certain all it needed was his music. His attitude was the opposite of other Hitchcock composers like Roy Webb, who thought they should remain discreetly in the background. As self-destructive as Herrmann was alleged to be in his dealings with the Hollywood establishment, flying into rages at the most inopportune times, alienating those he needed to befriend, he had a healthy confidence during this period with Hitchcock and a keen sense of how much the director's limits could be tested.

Herrmann's relationship with Hitchcock was deeply empathetic in those days. Hitchcock's Old World sophistication needed Herrmann's New York brashness and iconoclasm, just as Herrmann's jagged style echoed Hitchcock's slashing, subjective montage. Sneering at the convention that the main title "has to have cymbal crashes and be accompanied by a pop song, no matter what," Herrmann held that it should "set the pulse of what is going to follow."[11] This precisely in line with Hitchcock's early assertion in the 1930s that music should set the tempo and underlying idea of the movie. Herrmann, who had produced five masterpieces for Hitchcock, seemed to know this one had the potential to be one of the most remarkable.

Another person who believed in the project, and came to love the music early on, was Stefano, who took Robert Bloch's tawdry shocker and turned it into the quintessential Hitchcock screenplay, one that was sparse and meticulous, allowing Hitchcock's camera and music to work maximum magic. Hitchcock hated "photographs of people talking," and thanks to Stefano there was little talking in *Psycho,* indeed, less than in any other Hitchcock sound film. Instead, Stefano invented brilliant cinematic ideas—Marion's interior-monologue voice-over in the driving rain, Norman Bates's long clean-up of mother's mess.[12] Hitchcock quickly became Stefano's mentor, as he often did with young people he invited into his projects. He invited Stefano to remain on the set long after his part in the project was complete. Stefano in turn took a quick liking for Herrmann, who was also a constant presence during filming, and who seemed to know right away how special this film was. According to Stefano, Herrmann was "the first person other than Hitchcock and I who dug the movie, the first who said 'Oops,— we've got something else here.'"[13]

Because Stefano was a composer, lyricist, and pianist as well as a screenwriter, Hitchcock was eager to get his reaction to the score; as the film progressed, he showed Stefano footage in a series of private screenings. Hitchcock was so large that they sat with a chair between them. "We didn't say more than five or six words to each other," Stefano recalls. "Seeing a Hitchcock movie with Hitchcock was like seeing the Vatican with the Pope. There was something almost spiritual about the experience." In the fourth screening, Hitchcock showed Stefano the version with music: "When I heard it, I nearly fell out of my chair. Hitchcock said the music raised *Psycho*'s impact by 33%. It raised it for me by another 30. Hitchcock expected that the score would knock my socks off, and it did." So vivid and present was the music that Stefano remembers seeing as well as hearing it, especially in the opening, when the illicit lovers rise from the bed and begin talking: "It was as if Bernie was lying on the floor at the feet of John [Gavin] and Janet [Leigh]. And as they talked, he sent a geyser of music that came up right between them. It was so breathtaking that I gasped."[14]

Others involved in the project had similar reactions. Hilton Green used the same image as Stefano: "When the music came in, it just knocked people out of their seats."[15] No one imagined music could make such a shattering difference. Robert Bloch, author of the grisly Grand Guignol that Stefano transformed, and who was invited to the screening, wondered if Herrmann had gone too far: "I simply didn't know how to take it. It was quite innovative, discordant—not the sort of thing one usually expected to accompany that kind of motion picture. . . . I was not quite prepared for such screeching."[16]

Of course, there never had been that kind of motion picture, any more than there had been that kind of music. The screeching shower scene was new, provoking unprecedented reactions consistent with the differing times. When the film was first released, the shower murder was denounced by many as unnecessarily cruel and graphic; eventually, it was seen as just the opposite: a model of what could be achieved when violence is suggested rather than shown. Janet Leigh said that Hitchcock took the audience "as far as they could go; they were so manipulated that they created the rest in their minds, so it would be more memorable. You take the plunge, and go for it."[17] This is a classic case of cultural relativity: Hitchcock was raising the ante on violence when he made the film in 1959; now the ante is up so high that the scene seems a model of restraint.

Reactions to the music have been more complex. The shower cue was always experienced as shocking, but the rest has elicited different kinds of responses. Some find that the opening cues set up a false sense of security. In Irwin Bazelon's words, the "slow, underplayed phrases behind much of the footage actually relax rather than tighten the dramatic suspense, thus setting up the audience for the knife murders that occur without warning"; similarly, in the finale of the film, one commentator speaks of a "curious serenity"; another finds it "curiously poignant." Many have exactly the opposite reaction. The opening music, says Christopher Palmer, "inform[s] the audience that something traumatic is going to happen"; Miklos Rozsa, *Spellbound's* composer, found that the "stark, jagged music, so redolent of Bartók and Stravinsky, is sufficient to grip the spectators in their seats, filling them with a nightmarish apprehension of the terror to come." Herrmann was clear about which side he was on: "I am firmly convinced, and so is Hitchcock, that after the main titles you know something terrible must happen. The main title sequence tells you so, and that is its function: to set the drama."[18]

The extreme divergences reveal how complex and subjective this music is. In "Bernard Herrmann and the Subliminal Pulse of Violence," Royal S. Brown demonstrates precisely how Herrmann gets at the deepest subcurrents of aggression and anxiety in American life: "A tension is created between the indefiniteness of the harmonic language and the exaggerated definiteness of the rhythmic idiom, which in many places is so relentless, so heavily accentuated, that the listener is aware not so much of temporal divisions as a subliminal pulse suggesting primordial violence."[19] Whether or not one is lulled into a false sense of security or cued right away that something dreadful will ensue, this subliminal level of unease is a key to the score's special nightmarishness.

Hitchcock stated that a third of *Psycho's* power came from Herrmann's music. If ever there was an admission from an auteur that the auteur theory has its limits, that we can "only collaborate," as Sondheim put it, this is it.[20] Despite his crusty individualism, Herrmann, too, believed in collaboration, contending that music and film were inseparable, that "cinema is music." As we have seen, Hitchcock always viewed cinema as musical, *Psycho* especially so. "I was directing the viewers," he told Truffaut: "You might say I was playing them, like an organ." Hitchcock had used the same metaphor when discussing *North by Northwest* with Ernest Lehman. In *Psycho*, he saw the design details as orchestration, an example being the high camera angle in the shocking Arbogast killing: "The main reason for raising the camera so high was to get the contrast between the long shot and the close-up of the big head as the knife came down at him. It was like music, you see, the high shot with the violins, and suddenly the big head with the brass instruments clashing."[21]

This may seem an odd analogy, since *Psycho* is a movie without brass instruments. Herrmann wanted to complement the black-and-white photography of the film with a "black-and-white score" (as well as meet the severely limited budget); strings alone producing such brutal power made the score all the more astonishing.[22] The Hollywood composer Fred Steiner, one of the earliest to recognize the score's brilliance, pointed out that the seeming limitations of strings add a perverse richness: strings "have an effective range of dynamics unmatched by other groups, and within the confines of their basic single tone-color they can command a great number and variety of special effects. . . . And when the expressive range of the strings orchestration is compared to that of black-and-white photography, Herrmann's analogy becomes perfectly clear. Both have the capability within the limits of one basic color of delivering an enormous range of expression and of producing a great variety of dramatic and emotional effects, with all the gradations in between."[23]

Before hearing the score, Stefano was intrigued but ambivalent: "I thought it was weird. No drums? No rhythm section? At the time, I didn't realize that he had prepared through several movies—*Vertigo* being a good example—for this score."[24] (A much earlier preparation was Herrmann's *Sinfonietta*, a concert piece that forecast the astringent string sonorities and "Madhouse" cue in *Psycho*.) According to Stefano, Herrmann conceived of the string ensemble early in the project. It was a novel idea, especially following the rich orchestrations of *Vertigo* and *North by Northwest*, where certain Herrmann signatures such as low, hollow winds and crisscrossing harp glissandos seem inseparable from his musical personality. After *Psycho*, the dense seventh and ninth chords exploding from string bows became associated with his sound even more than his earlier effects.

For Herrmann, orchestration was inseparable from content, not something that could be turned over to an arranger. He orchestrated his own scores and was contemptuous of those who didn't. Hiring an orchestrator, he once said, was like having someone else color your painting. (Some have accused Herrmann of hyperbole on this issue, pointing out that the best Hollywood composers make such detailed sketches that the orchestrator is really a glorified copier.) For someone who believed that music is cinema, the idea of a black-and-white score for a black-and-white picture was literal: music and movies had a one-to-one correspondence. The sound of *Psycho*—

its restless, monochromatic strings—is fundamental to the film: its look, its modernity, its bleak terror.

Although Hitchcock initially wanted little music, he was keenly interested in Herrmann's string concept. According to Marshal Schlom, the script supervisor, "Mr. Hitchcock had a wonderful relationship with Bennie, and the way to maintain that was to give Herrmann the latitude to do what he wanted. Mr. Hitchcock only wanted people around him who knew what they were doing."[25] As usual, Hitchcock gave Herrmann latitude but still made precise suggestions. Initially, he wanted a nerve-jangling bop score, something suspenseful and of the period. But Herrmann stuck to his vision, and once again Hitchcock got something groundbreaking as well as perfect for the film.

In addition to being viscerally terrifying on their own, the slashing glissandos seem to stand in for the stabbing knife and Marion's cries—as well as our own: an outburst of cold dread. Sight and sound are insidiously united; Hitchcock's devastating montage seems cut with a musical knife, Herrmann's stabbings launching the attack. Even after the murder, Herrmann refuses to let us off the hook. After an eerie silence, the glissandos suddenly erupt again, melting together in a different kind of scream, one coming from Norman, establishing his point of view: "Oh God, mother, blood!" Viewers reported hearing synthesizers, screaming birds, and much else, even though these things existed only in their imaginations, just as they saw the knife slashing when no penetration actually appears on the screen. The art of suggestion in Hitchcock's montage parallels Herrmann's music.

Strings, of course, are associated in movie music with lushness—the "terrible" strings Hitchcock deplored in *Spellbound,* and the violin-romance cues in his British pictures. *Psycho* upset musical conventions as it did others: opening with an extramarital love scene in a seedy hotel, killing off the star midway through the picture, and (what worried Hitchcock the most in terms of the censors) showing a toilet. Herrmann's strings connote the opposite of romance: a gray, somber world where violence can strike any second.

Even more than usual in a Hitchcock picture, we see the fingerprints of Poe: Gothic imagery, split identities, fixation on a dead beloved, claustrophobic horror, and the sense of life being a descent into a maelstrom. Most important here is Poe's advocacy of a unified tone, a maximum power from minimal means. Hitchcock financed *Psycho* himself and used his black-and-white television crew from Shamley Productions to ensure that the movie came in under a million dollars. Herrmann's limited orchestration was partly due to these financial constraints, which became an artistic stroke of good fortune; it is hard to imagine either the film or its music without its austere look and sound, so perfect for its unique despair.

What Fred Steiner calls "great variety" within "one basic colour" gives *Psycho* a special power. Marion drives frantically on a lonely freeway propelled by the restless main title—pulsing chords on a road to nowhere. Right away we are gripped by the taut Prelude, its lonely theme winding in and out of relentless dissonance. With the exception of *Vertigo*, this is the most influential main title in any movie. Composed before Saul Bass designed the famous intersecting lines, it sets everything up, becoming progressively darker during Marion's panicky drive through the rainy night. Like Marion, this theme disappears from the movie, returning in a poignant fragment during Arbogast's fruitless search. Everywhere the colors are limited yet generate surprising variety. Arbogast goes up the fatal stairs and Lila approaches mother's basement to near-subliminal harmonies. Lila approaches Bates's Gothic manse to ascending-descending strings cross-tracking with the images between her point of view and that of the house, as if the latter were a living entity; she moves fearfully through the bedroom on an extended pedal of mysterious beauty leading her to mother's indented bed, Norman's nursery, and an enigmatic sculpture of folding hands. Along with the unfulfilled love theme at the beginning—the geyser of longing that took Stefano's breath away—this is the only moment in the score approaching gentleness, but the context makes it as threatening as everything else.

Lila opens a book that is apparently pornographic: the clue is a close-up of an LP—Beethoven's "Eroica" Symphony, chosen by Stefano because of its resemblance to *erotica*. This is typical of Hitchcock's mischievous humor, but we never get to hear the "Eroica" or any other phonograph or radio music. For once, Hitchcock eschews source music and its attendant witticisms. Hitchcock insisted that *Psycho* was a black comedy; though some of the lines (Norman's "mother is not quite herself today") have a perverse mirth, most of us don't find it very funny.

In *Vertigo*, Herrmann wrote plenty of anxiety into the score but also romantic passion and glimmers of light: Scottie chooses fantasy over reality, Madeleine over Midge, but at the end is able to take responsibility, cut loose the past, and look down into the abyss. *Vertigo* ends with a cadence after the final desperate suspension, a hard-fought major chord. It may be darkly colored and arrived at with difficulty, but it is there, the final say. In *Psycho*,

Marion tries to make amends, to claw her way out of the cage described so well by Norman by returning the money and starting over, only to be stabbed to death in the purifying water of a shower at the moment of redemption by the man who evoked her epiphany. Everywhere the music suggests enclosure. The grim figures in contrary motion during "The Hill" draw Lila toward the house we desperately want her to not enter, the violins sliding down as the basses creep up—a brilliant evocation of entrapment; later in the scene, *moto perpetuo* scratchings beckon, then pull her down into the dreadful basement. The only escape from *Psycho*'s trap is madness or death, both signified by the horrific dissonance finishing the movie over Bates's lunatic grin dissolving into a skull and Marion's car being hauled from the swamp.

Leitmotifs, so crucial in *Vertigo*, are not as relevant here: *Psycho*'s music is driven by moods, most of them bad, not by characters or locations. The languid chords traveling with the camera as it sweeps over Phoenix and pans into Sam and Marion's hotel room seem associated with their unhappy love affair; but they return at other, very different points, such as Norman's nervous refusal to eat sandwiches in Marion's room and Sam's futile search for Arbogast. The first time these chords suggest melancholy sexiness, later mounting anxiety. The desolate chords during Bates's mop-up ("The Curtain" and "The Water") sustain our horror at Marion's murder even as they drive us into reluctant sympathy for Norman, who must clean up mother's mess—one of Stefano's most brilliantly insidious ideas. Later, they return during Arbogast's fatal return to the Bates Motel, combining with the "Madhouse" cue to establish the inevitability of his demise. The latter cue, which Herrmann called the *Psycho* theme, dissolves Norman's nervous, boyish charm into a sudden, terrible warning as Marion suggests putting his mother in an asylum; it returns following Norman's cleanup and at the end as the swamp is drained. The only instance where it actually appears in a madhouse is during the shivery fugue weaving through Norman's female voice-over as he tells us he "wouldn't even harm a fly."

Herrmann wrote this grim stuff in the highest spirits. According to Stefano, he was by no means the grouchy curmudgeon of legend. On the set he "oozed enthusiasm. I had just a wonderful time with him. He loved to talk about what he was doing even before he started." What he didn't talk about, much to Stefano's disappointment, was earlier Hitchcock scores. He was too absorbed in the moment: "He wouldn't talk about *Vertigo*, which was too bad. I'd talk; he just sat and waited for me to finish." Neither man knew that *Psycho* and *Vertigo* would become legends with cult followings. A movie was for right now. "When it's over it's over," Stefano told me wistfully. "This was before video and film schools. We didn't dream of the afterlife of movies."[26]

Yet afterlife *Psycho* certainly has, especially its music. Homages to the score abound—in *Carrie, Dressed to Kill, The Brood,* endless cartoons, Herrmann's own quotation of the "Madhouse" cue in *Taxi Driver*—but the most remarkable phenomenon is the durability of the actual score. Herrmann quoted a fragment in his haunting string quartet from 1965. The title of the work is "Echoes," but it turned out to be a premonition. Within a decade, *Psycho* was being recorded by numerous conductors, beginning with Herrmann in 1975, and has become a staple in the concert repertory. The conductor Jonathan Sheffer argues that the tautness and complexity of Herrmann's score liberate it from its status as movie music and move it into the realm of classical. Here is a poignant irony: Herrmann, who longed for acceptance as a concert composer rather than as movie man, has finally been accepted into the concert establishment—for *Psycho,* a movie that was denounced upon its release as lurid trash.

What this score really demonstrates is the rightness of Herrmann's cause: the unappreciated importance of film scores in the preservation of musical culture. As he is fond of pointing out, the *Psycho* score proves that audiences love modern music as long as it is in a movie. Just as cinema has kept the Romantic flame alive in music by Korngold and Steiner when Romanticism was being shunned by the intelligentsia, so has it enabled modernism to thrive in scores like *Psycho* when it was scorned by the general public. This achievement is not unlike Hitchcock's ability to sell a bleakly modernist vision—Norman's "we're all in our private traps" counterposed with what Janet Leigh calls Marion's "desperate grab for life"—as long as it's in a roller-coaster thriller.

After his rupture with Hitchcock, Herrmann maintained that the director resented his contribution precisely because of its importance. Stefano remembers it differently: "Hitchcock was so proud of the music." His open praise for the score was highly unusual, for he was not given to compliments: "As far as Hitchcock was concerned, if he decided to use you, that was compliment enough." Like everyone connected with *Psycho,* Hitchcock recognized that Herrmann's score was transformative. In Stefano's words, "Bernie had taken the picture and turned it into an opera."[27]

21

the birds: aviary apocalypse

> An electronic silence, a sort of monotonous low hum that might
> suggest the sound of the sea in the distance.
>
> —Hitchcock, on the finale of *The Birds*

In *The Birds*, Hitchcock achieved his most revolutionary sound track. The great paradox of the film is that it ostensibly has no music yet delivers one of the most daring "scores" in the Hitchcock canon. The murderous birds have their own music and don't need anyone else's, not even Bernard Herrmann's. In the most insidious sense, this is the music of nature, a natural world gone awry, not the benevolent force of Wordsworth and Whitman but the chaos of Poe—the raven, the black cat, the maelstrom.

It is also the nature of Daphne du Maurier, whose gripping and poetic novella is the film's ultimate source for its intense focus on auditory wizardry. Although Evan Hunter, who wrote the screenplay, insists that after mining the essential idea, he completely threw out du Maurier's book, this is true only for the narrative and characters. The basic sonic concept remains intact. This was Hitchcock's third treatment of a du Maurier work—the first, *Rebecca*, was a smash success, the second, *Jamaica Inn*, a notorious flop—and though it broadens the plot in terms of the human characters, giving critics a field day ferreting out connections between alienated relationships and bird attacks, it is utterly faithful to du Maurier's meticulous attention to the sound of aviary apocalypse.

Listen: "The tapping began at the windows, at the door, the rustling, the jostling, the pushing for position on the sills, the first thud of the suicide gulls upon the step. . . . The smaller birds were at the windows now. He recognized the light tap-tapping of their beaks and the soft brush of their wings. The hawks ignored the windows. They concentrated their attack upon the door. Nat listened to the tearing sound of wood, and wondered how many million years of memory were stored in those little brains, behind the stabbing beaks, the piercing eyes, now giving them the instinct to destroy mankind with all the deft precision of machines."[1]

I remember as a child reading this passage with shivery delight in a Dell paperback called *Alfred Hitchcock Presents Fourteen of My Favorites in Suspense*. This anthology came out three years before the film; the latter was a keen disappointment in terms of the talky exposition (at least for a young person) but succeeded only too well once the birds began shutting everyone up. The film uncannily enacts du Maurier's auditory metaphors. Indeed, it is hard to think of a movie that renders the sound of a story so exactly—the tap-tapping of beaks, the soft brush of the smaller birds, the tearing and thudding of the bigger ones. Although not the exact phrases, these are very close to the descriptions Hitchcock uses in his notes to the sound engineers. That many of Hitchcock's effects are electronic is appropriate: his birds, like du Maurier's, have the deft precision of machines.

Hunter was eager for Hitchcock to get a terrifying score. His only worry was that, combined with the overpowering bird onslaughts, the music might make the film *too* frightening. What would happen, he wondered deliciously, if audiences simply couldn't take it? To his surprise, Hitchcock demurred: sorry, no music this time. Hitchcock was determined to create a new sound, one utterly removed from the Hollywood norm. He had allowed Herrmann to insert music in *Psycho*'s shower scene, originally an exercise in silent terror; this time he would have his way. Austerity would reign supreme. *Psycho*, which had its own obsessive aviary imagery, had pushed the symphonic Hollywood score as far as possible, unleashing screaming, birdlike string glissandos in a bathroom decorated with crow pictures. Now the strings would be eliminated. Only the birds would remain.

"There will be two kinds of sounds in the background of this picture," begins a voluminous memo dated October 23, 1962, called "Mr. Hitchcock's Notes: Background Sounds for '*The Birds*'": "One will be natural sounds and the other will be electronic sounds."[2] These simple, declarative sentences announce a new concept in mainstream film scoring whereby melody, harmony, rhythm, orchestration—all the traditional elements of Western music—simply vanish from the film. Anyone who doubts how radical this sound track is should watch the special feature on the Alfred Hitchcock Collection DVD of *The Birds*. Rather than trust the silent menace of the film, the producers interpolate symphonic film music (mainly scores from other Hitchcock movies) into clips from *The Birds,* thereby eviscerating the special atmosphere of the film. The scenes suddenly become conventional scary-movie stuff, strikingly photographed but clichéd and normalized. The pungent austerity that is the film's hallmark is lost. The severely restricted music of *Lifeboat, Jamaica Inn,* and *Rope* had paved the way; this time, even the title sequence and the finale would be silent.

Yet "Mr. Hitchcock's Notes" are full of musical tactics. Immediately in reel 1, we get this directive: "Title backgrounds . . . we have silhouetted flying birds. These will vary in size, start in very close. In fact, so close that they almost take on abstract forms. For the electronic sounds we could try just wing noises only with a variation of volume and a variation in the expression of it in terms of rhythm. We could also consider whether we have any bird sounds such as crow or gull sounds or their electronic equivalents, or a combination of both wing and bird cry sounds. Whatever sounds we have . . . the question of volume should be carefully gone into in view of the fact that we are not using any music at all."

This directive conveys an expansive attitude toward experimentation, an eagerness to try all possible permutations of the natural and unnatural. "We are not using any music at all," yet Hitchcock describes minute details of texture, rhythm, and dynamics, the details one would find in a score. The musical pattern is crescendo-decrescendo; the bird cries rise in intensity as Hitchcock's name appears and Tippi Hedren, as Melanie Daniels, crosses the street to the clang of a San Francisco cable car, a counterpoint between the natural and mechanical world that sets up the movie. As the notes request, the wing noises have their own entrancing rhythm. The entire sequence has a startling sense of depth, as if some birds are swooping in from far away as others are flying in our faces. The result is both abstract and immediate, stark and colorful, one of the most daring of all main title sequences, including those in *Vertigo* and *Psycho.*

As usual, the French understood Hitchcock's achievement before anyone. Truffaut first articulated the film's great paradox: "There's no music, of course, but the bird sounds are worked out like a real musical score."[3] Truffaut's favorite instance is "the attack on the house," which is carried "solely by sound." It is not clear from the editing and translation of the Truffaut interview which attack on the Brenners he means, but it does not matter. Both are musical masterpieces, with utterly different sounds and effects. Indeed, the sonority of each of the seven attacks has its own color and character, from the single, silent streak across the sky when Melanie is crossing Bodega

10/23/62

BACKGROUND SOUNDS FOR

"THE BIRDS"

There will be two kinds of sounds in the background of this picture. One will be natural sounds and the other will be electronic sounds.

In the following lists of sequences, following the number of the sequence we will indicate in parenthesis which is natural and which is electronic.

As far as can be indicated at present, it is our intention to do the natural sounds in the studio here and leave the electronic sounds to be shot in Germany.

REEL 1

1. (ELECTRONIC) Title backgrounds as will be seen behind the titles, we have silhouetted flying birds. These will vary in size, start in very close. In fact, so close that they almost take on abstract forms. For the electronic sounds we could try just wing noises only with a variation of volume and a variation in the expression of it in terms of rhythm. We could also consider whether we have any bird sounds such as crow or gull sounds or their electronic equivalents, or a combination of both wing and bird cry sounds.

Whatever sounds we have in behind the titles the question of volume should be carefully gone into in view of the fact that we are not using any music at all. So therefore in a sense the volume is a very important factor here.

2. (NATURAL) This sequence calls for San Francisco street sounds including that of the cable car and general passerby sounds. When Melanie looks up to the sky, we should put in some faint cries of gulls in order to create the unusual nature of their numbers. It should be debated whether this faint distant sound should perhaps not be a natural one but a stylized one electronically made.

3. (NATURAL) The bird shop, the existing background sounds of birds singing, twittering should remain. In the opening shot as Melanie comes through the door, we should hear the traffic noises coming from outside including perhaps another cable car sound. As the camera pans her around the top of the stairs, removing the front door from our view, we should fade away the traffic noise. When we cut back to the arrival of Mr. Brenner, we should bring up the traffic noises again and, in order to avoid a jar, we should just softly bring it up before we cut to the entrance. Again the traffic noise should subside as we pan him up the stairs and the front door disappears from view.

Traffic noises should resume when Melanie is panned down the stairs to the front door. As she looks out, we see Mr. Brenner's car going away so we should now put in full traffic noises.

Sound notes for *The Birds*, Hitchcock's most precisely planned "score."

(Margaret Herrick Library)

Bay to the shocking counterpoint of beating wings and children's cries during the assault on the school. The children's party has the highly differentiated cawing of gulls, the school scene the ugly squawking of crows, the filling station inferno a fiery explosiveness, the finale a strangely beautiful cooing and humming. These birds have an intense musicality that provides welcome relief from the drab monotone of the bickering humans they silence.

Hitchcock continued to conceive of his movies operatically, this time in an especially daring way: "To describe a sound accurately, one has to imagine its equivalent in dialogue . . . as if the birds were telling Melanie, 'Now, we've got you where we want you. Here we come. We don't have to scream in triumph or in anger. This is going to be a silent murder.' "[4] Just as Hitchcock heard the timbre of actors' voices in relation to the total sound track, so he heard the "murderous birds" in relation to dialogue. They have a silent libretto, an untranslatable recitative, but it is disturbingly easy to imagine what they are singing. The notes set up a dynamic in which the director acts as the composer, the sound team as the orchestra, the birds as the singers.

The sound of *The Birds* was new. Hitchcock had been moving in a modernist direction in the minimalist churnings of *North by Northwest* and the bleak expressionism of *Psycho*. In *The Birds*, he took the next step: electronic music, something that was gaining ground on the new music concert scene but was rather unusual in movies. For better and worse, he temporarily abandoned the rich symphonic tradition he himself had brought to perfection in the scores he inspired for *Rebecca, Notorious, Vertigo*, and other films, to inaugurate the brave new world of electronic scoring. Electronic music was not completely new, of course. Hitchcock himself had used the theremin, an electronic instrument, in *Spellbound* 20 years earlier—something novel and exotic at the time. And those who grew up to the electric shivers in *The Day the Earth Stood Still* and *Forbidden Planet* know that electronic scores were not unknown in the 1950s. But *The Birds* went further: it is a sustained attempt to merge electronic sounds with real ones, a fusion of created and "found" music, actual birdsong and mimicked, a mélange worthy of Varèse and Cage, a forerunner of the downtown noise music of Charles Amirkhanian and Eric Schwartz.

As he demonstrated as early as *Blackmail*, Hitchcock plunged forward aggressively when he had something sonically new at his disposal. The sound track notes, though highly technical, convey a sense of excitement in a confident, imperious tone. "It is our intention," they state, "to do the natural sounds in the studio here and leave the electronic sounds to be shot in

Germany." The latter were created by Herrmann working with Hitchcock in Berlin—the seventh Hitchcock-Herrmann collaboration, and certainly the riskiest—but were conceived and recorded by the avant-gardist Remi Gassmann, who cocreated a gadget called the Trautonium, an electronic keyboard instrument first used by the New York City Ballet. The Trautonium was unveiled with considerable fanfare. In a breathless letter to Hitchcock written in 1962, Gassmann claimed that "familiar sounds—from common noises to music and esoteric effects—as well as an almost limitless supply of completely unfamiliar sounds, can now be electronically produced, controlled, and utilized for film purposes. The result is much like a new dimension in film production."[5] This symphony of the common mingled with the completely unfamiliar became the music of *The Birds.*

Gassmann's point about control was crucial for Hitchcock. Electronic music suddenly gave him an advantage in this ever-important issue, drolly summarized when he told Ernest Lehman his dream of directly playing his audience like an organ or hooking them up to electrodes. In *The Birds,* the fantasy was enacted. If Hitchcock wasn't directly hooking his audience up, he was achieving the next best thing: linking his directions with a sound team's precise enactment. With an electronic score, Hitchcock could get what he wanted more reliably than in a symphonic one. He had always been able to control source music, but not the underscore. Now he could manipulate that too. Indeed, just about every noise, nuance, and silence he asks for in the notes emerges in the film. (Later directors like David Lynch and Sam Raimi would use electronic synthesizers routinely for terrifying effects, saving considerable money in the process.)

In the forties and fifties, Hitchcock had presided over lavish Hollywood scores. In *The Birds,* however, he was a pioneer who inadvertently contributed to the decline of symphonic movie music, just as he helped set the trend, in films ranging from *Blackmail* to *Rear Window,* of licensing popular songs rather than creating original material. *The Birds* represented a Hitchcockian musical ideal, allowing him to have it both ways: he could more or less control what he wanted, rather than trust a composer to create it, yet still get many of the subtleties of a real score. No music became the ultimate music.

Nonetheless, the teasing question remained: did Hitchcock completely control the sounds of *The Birds*? He was not the only one who took great satisfaction in this project. So did Bernard Herrmann, who spent a month with Hitchcock in West Berlin supervising the project. Indeed, Herrmann said he felt he was the codirector of *The Birds,* a remark that could not have sat well with Hitchcock. Alistair Reid recalled that *The Birds* was the only Hitchcock movie Herrmann talked about a lot: "He regarded himself as one of its prime movers."[6] The issue of control did not quite go away, even here, and another seed was planted in the Hitchcock-Herrmann rift.

Before *The Birds,* there is no evidence that Hitchcock was interested in nontonal or nonacoustic composers. (The tonality of the expressionist score for *Blackmail* is shaky, but still intact.) His tastes were catholic, but only up to a point. Although he liked everything from Elgar to various kinds of American vernacular song, his enthusiasms apparently did not include the electronic avant-garde. But after this project—perhaps because of it— Hitchcock did develop an adventurous curiosity about new music and its cinematic potential. (During the same period he evinced a similar taste for experimental cinema, diligently screening European New Wave films, including those of Truffaut.) He ordered recordings of Stockhausen, Boulez, and other composers and considered using Shostakovich and Richard Rodney Bennett (who was a progressive in those days) in his final films. None of these fantasies came to fruition, but *The Birds* apparently opened new aesthetic possibilities in his musical imagination. One can only wonder what might have developed had Hitchcock not come under increasing pressure from Lew Wasserman and the studio to bow to commercial trends rather than striking out into new territory as he had done in *Psycho* and *The Birds.*

Hitchcock was proud of the daring experiments in *The Birds,* and one can see why. The assault on the children's party, for example, is a brilliant percussion piece full of clacking wings, popping balloons, smashing dishes, and the shrieks of gulls and children, which Hitchcock insisted should be distinct entities rising and falling together: "It will be very necessary to watch that the screams of the children and the screams of the gulls do not sound the same. . . . The screams of the gulls should fade away in the distance at the same time that the children's cries finish off, so that we end with a silent background broken only by the dialogue of the characters."

This is the basic movement of much of the film: carefully adjusted sounds rising to screechy climaxes, then dying to an even more unsettling silence. Throughout the movie, the birds strike, vanish, then begin massing again for another assault, each one with a unique sound, in a scrupulously planned musical pattern.

A contrast to the school party occurs in the all-electronic sparrow attack down the chimney of the Brenner house, which Hitchcock wanted to "assail the ears of the audience to perhaps an almost unbearable degree." Sparrows, of course, are delicate creatures; the havoc they wreak here derives not from brute loudness but from quality and timbre: "It should not necessarily have volume, but the quality of the shrill notes should be something like the effect of the screech that you get if you scrape two pieces of metal together." Again, the degree to which Hitchcock heard these sounds in his imagination—and could make precise aural analogies—is striking. He clearly wanted this scene to have a different musical quality than the other attacks, something resembling a scherzo, a consistent flurry of noise. In most of the assaults, a crescendo is requested, but not here: "In view of the sudden rush and such a quantity coming in together . . . the sound should start with a fairly comprehensive amount at the beginning of the scene." He cues the texture as well: "Naturally accompanying this but in a much lesser degree, we have the sound of the little wings beating . . . some sprinkling of thuds where birds hit the walls and other objects in the room . . . the NATURAL sounds of the flicking of the napkin by Mitch, the tipping of the table and the thrusting of it in the fireplace."

Even more riveting is the second attack on the house, a demonstration of the Hitchcock dictum that what you can't see is often more unnerving than what you can. Here the birds are a percussive, savage pecking from behind the door, which rises incrementally—the film's most precise crescendo. (This was one of the earliest scenes to be tried out; in the final sound notes for this reel, Hitchcock simply refers the sound team to an earlier electronic sample.) As in Poe's "Fall of the House of Usher," one's own home becomes a deadly trap, full of invisible menace. This scene makes explicit what is implicit throughout the film, that every moment is dangerous and has been even in the film's slowest scenes. As Elisabeth Weis eloquently puts it, "The film eventually makes us feel just as vulnerable in moments of relative tranquility as in chaos. It is one thing to feel threatened when under attack, it is another to be frightened at all times, to feel that life is a permanent state of siege. Thus Hitchcock has achieved his career-long aim of making us wary, not so much of blatant evils but of our precarious daily condition."[7]

A children's schoolyard becomes another precarious environment, as Hitchcock indicates in one of the most symphonic passages in the notes: "We should have a silence with an odd flapping or two of the wings because we assume the children will tiptoe out. Suddenly we hear the running feet of the children. Immediately there is a tremendous fluttering of wings as the crows rise. In the long shot we should see the crows coming over the top of the schoolhouse and for the first time we hear the distant massing electronic sounds of growing anger as they descend upon the children. The sound increases now with the rest of the running sequence." The "silence with an odd flapping or two of wings" occurs as the camera cuts from the children to the birds; the "tremendous fluttering of wings as the crows rise" gives way to an aggressive sonority with all the stops pulled out: "We hear running feet, the odd screams of the children which should not be reduced by the croaking of the crows but should be continuous, but possibly not excessive so we do not get a monotonous humdrum all the time. All this continues until the distant screams of the children are heard going down the street, while Melanie picks up Michele and hurries her across to the station wagon. Once they are inside the wagon and the window is up, we hear the banging and flattening of wings and the groans all round the station wagon but with a reduced volume. Finally, the croaking dies away as do the screams of the children and Melanie drops her head on the wheel in complete silence."

Here is a nightmarish texture of screams, croaks, running feet, the flattening of wings—a surreal cacophony—all dying into the complete silence that this film inevitably sinks into. At all costs, Hitchcock is determined to avoid any auditory dullness, any hint of monotonous humdrum. Just before the final silence, Melanie blasts her horn, a detail not in the notes, a displaced emotional release similar to Jessica Tandy's roaring truck following her impotent attempt to scream.

The climactic attack is the attic scene with Melanie Daniels, the shallow playgirl who develops into a tragic heroine. The mysterious gentleness of these sounds was partly necessitated by the dramatic situation: "It is very essential . . . that we give the sound a quality that gives this volume but is not of such a serious quality as to cause the people downstairs to be awakened by it." The relentless beating of wings has a mesmerizing quality a bit like the clacking train rhythms in *The Lady Vanishes* and *North by Northwest,* a sound perversely soothing. Hitchcock was especially pleased with this scene, as indicated in his remarks to Truffaut: "We inserted the natural sounds of wings, but we stylized them so as to create greater intensity. We wanted to get a menacing wave of vibration rather than a single level . . . a variation of the noise, an assimilation of the unequal noise of the wings. Of course, I took the dramatic license of not having the birds scream at all."[8] Hitchcock did not automatically associate silence with realism. This film is pure Hitchcockian fantasy, its silences as brilliantly artificial as its sounds.

Omitting screams, whether the birds' or their victims', carries its own powerful charge. The stress on blankness, where quiet acts as a musical rest, was not new, but here its uncompromising intensity was unprecedented. The famous jump cuts from the farmer's shattered teacups through his house to his bloody eye sockets are all the more shattering without sound, as is the stifled scream of Jessica Tandy as she rushes at the screen from long shot to close-up to emit a nightmarish blast of nothingness. In the notes to this reel, Hitchcock did not merely state that he wanted to omit noise but that "we should be in silence." As with Anton Webern and Cage, silence is not simply the absence of sound but a state of being, a positive musical value. The quiet is so terrible that the sudden roar of Lydia's truck is as unnerving as the birds. Again, Hitchcock points out that the effects had little to do with realism: "We were really experimenting there by taking real sounds and then stylizing them so that we derived more drama from them than we normally would." The truck stands in for Lydia's suppressed scream: "It's not only the sound of the engine you hear, but something that's like a cry. It's as though the truck were shrieking."[9] The elaborate aural transferences in everything from *Blackmail* to *Strangers on a Train* here receive their ultimate refinement; less is infinitely more. The notes call for "the choking sounds of Mrs. Brenner when she dashes out and just the simple sounds of the roaring truck as she dashes back to her home." Conventional horror music would be a relief here, a release of tension.

The nontonal bird music—the electronically blended chirps, caws, flutters, and jabberings—does not release anything at all; it has the weird property of constantly building tension, then vanishing. In earlier films, music provided catharsis—the effulgent major-key cadence at the end of *Rebecca,* the fateful minor one concluding *Notorious,* the big concluding chords in "The Beach" and final tower scene in *Vertigo.* The only resolution we get in *The Birds* is a repetition of the final chorus in "Risseldy, Rosseldy" just before the crows sweep down on the children, hardly a restorative moment. This is a modern movie that provides no closure or resolution; it is also one of Hitchcock's most Poe-like pictures, sustaining a single mood—a vivid barrenness—without contrast or relief.

Hitchcock was most radical when revisiting the aesthetic of his silent films. His drama of silent murder is played out right until the end, in a movie that begins with the blaring of trucks, trolleys, and a wolf whistle, and gradually subsides into awesome quiet. The finale has some of the film's most subtle musical effects: the birds mass for their final attack, then suddenly scream in unison a crescendo that dies into eerie quiet. Their haunting hum in the final shot is a near-subliminal pedal point. At the last instant, in an exquisite final subtlety, the bird noises rise again in a tiny final crescendo, a preapocalyptic shiver.

As with sight, what we can't quite hear is often more powerful than what we can, as Hitchcock explained to Truffaut: "For the final scene, I asked for silence . . . an electronic silence, a sort of monotonous low hum that might suggest the sound of the sea in the distance . . . a strange, artificial sound, which in the language of the birds might be saying, 'We're not ready to attack you yet, but we're getting ready. We're like an engine that's purring and we may start off at any moment.' All this is suggested by a sound that's so low that you can't be sure whether you're actually hearing it or only imagining it."[10]

Here, Hitchcock is describing the actual achievement of the film. The sound notes again show how much of the sound track was originally in his head, waiting only to be actualized by his sound team. This is the sonic dimension of the Hitchcockian storyboard, though the imaginary sound track is a work in progress, a series of carefully calibrated possibilities. More than any of the other notes, those for the final reel are full of conditionals, whatevers, suggestions for experimentation: "If it is at all feasible, what we would like to have electronically, is the equivalent of brooding silence. Naturally, to achieve some effect like this will necessitate some experimentation. Maybe the whole time there is a murmur of the lowest possible bird sounds. Whatever it is, however, should give us a feeling of a waiting mass, that if they were unduly disturbed, an attack would start again." The suggested "murmur of the lowest possible bird sounds" is the first mention of the monotonous low hum. The film's most distinctive mood is precisely described as brooding silence. Here we have a haunting instance of Hitchcock's vision of music as a preternatural presence, a living mass that inhabits the scene like a character.

To the end, Hitchcock fussed and worried over details. Would the hum be too monotonous? Should a scenario be constructed to allow for contrasting colors and effects? Should "individual crow sounds be interpolated at the sight of Mitch?" a question raised in the notes. The finished film does include these interpolations: a silent gull suddenly squawks and pecks Rod Taylor's Mitch, a small but unnerving contrast to the birds' gently sinister cooing. We hear other bird murmuring in layers, from various distances, a perversely pleasant ambiance. The jittery poetry of the finale sounds like formal electronic music. Close your eyes, and you think you are hearing Xenakis. Again, it is striking how abstract this score is, much like the bird silhouettes Hitchcock describes in the notes for the titles. By the end, we read the music of the birds as a real score, one that does everything a normal one would. Herrmann insisted that "there was no attempt to create a score by electronic means," but he helped create one anyway, intentionally or not.[11]

With *The Birds*, Hitchcock thus redefined source music; the sound of the birds comes from a visible, nonmusical source, yet acts exactly like a score. But he did not entirely abandon traditional music. First, there is Debussy; Melanie plays the first "Arabesque." As with *The Wrong Man*, where Hitchcock had Henry Fonda learn his Stork Club double-bass jazz numbers, he required Tippi Hedren to take piano lessons for twenty-one days (at two hundred dollars a week) so she could play her "Arabesque" herself, flowingly and convincingly. Melanie's piano is the calm before the storm, the elegance of art sounded out in a seemingly secure home before it becomes a trap. Is it a stretch to suggest that Hitchcock's musical choice is a reference to Poe's *Tales of the Grotesque and Arabesque*? Debussy was a fanatical admirer of Poe, whose *Tales* were a lifelong inspiration, as they were for Hitchcock. In *The Birds*, the arabesque—the elaborate florescence of sound and image, the oscillating bird noises over the Technicolor vision of Bodega Bay—carefully balances the grotesque: the farmer staring balefully with no eyes, the bloody assault outside Melanie's phone booth. We surrender to the malignant birds, awaiting their next attack between the incessant prattle of the human characters, partly because they are so artfully designed and choreographed.

The most memorable source music occurs during the schoolyard scene, where Melanie sits and smokes a cigarette as schoolchildren sing. When Evan Hunter asked his own kids for their favorite school song, they came up with "Risseldy, Rosseldy," a cheery tune that provides Hitchcockian counterpoint to the massing of the birds. Unfortunately, the lyrics were insufficient to cover this long scene, so Hunter had to write new ones— "enough to cover the whole bird kingdom arriving on that jungle gym," he said.[12] He also had another concern, voiced in a memo from Hal Landers to Peggy Robertson on June 4, 1962: "Evan is a bit concerned because he knows the song is a Kentucky folksong, and he wants to know if Revue's legal dept. is under copyright. (He says he doesn't want to have some mountain man come out of the hills someday to sue him first and ask questions later.)" But Hunter was in luck: not only did no one come down from the hills, but he made lots of money because writing new lyrics required him to join ASCAP, resulting in royalties every time the song was used.

"Risseldy" was good for Hitchcock as well. It turned out to be one of his most stunning and celebrated uses of vernacular song. The children's singing dominates the sound track as Melanie enters the school, then fades—but only slightly—when she goes outside to the playground. In real life, the sound would dissipate considerably; the camera follows Melanie in a long shot, watching her move slowly toward the playground, the sound dying a little, then settling into a Mezzo Forte level even as she walks away. Again, we have poetic license, the singing serving as a kind of aural cover for the gathering terror. Seen only by the audience, a single crow swoops down and lights on the jungle gym, then two more, then several. They continue to amass—now seen by no one—as the camera watches Melanie in lingering close-up anxiously drawing on her cigarette, twitching her head this way and that, the song continuing uninterrupted with its nonsensical lyrics. Only when Melanie's eye finally catches a crow flying across the sky, then plummeting to the playground to join its fellow marauders in a huge black mass, does she realize the danger. Throughout this daringly languid scene, the singing pours out of the school with monotonous cheeriness, in one of Hitchcock's most chilling and sustained uses of musical irony.

The Birds is an icon of modern culture, alluded to in newspaper stories whenever birds behave unpleasantly, in TV commercials, and in parodies both affectionate and jeering. It was Hitchcock's last globally influential film, the final one to work its way deeply into our collective subconscious. The film has gradually come to be read as a study of blocked human relationships in which the birds are a metaphor. Although this is undoubtedly accurate, it is still the birds themselves, possessing what Yeats would call a "terrible beauty," that rivet audiences and have become an indelible part of popular culture. "All you can say about *The Birds*," Hitchcock told an interviewer, "is nature can be awful rough on you." Indeed. And that roughness is communicated in large part by musical sound, so much so that Hitchcock had a timpanist play an amplified side drum inside the Brenner house during the shooting so the cast would be properly unnerved. Here was a new kind of invisible music, seen and heard only by the actors, a testament to how closely Hitchcock connected terror to music. (It is also a testament to Hitchcock's grounding in the silent film era, when directors often had musicians playing on the set.)

Thanks to Hitchcock, it is impossible to see or hear birds the same way after experiencing this movie, just as it is impossible to think the same way of a wine cellar after *Notorious*, a shower after *Psycho*, a blank alleyway after *The Man Who Knew Too Much*, or Mount Rushmore after *North by Northwest*. The film does not, of course, explain why the birds attack; enigma is the key to their power. Hitchcock's most powerful villains, the birds have it all: they are uniquely formidable simply being themselves, yet given their stylized, arabesque vagueness, they can also become any fear we like. The best answer I've heard as to why they attack is the one Evan Hunter gave at an academic conference, after many elaborate and laborious papers: "be-cause Mr. Hitchcock told them to."

The Birds is not about explanations but about a strange new world of sound and silence. The latter gradually takes over as the film winds down from violent noise through delicate flutters to ghostly quiet—the final iso-lation in a hostile universe. This film is exactly what its title implies. At the end, there are only the birds. "We are left alone with the birds," Hitchcock says in the final, eloquent passage of his sound notes. "All we hear is this brooding, massing murmur which should continue until the picture fades out."

22

the music ends:
hitchcock fires herrmann

It was really all Hitchcock's fault.

—Claude Chabrol

We'll never know what really happened.

—Christopher Palmer

The swift and permanent rupture between Bernard Herrmann and Alfred Hitchcock over the score for *Torn Curtain* was a tragedy for both artists. A decade of collaboration had established Hitchcock-Herrmann as the greatest director-composer team in cinematic history. Neither artist entirely recovered, though claims of their mutual collapse are exaggerated. Herrmann went on to write powerful music for Truffaut, De Palma, and Scorsese; Hitchcock got imaginative scores from Maurice Jarre, Ron Goodwin, and John Williams. Yet the shadow of Hitchcock-Herrmann lingered over the last works of both artists: *Obsession* is an extended meditation on the music for *Vertigo, The Bride Wore Black* an affectionate Hitchcock homage; *Taxi Driver,* which Herrmann finished on Christmas Day of 1975, the day he died, concludes with a traumatic quotation from *Psycho.* Hitchcock stewed in silence about the falling out but would occasionally vent his bitterness. He aired his side of the quarrel to Jarre during *Topaz;* indeed, he took to Jarre partly because his music sounds so unlike Herrmann's, just as he fired Henry Mancini during *Frenzy* for sounding too much like Herrmann. Christopher Palmer called the severance Herrmann's great professional tragedy; it was a personal one as well: increasingly lonely and estranged from the Hollywood establishment, he had enjoyed an affectionate relationship with Hitchcock and his family and was shattered by the breakup. He attempted reconciliation, but Hitchcock, who never looked back, refused to speak with him. According to Donald Spoto, Hitchcock actually hid behind a door to avoid being seen when Herrmann came to his office for a visit.

Most commentators blame Hitchcock for the breakup, but both men were propelled by larger cultural and corporate forces, as well as by their equally stubborn and uncompromising personalities. An eloquent gloss on the outer stresses was provided five years after the firing by another Hitchcock composer, Dimitri Tiomkin, in an elegy for the end of Hollywood's Golden Age: "[Hollywood] was a bright dream about a beautiful democracy in a world under the shadow of tyranny. I suppose there were fakers and phonies, but I can't help thinking there was an innocence which has now vanished. Once Hollywood forgot the dreams and got down to reality, it failed."[1] The reality, the breakup of the studio system and the abandonment of creative risk for ever more instant profits and blockbusters, was paralleled by a lust for pop scores—one Tiomkin himself had helped ignite with his huge hit song for *High Noon*. Hitchcock and Herrmann, both strong individual artists, suffered profoundly under these pressures, although it is hard to explain the rupture on these grounds alone. Hollywood-made-me do-it only goes so far; powerful personal and aesthetic issues were enacted as well.

THE UNRAVELING BEGINS: *MARNIE*

The background to disaster was *Marnie*, a film that has many admirers in contemporary academia but was roundly panned by audiences and critics at its release. Hitchcock envisioned this "sex mystery," as he called it in the trailer, in the tradition of *Rebecca* and *Spellbound*, but it strikes most viewers as utterly singular—daring in the view of Hitchcockians, merely odd in the opinion of most others. Jay Presson Allen, who wrote the screenplay, confessed in 1999 to being puzzled by the current revisionism. She didn't think *Marnie* was good in 1964 and doesn't think so now: "It's not a very good movie because I didn't know how to write it. Hitchcock was an unbelievably marvelous teacher, but my ignorance was glorious—I hadn't a clue." And she doesn't buy the rapturous reappraisals of Tippi Hedren: "Tippi's too brittle." Academic deconstructions of the movie puzzle her too: "I've been in this business for 50 years, and I don't ever remember meeting an intellectual. It comes from the gut, from instinct."[2]

One intellectual who did admire *Marnie* was Truffaut, who called it a "great flawed film," a "fascinating" work "underrated by the critics." The critics may have caught up, but they were much too late: "Hitchcock was never the same after *Marnie*," states Truffaut, "and its failure cost him a considerable amount of his self-confidence." It is against this backdrop of gnawing anxiety and self-doubt that the blowup with Herrmann erupted.[3]

For all the innovativeness now attributed to *Marnie*, Hitchcock's production crew saw it as he did, as a psychological thriller about guilt and memory harking back to the Selznick era, with music to match. A memo dated November 11 following an "Art Meeting on Marnie" states that "Hitchcock's conception of *Marnie* is that of a psychological suspense drama in the same genre as *Rebecca*," with "many psychological undertones." Hitchcock's direction would emphasize "tempo and pace," two of his favorite musical concepts, and would "have a musical theme along the lines of *Spellbound*."[4] Whether accidentally or deliberately, Herrmann delivered in his main title exactly what we experience in Rozsa's for *Spellbound*, though in his own unmistakable style: a jagged paranoia theme followed immediately by a resplendent love melody, a *Spellbound* design that repeats throughout the film in scenes juxtaposing attraction with repulsion. As Marnie literally sees red and goes into traumatized trances, the anxiety motif stabs violently into the sound track, often just before the love melody soars above it. (The dread-inducing red is similar to the parallel lines that spook Gregory Peck in *Spellbound*.) In the exposition, the two themes play separately, the latter during Marnie's traumas and nightmares, the former during happier moments, such as her ride on her beloved horse, Forio; they first sound together when Marnie spills red ink and flees past a concerned Mark Rutland, played with suave intensity by Sean Connery.

These two ideas, one a bleak fragmentation of the other, provide most of the musical substance in this tightly unified score. Many of the themes—the moody driving music as Mark takes Marnie to meet his father, for example—are variations on the main title. As Royal S. Brown points out, this type of traditional theme score was a departure for Herrmann, who in *Vertigo* and *Psycho* reprised the title motif only in subtle, restrained ways while spinning out a multiplicity of contrasting ones. Herrmann does deliver strong subsidiary inventions: a wistful theme for Forio, a *Vertigo*-style sequence of cha-cha chords during the office manager's nervous reopenings of the company safe; a terrifying series of ascending scales during the "men in white" flashback; and sighing chords at the end releasing Mrs. Edgar's suppressed memories, a superb example of Herrmann's ability to deliver a complex epiphany with harmonies and colors. The tour de force is the spectacular hunting scene, a pure cinema extravaganza that begins with Haydnesque hunting calls (an homage to those in *Suspicion?*) and builds to a climax of snarling dissonance. This was Herrmann's last great sequence in a Hitchcock film: at least he went out in style.

None of this was good enough for Hitchcock, who thought *Marnie* was too much like Herrmann's usual, indeed a travesty of self-plagiarism. (Never mind that Hitchcock repeated a source music device right out of *The Birds:* the children's song framing the scenes with Marnie's mother.) Even among admirers, the music has a reputation as one of Herrmann's most traditional scores, a retreat from the innovations of *Psycho* and *The Birds.* That it works splendidly for the movie, providing a far more eloquent dramatization of tortured passion than Tippi Hedren, didn't matter to Hitchcock. Perhaps more important, it didn't matter to the executives at Universal: they too thought it was a retro score and pressured Hitchcock to get rid of Herrmann.

The music was planned with the usual care, as indicated by a "preliminary music note" from January 17, 1964: "After the main title music fades out, the opening shot of Marnie walking down the railroad station will be without music—just the clipetty-clop of her walk. When we jump to the big head of Strutt, we may possibly start music here." Herrmann's melancholy score followed by the stark percussion of that "clippety-clop" sets up *Marnie*'s uncompromising expressionist tone, its most successful feature. (In the final cut, there was no music in the opening scene with Strutt, the robbed businessman; his ominous tirade is allowed to speak for itself.)

One advantage Universal thought it had for this problematic film was "Marnie," a song recorded by Nat King Cole ("Your world is lonely, Marnie"), along with sheet music for a piano solo with sketches of Hedren and Connery on the cover.[5] Since Herrmann's love theme was so romantic, there was no need to create a new tune for the lyrics. For the public, however, the idea of a "Marnie" hit tune was just as unlikely as it sounds: a frigid, hallucinating kleptomaniac was not exactly the ideal subject for a pop love song. The song, originally planned for the main title, sank into oblivion with the movie; unlike the latter, it never resurfaced. Herrmann's music had enhanced the reputation of other Hitchcock films, but this time its only impact was as a sharp point of contention for the next project.

THE RIP THAT WOULDN'T MEND: *TORN CURTAIN*

Torn Curtain, like *Marnie,* was also a dismal flop, and a more painful one for Hitchcock, who now had less control over his product than ever before and who knew from the beginning that this film was shaping up as a failure. The script, as acknowledged by Brian Moore, who wrote the screenplay, was unsuccessful (Peggy Robertson tried, without success, to bring back John Michael Hayes), and Hitchcock was convinced that his two leads, Paul Newman and Julie Andrews, both foisted on him by Universal, were dreadfully miscast. He regarded their $1.8 million salary as a "disgrace . . . just because they happened to be hot!"[6]

Herrmann always insisted that he was terminated from this unhappy project because he refused to lower himself to write popular music, but there was a great deal more to it than that. According to Rudy Behlmer, the issue had little to do with pop songs; as with Newman and Andrews, it was all about who had star power. The studio, especially Lew Wasserman, wanted Herrmann out because he was no longer a box office draw: "'Get something that's in,' they told Hitchcock, 'something hot, something contemporary.' It wasn't really about pop."[7]

But pop was certainly part of the equation; one reason Hitchcock worried about Julie Andrews was that audiences would expect her to sing. Universal condemned Herrmann's current writing as "lazy" and "derivative," but they also wanted a profitable title song because they too knew that *Torn Curtain* was going badly.[8] As we have seen, the pressure to produce a hit song went back to the Selznick era, but it was now more intense. At least when Selznick failed to get a good pop song, he had sense enough to simply let the matter drop. For him, a song was a bonus, not an obsession. The composer David Raskin maintains that personal animus was also to blame; Hitchcock had been "ruthless" and "cruel" to many people, and now they were getting their revenge: "They took advantage of Hitchcock on his way down. . . . They started giving him a hard time. . . . Some of the guys at Universal said 'You don't need that old-fashioned score. What you need is something "with it"—"now!"'"[9]

Then there was the issue of authorship. Alex Ross makes the provocative comment that the films Herrmann scored "seem to mirror his own concerns, rather than the other way round. How much of the emotional intensity we feel in these greatest achievements of Welles and Hitchcock—directors not otherwise noted for their romantic touch—comes from the dark passion of Benny Herrmann?"[10] Raskin (who loathed Hitchcock) put it more bluntly: "Hitchcock owed Benny *everything*." Hitchcock was giving Herrmann credit for some of the dark passion, especially in *Psycho*, and Herrmann suspected that Hitchcock was beginning to resent the extent of his contribution—who was the auteur, anyway? Certainly Ross's formulation, if correct, reverses normal expectations: with Hitchcock, the film was paramount—the composer or anyone else should adjust himself to it, not the other way round.

Perhaps Herrmann had simply overstayed his welcome. Given the work-for-hire nature of directing and composing in the studio era, seven consecutive collaborations were highly unusual. Waxman and Tiomkin had worked four times for Hitchcock, and each had had a long intermission between projects; Herrmann had nearly doubled the quota and was much more temperamental and willful than either man.

The story of the actual firing is as dramatic and troubling as a Hitchcock movie. It begins with a long, ominous telegram from Hitchcock on November 4, 1965, commissioning the score. "I am very anxious for you to do the music on *Torn Curtain*," it begins. Anxious is the correct word, for by now, Hitchcock was under pressure to get rid of Herrmann. "I was extremely disappointed when I heard the music for 'Joy in the Morning,'" the telegram continues, suddenly turning hostile. "Not only did I find it conforming to the old pattern but extremely reminiscent of the *Marnie* music." Hitchcock was mortified that Herrmann had cannibalized from the failed *Marnie* for a non-Hitchcock production (a downbeat teenage love story) that was an even greater flop. This was not a new issue: twenty years earlier, Hitchcock had engaged in a memo battle with Rozsa over that composer's alleged self-plagiarism, something that angered him even though that score and its film were a great success.

Conforming to the old pattern meant not only that Herrmann was repeating himself but that he was writing in an Old World symphonic style rather than a hip 1960s idiom: "We do not have the freedom that we would like to have because we are catering to an audience and that is why you get your money and I get mine. This audience is very different to the one to which we used to cater. It is young, vigorous, and demanding. It is this fact that has been recognized by almost all the European film makers where they have sought to introduce a beat and a rhythm that is more in tune with the requirements of the aforesaid audience." Hitchcock was blunt: if Herrmann could not come up with a 1960s beat and rhythm, whatever that meant, "then I am the loser"—and so, by implication, would be Herrmann. "I have made up my mind that this approach to the music is extremely essential."

As someone who was a member of that young, vigorous, and demanding sixties audience, I can attest that we adored the music for *Vertigo, North by Northwest, Psycho, The Birds*, and even *Marnie*. Herrmann *was* hot, and we would happily have gone along with the challenging music he wrote for *Torn Curtain*. Like his studio bosses, Hitchcock simply misread the culture, something sad and unprecedented for him, and sadder for Herrmann. Audiences of the 1960s endorsed pop music in films such as *The Graduate, Midnight Cowboy,* and Richard Lester's Beatles movies because it was appropriate and skillfully used—just like the pop music in *Rear Window* and *The Man Who Knew Too Much.* They rejected many other rock-infused movies (mercifully forgotten) and were far more sophisticated in their tastes and requirements than the studios realized, as demonstrated by the popularity of later Herrmann scores such as *Fahrenheit 451* and *Taxi Driver*— both dark, complex, and thoroughly Herrmannesque.

Hitchcock's sense that he and Herrmann did not have "the freedom that we would like" in an increasingly corporate era created feelings of intense vulnerability. Initially, his uncompromising perfectionism had endeared him to Herrmann, an artist like himself who had a vision compatible with his own. Both men saw life as a treacherous chaos fleetingly ordered by art. Clearly, Hitchcock was hoping to appeal to Herrmann as a sympathetic soul, a comrade in arms, using "we" in his memo rather than "I."

Nonetheless, under severe pressure, he was determined to limit Herrmann's possibilities: "I also have very definite ideas as to where the music should go in the picture, and there is not too much." The happy period of *Vertigo* and *North by Northwest,* when Hitchcock trusted Herrmann and allowed him great flexibility, seemed long in the past.

Part of Hitchcock's dark mood was his suspicion that in *Torn Curtain* he had another disaster on his hands. Projecting his anxiety onto Herrmann, he dragged other composers into his diatribe: "So often I have been asked by Tiomkin, for example, to come and listen to a score and when I express my disapproval his hands were thrown up and with the cry of 'But you can't change anything now, it has all been orchestrated.' It is this kind of frustration that I am rather tired of . . . getting music scored on a take it or leave it basis." Here we get a rare glimpse of the director's frustration at not being able to get exactly the music he wants. It is not clear which Tiomkin pictures Hitchcock is bemoaning, but since all except *I Confess* were successes (even it was praised for its music), we can speculate that Hitchcock was expressing a general weariness during a bad moment in his career.

And there was "another problem: this music has to be sketched in advance because we have an urgent problem of meeting a tax date. We will not finish shooting until the middle of January at the earliest and Technicolor requires the complete picture by February first." Herrmann was therefore put in the awkward position of being asked to write the music before the scenes were ready.

Herrmann later told the press that he resisted Hitchcock's request: "If he wanted that kind of music, I told him, he ought to get that kind of composer."[11] But in his letter back to Hitchcock on November 5, he quickly assented to the grudging commission: "Delighted to compose a vigorous beat score for TC. Always pleased to have your views regarding the music for the film. Please send script indicating where you desire music. I can then begin." All seemed well; the agreement to write a "vigorous beat" score designates a commitment, however vague, to come up with something snappy and sixties. But speaking of Hitchcock's views was the worst thing Herrmann could have uttered; this director issued instructions, not views. When Hitchcock did not respond, the uncharacteristic silence filled Herrmann with anxiety, as indicated by a November 18 telegram to Peggy Robertson:

> Dear Peggy:
> Nearly 2 weeks ago I replied to Hitch's cable as follows: "Delighted to compose a vigorous beat score for TC . . ."
> As of today I have not received the script and am anxious to have it. I would also like to have Hitch indicate where he wishes music and also his ideas about the kind of music for each one. If he could describe these in the same manner as he does when he gives the sound department his notes on sound . . . I have been asked to do Truffaut's new film next May or June. I am certain that this is because of Hitch and I thank him for it. I have not seen his book on Hitch as yet. . . . I am most anxious to read it. . . . All the best for the *Torn Curtain*. Indeed, I feel certain it will be one of Hitch's greatest films. I just know it will be so.
> Love Benny

The nervousness at the beginning—asking Robertson to intercede on his behalf—is matched by the obsequiousness at the end. Herrmann was usually blunt, not given to flattery. There was certainly no harm in saying twice that *Torn Curtain* would be one of the great Hitchcock films when all the advance signs indicated otherwise; many would say such a thing reflexively as a way of ingratiating themselves to the boss. But this was not Herrmann's way, and he was hardly a stranger to Hitchcock. On the other hand, he was obviously happy about the Truffaut assignment, and grateful to Hitchcock for it. What he did not know was how timely the Truffaut commission was, given how grimly things were about to go.

He certainly had plenty of warning. Paul C. Donnelly, a member of the production team, wired Herrmann on November 11, 1965, offering $17,500 and concluding with the following ominous caveat: "Benny, there is one point that Hitch asked me to stress and that is the fact that you should not refer to his 'views' toward the score, but rather his requirements for vigorous rhythm and a change from what he calls 'the old pattern.'" Here it was, as terse and blunt as one of Herrmann's motifs: do it my way—write something hip and jettison the old pattern—or else. Herrmann must have known that Hitchcock meant it; a chronic avoider of unpleasantness, Hitchcock invariably had someone else issue significant warnings and threats. Furthermore, he met with Herrmann briefly in late December, heard a few motifs Herrmann had sketched, and declared them too heavy; he also, in a moment reminiscent of his instructions for *Psycho*, insisted that Herrmann write no music for the murder sequence.[12]

Still, the assignment seemed intact, as Robertson's December telegram to Herrmann indicates: "I think [*Torn Curtain*] will be Hitch's greatest. I read your letter to him and he was most pleased, as you can imagine." Hitchcock sent music notes on February 15 calling for an "exciting, arresting, and rhythmic" main title. By March 1, Herrmann was well along, as his music notes for the gruesome murder sequence indicate: "2nd Reel . . . music after Armstrong throws object at telephone . . . out on hand opening gas jets . . . music as second gas jet is closed . . . out at end of reel." Plans were made to record the score at the Goldwyn Studio on March 24 and 25 and April 4.

All seemed normal—except for one thing: "The orchestra: 12 flutes, 16 horns, 9 trombones, 2 tubas, 2 kettle drums, large group of cellos and basses." This heavy, bizarre ensemble must have raised eyebrows. And what Herrmann wrote was entirely suited for it. Vigorous it certainly is—harrowing would be a better word. But a 1960s beat is nowhere to be found, by any stretch of the imagination. Nor does it eschew the old pattern; in fact, it carries it to the furthest, most strident extreme. Grim, shattering, unremittingly bleak, this is Herrmann at his most expressionistic, without any hint of 1960s pop.

Given Hitchcock's emphatic demands and warnings, did Herrmann really have to write a black, angry score for a dozen horns and flutes and only the darkest strings? His *Torn Curtain* Prelude is so ostentatiously grim that one wonders what his motives were. Did he write it to test or irritate Hitchcock, to show who was really in charge of the music? The score seems to be another manifestation of his legendary irascibility, what Oscar Levant termed his "apprenticeship in insolence."[13]

But Herrmann's prickliness was only one side of a complex personality. My friend Seymour Solomon, president of Vanguard Records, told me on several occasions that Herrmann was kind and compassionate, his flashes of bitterness mainly symptoms of a bad marriage. Miklos Rozsa, Joseph Stefano, Royal S. Brown, Steven Smith, Oliver Daniel, and Christopher Palmer all speak of a fundamental generosity, sincerity, and warmth beneath the shell of insolence. It is possible that Herrmann genuinely believed his score would jolt some dark energy into a movie he had heard was moribund and that he was hoping to get Hitchcock on board, as he had done in *Psycho*'s shower cue. Stranger things have happened in show business; it is always risky to over-psychoanalyze such a situation. Artistic considerations were surely in play. Like Hitchcock, Herrmann loved risk and experimentation; he never chose the easy way out, though he misread the political moment, underestimating the pressure his boss was under from the studio. Certainly, his own comments about the score—he was especially proud of the orchestration—betray nothing but boyish enthusiasm at discovering a new sonority. ("The sound of twelve flutes," he said, "will be *terrifying*.")[14]

Royal S. Brown provides the most convincing assessment: "[Herrmann] apparently—and quite rightly—saw *Torn Curtain* as a film that justified neither the pop tune approach nor the type of John Addison fluff it finally ended up with. And so, for the first time in his Hitchcock collaborations, the composer turned, perhaps somewhat spitefully, to an outrageous but quite effective orchestration."[15] Herrmann's idiosyncratic score was thus the result of artistic calculations, with a bit of spite as well.

Hitchcock's reaction was ugly, swift, and exactly the opposite of what Herrmann hoped. He came to Goldwyn Studio, listened to a playback of the prelude, and angrily declared the music unsatisfactory. Herrmann tried to get him to hear another cue, but Hitchcock fired him on the spot, humiliating him in front of his colleagues.

As Meryl Seacrest once observed, show-business memories are always Rashomon. Everybody has a different account of what really happened; as Christopher Palmer points out, no one knows the full story. Herrmann claimed he was not fired at all but resigned because he wouldn't cave in to philistines: "I wouldn't sell myself to that MCA boardroom nonsense."[16] He told Brown that he blasted Hitchcock on the phone later in the day: "I said, 'I had a career before, and I will afterwards. . . . Look, Hitch, you can't outrun your own shadow. And you don't make pop pictures. What do you want with me? I don't write pop music.'"[17] Raskin says Herrmann pleaded with Hitchcock to at least finish the recording session, then decide what to do, but Hitchcock cancelled the session to embarrass Herrmann in front of the orchestra players, who had cheered the score after recording the main title.

Most accounts cast Hitchcock as the villain, Herrmann as the valiant defender of high art. "You can't really call it a falling out; it was really all Hitchcock's fault," said Claude Chabrol; Raskin accused Hitchcock of having "the loyalty of an eel."[18] What this mythology ignores is that it was Hitchcock who defended Herrmann in the beginning, even though he agreed the composer had become "a very difficult man" and insisted he be hired when Universal sought to keep him off the project.[19] After sticking his neck out, Hitchcock felt burned when Herrmann spurned his directions; he was a director, after all, one who knew what he wanted. Alan Robinson, a horn player, remembers that Hitchcock simply said, "What is this? It's not what I want."[20] When Hitchcock was told after hearing the main title that Herrmann had scored the murder sequence against his directive, he felt further betrayed.[21] In yet another version of what happened, Truffaut insists that the studio pressured Hitchcock to discard Herrmann's score after it had been recorded.[22]

There is plenty of blame to go around, and no winners: not Hitchcock, Herrmann, the studio, the film, or even John Addison, whose replacement score was so undistinguished it hurt his legacy—the opposite of the case with other Hitchcock composers. Hitchcock and Herrmann, locked in a stubborn struggle over control and authorship, misread all the cues; Wasserman and company were misinformed about their audience. No one would have cared about this behind-the-scenes drama had it not been for the universal acclaim of the Hitchcock-Herrmann collaborations. At least that much is affirmed by the notoriety of this sad incident.

There are many ironies here. No one was able to pressure John Addison into writing anything remotely resembling sixties music. Indeed, Addison gave an interview to the *Los Angeles Times* in which he boasted that "the PR people are quite happy" with his "simple, straightforward waltz" that became the *Torn Curtain* love song, "The Green Years," replete with Livingston-Evans lyrics.[23] So much for hip, happening music with a sixties beat! The powers-that-be turned out to be not happy at all; after much dithering and indecision, Hitchcock and the studio dropped the song from the film, though, as with "Marnie," they released a sheet-music version with the stars on the cover in a final effort to plug the film.

The composer who *was* hot was Herrmann; he had just been hired by Truffaut, the most prominent of the New Wave Europeans Hitchcock had warned Herrmann against as exemplars of sixties beat and rhythm. This

The LOVE THEME from

TORN CURTAIN

(GREEN YEARS)

Music by JOHN ADDISON • Lyrics by JAY LIVINGSTON and RAY EVANS

PAUL JULIE
NEWMAN ANDREWS
in
ALFRED HITCHCOCK'S
'TORN CURTAIN'
TECHNICOLOR®

LILA KEDROVA · HANSJOERG FELMY · TAMARA TOUMANOVA
LUDWIG DONATH · DAVID OPATOSHU · JOHN ADDISON · BRIAN MOORE
Directed by ALFRED HITCHCOCK · A Universal Picture

SHAMLEY MUSIC CORPORATION
Sole Selling Agent **MCA MUSIC** a division of MCA INC.   75c IN U.S.A.

"Green Years," love theme from *Torn Curtain*. The song could not save the movie.

was doubly ironic given that Truffaut would soon provide Hitchcock enormous new cachet by publishing a book-length interview that became an international hit. The crowning strangeness was that Herrmann was hired in the early 1970s by Brian De Palma, the hip young director of the moment in America, to score *Obsession* and *Sisters*—both homages to Hitchcock, and in the case of *Obsession,* to Herrmann's music for Hitchcock.

Although Herrmann said he wasn't fired from *Torn Curtain*, Hitchcock officially terminated him on March 25 after apologizing to Universal and offering to pay Herrmann's salary. Four days later, he was sent John Addison's credits, which looked impressive. He had thirty-three films under his belt, some of which—the Oscar-winning *Tom Jones, A Fine Madness, Look Back in Anger, School for Scoundrels*—were highly regarded. In addition, Addison was a well-known television composer. Maurice Jarre was first choice because of the enormously popular *Doctor Zhivago*, but he was unavailable.

After hearing that Herrmann had gone down, Dimitri Tiomkin tried to put himself back in the Hitchcock family: "Understood no composer set for your picture," he wrote Hitchcock in a telegram; "will love to be associated with you once more." But as his cranky telegram to Herrmann implied, Hitchcock was through with Tiomkin, who represented the Old Guard. And in any case, Tiomkin would have wanted to keep more of the rights to his music than the studio cared to grant.[24] In April, Addison was hastily hired for $12,500, and Hitchcock began preparing new music notes, but postproduction was by now such a scramble that he had to communicate with Addison by transatlantic telephone. This unsatisfactory arrangement may have influenced the result: the dullest score for any Hitchcock film, and the least Hitchcockian. Royal S. Brown speaks of a "Hitchcock chord," an anxious Herrmann dissonance that simultaneously employs major and minor intervals, invoking the world of the irrational that exists beneath Hitchcock's rational surfaces; as we have seen, Rozsa and Webb could create convincingly disorienting harmonies of their own, but Addison apparently couldn't, at least not for this film. What he produced, ironically, was watered-down Herrmann: for example, the close-up of Michael's telegram response in reel 1, backed by harsh string figures against low winds, but without Herrmann's uncanny harmonies; or the dissonant strings in Paul Newman's men's room scene (Addison called this the "brain theme"), which sounded like a tame version of *Psycho*.

A comparison between Herrmann's score and Addison's is telling. Herrmann's pounding prelude, the occasion of his termination, rivets our attention; despite the exotic scoring, there is something fundamental and primordial about it—Herrmann stripped down to his essence. Addison's waltz, on the other hand, colorfully orchestrated with snare drums and saxophones, is skillful boilerplate, too mild for the apocalyptic images on the screen but too dour for counterpoint. For the opening bedroom scene, Addison provided Hollywood romance music followed by what his notes call "gay phrases," setting an off-key mood for this furtive love scene, where

Michael must jump out of bed and lie to the message boy—and, implicitly, to Sarah—to protect his double-agent identity. Hitchcock's basic espionage-romance-betrayal narrative is set in motion, but with little help from the music.

Herrmann avoids love themes and character motifs. His icy brass harmonies are pure mood, malevolent and gripping. Newman and Andrews as Michael and Sarah move furtively through the film as if pursued by his stalking chords. We forget (or at least overlook) what's coming so unconvincingly out of their mouths.[25] Herrmann's starkness pays off again and again: Sarah's bookshop scene, with the professor appearing and disappearing behind bookcases, is insidiously unnerving thanks to a motif ascending to nowhere; Addison's sour woodwind descent tells us something bad is afoot without evoking any mystery. With Herrmann, the simplest devices are effective, as in the whispered woodwinds when Sarah discovers that Michael is flying to East Berlin, a moment when this brutal score takes on great subtlety. Similarly, when Michael harshly orders Sarah to go home, gently swirling woodwinds suggest her gathering pain and chaos.

Instead of the anxious ambiguity Hitchcock usually elicited, Addison's score delivers stock responses: the breezy waltz playing as Sarah leaves the hotel in reel 2, the stinger chord when she tells the professor she is engaged to Michael, the gloomy fugal variant of her theme after Michael rebuffs her at the restaurant, which does little to convey her hurt. Addison's music is as unsuited for Hitchcock as his saucy score for *Tom Jones* was dead-center perfect for Tony Richardson. Rather than invoking mystery and tension, it imitates and italicizes, telling us what we should feel rather than making us feel it. These emotions—the kind Hollywood composers were coming to increasingly rely on—are virtual rather than real.

The most revealing contrast between scores is the lightest cue, Hitchcock's cameo holding a baby. Addison's "tune on a trombone," standard fat-joke music, is embarrassing. Herrmann's version, a moment of charm in an otherwise grim score, is a rich horn fanfare followed by twirling woodwinds, another "portrait of Hitch" by someone who knew him well, especially touching because it shows his continued affection for Hitchcock even in the midst of their deteriorating relationship.

Herrmann's score has a mysterious beauty never attempted by Addison, as illustrated by seductive brass chords when Michael discovers the "Pi" code in the men's room, a daring contrast to Addison's standard stinger chords. With Herrmann, the film takes on a larger emotional dimension that might have helped it immensely had he been allowed to finish his job.

His last finished cue, the brutal, endless killing of Gromek, is one of the most gruesome things he ever wrote, a sustained explosion of rage and violence in the lower winds, appropriate not only for this troubling scene but for the gathering storm in his friendship with Hitchcock.

The final version of the Gromek killing has no music, as Hitchcock instructed, a striking illustration of his preference for silence during scenes of disturbing violence. And *Torn Curtain* does have his usual expert spotting. The long shot of Michael and Sarah on a hill where they are observed but not heard by the professor delivers its epiphany entirely through music, as a sappy version of Sarah's theme tells us that Michael has come clean with the truth. What a great moment this might have been had the music been Herrmann's! And there are wonderful, characteristic touches, including the timpani solo during the bus escape and Strauss waltzes playing as stately counterpoint in the restaurant scene where Michael is softening up Professor Lindt for the blackboard duel.

The most striking indication of the score's pallidness is its painful contrast with the Tchaikovsky ballet scene. Hitchcock originally planned five minutes from Ravel's *Daphnis and Chloe*, but according to a Peggy Robertson memo of October 1, 1965, "the finicky French" wouldn't allow it without the original orchestration. Hitchcock was always attracted to impressionist music, as evidenced by the Delius scene in *Saboteur* and Melanie's Debussy solo in *The Birds;* the endless search for the lost "Mary Rose" music shows he was especially fascinated by offstage choruses (an effect he would finally get from John Williams in *Family Plot*), but he would not get them here: the *Daphnis* plan was scrapped, even though the timings had been planned (one and a half minutes for the Prima Ballerina, three and a half for the Corps de Ballet). Hitchcock considered other intriguing possibilities, ordering the Eugene Ormandy–Philadelphia Orchestra recording of Bartók's Concerto for Orchestra (a work that is invoked in Robert Bloch's novel *Psycho*) and Boulez's *Le Marteau sans maître*, the latter a manifestation of his interest in the avant-garde cultivated during *The Birds*. (It's not clear how he would have used these had he chosen them.)

Finally he settled for *Francesca da Rimini*, which Stanley Wilson (a composer for Hitchcock's television show) conducted with a thirty-six-piece orchestra. Suddenly, *Torn Curtain* comes to life. Tchaikovsky's tone poem is perfectly timed with Hitchcock's jarring camera as it records the accusing eyes of the ballerina and Michael's escape epiphany as he watches flames leaping from the ballet stage. As in the music-hall finale of *The 39 Steps* and the Royal Albert Hall scene from *The Man Who Knew Too Much,*

Hitchcock integrates movement and sound with a concert layout to produce a stunning music-suspense sequence. This time he incorporates ballet, a metaphor in chase movies that here becomes literal. The choreography extends from the ballet proper through panicked mob gyrations to an elaborate chase down the stairs, concluding with Michael and Sarah jumping into costume baskets, a marvelous comic touch. For a glorious moment the old Hitchcock, the cinema's musical master, bounces back.

Two years after the *Torn Curtain* debacle, Herrmann, still smarting from his wounds, gave an interview to the *Los Angeles Times* entitled "Composer Settles a Score." By turns rambling, self-pitying, feisty, and deeply touching, it reveals Herrmann still hurt and angered over his firing, yet rising to Hitchcock's defense. "Everybody's looking for a new sound," he stated, referring to the fetish for up-to-dateness that ruined his collaboration with Hitchcock, "which means taking an old sound and jacking it up and amplifying it till your ears hurt. There are no new sounds, just new ideas. . . . They don't come along very often." When asked about his termination, he gave his stock answer: "The studio and Hitchcock felt they wanted a pop score. If that's what they wanted I wasn't fitted for it."[26]

Not entirely buying this, Kevin Thomas, the interviewer, asked, "What of Que Sera Sera, which had a score admired by Hitchcock more than the one for the original film?" That score, of course, was by Herrmann, and in the case of *Torn Curtain,* Hitchcock could again have hired someone else to write a song. It was Herrmann's explosive prelude that caused the firing. Yet Herrmann strongly defended Hitchcock's decision to use the Livingston-Evans song: "It was imperative that he have something while he was panning down that staircase. So Doris Day came up with three songs, and this was the best." It was not, Herrmann argued, "a pre-meditated attempt at song plugging." And Herrmann continued praising Hitchcock: "Many directors can make one or two great movies, but how many can make 50 great ones, like Hitchcock? Somerset Maugham once said, 'Anyone has a good novel in him—it's the second one I'm interested in.'"

In a poignant moment, Thomas called Herrmann "an extension of Hitchcock and his only heir apparent" and stated that Herrmann "hopes to be working again with Hitchcock." This, however, was not to be. Right or wrong, Hitchcock's wishes regarding music were explicit; Herrmann had deliberately ignored them. For Hitchcock, there was no forgiveness or turning back.

Perhaps the definitive statement on the rupture comes from John Williams, who, like his timpanist father, was close to Herrmann. His sources are impressive—Peggy Robertson and Herrmann himself—but he admits the reasons for the termination are ultimately mysterious. "I tried through Peggy Robertson to understand what had happened between the two of them; it's a mystery. I even asked Benny about it, and he said, 'Oh, I know things about him that can't be told'—all this kind of allusion to personal difficulties that I think had nothing to do with music or film. But I can't even surmise what it could be."

There is a tantalizing clue: "One thing Peggy offered to me one day when we were sitting alone in his projection room: she said that Hitchcock had heard some of Herrmann's music in other films that he thought sounded too familiar to the music he'd written for his films, and he felt that Benny was repeating himself and quoting himself." This statement is consistent with Hitchcock's telegram expressing his "disappointment" in Herrmann quoting *Marnie* in *Joy in the Morning*. Williams feels that on its face, the charge is not unreasonable: "It could be true: Herrmann's music was very insistent and consistent—you could also say 'repetitive,' in the good sense of that word, and also idiosyncratic—nobody else could have written it."[27]

So we come full circle: Herrmann was repeating himself—but what he was quoting was his own lonely, unique voice. Did Hitchcock really want a chameleonlike composer who adjusted his style to suit changing taste, when his own films were also quirky, daring, and full of obsessively repeating motifs? If Hitchcock could repeat himself, why couldn't Herrmann? Perhaps the two were actually too similar, a theory Williams got from various Hitchcock associates: "Hitchcock may have felt that his style was too dependent on Herrmann's music and that might have wounded his pride: they ended up being two matadors opposing one another."

Herrmann preferred another animal metaphor for his personality, concluding his *Times* interview with a quote from Tolstoy: "Eagles fly alone, and sparrows fly in flocks." What he never quite grasped was that Hitchcock hired eagles—but only those who learned to behave like sparrows once they flew onto his set.

23

topaz: the music is back

I didn't give you a great picture, but you gave me a great score.

—Hitchcock to Maurice Jarre

Conventional wisdom has it that after Hitchcock lost Herrmann, every-thing went downhill. Claude Chabrol went so far as to assert that after the firing, Hitchcock's music "was only good when it imitated Herrmann."[1] *Torn Curtain*'s score is indeed undistinguished, but what Hitchcock got from Maurice Jarre, Ron Goodwin, and John Williams was topflight. In-deed, as Hitchcock lost some of his touch with actors, scripts, and audi-ences, he retained his mastery of the sound track.

Certainly this was the case with *Topaz,* an elegant, fascinating, though curiously inexpressive Cold War thriller about defectors and double agents set against the Cuban Missile Crisis. Even in decline, Hitchcock continued to be an enormous draw for composers. Michel Legrand, fresh off his suc-cess with *The Thomas Crown Affair,* applied for the job as composer, as did Richard Rodney Bennett. The most bizarre application came from Ravi Shankar: "As you know," stated a breathless July 1968 memo from one of his representatives, "he is a great admirer of yours." The PR accompanying Shankar's submission called him "hippie culture's newest guru," adding the odd caveat that "he never wanted to be a hippie heir in the first place."[2] Hitchcock surely got a much needed laugh out of this pop-Indian, reluc-tant-hippie sitar composer applying for a job requiring European music with Russian overtones evoking balalaika sounds.

The most fascinating part of the search for a composer was an ambi-tious attempt to enlist Dmitri Shostakovich, whose searing "Babi Yar" Symphony interested Hitchcock so much that he ordered research on the work and set in motion a series of inquiries. (Though mainly a symphonic composer, Shostakovich had written numerous film scores for Soviet cinema.) A music department memo from John McKellen to Harry Garfield, dated February 27, 1969, expressed skepticism: "There are various reasons why we do not think this is feasible. . . . Any motion pictures for which Russian music is being considered must be ok'd by their cultural attaché. The general lines for guidance are that anything in the motion picture that might have anti-Russian or anti-Communist overtones would cause the Russians to prohibit the use of their music. . . . It appears that in the case of *Topaz* . . . there are certain Communist implications in the plot. . . . [It] would certainly appear that the Russians would not approve. . . . We do not want to run any risks in damaging our relationship with them by raising the question. It is extremely doubtful that Mr. Shostakovich could get a visa to come to work in Hollywood to write music for this film." This attempt to get the world's premier symphonic composer shows how high Hitchcock set his musical sights even in a film that was going into free fall.

Once Hitchcock gave up on Shostakovich, he again chose Maurice Jarre, a composer he had unsuccessfully tried to hire after firing Herrmann, and this time landed him. (Jarre calls Shostakovich, whom Sam Spiegel tried to hire for *Lawrence of Arabia,* "my main competitor.")[3] Hitchcock and Jarre got along splendidly, as indicated by the amount of time they spent eating and drinking at Chasens, ordering the best dishes and bottles of Château Margot—always a good sign during a Hitchcock project. The health of the collaboration was striking, given that just about everything else on the set was malfunctioning. Hitchcock despised Leon Uris's script so much that he dumped it, forcing him to scramble on a day-by-day basis with a new one by Sam Taylor, the writer of *Vertigo;* Universal rushed the production, and the total lack of preplanning depressed Hitchcock profoundly. A creature of the studio, where he could create exactly what he needed, he chafed at being forced to use three international locations; not surprisingly, the scenes in Cuba, which obviously had to be constructed in the studio, and in Harlem, where the defunct Hotel Theresa had to be re-created, are by far the most controlled, exciting, and authentically Hitchcockian.

Hitchcock's productive rapport with a composer in the midst of an obviously doomed project resembles *The Paradine Case.* Nonetheless, Jarre was happy to get the job after being "very disappointed" that scheduling had forced him to turn down *Torn Curtain.* "I was afraid I would never be asked by Hitch again. When he called me for *Topaz,* I was thrilled." In 2004, when

I spoke with Jarre, he was still enthusiastic about having worked for Hitchcock and happy with what he produced.

Hitchcock employed his typical method of setting the design, then getting out of the way. Having settled on Jarre, he let him work in a state of freedom, something the composer at first found troubling. After watching scenes, he wrote several themes and offered to show them to Hitchcock in advance, just to make sure the director still thought he was right for the job. "Why?" Hitchcock asked. "I chose you to be the composer; do what you want." Again, Jarre offered to read the script (such as it was) and show Hitchcock cues. Again, Hitchcock demurred. He wouldn't tell a composer he hired how to compose any more than he would tell Cary Grant how to act. Jarre persisted: "I told Hitch it was too scary; he said, 'No, Maurice, do what you want.'"

Jarre finally went home and got down to sustained work. When he had finished, a recording schedule was worked out, with Hitchcock's assurance that any problems could be resolved at the sessions. (A meticulous professional, Jarre requested four sessions for June, then a fifth in July.) Jarre asked Hitchcock when he would attend and was amazed at the response: "Do you really want me there?" When the answer was an emphatic yes, Hitchcock showed up punctually at 9 AM on Monday. After hearing the first sequence, he turned to a nervous Jarre and told him he liked the score very much. Jarre's relief was only temporary; after the second sequence, he turned to ask Hitchcock what he thought—and he had vanished. "He'd disappeared—and was gone for one week!" The agitation returned, worse than ever. "Maybe he doesn't like it!" The next week, Hitchcock popped up again, heard the rest, and made a definitive pronouncement: "I love it. I won't cut a single second." Even then, Jarre was worried. "Usually, directors want to change things. Other composers warned me about Hitchcock: 'Good luck! He'll change his mind.'"

But he didn't; the music survived unscathed. What seemed to be Hitchcock's indifference—especially since *Topaz* was shaping up so dismally—was professional confidence. Although Hitchcock couldn't control the actors' false notes—"all those foreigners speaking English," as he ruefully put it—he knew he would get correct ones from Jarre.[4] The only question was where to put them, how to adjust the dynamics, and how to connect them with the rest of the sound track, all of which Hitchcock manipulated with his usual authority. By the end of the project, Jarre understood the Hitchcock paradox: you can create anything—as long as you follow his directives: "He said 'Do what you want—but he knew what *he* wanted.'"

What he wanted, as he made clear, was counterpoint, and what Jarre gave him was perhaps the purest in any Hitchcock film except the Poulenc piano music in *Rope* and Herrmann's fandango in *North by Northwest*. Jarre's two main ideas are a steely march and an exotic "Topaz Theme" colored by organ, guitar, electric harpsichord, accordion, synthesizer, and Fender bass. (According to Jarre, the uncannily convincing balalaika sounds are achieved with conventional instruments.) These instruments sound through the film as obbligato rather than moment-to-moment commentary. Only occasionally does the stream of sound fragment or distort to italicize a specific action.

Knowing Jarre could write terrific marches (the *Lawrence of Arabia* march is one of the finest in film), Hitchcock asked for a Soviet military march to begin the film and periodically erupt through it. Often it behaves as if coming from a marching band playing near the action, much the way Hitchcock used waltzes. When the Soviet agent Boris Kusenov is offered American protection by Michael Nordstrom if he agrees to betray his country, the march blares into the room and continues during his daughter Tamara's entreaties to stay in the West; as Kusenov is led into another room and interrogated about Cuban missiles, it dies away. The ambiguous Topaz theme works the same way. When the elegant French Embassy operative André Devereaux confronts accusations that he is too cozy with the Americans, the thumping bass, mocking winds, and melancholy harmonies are at odds with one another as well as with the brittle conversation. The jazziest variations appear during the most tense scenes: the Harlem hotel theft, perhaps the most thrilling in the film; and the capture of the Mendoza couple as they spy on the Cuban missile operation, a grimly ironic prelude to their fatal torture. (Birds, treacherous as ever in Hitchcock, give them away.) This detachment is very different from Jarre's emotional fervor and voluptuous tone painting in *Doctor Zhivago* and *Lawrence of Arabia*.

Hitchcock's loss of control during this project did not extend to musical choice and placement: a crowd belts out a rousing patriotic song during a Castro rally against the Communists' discovery of André's spying; another chorus erupts from a truck during the establishing shot of the Mendozas' capture (Hitchcock requested a Russian chorus for these scenes); a tense interrogation regarding a mysterious spy operation called Topaz occurs as Tamara practices Russian piano music in the next room. Eschewing a traditional suspense cue, Hitchcock opted for something deeper that would communicate rupture and homesickness: the girl's playing should be "evocative of Russia," he told his postproduction crew, ordering recordings of Tchaikovsky, Scriabin, Rachmaninoff, and Borodin in preparation for the scene. (He initially asked for Rubenstein playing a Chopin Nocturne, then decided the music should be Russian.) One directive requested that the performance "should not sound too professional and should be played in the form of improvisation"; another stated that "the music should have grace and simplicity to counterpoint the argument downstairs."[5]

"Hitchcock wanted counterpoint, not sugar on a cake like most Hollywood directors," says Jarre. The closest Jarre gets to sugar is the soaring melody for André and the doomed Juanita de Cordoba during their affair. This is a typical Hitchcock love theme; the sensuality evoked by Jarre's harmonies and accordion solos is cool rather than sentimental. (Hitchcock requested theaters to use this beautiful cue, "Juanita's Theme," as walkout music.)

The musical structure is pure Hitchcock even though the architecture of the narrative is flaccid. Rising and receding marching bands, a sound track staple since *The 39 Steps,* are an important part of the picture, as indicated by Hitchcock's precise August 25 cutting notes for reel 1: "The music is to continue right up to the square, but naturally it will be brought partially down over the Foreword and stay further down as the Copenhagen shot comes on the screen. The last part should just be heard faintly."[6] Rico Parra's graceful killing of Juanita when he discovers she has betrayed him politically and sexually, one of Hitchcock's most morbidly beautiful ballets, occurs in silence, after Jarre's darkest cue has run its course.

What must have been refreshing to Hitchcock was that the score did not sound like Herrmann. The grim heaviness of *Marnie* and *Torn Curtain* is nowhere to be found. This is a cool, modern score, more neoclassical than expressionist. It was sufficiently hip that that no one at Universal regarded it as old-fashioned; the usual pressure for a popular song was light this time. (The file mentions a "Topaz Bossa Nova" and two lyrics by Paul Francis Webster, the title song and "Strange, My Love," but none of these materialized.) One bond between director and composer was their distaste for Herrmann's moodiness. "He was a bitter man," Jarre told me. "He said bad things about everybody, including me." Hitchcock's comment to Jarre was simply that "his head started to be too big." Here again is evidence that the Herrmann-Hitchcock breakup involved issues of authorship and envy.

Despite manifold problems associated with *Topaz,* Hitchcock, his composer, and his sound technicians were all proud of the European ambiance and elegance of their creation. (*Topaz* actually did well in Europe even though it failed in America.) If production was a nightmare, postproduction was much happier, as indicated by a note of September 8 from the Universal sound department thanking Hitchcock. Attached to the note is a newspaper clipping: "Hitchcock likes to keep his finger on his picture's pulse, and during the making, his bustling figure will turn up sooner or later in every corner of the studio. . . . 'Directing a film for me is not just lining up shots and going home. It's involving myself in every aspect of a film right from the time I research locations, just as an author would do for a book, until the fine shadings of dubbing, music, and effects.' "[7] The finer shadings are there, at least in *Topaz*'s sound.

Until the very end, when a catastrophic audience preview compelled the creation of two new endings (requiring, of course, additional music measurements), Hitchcock proceeded with his usual aural assurance. He made extensive music and dubbing notes, including last-minute addenda on dynamic adjustments. In the final scene, things started to go wrong. An urgent memo from Peggy Robertson on September 2 asked Jarre to "immediately" start work on music for an alternate ending involving a two-shot sequence at Orly airport, in which the American and Soviet agents would be boarding different planes. The same day, Hitchcock met with Jarre to discuss the revision. He wanted Jarre to write a jauntier version of the Topaz theme but then decided to use the march, beginning it softly during the double-airline shot and bringing it to a crescendo during the end credits. This elegant bit of symmetry reverses the film's opening, where the march begins loudly and dies.

Hitchcock's distress by the end of the project is revealed in testy back-and-forths with Peggy Robertson that occurred on September 23.

Hitchcock: Tell Jarre that I don't want the film to die out, and that's what the effect of the Topaz theme is doing. The music should start from March of the Red Square the moment that Piccolo [*sic*] appears on the screen.

Robertson: Now he wasn't going to do that. . . . He was going to do the Topaz theme for the end, no music at all at the airport.

Hitchcock: Is he going to do it with a livening lift-up? It doesn't have that. . . . It has a dying out effect.

Robertson: Well, this is why he's doing it with an upbeat ending. . . . Would you like him to change it and do the Red Square March over Piccolo?

Hitchcock: I want the Red Square March over Piccolo very low, and
the moment the newspaper appears, bring it up to the full
and go out on the livening March.
Robertson: All right, instead of the Topaz theme . . .
Hitchcock: To hell with the Topaz theme.

The two-shot ending thus concludes with the stinging irony of Soviet
music rising in heroic crescendo as Jacques Granville genially waves good-
bye to his adversary (sexual as well as political, for Jacques has been having
an affair with André Devereaux's wife). Yet such was the terrible luck Hitchcock suffered during this project that after all the adjusting and readjusting,
this ending was not the one released. To assuage those who might object to
the villain escaping, he was forced to consider an alternate ending, cobbled
together by Universal: a camera shot of the doorway of Jacques, the Soviet
double agent, is overlaid with a gunshot, implying that he commits suicide;
the march rises from the newspaper close-up during a quick montage of
three dramatic deaths in the narrative rather than counterpointing Jacques's
escape on the airplane. Hitchcock had already discarded one ending, a duel
between André and Jacques that was ridiculed by preview audiences.

There is much confusion about the final release. Critics prefer Universal's suicide version, debunking both the duel and getaway codas. According
to conventional wisdom, the Orly ending is too flip, the duel too melodramatic; the suicide option works best. But the files reveal that Hitchcock deplored it as a sop to conventional morality in which the villain must not escape—a censorship issue with which he had struggled since *Blackmail.* In a
behind-the-scenes gambit worthy of any espionage film, Hitchcock secretly
instructed Peggy Robertson to hide Universal's ending and release it only as
an emergency: "Ditch the suicide version and don't tell anyone. . . . The only
reason the suicide came up [was] 'oh my God, what will the French government say by letting him get away with it??' . . . So that ending with the shot
on the secret house is an emergency. . . . Score and dub it in case of emergency." In the end, weary and dispirited, he gave up the fight with Universal,
and the emergency was used. (Robertson apparently didn't ditch it after all.)
Hitchcock was therefore stuck with the worst of all possible worlds: the
master of the perfect ending delivered, under pressure, a conclusion that
he deemed unacceptable but that everyone thought he endorsed. That he
never cleared the matter up probably indicates his embarrassment over the
entire incident. As with *The Paradine Case,* he disassociated himself from
Topaz as quickly as he could. (In a final muddle, the Alfred Hitchcock Col-

lection DVD has the Orly ending, yet the special-feature commentary dismisses it as untenable.)

Despite all this, Hitchcock continued to enjoy a pleasant time with Jarre, who confirmed all the stories about the director's boredom with the actual shooting of a scene after he conceptualized it. He was "extremely careful about details," yet sometimes in the middle of a scene, he would grab Jarre and head for Chasens: "He would just leave the stage. 'Aren't you going to watch the scene?' I'd ask. 'No, the actors are ready; the cameramen are ready. If not, I'll cut it.'" After the picture was over, Hitchcock gave Jarre a slide carousel with remote control, a chic gift in those days. "He was a real gentleman, so charming; it was absolutely adorable, the first present I'd ever gotten from a director."

An even better token of appreciation was Hitchcock's admission to Jarre that the music was the best thing about the film. (John Huston later said the same thing after Jarre scored *The Man Who Would Be King*.) "I didn't give you a great picture," he said, "but you gave me a great score."

24

frenzy: out with mancini, hold the bach

If I wanted Herrmann, I'd ask Herrmann.

—Hitchcock, on why he fired Henry Mancini

Like *Strangers on a Train, Frenzy* marked Hitchcock's return to form after a debilitating series of failures. It was his final comeback, and also his last journey back to England. Clearly, England had changed, and so had he. He always distrusted nostalgia, but the vision communicated in *Frenzy* is strikingly coarse and cynical, a world of predatory cruelty relieved only by the charm of Alec McCowen, Hitchcock's most winning detective since John Williams in *Dial M for Murder*. The dark tone is set in the score, which was created with the help of some of Hitchcock's most detailed, insistent, and illuminating music notes—two sets of them, for once again Hitchcock fought with and fired a famous composer, this time Henry Mancini.

Even in decline, Hitchcock's star was bright. The list of those applying for the project reads like a Who's Who of British and American composers of the early 1970s. Some of the more prominent are Malcolm Arnold, who was carefully considered; Richard Rodney Bennett, who applied for more than one Hitchcock project but never prevailed; John Addison, who got along with Hitchcock but was associated with the *Torn Curtain* fiasco; James Bernard, who wrote lurid scores for Hammer productions, the British horror machine (luridness should not have been a problem for *Frenzy*); Humphrey Searle, who was responsible for *The Haunting*, the classiest spook score of the period; Ron Grainer, who was recommended for his "interesting stuff with the BBC Radiophonic Workshop"; Howard Blake, who wrote several episodes of *The Avengers;* and Benjamin Frankel, who composed the tight, noirish score for Hitchcock's "Bon Voyage" and the exquisitely moody one for John Huston's *Night of the Iguana*. The production file also contains an unsigned memo from someone in postproduction who wanted to consider bringing back Herrmann, but the Hitchcock-Herrmann era was over, no matter how many associates of both artists tried to revive it.[1]

Ron Goodwin ultimately got the job, but only after an enigmatic behind-the-scenes melodrama. Hitchcock's firing of Henry Mancini is a mysterious business. There were no warning signs as in the Herrmann case, at least none revealed in the records.[2] Mancini was hired for a flat fee of $25,000. By November 23, 1971, he had full music measurements sheets; on November 30, a memo from Peggy Robertson stated, "Mancini will pay all transportation and hotel accommodations himself." Four recording sessions were scheduled in mid-December; a memo from Mancini insisted these needed to last only last three hours, not four as suggested in Robertson's memo. Musical directions for the two killings and the dramatic finale were clear: there was to be music at the beginning of Brenda's terrible rape and murder and throughout the unforgettable backtracking down the stairs in the disturbing scene Hitchcock called "Babs' Farewell," but there was to be none during Blaney's invasion of Rusk's apartment during the final tracking shot.

Then rather suddenly, Hitchcock quarreled with his composer and fired him. The final, stark note in the Mancini-Hitchcock file simply says, "No Mancini music was used. Ron Goodwin did the music, for which Mr. Hitchcock dictated new music notes." New indeed: they reversed all of the above directions, eliminating the music in both murder scenes and adding it to Blaney's vengeful stair ascent. Wiping out Mancini's piquant main title, Hitchcock instructed Goodwin to write a soaring, effulgent one. It was as if Hitchcock wanted to obliterate every vestige of Mancini's brief existence in the project.

Hitchcock's termination of Herrmann was still reverberating in odd revisitings and repetitions. Peter Bogdanovich rates Ron Goodwin's *Frenzy* score as one of the best of any non-Herrmann picture, but its initial reception was mixed at best. Many believe Hitchcock fired Mancini for creating faux Herrmann. According to Herrmann himself, "Hitchcock came to the recording session, listened awhile, and said 'Look, if I wanted Herrmann, I'd ask Herrmann. Where's Mancini?' He wanted a pop score from this Academy-Award winning song writer, and Mancini wrote what he thought was one."[3]

Again Hitchcock fired a distinguished composer for not producing a pop score, then hired another, who proceeded to write something utterly symphonic, not remotely pop—and Hitchcock seemed perfectly happy with the outcome. There are further ironies: Goodwin's score was criticized for being overly thick and retrograde; indeed, Mancini's main title is lighter in orchestration and sensibility than Goodwin's full-blown symphonic statement. Again, the issue was not so much a pop score as the pressure Hitchcock was under to produce something hip and contemporary. Like Addison, Goodwin was a popular, sought-after composer, and Mancini's popularity had peaked.

Goodwin got right to work and then waited breathlessly for Hitchcock's reaction. "It has been a long ambition of mine to write music for a film which you have directed," he wrote Hitchcock on February 18, 1972, but "my joy was mixed with trepidation." Given what had happened to Herrmann and Mancini, it must have seemed a high-risk job. Hitchcock phoned Goodwin personally to tell him he liked the score; from there, everything apparently went well.

A versatile artist, Goodwin could produce old-fashioned cinema music if requested. Hitchcock wanted a main title "grandiose in style, symbolizing the entry through the gates into London. The section continues until the speaker (Minister of Health) is both seen and heard. The composer should stress the music on the word 'Frenzy,' but this should not be done too obviously." The "grand and British" theme (which resembles Universal's fanfare) "continues until the speaker . . . is both seen and heard," quoting Wordsworth and discoursing on the cleanliness of London's great waterway, as Hitchcock himself listens intently in his cameo—until a naked corpse floats suddenly into view. The Wordsworthian splendor turns out to be a fraud. Beginning with *Shadow of a Doubt*, Hitchcock used music to show the unreliability of celebrating past glories, whether American or British; the banishing of pollutants promised by Sir George, the Minister of Health, has manifestly not occurred. This brutal intrusion into British pomp is rendered in shocked silence, a quality that increasingly haunts the film. (According to Goodwin, Hitchcock, at their first meeting, plopped out a replica of his head, originally planned in his cameo to float on the Thames, and asked him what he thought: 'Very nice. . . . I mean, what do you say when someone shows you a perfect replica of his own head?")[4]

The title music ends up as a dark joke, its majesty utterly undone. Hitchcock wanted "sparkling, early-morning music for the opening," says Goodwin, "woodwinds and glockenspiel. If Hitchcock hadn't directed me, I would have written something with a macabre lilt to it. But he wanted no hint of the horror to come."[5] Two myths are undone here: that Hitchcockian suspense is always premised on inevitability rather than surprise; and that he simply stayed out of the way of composers. Goodwin was clearly directed, having been given specifications of mood, color, and even a bit of orchestration. Hitchcock had an instinct for when to specify what he wanted and when to let creative artists be creative; it was the same counterpoint between imposing control and allowing freedom that he struck with actors: Barry Foster, who played *Frenzy*'s necktie murderer, Rusk, recalls that Hitchcock gave him no direction until the end, when he instructed him not to bow his head in defeat when caught in the act by Alec McCowen's detective but to look straight on with indomitable serial-killer tenacity.[6]

Hitchcock wasn't quite through with the grandiose music. His music notes for the first Covent Garden scene are a kind of musical storyboarding that parallels the visual: "Music starts on the newspaper signboard—'Another Necktie Strangling'—continues over the high shot of Covent Garden. The music should die away just before Blaney reaches Rusk—before the start of dialogue. This high shot music should be 'Broad scope music,' such as is commonly used in movies for open sea, sailing ships, or open range—but it should also continue the menace."

Goodwin delivers the undertone of menace with a resounding seventh chord as Jon Finch as Blaney, Hitchcock's final and least sympathetic wrong man, passes the newsstand: the score then soars into broad scope music, a scherzo-like variant of the main title played by high winds. As the camera pans over the noisy vendors of Covent Garden, the tempo slows to a full-bodied statement of the opening music—but that single sinister chord played against the necktie murder headline plants a subversive undertone.

Hitchcock's post-Mancini music notes are an instruction to take out the scissors. The score is laid in with a concision that parallels the superb cutting throughout the picture. By the time he presented these notes on New Year's Day, 1972, he had apparently abandoned all notions of a pop tune. They emphasize elision, a determination to eschew sentimentality, to produce just the right nuances: "Put in a faint 'Frenzy' touch as Blaney and Brenda arrive outside Brenda's apartment. This music should start when Blaney says, 'I'd like to see where you live.' It ends on a cut to the Salvation Army." The "Frenzy Theme," a series of metallic discords resembling snatches of a death march, displaces the noble main title, which never appears again. Hitchcock continually insists on subtlety. At one point, he asks for "a subtle touch of music as Blaney examines the money in the Salvation

Army Hotel." Apparently the volume level was a bit *too* subtle, for Hitchcock requested more sound: "Front part o.k.," states a memo, "but Rusk's entry needs to be brought up in volume so we get more shock value."

A much bigger shock is soon to come: "On the cut to Brenda powdering her face, the music should drop a shade, but on Rusk's entry it rises to a sharp chord and then comes to a sharp stop." This fleeting moment of sharp chord–sharp stop, a violent pizzicato pluck, is the sole prelude to Brenda's ugly, cruel, gratuitous, thoroughly un-Hitchcockian rape-murder, an unbearably long, nearly unwatchable scene. Originally, this ghastly sequence was to be accompanied by Mancini's music up to the point where Brenda crashes to the floor, but Hitchcock decided—as he had in *Blackmail, Sabotage, Torn Curtain,* and other films—to make the violence more palpable by going against convention and leaving music out. He was certainly successful, though one wishes he had followed his usual principle, even in *Psycho,* of leaving the details to our imaginations.

Music does not commence again until this scene is mercifully over: "Music starts as we see Brenda, now dead, sprawled in the chair." The wrenching dissonance at the close-up of Brenda's eye-popping, tongue-lolling face initiates a return to music. Harps and woodwinds establish the tempo of Blaney's wrong-place-at-the-wrong-time movements in the elaborate, fateful ballet when he ascends Brenda's stairs and is spotted by her secretary as both turn the corner. Hitchcock wanted "another aspect of the 'Frenzy' music as Rusk departs. This should be quite agitated in its undertones and it should carry on as he enters Oxford Street and Blaney approaches. The music should continue with a tremolo as the audience is ahead and will possibly realize that Blaney is going to be wrongfully accused." The "tremulous undercurrent" continues as Brenda's secretary, after seeing Blaney, enters the building. Then Hitchcock ordered one of his classic music-suspense devices: "As she enters, we should quickly fade out the music leaving just the distant traffic noise—until the scream."

Directives like "tremolos" and "agitated" chords reveal how far Hitchcock went to get what he wanted; he was not afraid to specify special effects. The notes also show how closely music and its absence are allied to suspense: the score keeps "the audience ahead" (the shock of the deceptive main title was a brief novelty after all): we know Blaney is in trouble when the music fades to a long silence breathlessly waiting to be filled by the secretary's scream. As indicated in the intricate, twelve-page "Final Dubbing Notes Made by Mr. Hitchcock" on November 26, 1971, the director had always planned to hold the silence even longer than usual, with street noises, then the chattering of two women rounding the corner: the audience's anticipation of the scream is stretched to the breaking point: "Oxford Street sounds again as Monica comes along and sees Blaney. Reduce these sounds because we are receding from them. Now we should just hear general faint traffic noise while Monica enters the building. We should take a little license and bring the traffic noise down—almost subliminal." Here again is the little license in Hitchcock's sound track to create almost subliminal effects from the noises of real life. These slight departures from reality are what create the dreamlike sonic poetry characteristic of his best work. Monica's scream is similarly orchestrated in the dubbing notes: "THE SCREAM: we should hear the chatter from the two girls—but not very loud—otherwise it will spoil the silence. The scream could be a shade louder."

In the hotel scene again, the music notes demand understatement and silence: "Music starts on the close shot of newspaper under the door. Please try to avoid hitting this is a corny way. Now continue the music into a very unusual agitato (if at all possible)—right through until the police open the door, and we see the empty room—in silence." Avoiding the corny way, Goodwin slid a muted version of the "Frenzy" chords under the door with the newspaper; the unusual agitato, a gradual crescendo, underlines the hotel manager's outraged reaction to the latest necktie murder, a summary of the film's horrendous vision: "Sometimes just thinking of the lusts of men makes me want to heave." When the police arrive, insistent chords drive them into Blaney's love nest, then suddenly shut off: "We see the empty room—in silence." (This was a Hitchcock tactic John Williams admired in a similar scene in *Family Plot.*)

The park scene offers a moment of lyrical respite, at least in the music notes: "Purely as an experimental piece, I would like to try music over the Park Bench sequence. It should start over the close two shot—Blaney's dialogue, 'But I ask you . . . ' This music should express a kind of dramatic anger, following Babs's attitude, as she begins to believe Blaney's story, so the music should slowly become more romantic. When we have reached the complete dramatic climax, it should be cut off by the shout, 'Blaney.'" Even at the end of his career, Hitchcock was open to sonic experiment, though he decided to abandon this one. The anger and ambivalent romanticism are carried solely by the compelling performances of Jon Finch and Anne Massey.

The decision to cut the park cue is consistent with an increasing reliance on spareness as Hitchcock continually refined *Frenzy's* music. The most chilling example is the second murder, the film's great set piece. Babs bursts out of the pub into the crowded streets after a row with the owner; suddenly, as her face appears in dramatic close-up, all sound ceases except Rusk's voice—"Got a place to stay?"—as his face floats on screen with recommencing street sounds. "Silence in the pub as Babs storms out," command Hitchcock's dubbing notes: "Drop all sounds—traffic and everything. And bring it up again when the camera tracks to the two-shot of Rusk and Babs so we get the effect when his voice is heard behind her big head. . . . This is dramatic license, but I think it is necessary to get the fullest effect out of Rusk's sudden appearance."

Killer and victim ascend Babs's staircase, again in deathlike silence, the camera one step ahead; it then watches them from behind as they enter her apartment door—as Rusk, slowly and from a great distance, says the line that was the prelude to Brenda's murder: "You're my kind of woman." The camera backs slowly down the stairs and into the street as the Covent Garden sounds—sounds that Babs will never hear again—come back noisier than ever. We only think we're safe, this insidious scene implies: the reassuring noises of commerce and civilization do not protect us from the lusts of men. The dubbing notes call for a gradual crescendo, a purely musical effect that abandons realism: "Now we start the pan down of the camera in silence; we go down the stairs—no sound of any kind. Now, as we go under the fan light, slowly bring up the traffic noise—it'll get louder and louder—and louder—and build it up along the corridor, pass the hall stand—traffic getting even more loud—and as we go through the door, bring it up with a roar—and now exaggerate all the traffic noise as we pull back to show the facade of the building—and make it almost a roar of traffic—louder than it would normally be." This scene represents the kind of daring that moved Truffaut and Bogdanovich to declare that *Frenzy* seemed the work of a young man.

A fascinating sidelight is Hitchcock's original musical decision versus his final one. According to Mancini's musical measurement sheets for November 23, 1971, music was to continue "throughout back tracking after Babs' murder even out into the street." It is as odd to contemplate music during this awesomely quiet sequence as it is to think of no music during Marion's demise in *Psycho;* in both cases, Hitchcock's second thoughts proved correct, though in *Psycho's* case they came at Bernard Herrmann's insistent prodding; Hitchcock usually regarded violence as best served by silence.

Silence also envelops Hitchcock's courtroom. The ruthless concision of *Frenzy*—we've seen these court bits before, so let's get on with it, Hitchcock seems to be saying—mandates we need only view the constables outside as the camera looks into the courtroom in a long shot. (Hitchcock used a similar approach in *Murder!*) Blaney screams out his innocence and Rusk's guilt; the camera looks down from a frightening aerial as he is brutally shoved into his cell, then down at Alec McCowen worrying over the verdict.

Distant bells ring through the somber sound track; Big Ben chimes as Rusk cheerfully disposes of Babs's body. The original direction that it strike 1 AM "as he is wheeling the wheelbarrow" was changed to an instruction to "save Big Ben" until Rusk's dramatic sofa scene: "The music stays after [Rusk] has disposed of the trolley. It should be in a light vein—he is pleased that he has unloaded the body—the music should express his relief as he crosses the road. Perhaps we might even go so far as to have a lilt in the tempo." This was the macabre lilt Goodwin would have written for the main title had Hitchcock not requested grandiosity.

As the killer reclines on his couch after what Bruno in *Strangers on a Train* would call a "strenuous day," high woodwinds play another Hitchcockian trademark, a dark waltz, which "comes to a sudden stop when he misses his tie pin." Suddenly, the music abandons restraint, striking like a snake. Rusk searches frantically, then "Angry 'Frenzy' music. This should really burst upon us at the start of the flashback murder. However, it should drop back down low enough at the end of the flashback so that we can hear Rusk's dialogue: 'Christ all bloody mighty!' 'Frenzy' music comes again as he dashes out of the room . . . extremely agitated and urgent. . . . We should never hear it finish because the sound of the engine starting must take over. Naturally of course the music, though agitated, should be low enough not to interfere with the starting of the engine." Goodwin's contribution before Rusk's realization was a bit too "urgent"; Hitchcock sent a February 3 memo requesting restraint: "The music is fine in Rusk's apartment. However, once he is in the open, the music should be kept down and must be very stealthy. This could be done in dubbing, or maybe Ron Goodwin would like to have another go at it." Hitchcock storyboarded this unsettling flashback so that its brutality is implied, without the explicitness of Brenda's murder; the music stands in for the violence.

For the notorious night journey of the potato truck, Hitchcock employed a trademark device, ironic whistling. Robertson requested the rights to "Baby It's Cold Outside," then sent another memo "*very urgently*" on May 5, 1971, for another permission: "The script now calls for the truck driver to sing or hum another song, 'Put Your Arms Around Me Baby, Hold Me Tight.'" In addition, Hitchcock considered "Pale Hands," "In My Arms,"

"Here in My Arms," "Full Moon and Empty Arms"—all grimly apt accompaniment to Rusk's entanglement with the corpse of his victim. The notes state that when the truck pulls up at the all-night cafe, "we should hear Juke box music," its volume deftly adjusted so it is just loud enough to put this tiny but critical scene in our memory. In *Frenzy*, no sound was too small for precise planning.

Intercut with the potato truck's grotesque black comedy is the lighter scene of Alec McCowen's poor Inspector Oxford longing for an English breakfast as Vivien Merchant as his wife serves pig knuckles, quail with grapes, and other haute-cuisine challenges. McCowen and Merchant provide the only levity in this unpleasant movie. Again, the original soundscape was pared down. While Mancini was still on board, Hitchcock planned radio music: "The whole of the Oxford Apartment should be silent, except for the b.g. radio, which I believe is to be put on by Mr. Mancini . . . some Bach . . . or something that suits the taste of the cultured Mrs. Oxford." Perhaps Hitchcock feared that Bach would distract from Mrs. Oxford's crucial observations: it is she who solves the crime, filling in Inspector Oxford's doubts about Blaney's guilt with precise, accurate "feminine intuition." As with Lisa in *Rear Window*, a woman's insight into the mechanics and customs of marriage provides the key to the mystery.

For Blaney's escape from the prison hospital, Hitchcock called on Goodwin to create the kind of double mood he'd asked for in *To Catch a Thief* and *The Trouble with Harry*. The sounds should be "furtive but humorous. . . . Dear Mr. Musician—Please do not make the error that this is a heavy dramatic scene of escape—it is a comic one yet a daring one. It is only when Blaney is walking down the corridor that the amusing part has been left behind, and we now have an angry man setting forth on a desperate mission." Mocking winds, delicate pizzicato, and shimmering strings set the furtive but humorous mood. After the amusing part, the score "should give the audience tension and excitement . . . continue with a sense of low urgency. . . . When Blaney gets out of the car, wrench in hand, we should continue the low agitato, to counterpoint Blaney's stealth. . . . The music should be exciting, very low and subdued because in an abstract way, while Blaney is inside the house, we don't want the music to be loud enough to awaken his intended victim. But please maestro, don't let's have '1910' agitato." Here is one of the fullest revelations of Hitchcock's precision when eliciting a mixed emotion. Goodwin created exactly what was requested, slithering chords underlined with thumping ostinatos, very low and subdued.

This passage also reveals Hitchcock's belief in music as a quasi-mystical force hovering over the action. The score needs to be subdued because "we don't want the music to be loud enough to awaken [Blaney's] intended victim." This is illogical, of course, but to Hitchcock it was real "in an abstract way." A movie was about abstraction and emotion; underneath the fanatical attention to logic and detail was a deep engagement with the irrational, what Poe, in "The Poetic Principle," called the "supernal" force represented by music. As we have seen, this doubleness is consistent throughout Hitchcock's career. His question in *Lifeboat*—"Where would the music come from?"—is usually interpreted as naïveté, but as the *Frenzy* notes show, it is an eccentric belief that worked very well for him: it made perfect sense to turn the music down to avoid waking up the victim, and it certainly made for a powerful scene. This is what Truffaut meant when he said Hitchcock's cinema has a dreamlike logic.

Following Alec McCowen's chillingly funny final line—"Mr. Rusk, you're not wearing your tie"—the camera freezes villain, policeman, and wrong-man hero into a powerful three-shot; Rusk's trunk crashes to the floor, cuing the black backdrop for the final credits. The end-title music was the subject of much discussion. Hitchcock first wanted the romantic park music, but since he had eliminated it, there was no music to use. Robertson handwrote a note specifying that the final sounds should offer "relief from mood but not in majestic way." Finally, Hitchcock weighed in: "For our final cast music let us reprise in a different way, the opening title music, interwoven with a slow version of the 'Frenzy' theme." What he finally used was only the latter, dark and haunting, building to a grim climax on the Universal title, then fading on a minor chord. It's as if Hitchcock realized that he could not really hide the grimness of *Frenzy* or cover it with a different version of the lyrical opening.

It would have been sad had Hitchcock ended his career with *Frenzy*'s cynicism and nastiness. Fortunately, he had one more movie to make and one more memorable score to inspire, with a new composer who would become the avatar of both Korngold and Herrmann.

25

family plot:
hitchcock's exuberant finale

> He was a wily professional who knew his business and could be of
> great assistance to a youngster such as I was at that time.
>
> —John Williams

In a delicious irony, Hitchcock chose for his final composer John Williams, a close friend of Bernard Herrmann and soon to be the bearer of the old-fashioned legacy Hitchcock and his bosses repudiated when they terminated Herrmann's contract. When Herrmann died, on Christmas Eve, 1975, having completed *Taxi Driver* that day for Martin Scorsese, many thought the age of symphonic movie music had perished with him—until Williams burst on the scene. *Jaws*, which came out as *Family Plot* was in its early stages, was an enormously popular score widely credited with helping that film attain the largest box office of all time. The history of the score was strikingly similar to *Psycho*'s: after *Jaws* was shot, Steven Spielberg's team worried that the film was too ordinary until Williams's music jolted them out of their chairs—exactly what had happened in *Psycho*'s postproduction. Like Hitchcock, Spielberg credited his composer with being responsible for at least half the movie's terror. Clearly, the traditional symphonic cinema score still had enormous vitality.

The music for *Family Plot* sustained the charming yet sinister tone of Hitchcock's comedy thrillers; it is Williams's most subtle music until *Catch Me If You Can* (an homage to the kind of slinky 1960s sound Hitchcock vainly sought from Herrmann during the *Marnie* era). Compared to the heavy orchestral rhetoric of *Close Encounters of the Third Kind, Indiana Jones,* and *Schindler's List, Family Plot* is a divertimento. Its light touch was

John Williams. (Courtesy of Jamie Richardson)

ideal for *Family Plot*, a genial swan song that was a relief after the grim misanthropy of *Frenzy*.

In choosing Williams, Hitchcock showed that his musical instincts were superb right to the end. Among the composers he considered were Jerry Goldsmith, Lalo Schifrin (who had contributed to his television shows), Laurence Rosenthal, David Rose, Richard Rodney Bennett (his third consideration for a Hitchcock film), and Robert Russell Bennett (a Rodgers and Hammerstein orchestrator who wrote *Victory at Sea*).[1] According to the Hitchcock biographer John Russell Taylor, who was on the set, Williams was hired very late in the game: "When Hitch was halfway through shooting the film I asked him who was going to write the music. To my surprise, considering how important music has been in many of his films, and how exhaustively he prepares just about everything in advance, he said he had not decided: 'Possibly Maurice Jarre—he's flexible,' and proceeded to tell me about his troubles and dissatisfaction with Henry Mancini."[2]

In November, Alma suggested Michel Legrand and Miklos Rozsa. Neither was chosen (not a surprise in Rozsa's case given Hitchcock's complaints about *Spellbound*). Hitchcock was musing about various moods and colors for the film: he purchased recordings of diverse classics, including Stravinsky's *Petrouchka* and (again) Bartók's Concerto for Orchestra. Finally, John Williams was brought to Hitchcock's attention by the composer and music executive Harry Garfield. According to Williams, the success of *Jaws* was key to his hiring. "I was thrilled to be asked; I had just done *Jaws*, and I think that's the reason he called me. It was a very gratifying and very flattering thing to me, as you can imagine, at that point in my life."[3]

Williams was eager to get started, but there was one "delicate" problem, as he put it, and that was Bernard Herrmann, whose shadow still hovered over Hitchcock nearly a decade after the *Torn Curtain* debacle: "I had great affection for Bernard Herrmann, if it's possible for anyone to say that, because he was such a character." Williams affirms that contrary to legend, Herrmann was only sporadically curmudgeonly and could be thoroughly congenial: "He was very fond of my late wife; whenever Benny got troublesome, she would say, 'Oh, Benny, shut up,' and then he'd giggle, and put his arm around her."

Williams was not comfortable saying yes to Hitchcock without Herrmann's permission: "So I said to Mr. Hitchcock, 'Nothing would thrill me more than to work with you, but I and the rest of the world are asking, "Why not Bernard Herrmann?" And he's a great friend of mine. Hitchcock was clear on the matter: 'Oh no, our relationship—our working relationship—is finished; I wouldn't be inviting him to compose a score in any case, so you don't need to feel delicate about that.'" Williams wanted the matter clear from both ends: "I followed up with a phone call to Herrmann [in Regents Park] and said, 'Benny, I've been asked to do this film,' and he said, 'Ah, go ahead and do it; it's fine. It means nothing to me: I'll never work with Hitchcock again.'"

In fact, it meant a great deal. Herrmann had attempted, without success, to mend his painful breach with Hitchcock. But he was professional enough to want the best for Williams, so he kept any diatribes—supposedly one thing he could always be counted on to unleash—to himself. Williams was relieved: "Having been given Herrmann's blessing, I went back to Hitchcock and said, 'I'm so happy to do this; I've talked to Benny, and I feel more comfortable.'"

Williams had a small composer's bungalow on the Universal lot immediately behind Hitchcock's studio: "Our physical proximity was pretty intimate. Once it was understood I was going to write the score for the film, and Peggy Robertson understood how close I was, she would occasionally call me over in my little room and say, 'Hitch would like to have lunch with you.' This would be at a quarter to twelve, and if I had a lunch date, I would cancel it, and go sit with him. His habit was to eat lunch in his office; someone would bring over a bottle of red wine and a sirloin steak every day. The luncheons I shared with him were just à deux."

Over that bottle of red wine the two had free-ranging, sometimes wild conversations. Hitchcock talked expansively about one of the great loves of his life, the theater: "He was very knowledgeable, particularly about the 1920s in London; he remembered the casts of many plays by Barrie and others." When Williams asked Hitchcock about his relationship with Ernest Lehman, who was again his script writer, he whipped open his shirt, pointed at his pacemaker, and said, "Do you want to know how I feel about Ernest Lehman? Ernest Lehman did *that* to me!"

And then, there was music. Williams was astonished by Hitchcock's sweeping knowledge and enthusiasm: "He talked a lot about English music, which he was very interested in: Britten, Walton, Elgar, Arthur Bliss, and Vaughan Williams, whose widow I knew very well and with whom I attended concerts. He would have known Walton because of the Olivier films, but I don't know where his larger knowledge came from." The depth of Hitchcock's musical prowess remains a mystery, even to Williams.[4] His restless curiosity extended to numerous genres and styles, from Beethoven to electronic music: "He was a man of broad interests. I remember when Benny Herrmann was working with him on *The Birds*—Benny was discussing the electronics with Hitchcock—just the fact that he was aware of all this is unusual." Williams recalls talking about Walton's string concertos and Heifetz's collaboration with Walton in the Violin Concerto: "That's pretty far off the mark from what he would have been doing in films. I haven't met many film directors in my lifetime who had that breadth of interest and intimacy in the concert repertory. Delbert Mann is one that does come to mind; Irving Kirshner was another who knows a lot of music—but generally speaking, they don't."

Williams's work with Hitchcock deeply influenced his career. "He was a wily professional who knew his business and could be of great assistance to a youngster such as I was at that time." Like so many, Williams had admired Hitchcock-Herrmann films for a long time: "Some of my earliest influences and strong impressions were from the Hitchcock-Herrmann collaborations. Herrmann's contribution was very striking and very strong, but Hitchcock was a director who placed his faith in that. Many directors would be afraid to have music that loud, that emphatic—they might think it's too operatic."[5]

Hitchcock was happy with Williams's score. With its harpsichord obbligato and ethereal women's chorus, it is neoclassical with a touch of Romanticism, a combination close to Hitchcock's sensibility and ideal for a comedy-suspenser with a touch of magic. Barbara Harris's séances with the elegant but naive Cathleen Nesbitt are an elaborate fraud, but they are so beautifully filmed and scored that we submit to them as much as she does.

According to Williams, Hitchcock conceived the most distinctive aspect of the score: a wordless women's chorus to evoke an impressionistic ambiance. "In the opening scene, the séance, he wanted to hear voices; that was his idea, that we should have a chorus of women's voices or otherworldly sounds that could be produced only vocally. That was definitely from his direction." In his last film, Hitchcock again set the conception, tone, and color, then left everything else to the composer. His decision to use a ghostly female chorus was a final manifestation of the search for the lost *Mary Rose* music; it was also inspired by Debussy's orchestral nocturne *Sirènes,* a recording of which he ordered during postproduction. The chorus chants through the main title and continues in the opening scene without pause; at the end, in "Blanche Wakes Up," it glides through Barbara Harris's final séance and her famous wink at the camera. So prominent did Hitchcock want the chorus that he eliminated all background sounds to reinforce its aura.[6]

Yet the cue is ironic, the ethereal chorus singing against Blanche's transparent fakery. To the end, Hitchcock preferred counterpoint to imitation. Later, Williams would create eerie choruses (for *Close Encounters, A.I.,* and *Minority Report*) and mean it; the otherworldly choral sounds set the mood for extraordinary events that really do occur. Here they are an aural disguise for Blanche's spiritualist scam.

Hitchcock wanted airiness and playfulness. "You can't always communicate with composers," he told Williams. "I had this composer in London; it was a film about a murder, and I wanted something whimsical. I gave him some instructions on the way the score should be. I went to the recording session, and the composer had every double bassoon and timpani in the city of London capable of making a lugubrious, ominous sound playing the music." Williams was puzzled: "Mr. Hitchcock, for a film about a murder, this sounds very appropriate," to which Hitchcock replied, "Well, Mr. Williams, you don't understand [here, Williams imitated Hitchcock's double-bassoon voice], murder can be fun."

Williams came up with some ominous, lugubrious sounds of his own, but in the context of murder being fun. His darkest moments counterpoint comic lines or body language. In "The Shoebridge Headstone," the caretaker, in a blurry long shot, rises from the grave behind Bruce Dern as Williams unleashes terrifying organ and string dissonance, but the scene is comic. Dern's Lumley trips over the tombstone and apologizes to whichever Shoebridge corpse lies beneath the earth; the caretaker complains about his double shift: "Never liked them multiple funerals."

Family Plot was Hitchcock's final game of musical doubles: two thieving couples, one ordinary and funky 1970s (Blanche and George), the other polished and deadly (Arthur and Fran) engaging in a frenetic ballet of criss-crossing con artists accidentally invading one another's turf, then coming together for a final confrontation. The conflict between the heroines is musically dramatized. "Blanche's Challenge" is a witty Poulencian harpsichord melody; "Mystery Woman" is oppressive and noirish. It's clear whose side Hitchcock is on.

For a comedy, the score has considerable variety and color. A harp mingles with glittery percussion in "The Diamond Chandelier," a sensuous sound associated with the lure of money and sex. The score is full of daring effects and abstractions, the kind of music we might find in Williams's concert works—the slithery dissonance in both graveyard scenes; the menacing switchblade cue, "Maloney's Knife"; the terrifying jolt in "Blanche Gets the Needle"; the high-percussion pedal point in "The Search Montage," a sound resembling the piercing electronic sound of *The Birds.* Hitchcock's late immersion in contemporary symphonic music, from late Shostakovich to Stockhausen and Boulez, makes one wonder what would have happened had he made more films with Williams. Both were on similar aesthetic wavelengths, fond of mixing the popular with the avant-garde, and both were fast workers.

Williams, who was hired late in the game, had to work rapidly, yet he produced music that was both original and suitable for Hitchcock's rhythms, moods, and spotting patterns. He did so with detailed dubbing instructions but without the benefit of Hitchcock's usual music notes. Williams laments not having had these: "They would have been an enriching experience." Nonetheless, in this rich score—more music in its thirty-five cues than in *Torn Curtain, Topaz,* or *Frenzy*—he deftly recapped a number of signatures from Hitchcock's long career: sinister harp, agitated pizzicato, churning ostinatos, orchestral chimes blending with real ones, a lyrical but cool romantic theme ("Share and Share Alike," for the slapstick aftermath of the mountain car chase), and a succession of lonely timpani solos.

The latter, which pound during the detective interview, the arrival of Maloney's car, and Blanche's final car scenes, are played with enormous brio by Williams's father, a timpanist who had performed in the CBS radio orchestra under Herrmann. "My father and Herrmann had a long and stormy, but good relationship," Williams explained. "He liked the way my father played, and they were old pals from New York. At the end of his career, my dad was playing timpani for me at Universal Studios." The generosity of the timpani cadenzas therefore has a personal origin. Not since "On the Rocks" in Herrmann's *North by Northwest* had Hitchcock unleashed so much thunder from the big drums.

Family Plot showcases for a final time Hitchcock's witty manipulation of source music. The shuddery sonorities from the king of instruments during the cemetery scene is suddenly displaced by a very different organ chart, "The Stonecutter," a 1970s rock-and-roll tune (written by Williams) that blasts away on the radio of a young girl engraving a tombstone for someone named George during Lumley's grimly comic interview with the stone mason. "Turn that damn thing down, Marcella," shouts the mason; she does, and the sudden cessation of 1970s rock clears his brain for an important epiphany. An echoing choir sings "Ye Holy Angels Bright" during the cathedral kidnapping, followed by a mounting whisper from the congregation. "Outside the cathedral the sounds should be very faint," Hitchcock instructed, "and continue so until we come inside the cathedral with Lumley. . . . the sound of the choir should have some echo or something of the quality that it is away in the back of the cathedral. A murmur from the congregation should start the moment the woman falls in front of the bishop. This murmur should increase gradually and get louder and louder as the Bishop is carried out of the cathedral." The faithful, it seems, are too reverentially polite to interfere with the abduction of their bishop; they watch in befuddled fascination as he is stuck with a needle and carried away in a getaway car.

Family Plot is also a final demonstration of Hitchcock's uncanny ability to know when to leave music out. Police rush into the villain's room accompanied by heavy timpani and an exciting orchestral crescendo and find an empty window as the music suddenly vanishes rather than climaxing. All we hear is the empty wind. "Start as Joe opens knife," say the notes; "carry through dialogue with Eddie through arrival of police through Eddie's dialogue with them through Eddie back to room, out on cut to open window." Williams vividly remembers this scene. "I can't recall in general how specific Hitchcock was in the spotting session, but I remember one particular incident: there was a chase sequence where a man was being pursued by police. There is a room where we believe the pursued has entered. Music accompanies all this. We cut to the inside of the room and we don't see anything, and the pursuers are still in their pursuit mode, and you cut to an open window of curtains blowing indicating that the man has escaped. Originally, I had music there on the cut to the window; in the scoring session, Hitchcock said, 'You should really stop the music when we cut to the window rather than having music there.' He felt the sudden silence would indicate the absence of the pursued. Of course, he was completely right." Hitchcock's notes further detail the effect he was after: "The moment Adamson sees the open window of his office we should hear faint city traffic sounds again. This will accentuate the open window." Williams calls this an excellent lesson for a young composer in where to position music in any film.

Hitchcock used everyday sounds to establish a suburban ambiance: "Outside Blanche's house just a faint car or two passing by, maybe a barking dog in the distance, just some sounds to give us the atmosphere of the suburbs of a city." We also get piano scales wafting through an open window, a subtle counterpoint with the many keyboard sounds in Williams's score. The most extended comedy-suspense sequence, the downhill plunge to near death in Lumley's sabotaged car, is also without music. The screams of objects and machines stand in for those of actors and musicians: "During the wild ride we will need a lot of screeching tires, the gears getting entangled. . . . Passing cars should scream their horns at them as they pass them and when they reach the motorcycles we should hear a roar as they thread their way through the whole group of motorcycles. Bring the noise up as loud as we can as they go through the fence and when they come to a stop." When Lumley and Blanche emerge in shock from their ruined car, "there is utter silence, with just a few birds twittering. Continue the chirping of the birds until Blanche and Lumley reach the road." Here one more time is trauma bathed in silence and birdsong, a device Hitchcock had first used fifty-four years earlier in *Blackmail*.

According to Williams, music is not only a Hitchcock signature but a presence, very much like a character. Hitchcock himself hinted at this mysterious aural personification when he told Truffaut that he imagined every sound as possible dialogue, even the deadly singing of *The Birds*. Characters become their music—the young Strauss blends with "The Blue Danube," Uncle Charlie with "The Merry Widow," Bruno with "The Band Played On," Jo with "Que Sera Sera," Lisa with "Lisa." Music often speaks for them: when the Fran-Arthur team perceive the truth about Blanche during the keyhole scene, pizzicato strings and agitated harp say "It's her!" before they do.

Williams, like Hitchcock, didn't mind music's subversion of realism. Both saw movies as communicating subjective truth through image and sound; as in Poe, Conrad, du Maurier, and other favored Hitchcock authors, realism is psychological, the reality of the mind. Hitchcock's final scene is a witty demonstration. George says, "If we could find the diamonds," and the séance chorus sails in on cue, fulfilling his fantasy: Blanche, the fake psychic, goes into a trance, floats through the house on the chorus's dreamy chords, and leads Lumley to the diamond in the chandelier. It's a trick, Blanche's final joke on her boyfriend, but the rapture of Williams's score makes us wish it weren't. "Blanche, you did it!" George cries in ecstasy; Hitchcock reprises the mocking harpsichord motif, and Barbara Harris moves in for a close-up to wink at the audience. Hitchcock's final image, that wink obliterates what's left of realism, ending the master's career in the realm of comedy with a reunited couple and glittering music.

Everyone in the *Family Plot* production knew that Hitchcock, ill and in pain, would probably not have the stamina to make another film. Bruce Dern tried to talk him into coming up on the staircase and winking himself, a final good-bye to his audience. But that would be too intimate for an intensely private artist who prized subtlety and indirection. Happier with these actors than he had been in any recent film, Hitchcock decided to let one of them do the winking for him.

Williams went on to become the house composer for Steven Spielberg, and together they formed the longest composer-director collaboration in history. Spielberg and Hitchcock are profoundly different artists, but they have a few important similarities. The most striking, says Williams, is their

> great trust in music. When I was working for Hitchcock, I was a young man; he was an elderly senior, a legend, of course, but a man who wasn't feeling well and whose energies were down a bit. Spielberg is a dynamo and a much younger man than I, so the workaday ambiance is quite different. What is similar is that both were very comfortable with music, very happy to have the orchestra playing a lot, both interested in intimate details like tempo and spotting. In both cases, much of their image

and filmmaking style has to do with their use of music—music that has an idiosyncratic stamp, that might include very specific melodic identification with characters. Music is a signature with both of them, despite the differences in age, energy, and styles. Steven is a different personality, sunnier, more optimistic, less skeptical—a very different approach to a view of life. But where music is concerned and its function, they are very similar.

Here is a firsthand summary of Hitchcock's musical predilections from his final composer. The absorption in "intimate details of tempo and spotting," the tight linkage of music with "image and filmmaking style," the comfort and sheer pleasure in hearing an orchestra playing, the "idiosyncratic stamp" of music in every film—all these were an indelible and enduring signature.

But there was a sad undercurrent; throughout *Family Plot*, Williams observed Hitchcock's health visibly deteriorating: "One thing I regret, because being with Hitchcock was such a wonderful experience, was that as I worked through the weeks and prepared the score, he seemed to be feeling worse. He came to the recording session only for about an hour. He sat there, I played him some music, he said 'fine,' and indicated he was very happy. Then he concluded, 'I'll leave this to you,' and left the stage."

Hitchcock did not improve. In addition to the stress of a heart pacer, he suffered from colitis and a kidney stone. Still, he fussed and fidgeted over tiny details until the very end, which came abruptly: "We moved on a week or so later to the dubbing; that process took in those days eight or ten days. I was present for all of it. I think he came on the stage once, made some comments about sound effects in a car chase, and something about some dialogue. Then he thanked everyone, and left." Hitchcock never came on a soundstage again. The exuberant credit music at the end of *Family Plot* was his coda.

finale: hitchcock as maestro

Hitchcock once said that the ideal death would be to drop dead on a set in the middle of making a movie.[1] He almost got his wish. In late 1977 he was working on *The Short Night,* an espionage-love story he had been contemplating since 1969. Bad weather and arthritis kept him from visiting the proposed location, Finland, but he was busy fussing over details. He had considered several composers from the *Topaz* era, including Michel Legrand, Burt Bacharach, and "Shoster Kovich." (Hitchcock phoned Harry Garfield to make inquiries about the latter and joke about the spelling.) He also discussed Leroy Anderson's "Summer Skies" and the possible use of a Russian lyre for other songs. "We need a composer who will give us tempo," he said, returning to one of his basic concepts. He chose a Finnish vernacular piece, Minum Kultani's "The Lumberman's Song," and ordered the music.[2] But kidney and heart problems forced him to halt production, and in May 1979 he shut down his company. He died in his sleep eleven months later. Unable to make another movie, what else could he do?

He left behind a unique musical legacy. As John Williams put it, "There is something at the core of his faith and trust and belief in music as a character in the film métier that was uniquely strong and high. . . . Every composer who worked for him benefited."[3] This includes those he fired. Herrmann defended him until the end; Henry Mancini commented that working with Hitchcock was "the quintessential composer-director relationship," every minute an all-or-nothing engagement.[4]

Hitchcock saw himself as a maestro. Conductors, he believed, illuminated solos and colors in ways analogous to camera shots. "I have the feeling I am an orchestra conductor," he told Truffaut, "a trumpet sound corre-

318

sponding to a close shot and a distant shot suggesting an entire orchestra performing a muted accompaniment."[5] Since Hitchcock viewed cinema in musical terms, it is not surprising that his movies are full of maestros and ensembles, their scenes depicted with elaborate close-ups and long shots that counterpoint the narrative and provide tempo. More than any director, Hitchcock enacted Herrmann's dictum that cinema is music; he used music as a visual as well as auditory presence, a self-enclosed design signifying that the film's meaning should be drawn not from the world beyond the movie theater but from within it. Rather than imitating life, Hitchcock's films re-invent it; as Oscar Wilde would want it, they make life imitate them. When Hitchcock "conducts" a movie, it changes our view of things. After the string glissandos in *Psycho*, a shower is no longer a place of comfort; after the electronic score in *The Birds*, birdsong is sinister; after the sounds cas-cading across courtyards in *Rear Window*, street and radio music become poetry; after the waltzes in *Waltzes from Vienna, Shadow of a Doubt*, and *Suspicion*, this seemingly staid form becomes a complex drama charged with multiple meanings.

Because Hitchcock saw film directing as analogous not only to con-ducting but to musical composition, he was particularly drawn to maestros who also composed. Waxman, Herrmann, and other Golden Age conduc-tor-composers were by no means the only ones. When Pierre Boulez was chosen as music director of the New York Philharmonic, Hitchcock placed an article on the appointment in his files. His interest in Boulez was under-standable: here was another perfectionist obsessed with details, a cool tech-nician who evoked passion through precision, not only in his podium art but in dreamlike works like *Le Marteau sans maître*, a recording of which Hitchcock ordered for his own listening. Boulez was a cerebral artist who knew how to thrust himself onto a large public stage and remake himself into a celebrity; if Hitchcock reversed the pattern, capturing the public first and the intellectuals later, the parallel was nonetheless meaningful.

All aspects of music, including its performance, were central to Hitch-cock, because they were a key aspect of pure cinema. In a Hitchcock picture, sound and image conspire to create an alternate reality beyond words. The most dramatic examples of this method—the *Tristan* radio epiphany in *Murder!*, the "Blue Danube" premiere in *Waltzes from Vienna*, the Royal Al-bert Hall assassination in *The Man Who Knew Too Much*, the dressing scene in *Vertigo*, "The Murder" in *Psycho*—take music out of the pit and thrust it onto center stage, where it roams about freely. Music is indeed a character in the métier, and it is a central player, not an extra. So vivid is the musical presence that even the invisible score has a curious palpability: Joseph Stefano's fantasy of Herrmann lying on the floor and sending forth a musical geyser in *Psycho* is not as fantastical as it sounds. Nor is his assertion that *Psycho*'s music is so provocative that it transforms the picture into opera: from the beginning, Hitchcock compared talkies to opera, moving from the Viennese operetta of *Waltzes from Vienna* to the pop song surrealism of *Rear Window*. Many of Hitchcock's characters are singers, but as Robert Walker and John Forsythe demonstrate in *Strangers on a Train* and *The Trouble with Harry*, they don't have to be to suddenly burst into song. For Hitchcock, even purely symphonic scores are operatic, so forcefully do they comment on the action and counterpoint actors' voices: it is no accident that Ingrid Bergman's most passionate soliloquy in *Under Capricorn*, set against Richard Addinsell's ravishing score, is called "Henrietta's Aria" on the cue sheet.

Hitchcock's musical signatures were present from the beginning, including general devices such as counterpoint and specific effects such as chimes, lonely bass and timpani solos, ambiguous bitonal chords, and sudden silences, but they are not reducible to a single pattern. Indeed, they bristle with tensions and oppositions: music can be a consolation or treachery, a force of healing or destruction, revelation or obfuscation, truth or evasion, innocence or guilt. In *The Wrong Man* and the remake of *The Man Who Knew Too Much*, it enables parents to save their children; in *Waltzes from Vienna* it is connected to bitter paternal conflict as well as its resolution. Nor is a particular type of music linked to a predictable outcome: classical music is a force of revelation in *Murder!*, but it fails to brighten the darkness in *Vertigo;* popular song is a Shakespearean healer in *Rear Window* but an occasion of violence in *Blackmail.* The closest Hitchcock comes to a consistent pattern is his treatment of jazz, which is invariably an exuberant energy covering up anxiety and danger. In that regard, Hitchcock aligns himself with Ravel, Milhaud, Constant Lambert, and other European concert composers, who viewed jazz as an emblem of life's precariousness in the modern age. Hitchcock valued musical taste and linked it with his most noble characters—but also with his most evil ones; the Nazi conspirator in *Saboteur* who frames Robert Cummings has as much musical erudition as the blind pianist who helps him. For Hitchcock, music was as full of unsettling paradox as everything else in life, even as it lifted life to a loftier level. Nevertheless, the pianist Philip Martin in *Saboteur* articulates a philosophy of music that comes close to Hitchcock's, at least in his more benign moments: musical sound, says Philip, can allow us to see "intangible things" and create connectedness in a fractured world. For Hitchcock, too, music was a way into the intangible, a means of tapping the underlying idea in any narrative.

His way with music paralleled his other achievements. As Maurice Jarre put it, "He was very calm, very careful, but very strong. And he was a bit ahead of his time."[6] Even smaller pictures like *The 39 Steps, The Lady Vanishes,* and *Stage Fright* opened new possibilities for musical setting, characterization, symbolism, and memory; music itself became a subject in the cinema, paving the way for directors as diverse as Ken Russell, Stanley Kubrick, Bob Fosse, and Mike Leigh. Bigger Hollywood scores like *Spellbound, Vertigo, Psycho,* and *The Birds* were profoundly influential; both symphonic and electronic film music were never quite the same after them, nor were the psyches and expectations of moviegoers. These are some of the last indisputably original specimens of the art of film music.

Hitchcock's music resonates in overt spin-offs, homages, installations, and pastiches, but also in subtle echoes: in Danny Elfman's *Vertigo*-like main title for *Spider-Man,* for example, or in the 1992 version of *The Fugitive,* where marching bands camouflage the wrong-man hero, party music counterpoints disaster, mysterious modal chords (by James Newton Howard) signify unconscious thoughts, and poetic noise effects—trains, sirens, horns, helicopters, and subways—set the tempo for a Hitchcockian double chase. These audio designs, which hark back to *Blackmail* and *The 39 Steps,* have become an indelible part of cinema tradition.

Often, it was not a single score or composer that was revolutionary but the way Hitchcock used popular song or commented on how it moves through space: in that regard, *Rear Window,* whose legacy is endless, is Hitchcock's most influential musical experiment. But Hitchcock's achievement was so singular that it was often invulnerable to imitation or cannibalization; the only logical postlude for the *Storm Clouds* Cantata, the most spectacular symphonic set piece in film, was a remake of the movie by Hitchcock himself. No one else attempted anything like it.

At the heart of Hitchcock's music is an enigma. He oversaw more music over a longer period than any other director. Even silent films like *The Pleasure Garden, Downhill, The Ring,* and *The Lodger* are filled with images of musicians, music halls, and dances woven intricately into the story. Hitchcock oversaw a sophisticated score the moment sound became available in 1929 and through five decades worked with symphonic, pop, folk, cabaret, electronic, and every other genre of music he could get his hands on. He experimented with waltzes, an Old World form, more than any moviemaker, even as he reinvented modernism through *Psycho, The Birds,* and an endless procession of noise effects. Some of his most distinguished composers, such as Arthur Benjamin, credited him with being far more serious about music than any other director. Yet according to his daughter, Pat, he had no formal musical training and no musical talent, though she recalls that he went to numerous classical concerts.[7] In some ways, this was an advantage. According to Stefano, he had an enormous respect for composers precisely because they spoke a language he did not know. What he did have was an openness to new sounds, an unappeasable curiosity about composers, songwriters, concert halls, acoustics, and the ways music defined identity. He undoubtedly learned a great deal about music from Herrmann, with whom he collaborated for a decade; he also learned from his first love, theater: moments such as the spastic drum riffs in *Young and Innocent,* the Cole Porter songs in *Stage Fright,* and the carousel sing-along in *Strangers on a Train* are very close to musical theater and opera. But how he put together such a vast, intricate musical canvas will always be a mystery.

Another mystery is clarified by music: given Hitchcock's rigid preproduction planning and predilection for mathematical gamesmanship, why does the end product have an intense emotional resonance, an uncanny aura that permeates our subconscious? A supremely calculating technician often accused of coldness, Hitchcock needed music more than most moviemakers. Music tapped into the Romanticism beneath his classical exterior. Certainly his most dreamlike moments—the ones we never forget—are profoundly connected to music. The filmmaker Ric Burns, a lifelong Hitchcock admirer, maintains that music has a jump on the other elements in film: "Movies are forms of dreaming continuously aspiring to the condition of music, the highest form of dreaming. The more the music evokes the dream-state, the more powerfully in touch you become as a film-maker and your audience becomes with the most potent and creative forces in the subject matter."[8] Hitchcock put it more succinctly. Through music, he said, we "express the unspoken."[9]

NOTES

The following film archives have been central to my research. Within a chapter, these sources are cited only at their first reference; any undocumented material thereafter is from the same archive.

British Film Institute, Library and Information Services, London, U.K.
Margaret Herrick Library, The Alfred Hitchcock Collection, Academy of Motion Picture Arts and Sciences, Beverly Hills, California
Museum of Modern Art, Film Study Center, New York, New York
RKO Studio Collection, Arts Library Special Collections, Young Research Library, University of California, Los Angeles, California
David Selznick Collection, Harry Ransom Humanities Research Center, University of Texas, Austin, Texas
Syracuse University Library, Department of Special Collections, Syracuse, New York
Warner Brothers Archive, School of Cinema-Television, University of Southern California, Los Angeles, California

All requests for musical archives in these libraries should be made by phone in advance. This book incorporates a great number of interviews; because these conversations flowed over a five-year period, with numerous addenda and follow-ups, a few of the interview dates are approximate.

Overture

1 This aspect is frequently overlooked. A 2005 television documentary on Stanley Kubrick, for example, claims that Kubrick was the first director to use music as a crucial part of the narrative, even though Hitchcock was doing this before Kubrick was born.
2 Another standout, as Rudy Behlmer reminded me, is Erich Korngold's magnificent fifteen-minute suite from *The Adventures of Robin Hood,* released in 1938. Rudy Behlmer, interview with the author, March 7, 2006. For authoritative commentary on Hitchcock's Selznick productions, see Rudy Behlmer, *Memo from David O. Selznick* (New York, 1972).
3 Peter Conrad, *The Hitchcock Murders* (New York, 2000), xi.
4 Camille Paglia, *The Birds* (London, 1998), 88.
5 Stephen Spender, *World Within Worlds* (London, 1951), 2–3.
6 Steven DeRosa, *Writing with Hitchcock: The Collaboration of Alfred Hitchcock and John Michael Hayes* (New York, 2001), 193.
7 Steven Smith, *A Heart at Fire's Center: The Life and Music of Bernard Herrmann* (Berkeley, 1991), 360.

CHAPTER 1 **The Music Starts**

1 Special feature, *Family Plot*, Alfred Hitchcock Collection, Universal Pictures, DVD 20659.

2 Widely known as the "first British talkie," *Blackmail* came after *Sunrise, Don Juan, Seventh Heaven, The Jazz Singer*, and the Warner Brothers Vitaphone shorts; though some of the music in these films was synchronized, they were essentially silent movies with sound effects. For a concise history of this subject, see Tom Ryall, *Blackmail* (London, 1993).

3 S. M. Eisenstein, "A Statement"; rpt. Sergei Eisenstein, in *The Film Form: Essays in Theory*, ed. and trans. Jay Leyda (New York, 1949), 257–60.

4 According to Christopher Husted, "Campbell and Connelly," which receives a byline in the main title, is actually the music publisher.

5 Jane E. Sloan, *Alfred Hitchcock: The Definitive Filmography* (Berkeley, 1993), 88.

6 According to the British Film Institute, Hitchcock "burned all his musical bridges" when he left for America, leaving behind little archival musical material.

7 Elizabeth Weis, interview with the author, May 30, 2002.

8 For more on Hitchcock's transition to sound, see Charles Barr, "*Blackmail:* Silent and Sound," *Sight and Sound* (Spring 1983). A thorough listing of Hitchcock's musical motifs in his talkies can be found in Eva Rieger, *Hitchcock und die Musik* (Bielefeld, 1996).

9 Sidney Gottlieb suggested this idea to me.

10 Special feature, *Family Plot*.

11 Oswell Blakeston, "Advance Monologue," Close Up 7, no. 2 (August 1930): 146–47.

12 John Russell Taylor, *Hitch: The Life and Times of Alfred Hitchcock* (London, 1978; 2d ed., 1996), 110.

13 William A. Shack, *Harlem in Montmartre* (Berkeley, 2001), 77.

CHAPTER 2 *Waltzes from Vienna*

1 Cited in "Sixty-five Years of British Cinema," Esmond Knight, *Seeking the Bubble, Sight and Sound* Supplement 18, Museum of Modern Art (September 1971): 19.

2 Cited in Donald Spoto, *The Dark Side of Genius: The Life of Alfred Hitchcock* (Boston, 1983), 135.

3 Jane Sloan lists Julius Bittner as an uncredited coarranger (*Alfred Hitchcock*, 114).

4 Spoto, *Dark Side*, 135.

5 Clipping from "Sixty-five Years of British Cinema," *The Observer*, October 22, 1933.

6 Cited in Sidney Gottlieb, ed., *Hitchcock on Hitchcock* (Berkeley, 1995), 244.

7 Sidney Gottlieb, interview with the author, March 14, 2004.

8 Gottlieb, *Hitchcock on Hitchcock*, 245.

9 Ibid., 242–43.

10 Ibid., 244–45.

11 Ibid., 242–43.

12 Ibid., 243, 245.

13 Ibid., 242–43.

CHAPTER 3 *The Man Who Knew Too Much:* Royal Albert Hall

1 François Truffaut, *Hitchcock/Truffaut* (New York, 1983), 94. According to William Rosar, editor of the *Journal of Film Music*, Benjamin's original title for his cantata was "Choral Symphony"; Rosar, interview with the author, March 18, 2006.

2 John Waxman, interview with the author, February 27, 2004.
3 John Williams, interview with the author, January 29, 2003.
4 Taylor, *Hitch*, 125.
5 For a different view, see Robin Wood's incisive comparison of the two heroines in *Hitchcock's Films Revisited* (New York, 1989), 365–70.

CHAPTER 4 Musical Minimalism

1 According to Guenther Koegebehn of Bernardherrmann.org, it is questionable whether Levy wrote the music attributed to him: "It appears mostly he either employed Jack Beaver, Hubert Bath or Charles Williams to actually write it"; correspondence with the author, March 13, 2006. The British scholar A. R. Gleason emphatically agrees: "Levy is credited with musical direction of some 250 talkies—again, I must stress he did not compose or arrange a single one"; correspondence with the author, January 23, 2007. On the other hand, ASCAP does list cues by Bath, Beaver, and Williams in Hitchcock films for which they are given no credit, but lists cues by Levy in those films as well. Other sources such as Jane Sloan and Donald Spoto give Levy broad credit. Barry Sherman, the annotator for the recording *Alfred Hitchcock: Music from His Films* (Museum of Modern Art, 1999), cites Levy as the composer for *The 39 Steps, Sabotage,* and *Young and Innocent.* David Wishart parcels out the credit among Levy, Beaver, and Williams.
2 Truffaut, *Hitchcock/Truffaut,* 98.
3 Smith, *Heart at Fire's Center,* 253.
4 For a probing analysis of the expressionist aspects of this sound track, see Elisabeth Weis, *The Silent Scream* (East Brunswick, N.J., 1982), 63.
5 Cited in Philip Clark, "Manufacturing Dissent," *Wire* (June 2002): 34.
6 Truffaut, *Hitchcock/Truffaut,* 115.
7 "Margaret Lockwood Tops in Good Cast," *Hollywood Reporter,* March 22, 1939.

CHAPTER 5 *Rebecca*

1 Cue sheet, March 22, 1940, courtesy of John Waxman.
2 For a detailed account of the relationship between Hitchcock and Selznick, see Leonard Leff, *Hitchcock and Selznick* (Berkeley, 1987).
3 Christopher Palmer, *The Composer in Hollywood* (London, 1990), 94.
4 John Williams, interview with the author, January 29, 2003.
5 Leff, *Hitchcock and Selznick.*
6 Taylor, *Hitch,* 157.
7 John Waxman, interview with the author, December 21, 2002.
8 Taylor, *Hitch,* 157–58.
9 Donald Spoto, in *The Art of Alfred Hitchcock: Fifty Years of His Motion Pictures* (New York, 1976; rpt. 1992), is one of the most influential exponents of this argument.
10 Rudy Behlmer, interview with the author, September 19, 2002.
11 See Leff's superb *Hitchcock and Selznick.*
12 David Selznick Collection.
13 David Selznick to Franz Waxman, October 11, 1939. Selznick also considered Erich Korngold as musical director, but that apparently never materialized.
14 David Selznick to music department, September 21, 1939.
15 Joseph McBride: "Alfred Hitchcock's Mary Rose: An Old Master's Unheard Cri de Coeur." *Cineaste* 26, no. 2 (2001): 25.

16 Christopher Husted, "The Scoring of Rebecca," CD liner note, *Rebecca*, Varèse Sarabande 302 066 160.

17 John Waxman, interview with the author, March 9, 2004.

18 Franz Waxman to David Selznick, March 13, 1941.

19 David Selznick to Daniel O'Shea, March 15, 1941.

20 The lost Beatrice music can be heard on a Marco Polo CD, the uncorrupted Mrs. Danvers cue on a recording from Varèse Sarabande. The notes for the latter call Selznick's meddling "inexplicable."

21 Waxman, interview with the author.

22 Palmer, *Composer*, 103.

23 Husted, "Scoring," 16.

24 Robert Townson, Varèse Sarabande annotation.

25 Truffaut, *Hitchcock/Truffaut*.

CHAPTER 6 **Waltzing into Danger**

1 "A screwball dame," the name attached to Lombard following *Nothing Sacred*, became the label of this genre.

2 "Mr. Hitchcock Meets the Smiths," the special feature in the Warner 2004 DVD, asserts that the film "is nothing like his others." John Russell Taylor states it is "quite unlike anything he had done before, or was to do subsequently" (*Hitch*, 171).

3 Truffaut, *Hitchcock/Truffaut*, 222.

4 "[Webb] did two of Hitchcock's films—the comedy *Mr. and Mrs. Smith* and *Notorious*," CD annotation, *Music from Alfred Hitchcock Films*, Varèse Sarabande 47225.5.

5 Cue sheet, March 2, 1942, courtesy of John Waxman.

6 RKO Studio Collection.

7 The horn cues are called "First Assembly Call" and "Second Assembly Call."

8 For a detailed analysis of the controversy over the ending, see Bill Krohn, "Ambivalence (Suspicion)," *Hitchcock Annual*, Fairfield, Connecticut, 2002–3.

9 Teresa Wright, interview with the author, October 15, 1999.

10 Olivia Tiomkin, interview with the author, October 16, 2002.

11 For an investigation of the vampire theme in *Shadow of a Doubt*, see David Sterritt's *The Films of Alfred Hitchcock* (Cambridge, 1993).

12 Dimitri Tiomkin, *Please Don't Hate Me* (New York, 1959), 225.

13 Ibid., 225, 226.

14 Special feature, *Shadow of a Doubt*, Alfred Hitchcock Collection, Universal Pictures, DVD 20672.

CHAPTER 7 **Sounds of War**

1 "Core of the Movie: The Chase," *New York Times Magazine*, October 29, 1950, 22–23, 44–46.

2 Ibid.

3 Ibid.

4 Review of *Foreign Correspondent*, *Variety*, August 28, 1940, 3–4.

5 "McCrea, Marshall Top Swell Cast," *Hollywood Reporter*, August 28, 1940.

6 Cue sheet, *Foreign Correspondent*, October 7, 1940. British Film Institute.

7 See Spoto's *Dark Side* for circumstances behind Hitchcock's patriotism.

8 See Sergio Leemann, "Alfred Hitchcock's Bon Voyage and Aventure Malgache," annotation, DVD 419, British Film Institute, Image Entertainment.

CHAPTER 8 *Spellbound*

1 Michael Wood, interview with the author, September 20, 2002.
2 Taylor, *Hitch,* 195.
3 Leff, *Hitchcock and Selznick,* 140.
4 See "From Spellbound to Vertigo: Alfred Hitchcock and Therapeutic Culture in America," in *Hitchcock's America,* ed. Jonathan Freedman and Richard Millington (New York, 1999) , chap. 4.
5 Michael Dirda, interview with the author, January 12, 2006.
6 Spoto, *Dark Side,* 278.
7 Rudy Behlmer, interview with Miklos Rozsa, *Spellbound,* Criterion DVD 136.
8 November 20, 1944, David Selznick Collection.
9 Miklos Rozsa, *Double Life* (New York, 1982), 146.
10 Christopher Palmer, "Biography of Miklos Rozsa," 1975, The Miklos Rozsa Society Web site, http://members.iinet.net.au/~agfam/miklos/index.html.
11 Truffaut, *Hitchcock/Truffaut,* 165.
12 Rozsa, *Double Life,* 147.
13 *Spellbound* Music Notes, Syracuse University Library.
14 Rozsa, *Double Life,* 147.
15 Ibid. According to John Fitzpatrick, of the Miklos Rozsa Society, the tune came to Rozsa while he was driving on the freeway.
16 Albert Glinsky, "The Fishko Files: The Theremin," National Public Radio, 2002.
17 Ibid.
18 Leff, *Hitchcock and Selznick,* 139.
19 *Spellbound* music notes, October 6, 1944, Syracuse University Library.
20 Palmer, *Composer,* 229.
21 In some cases, the ondes Martinot was used; in truth, it is sometimes difficult to distinguish between the sounds of the two, but the theremin has acquired a far more cultish following.
22 The year after *Spellbound* appeared, Olivier Messiaen used the ondes Martinot, which sounds much like the theremin, in his Turangalila Symphony; it eventually became a staple in classical music.
23 Audray Granville to David Selznick, October 10, 1945, David Selznick Collection.
24 Rozsa interview, Criterion DVD. In Rozsa's version of the controversy, Selznick and Hitchcock were accusing him only of reusing the theremin, whereas Selznick's memo and Granville's rejoinder indicate the plagiarism charge was broader.
25 Granville to Selznick, October 10, 1945.
26 Scholars have assumed that Rozsa finished the score in time for an early preview in February 1945, but these memos indicate that only part of it had been done. (Leff, *Hitchcock and Selznick,* 166). The sound notes for "The Awakening," for example, are dated February 15, 1945, whereas those for "Rooftop Dream" and "Gambling Dream" are from September 14, 1945. Numerous memos from Selznick and his associates through the summer and early fall of 1945 express concern that Rozsa had not completed the score.

27 Don King to David Selznick, June 6, 1945.

28 David Selznick to Robert Dann, June 7, 1945.

29 The publishers included Southern Music, Chappell, and Shapiro Bernstein. Among the lyricists were Doris Fisher, Al Roberts, Kermit Goell, Harold Adamson, Al Stewart, and Al Neiberg.

30 John Waxman, interview with the author, June 19, 2003.

31 Cited in annotation for *Spellbound: The Film Music of Miklos Rozsa*, RCA 0911.

32 Paul MacNamara to David Selznick, July 25, 1945.

33 Spoto, *Dark Side*, 278.

34 ARA Records contracted to record the score on September 19, 1945.

CHAPTER 9 *Notorious*

1 Truffaut, *Hitchcock/Truffaut*, 170.

2 Rudy Behlmer, interview with the author, September 18, 2002.

3 Christopher Husted, interview with the author, October 14, 2002

4 Smith, *Heart at Fire's Center*, 94. See this source for an exhaustive account of Herrmann's relationships with other composers.

5 Behlmer, interview with the author. Because of the lack of archival material from the 1930s, it is not clear how much involvement Hitchcock had with Louis Levy's music, although his signatures are astonishingly consistent.

6 Ibid.

7 *Spotting*, a technical term, refers to deciding which scenes should have music and where it should go.

8 David Selznick Collection.

9 Correspondence between Barbara Keon and Ann Harris, April 4 and 10, 1945.

10 Natt Winecoff to David Selznick, April 12,1945.

11 RKO Studio Collection.

12 Brian Wise, "What Brazil Offers to Classical Music," *New York Times*, July 27, 2003, sect. 2, 27.

13 Palmer, *Composer*, 176.

14 Roy Webb, "Things a Motion Picture Composer Has to Think About," *Film Music Notes*, October 4, 1941, 2.

15 Smith, *Heart at Fire's Center*, 94.

16 The score is housed in the RKO Studio Collection.

17 Other notable Webb scores from the late 1940s such as *Crossfire* (one of the earliest cinematic treatments of anti-Semitism) and *The Window* are even more obscure, though the movies themselves are relatively well known.

18 CD liner note, *Digital Premiere Recordings from the Films of Alfred Hitchcock*, Varèse Sarabande, 47225. See Palmer's *Composer* for the definitive account of Webb's career.

CHAPTER 10 *The Paradine Case*

1 For "excessively cutty," see Leff, *Hitchcock and Selznick*, 258.

2 David Selznick Collection.

3 Ted Wick was instrumental in getting the *Spellbound* score on the radio ahead of its release.

4 Leff, *Hitchcock and Selznick,* 259.

5 Cue sheet, March 30, 1948, courtesy of John Waxman.

6 Ibid. Leonard Leff argues that Selznick "shopped around for a composer who could give *Paradine* the warmth that Hitchcock had perhaps sapped with his cold lighting and occasionally labored tracking shots."

7 Margaret Herrick Library.

8 Truffaut, *Hitchcock/Truffaut,* 256.

9 Music timing sheet, November 12, 1947: "We see Keane coming out carrying his bag and we see Hitchcock coming out carrying his cello case."

CHAPTER 11 Hitchcock in a Different Key

1 Special feature, Arthur Laurents, Alfred Hitchcock Collection, Universal Pictures, DVD 20671.

2 The credits list Leo F. Forbstein as the musical adapter, but the cue sheet credits David Buttolphe.

3 The first scholar to comment on the connection was Elizabeth Weis in *The Silent Scream.*

4 Paul Crossley, CD annotation, "Poulenc: Complete Piano Music," CBS Records 44921.

5 For an analysis of the other assets, and a vigorous defense of the film overall, see Mark Rappaport, "Under Capricorn, Revisited," *Hitchcock Annual,* Fairfield, Connecticut (2003–4): 42–66.

6 Victor Peers to Roy Orbinger, November 19, 1948, Warner Brothers Archive.

7 Rappaport calls this "a virtuoso nine-minute take" (53).

8 Carlisle Jones, "From the Warner Brothers Studio," Warner Brothers Archive.

9 Joseph I. Breen to J. L. Warner, August 17 and November 16, 1949.

10 Alfred Hitchcock to Jack Warner, July 18, 1949.

11 Alma Reville, Treatment, March 23, 1949.

12 The cue is called "Eve and Smith in Car," cue sheet, May 16, 1950.

CHAPTER 12 The Band Played On

1 Warner Brothers Archive. All archival quotes are from this source unless otherwise indicated.

2 Cue sheet, May 21, 1951.

3 Palmer, *Composer,* 151.

4 Special feature, *Strangers on a Train,* Warner Brothers, DVD 31975.

5 Tiomkin's detractors include Royal Brown, Donald Spoto, and Sedgwick Clark; Olivia Tiomkin, interview with the author, October 16, 2002.

6 Joseph Stefano, interview with the author, April 15, 2005. According to Stefano, Hitchcock almost heard the script in advance as well.

7 Truffaut, *Hitchcock/Truffaut,* 204.

8 Cue sheet, January 26, 1953,

9 Olivia Tiomkin, interview with author.

10 *Hollywood Reporter,* February 5, 1953.

11 Olivia Tiomkin, interview with author. According to Donald Spoto, Hitchcock became aware of Kelly from a test she did in New York (*Dark Side,* 342).

12 Warner Brothers Archive.

13 Special feature, *Strangers on a Train*, DVD.
14 Ibid.

CHAPTER 13 *Rear Window*

1 Truffaut, *Hitchcock/Truffaut*, 165.
2 Cue sheet, July 6, 1954, courtesy of John Waxman.
3 John Waxman, interview with the author, December 21, 2002.
4 Ibid.
5 "Description of the Manner in Which Music Is Used," memo, Elinore Dolnic to Richard Healand, Paramount Corporation, document courtesy of John Waxman.
6 Prelude courtesy of John Waxman. Other parts of the score are housed in the Syracuse University Library.
7 DeRosa, *Writing with Hitchcock*, 47–49. DeRosa provides insightful commentary on Hitchcock's use of street noise and sudden silence.
8 Elizabeth Weis points out that this is often a red herring: "Hitchcock's favoring of low-brow over high-brow music can be taken as evidence of the anti-intellectualism that so offends Charles Thomas Samuels in Hitchcock's work. Yet . . . it is less musical taste than moral and psychological questions that are at stake" (*Silent Scream*, 93).
9 Truffaut, *Hitchcock/Truffaut*, 216.
10 Steven DeRosa notes that in the prescript treatment of the film, the powerful effect of the song is not limited to Miss Lonely Hearts: "Lisa reveals that the song inspired her to fight for her life" when she is caught by Thorwald entering his apartment. See DeRosa, *Writing with Hitchcock*, 29.
11 The trailer for the film accentuates the brooding and even threatening qualities of this character: an ominous voice-over introduces him as "The Songwriter, who plays the same melody over and over again—a genius? or insane?"
12 Truffaut, *Hitchcock/Truffaut*, 216.
13 Cited in DeRosa, *Writing with Hitchcock*, 50.
14 John Waxman, interview with the author, February 24, 2004.
15 For examples, see Alfred Hitchcock, "On Music in Films," 1933, rpt. in Gottlieb, *Hitchcock on Hitchcock*, 244; Spoto, *Dark Side*, 204; Truffaut, *Hitchcock/Truffaut*, 276.
16 The ending as filmed is different from what was in the first draft of the script, where, as DeRosa points out, "Miss Torso compliments the Songwriter for his lovely tune, and he invites her up to his apartment" (*Writing with Hitchcock*, 37).
17 For a reading that emphasizes the "closed" and "selective" use of song in the film, see Elizabeth Weis's pioneering analysis in chapter 6 of *The Silent Scream*.
18 Special feature, "Rear Window Ethics," *Rear Window*, Alfred Hitchcock Collection, Universal Pictures, DVD 20011.

CHAPTER 14 Lethal Laughter

1 See Leslie Brill, "Redemptive Comedy in the Films of Alfred Hitchcock and Preston Sturges: 'Are Snakes Necessary?'" in *Alfred Hitchcock: Centenary Essays*, ed. Richard Allen and S. Ishi Gonzales (London, 1999).
2 Special feature, *To Catch a Thief*, Paramount DVD 06308.
3 Smith, *Heart at Fire's Center*, 191, 192; Royal S. Brown, *Overtones and Undertones: Reading Film Music* (Berkeley, 1994), 148, 149; Spoto, *Dark Side*, 355.
4 Donald Spoto, correspondence with the author, January 14, 2005.

5 Smith, *Heart at Fire's Center*, 193.
6 Spoto, *Art of Hitchcock*, 237.
7 Special feature, *The Trouble with Harry*, Alfred Hitchcock Collection, Universal Pictures, DVD 20670.
8 DeRosa, *Writing with Hitchcock*, 149; Spoto, *Art of Hitchcock*, 235.
9 Smith interview, special feature, *Trouble with Harry*, DVD.

CHAPTER 15 *The Man Who Knew Too Much:* Doris Day
1 Taylor, *Hitch*, 236.
2 James Stevens applied for the composer's job, but on April 1, Hitchcock politely turned him down.
3 DeRosa, *Writing with Hitchcock*, 177.
4 Smith, *Heart at Fire's Center*, 197–98.
5 Margaret Herrick Library.
6 According to James Wierzbicki, at the University of Michigan School of Music, the additional music comes from the main title in the original film; interview with the author, March 18, 2006.
7 Murray Pomerance, "Finding Release: 'Storm Clouds' and *The Man Who Knew Too Much*," in *Music in Cinema*, ed. James Buhler, Caryl Flinn, and David Neumeyer (Hanover, N.H., 2001), 243. This article offers an extensive formal analysis of Benjamin's cantata.
8 Film music books such as Irwin Bazelon's *Knowing the Score* (New York, 1975) list the main title as simply an excerpt from Benjamin's cantata, but it is really a Herrmann re-creation.
9 Bill Krohn, *Hitchcock at Work* (London, 2000), 171.
10 See ibid., for example.
11 Spoto, *Dark Side*, 65.
12 Claudia Gorbman, *Unheard Melodies: Narrative Film Music* (Bloomington, Ind., 1987), 24.
13 Bazelon, *Knowing the Score*, 133.
14 Spoto, *Dark Side*, 355.
15 See Robin Wood, *Hitchcock's Films Revisited* (New York, 1989), for a powerful analysis of Jo's representation and repudiation of her culture.
16 Ibid., 370.
17 See Krohn, *Hitchcock at Work*.

CHAPTER 16 *The Wrong Man*
1 Reba Churchill and Bonnie Churchill, "Jazz Role in Movie," *Beverly Hills Citizen*, July 16, 1956, 12.
2 See Hitchcock's fascinating arguments with Truffaut on the subject of realism (Truffaut, *Hitchcock/Truffaut*, 239); Truffaut believed the film needed to be even more in the style of a documentary.
3 Warner Brothers Archive.
4 *Variety*, December 21, 1956; *New York Post*, December 24, 1956.
5 Louis Kaufman, cited in "Music for the Movies: Bernard Herrmann," Sony video 67169.
6 An exception is David Sterritt, who characterizes Manny's music as reflecting the "stagnant pattern" of his life. The voice-over in the trailer makes that pattern clear: "He

lived in a simple routine world; when the lights went out, the fiddle was put away. The same subway, the newspaper, home to Rose and the kids . . . straight and narrow until the night of January 14th, 1953, when, 'Is your name Christopher Emmanuel Balestrero?'" (*Films of Alfred Hitchcock,* 69).

7   Cited in Katherine H. Allen, CD liner note, *Jonny spielt auf,* Vanguard 8048.

8   "Music Notes made at first running of 'The Wrong Man,'" August 29, 1956.

CHAPTER 17 Sing Along with Hitch

1   Spoto, *Dark Side,* 399.

2   John McCarty and Brian Kelleher, eds., *Alfred Hitchcock Presents* (New York, 1985), 9–10.

3   Martin Grams, Jr., and Patrick Wikstrom, *The Alfred Hitchcock Presents Companion* (Churchville, Md., 2001), 50. According to this source, Herrmann arranged the opening and closing march for the second and third season of *The Alfred Hitchcock Hour.*

4   Historically, this was not completely new: Bach, Handel, Mozart, and many others plagiarized from themselves and others. But the basic authorship of a work was never in question. And the financial implications were much smaller: the economic arrangement for television and film cues involved shows that would be rebroadcast thousands of times.

5   McCarty and Kelleher, *Hitchcock Presents,* 30.

CHAPTER 18 *Vertigo*

1   The original score is housed in the Paramount vault. I am deeply grateful to Tegan Kossowicz and Heather Schwarz of the Famous Music Corporation for helping me find it and negotiate rights for the reprint of the prelude image.

2   Sterritt, *Films of Alfred Hitchcock,* 83.

3   Martin Scorsese, "Foreword," in Dan Auiler, *Vertigo: The Making of a Hitchcock Classic* (New York, 1998), xiii.

4   Donald Spoto, "Sound and Silence in the Films of Alfred Hitchcock." *Keynote Magazine,* April 1980, 12.

5   Alex Ross, CD liner note, "Bernard Herrmann: The Film Scores," Sony 62600; Ross, "Casting the Spells of 'Vertigo,'" *New York Times,* October 6, 1996, H17.

6   David Cooper, *Bernard Herrmann's Vertigo* (Westport, Conn.), 2001. This is a helpful, detailed resource for anyone interested in the harmonic architecture of the score.

7   Margaret Herrick Library.

8   For an authoritative study of Poe's influence on Hitchcock, see Dennis Perry, *Hitchcock and Poe: The Legacy of Delight and Terror* (Lanham, Md., 2003).

9   Hitchcock shot an alternative, happy ending, in which Scottie and Midge hear a radio report of Gavin Elster's capture, but he did not use it.

10   For a thorough harmonic analysis of these themes, see Brown, *Overtones.*

11   Smith, *Heart at Fire's Center,* 222.

12   Truffaut, *Hitchcock/Truffaut,* 244.

13   The tapes of the Hitchcock-Truffaut conversations, along with partial transcriptions, are in the Hitchcock collection at the Margaret Herrick Library. I owe this reference to Sid Gottlieb.

14   Auiler, *Vertigo,* lists the LSO, but Ridge Walker, from Paramount's music department, quoted in Cooper, *Bernard Herrmann's Vertigo,* does "not find the name of any particular orchestra in London" (51).

15 These include the London cues on a 1958 Mercury recording reissued on CD; the complete sound track on Varèse Sarabande; a Royal Scottish National Orchestra version of the complete score on Varèse Sarabande; and numerous suites directed by Esa-Pekka Salonen (Sony), Elmer Bernstein (RCA), and Herrmann (London Phase-4).

16 Cited in Kevin Mulhall, CD annotation, *Vertigo: Original Motion Picture Soundtrack,* Varèse Sarabande 5759.

17 Chris Marker, cited in Auiler, *Vertigo,* 184.

18 Brown, *Overtones,* 148.

19 Alan Ryding, "In Art, Too, the Sound Is Spooky," *New York Times,* April 11, 1999. Gordon also created the 1993 *Twenty-Four Hour Psycho,* which projected slow-motion images of *Psycho* on a screen for twenty-four hours, without Herrmann's music.

CHAPTER 19 *North by Northwest*

1 Smith, *Heart at Fire's Center,* 227.

2 Roy Pendergast, *Film Music: A Neglected Art* (New York, 1977; rpt., 1992), 139.

3 Lehman, cited in Smith, *Heart at Fire's Center,* 227.

4 Spoto, *Dark Side,* 406.

5 Margaret Herrick Library.

6 Typescript from *Bernard Herrmann Journal* (n.d.), Museum of Modern Art.

7 Walter Pater, "The Condition of Music," from *Studies in the Renaissance,* 1893; rpt. in Jack Sullivan, *Words on Music* (Athens, Ohio, 1990), 338.

8 "Core of the Movie: The Chase," *New York Times Magazine,* October 29, 1950. Typescript in Margaret Herrick Library.

9 Telegram from Eva Marie Saint to Bernard Herrmann, July 17, 1959.

10 Truffaut, *Hitchcock/Truffaut,* 256.

11 Eva Marie Saint, Hitchcock Centenary Conference, New York, October 16, 1999.

12 Brown, *Overtones,* 173.

13 Palmer, *Composer,* 278.

CHAPTER 20 *Psycho*

1 Smith, *Heart at Fire's Center,* 239. The cue in its initial appearance is called "The Murder"; when a shorter version reappears during Arbogast's killing, it is called "The Knife."

2 For an authoritative analysis of the Sublime, see Jacques Barzun's article on Romanticism in Jack Sullivan, ed., *Penguin Encyclopedia of Horror and the Supernatural* (New York, 1986), 356.

3 Truffaut, *Hitchcock/Truffaut,* 268.

4 Joseph Stefano, interview with the author, October 16, 1999.

5 Stephen Rebello, *Alfred Hitchcock and the Making of Psycho* (New York, 1990), 138.

6 Smith, *Heart at Fire's Center,* 237.

7 Rebello, *Psycho,* 138.

8 Margaret Herrick Library.

9 Smith, *Heart at Fire's Center,* 240.

10 Rebello, *Psycho,* 136. Rebello's evidence comes from the screenplay, which describes only traffic noises.

11 Smith, *Heart at Fire's Center,* 238.

12 Joseph Stefano, interview with the author, April 15, 2005.

13 Rebello, *Psycho,* 139.

14 Stefano, interview with the author, April 15, 2005.

15 Rebello, *Psycho,* 143.

16 Ibid. , 144.

17 Janet Leigh, Hitchcock Centenary Conference, New York, October 16, 1999.

18 Bazelon, *Knowing the Score;* David Wishart, CD liner note, *Psycho: The Essential Alfred Hitchcock,* Silva Screen 1101; Palmer, liner note, *Psycho,* Unicorn-Kachana, 2021; Palmer, *Composer,* 275; Miklos Rozsa, Foreword to Edward Johnson, *Bernard Herrmann: Hollywood's Music Dramatist* (Rickmansworth, 1977), 2; Smith, *Heart at Fire's Center,* 238.

19 Royal S. Brown, "Bernard Herrmann and the Subliminal Pulse of Violence," *High Fidelity and Musical America,* March 1976, 75.

20 Cited in Jack Sullivan,"A Little Night Music," *Washington Post Book World,* September 6, 1998, 7.

21 Truffaut, *Hitchcock/Truffaut,* 269, 276.

22 Smith, *Heart at Fire's Center,* 237.

23 Cited in Palmer, *Composer,* 274.

24 Rebello, *Psycho,* 139.

25 Ibid., 138.

26 Stefano, interview with the author, September 20, 2001.

27 Stefano, interview with the author, April 15, 2005. Hitchcock loved to joke around with Stefano. When Stefano mentioned that he enjoyed the music of Eric Coates, Hitchcock said, "Oh, him. But don't you think that's tea-dance music?"

CHAPTER 21 **The Birds**

1 Daphne du Maurier, "The Birds," rpt. in *Alfred Hitchcock Presents Fourteen of My Favorites in Suspense* (New York, 1959), 47–48.

2 Margaret Herrick Library.

3 Truffaut, *Hitchcock/Truffaut,* 294.

4 Ibid., 297.

5 Smith, *Heart at Fire's Center,* 254.

6 Ibid.

7 Elizabeth Weis, "Style and Sound in *The Birds,*" in *Film Sound,* ed. Elizabeth Weis and John Belton (New York, 1985), 308.

8 Truffaut, *Hitchcock/Truffaut,* 297.

9 Ibid.

10 Ibid.

11 Smith, *Heart at Fire's Center,* 254.

12 Special feature, *The Birds,* Alfred Hitchcock Collection, Universal Pictures, DVD 20275.

CHAPTER 22 **The Music Ends**

1 Palmer, *Composer,* 321.

2 Camille Paglia and Donald Spoto are among Hedren's most passionate defenders. Paglia characterizes the attacks on her performance in *The Birds* as "disgraceful"; Jay Presson Allen, interview with the author, October 16, 1999. Remarks on the script and Hedren made at the Hitchcock Centenary Conference, New York, also on October 16, 1999.

3 Truffaut, *Hitchcock/Truffaut*, 327.
4 Margaret Herrick Library.
5 The file lists Herrmann, Peter Jason, and Gloria Shayne as the song's creators.
6 Spoto, *Dark Side*, 491.
7 Rudy Behlmer, interview with the author, September 18, 2002.
8 Spoto, *Dark Side*, 491.
9 "Music for the Movies: Bernard Herrmann," Sony video 67169.
10 Alex Ross, CD liner note, "Bernard Herrmann: The Film Scores," Sony 62700.
11 Museum of Modern Art, typescript of interview in the *Bernard Herrmann Society Journal* 1, no. 3 (n.d.): 9.
12 Smith, *Heart at Fire's Center*, 271. As Smith points out, Hitchcock's notes were scant compared to his usual.
13 Brown, *Overtones*, 148.
14 Smith, *Heart at Fire's Center*, 271
15 Brown, *Overtones*, 172.
16 "Music to Commit Murder By," *Soho Weekly News*, September 9, 1976, 14.
17 Royal S. Brown, "An Interview with Bernard Herrmann," *High Fidelity*, September 8, 1976, 65.
18 Chabrol and Raskin, in "Music for the Movies," Sony video.
19 Smith, *Heart at Fire's Center*, 268.
20 "Music for the Movies," Sony video.
21 Smith, *Heart at Fire's Center*, 272.
22 Truffaut, *Hitchcock/Truffaut*, 328.
23 *Los Angeles Times*, June 27, 1966.
24 Christopher Husted, interview with the author, March 3, 2005.
25 Hitchcock told Maurice Jarre that Julie Andrews was constantly complaining, "I don't feel this scene"; Hitchcock would reply, "Look, Julie, say what you want. I'll take care of it in the cutting room." Maurice Jarre, interview with the author, June 1, 2004.
26 Kevin Thomas, "Composer Settles a Score," interview with Bernard Herrmann, *Los Angeles Times, Calendar*, February 4, 1968.
27 John Williams, interview with the author, January 29, 2003.

CHAPTER 23 *Topaz*
1 "Music for the Movies: Bernard Herrmann," Sony Video 67169.
2 Jay Hoffman to Alfred Hitchcock, July 16, 1968; clipping from *Life* magazine ad in the *New York Times*, August, 14, 1967. Margaret Herrick Library.
3 Maurice Jarre, interview with the author, June 1, 2004. All Jarre quotes are from this interview.
4 Spoto, *Art of Hitchcock*, 369.
5 Harry Garfield to Peggy Robertson, March 31, April 3 and 7, 1969. The *Topaz* music file in the Margaret Herrick Library is one of the most detailed and specific in the Hitchcock collection, demonstrating Hitchcock's extensive research into folk, classical, and popular music during the project. In each case, Hitchcock listened to numerous options before making his choices.
6 Peggy Robertson gave Jarre numerous references for the types of marches favored by

the Soviets, including the Russian National Anthem, "Moscow in Italy," and marches by Glinka.

7 The clipping, from an unknown source, is taped to the note.

CHAPTER 24 *Frenzy*

1 Margaret Herrick Library.
2 My attempts to get information from Mancini's surviving colleagues proved fruitless.
3 Spoto, *Dark Side,* 515.
4 Ibid., 515–16.
5 Ibid.
6 Special feature, *Frenzy,* Alfred Hitchcock Collection, Universal Pictures, DVD 20661.

CHAPTER 25 *Family Plot*

1 Composer memo, August 28, 1975, Margaret Herrick Library.
2 Taylor, *Hitch,* 303.
3 John Williams, interview with the author, January 29, 2003. All other Williams quotes are from this interview, unless otherwise indicated.
4 Christopher Husted, who expressed surprise at Williams's remarks, speculates that some of Hitchcock's knowledge came from his association with Herrmann.
5 Special feature, *Family Plot,* Alfred Hitchcock Collection, Universal Pictures, DVD 20659.
6 *Family Plot* dubbing notes, December 10, 1975: "Reel 1 M-101 Start on F.I. emblem through M.T. card 0- through opening séance, carry through all dialogue until Blanche collapses to the side"; "Reel 13, ending. Start as Blanche starts to fake seance (leans away from George) through walk upstairs to point to chandelier through wink at audience through cast." The cue sheet: "Seance: no need for any external sounds because we're going to rely on the background music to accompany this scene and there will not be a need for passing cars etc." The dubbing notes are located in the Herrick Library; the cue sheet is housed in the British Film Institute.

Finale

1 Taylor, *Hitch,* 314.
2 Margaret Herrick Library.
3 Special feature, *Family Plot,* DVD.
4 Mancini, cited by John Waxman, interview with the author, December 21, 2002.
5 Truffaut, *Hitchcock/Truffaut,* 335.
6 Maurice Jarre, interview with the author, June 8, 2005.
7 Patricia O'Connell, interview with the author, June 8, 2005.
8 Jack Sullivan, "New York: A Documentary: An Interview with Ric Burns," *New York Stories* (Winter 2000): 4.
9 Gottlieb, *Hitchcock on Hitchcock,* 244.

INDEX

Page numbers in italics indicate photographs or facsimiles. "H" is used in subheadings as an abbreviation for Hitchcock.

Fenby, Eric, 56
film music: catharsis provided by, 268; as character/personification through, 76–77, 104, 315–16, 318–20; comedy and, 53; composition processes, 69–70, 110; corporate scoring, 70–72; electronic scores, 264–65 (see also *The Birds*); as foreground, 195; H on functions of, 28–29; H on music as sound, 44; for horror films, 245; H's preferences, 130–31, 251; modernism, 258 (see also *Psycho*); musical culture preserved, 113, 258; realism subverted, 316; Rozsa on conservatism of, 108; underscore eliminated, 170 (see also *Rear Window*); used to promote film (*see* concert music; popular songs; *Rebecca*; *Spellbound*); *Vertigo's* recording difficulties, 232–33; Waxman's vision, 69, 76–77. *See also* source music; *and specific films and composers*
Finch, Jon, 301, 303
Fishko, Sara, 123
Fjastad, Roy, 194
"Flaggin' the Train to Tuscaloosa" (David and Scott), 190
Fleming, Rhonda, 118, 121
folk music, 33, 46, 52–53, 140, 172, 270–71
Fonda, Henry, 146, 207, *208*, 212–13
Fontaine, Joan, 58, *59*, 60, 75, 84
Forbes, Lou, 64, *65*, 66–67
Foreign Correspondent (1940), 83, 96–101
Forsythe, John, 172, 190, 219, 320
Foster, Barry, 301
"Four O'Clock" (episode of NBC's *Suspicion*), 219–21
Francesca da Rimini (Tchaikovsky), 273–74

Frankel, Benjamin, 105, 298–99
Frenzy (1972), 273, 298–307
Friedhofer, Hugo, 104
The Fugitive (Davis; *1993*), 321
"Funeral March of a Marionette" (Gounod), 189, 214

Galsworthy, Mrs., 13
Garfield, Harry, 291, 310, 318
Garmes, Lee, 138
Gassmann, Remi, 265
Gaumont (studio), 2, 41, 43, 55, 194. *See also* Levy, Louis; *and specific films*
Gielgud, John, 44, 45
"Girl of My Dreams" (Clapp), 5
Goldsmith, Jerry, 245, 309
"Golly Gee" (Livingston and Evans), 193
Gone With the Wind (Fleming; *1939*), 61, 63–66, *65*, 70
Goodwin, Ron (*Frenzy* score), 273, 290, 299–303, 305–7
Gorban, Claudia, 200
Gordon, Douglas, 234
Gounod, Charles ("Funeral March of a Marionette"), 189, 214
Grainer, Ron, 298
Granger, Farley, 145, *147*, 157
Grant, Cary: in *North by Northwest*, 185, 231, 235, *236*, 237–39; in *Notorious*, 127–29, *128*; possible *Hamlet* film for, 97; in *Suspicion*, 84, *85*, 87; in *To Catch a Thief*, 184
Granville, Audray, 115–19, 121, 126
Grau, Gil, 133
"The Green Years" (Addison, Livingston, and Evans), 283, *284*
Gross, Walter, 170, 173, 176

Hallis, A., 13, 14
Hamlet film idea, 97
Hammerstein, Oscar, 62, 119

Hardwicke, Sir Cedric, 215

Harris, Barbara, 312, 316

Harvey, Laurence, 217

Hayes, John Michael, 184, 193, 277

Head, Edith, 173

Hecht, Ben, 113, 121

Hedren, Tippi, 146, 261, 270, 274, 276

Henderson, Jack, 32

Herbert, Frederick, 217, 219

Herman, Sid, 170

Herrmann, Bernard, 186, *188*, 196;
  AHP scores, 216; and *The Birds'*
  electronic score, 264–65, 311; concert music, 233, 254, 258; conflicts
  with musicians, 191; considered
  for Hitchcock scores, 107, 125,
  138–39, 184, 299; death, 308; on
  H's understanding of film music,
  xvi; Lehman introduced to H, 237;
  on main titles, 251, 253; and *The
  Man Who Knew Too Much (1956)*,
  as on-screen conductor, 16, 193,
  195, 197, *199*; —, score, 31, 33,
  195–96, 204–5; —, *Storm Clouds*
  approved, 193; —, *Storm Clouds*
  orchestration, 32, 195; *Marnie*
  score, 275–76, 289; on music's role
  in film, xix; non-Hitchcock scores,
  125, 130, 212, 226, 234, 273, 279–
  80; *North by Northwest* score, 235–
  42; orchestrations done by self, 254;
  personality, 282; popularity, 278–
  79, 283–84; *Psycho* score, 243–51,
  246, 304, 320; relationship with H,
  168, 186–87, 191, 241–42, 264–
  65, 273–74, 318, 322; —, rupture,
  273–74, 277–85, 288–89, 294, 299,
  310; *Sweeney Todd* as homage to,
  245; television music system objected to, 217; *Torn Curtain* score,
  117, 278–83, 285–87; *The Trouble
  with Harry* score, 14, 186–87, 189–

91; *Vertigo* score, 12, 67, 172, 222–
34, 256, 258; and Webb, 125; and
Williams, 310, 311–12; and
Williams' father, 314; *The Wrong
Man* score, *208*, 210–13

"He's a Jolly Good Fellow" (trad.), 18

Hichens, Robert, 138. See also *The
Paradine Case*

High Noon (Zinnemann; *1952*), 165,
166, 274

Hitchcock, Alfred: actors, method of
working with, xvii; on audience
laughter, 91; audience played like
organ, 237, 265; bored by shooting
of scenes, 297; on the chase, 96–97;
cinema seen as music, xiv, 28, 176,
253–54, 263, 318–20; citizenship,
214; as composer, xv; on contrapuntal use of sound, 29–30, 163;
Delius compared to, 103; emigra-
tion to Hollywood, 56, 60–61, 103;
FBI watch on, 129; first stint as producer, 187 (see also *The Trouble
with Harry*); Hollywood belittled,
22; illness and death, 311, 316, 318;
imprisonment feared, 208; invited
to "Spellbound Suite" premiere,
121; "It's just a movie" line, 234;
lunch habits, 311; musical knowledge, xv, 28, 311, 322; musical
legacy, 318; patriotism, 96; photographs, *151, 177, 188, 203, 216;*
production assistant (*see* Robertson, Peggy); relationship with composers (*see specific composers*); respect and recognition craved, 186;
sense of humor, 187, 190; Spielberg's similarities to, 316–17; Stefano mentored, 251, 257–58;
weight, 91. *See also* cameo appearances; *and specific films and television productions*

silent films by Hitchcock, xv, 16, 321
Sim, Alastair, 151, 153
Sinfonietta (Herrmann concert piece), 254
"Sing along with Hitch" (*AHP* introductory skit), 215–16
The Skin Game, 13
Skinner, Frank, 101–3
Smith, Steven, 186, 191, 282
Solomon, Seymour, 282
Sondheim, Stephen, 156, 245
"Sonny Boy" (Jolson), 8
sound notes: for *The Birds*, 260–64, 262, 266–69, 272; for *Family Plot*, 314–15; for *Frenzy*, 302–5; for *The Man Who Knew Too Much (1956)*, 196, 199, 201, 205–6. *See also* music notes
sound technology, Hitchcock's first use of, 4
source music: in *The Birds*, 270–71; in *Blackmail*, 2, 5, 7; in "Bon Voyage," 105; children's songs, 50, 268, 270–72, 276; in *Family Plot*, 314, 315; in *Foreign Correspondent*, 98, 100; in *Frenzy*, 305–6; fusion of score with, 23, 50; in H's British films, 60; in *The Lady Vanishes*, 53–54; in *Lifeboat*, 104; in *The Man Who Knew Too Much (1934)*, 33; in *The Man Who Knew Too Much (1956)*, 33–34; in *Murder!*, 11–13; in *Notorious*, 126–27; in *The Paradine Case*, 140; *Psycho* lacking, 256; in *Rear Window*, 170–72, 319 (see also *Rear Window*); in *Rebecca*, 69; revelation through, 11–12; in *Rich and Strange*, 16–18; in *Rope*, 145–46; in *Sabotage*, 47–48; in *Saboteur*, 101, 102–3; in *Secret Agent*, 45–47; in *Spellbound*, 109; in *Stage Fright*, 150–53; in *Strangers on a Train*,

154, 159, 320, 322; in *Suspicion*, 85; in *The 39 Steps*, 40, 42–43; in *Topaz*, 293–94; in *The Trouble with Harry*, 172; in *Under Capricorn*, 149; in *Vertigo*, 229–30, 232; in *Waltzes from Vienna*, 23; in war-propaganda films, 96. *See also* musical performance(s); radio music; whistling; *and specific films and compositions*
Spellbound (1945), 106–23; critics' opinions, 33, 107, 116; Dalí and, 106–7, 111, 113; score, 107–23, 321; —, concert pieces, 80, 117–18, 120–21, 122; —, hit song sought, 117–20, 176; —, H's opinion, 108–9, 117; —, *Marnie*'s similarities, 275–76; —, popularity, xvii, 116, 120–23; —, Selznick and, 74, 88, 107–17; —, theremin, 10, 108, 110–12, 115–16, 122–23, 263
Spender, Stephen, xv–xvi
Spiegel, Sam, 291
Spielberg, Steven, 308, 316–17
Spoto, Donald, xvii–xviii, 20, 186–87, 189, 223–24, 274
Stafford, Henry (*Blackmail* score), 3–4, 7–10
Stage Fright (1950), 132, 149–55, 151, 322
Stanley, Allen, 207
Stanton, Harry Dean, 220
"Star-Spangled Banner" (music trad.; words by Key), 98, 100
Stefano, Joseph, 252; on Herrmann's personality, 282; on H's relationship with composers, 168, 322; and *Psycho*, 247, 249, 251–52, 254, 256–58, 320; on the *Strangers on a Train* score, 162
Steiner, Fred, 254, 256
Steiner, Max, 59, 61, 64–66, 65, 124. *See also* Webb, Roy

Sterritt, David, 222

Stevens, Leith, 138

Stewart, Al, 119

Stewart, James ("Jimmy"; actor): on Day's acting, 202; on H as director, xvii; in *The Man Who Knew Too Much (1956)*, 192, 195, 198, 206; in *The Paradine Case*, 147; in *Rear Window*, 170, 197; in *Vertigo*, 228, 234

Stewart, James (sound engineer), 139

stinger chords, 112, 286

Stokowski, Leopold, xvii, 121, 193

Storm Clouds Cantata (Benjamin), 32–37, 58, 192–202, 321

Strangers on a Train (1951), 156–62; popular music, 154, 159–61, 172; score, 10, 156–62, 200; source music, 154, 159, 320, 322

Strauss, Johann, Jr.: "Blue Danube" waltz, 21, 23–27, 31–32 (see also *Waltzes from Vienna*); H's preference for, 144–45; music in *Foreign Correspondent*, 98, 99; waltzes used, 27, 59, 216; "Wiener Blut," 84–86

"Summer Night on the River" (Delius), 102–3

Suspicion (1941), 84–89, 85; score, 61–62, 84–89, 114, 139, 140; waltzes, 59, 84–86, 319

Sweeney Todd (Sondheim musical), 245

swing music, 98–99, 101–2, 185

Symphonie fantastique (Berlioz), 223

"Tales of the Grotesque and Arabesque" (Poe), 270

Tandy, Jessica, 267–68

Taxi Driver (Scorsese; *1976*), 212, 226, 273, 279, 308

Taylor, John Russell, 36, 63, 309

Taylor, Samuel, 226, 227, 291

Tchaikovsky, Peter, 172, 287–88

telepathy, musical, 90, 92–93, 159–61

television music, 215–19

terror, 112, 243–44. See also *The Birds; Psycho*

Tetzloff, Ted, 127

"That's Amore" (Warren and Brooks), 178

theremin, 10, 111–12, 115–16, 121–23, 185, 217; in *Spellbound*, 106, 108, 110–12, 115–16, 123, 263

The 39 Steps (1935), 6, 12, 31, 39–44, 41, 127–28

Thomas, Kevin, 288

"Three Blind Mice" (children's song), 50

timpani: in *Blackmail*, 3, 10; in "Bon Voyage," 105; in *Family Plot*, 314; in *North by Northwest*, 241, 314; in *Rebecca*, 67–68; in *Torn Curtain*, 287

Tiomkin, Dimitri, 61, 89–90, 92, 165; critics dismissed, 162; *Dial M for Murder* score, 165–67; on Hollywood's Golden Age, 274; on H's weight, 91; *I Confess* score, 162–65; non-Hitchcock scores, 117, 158–59, 164, 165, 167, 274; preferred by H, 130; relationship with H, 165, 167–68, 278, 279; *Shadow of a Doubt* score, 89–95; *Strangers on a Train* score, 156–62; *Torn Curtain* score offer, 285

Tiomkin, Olivia (wife of D. Tiomkin), 89, 161–62, 165

Titanic project, 18, 62

To Catch a Thief (1955), 115, 184–86

Tomasini, George, 172

Tom Jones (Richardson; *1963*), 285, 286

"Too Fast" (Waxman cue for *Suspicion*), 88–89, 114

Topaz (1969), 172, 273, 290–97

Torn Curtain (1966), 276–89; Addison score, 282, 283, 285–87; classical music in, 172, 287–88; Herrmann score, 273, 278–83, 285–87; popular song, 117, 277, 283, *284*
"To See You Is to Love You" (Burke and Van Heusen), 178–79
Townson, Robert, 80
Trautonium, 265
Tristan and Isolde (Wagner): echoed in *The Man Who Knew Too Much*, 200; in *Murder!*, xv, 11–12, 58, 172, 200, 319; *Vertigo* score influenced, 12, 223
The Trouble with Harry (1955), 14, 172, 186–91, 320
Truffaut, François: on *The Birds*, 261; book on H, xviii, 284; on *Foreign Correspondent*, 97; on *Frenzy*, 304; on the Herrmann-Hitchcock rift, 283; Herrmann's score for, 273, 280, 283; H's comments to, on *The Birds*, 267, 268–69; —, on drummer's off-beat rhythms in *Young and Innocent*, 51; —, on Granger in *Strangers on a Train*, 157; —, on *I Confess*, 164–65; —, on *Lifeboat*, 104; —, musical cartoon described, 34; —, on *Psycho*, 253–54; —, on *Rear Window's* "Lisa," 175; —, on self as maestro, 318–19; —, on *Vertigo's* dressing scene, 228; —, on war-propaganda films, 105; on *The Man Who Knew Too Much*, 32; on *Marnie*, 274–75; on Mr. Memory in *The 39 Steps*, 43; on *North by Northwest*, 143, 239, 241; on *Notorious*, 124; on *The Paradine Case*, 142; on *Rebecca*, 79, 80; on *Waltzes from Vienna*, 20
The Twilight Zone (television series), 115

Under Capricorn (1949), 148–49, 155, 194, 320
Universal (studio): H pressured to get rid of Herrmann, 276–79, 283, 285; and *Topaz*, 291, 294–96; Waxman, Skinner and, 102. *See also specific films*
Uris, Leon, 291

Valli, Alida, 140, 143
Van Heusen, Johnny, 178
Van Sant, Gus, 246
Variety, 97, 210
vernacular music. *See* dance music; jazz; popular music; popular songs; swing music
Vertigo (1958), 222–34; as experiment, 208; Judy's letter, 88; recognition (dressing) scene, xix, 228, 319; score, 222–35, *224*, 256; —, catharsis provided, 268; —, classical pieces, 172, 320; —, conductor, 195; —, echoed in *The Man Who Knew Too Much*, 204; —, "Echoes" quartet based on, 233, 258; —, hit song sought, 120, 231–32; —, impact and influence, 223–25, 232–35, 321; —, main title rarely reprised, 275; —, *Mary Rose* music and, 67, 225; —, and the *Obsession* score, 234, 273; —, popular songs rejected, 172; —, spirals and arpeggios, 3, 10, 222, 223; —, used in *North by Northwest*, 231, 238, 241; —, Wagner referenced, 12, 223; source music, 229–30, 232
Vienna Film Orchestra, 232–33
Vienna Symphony (Vienna Philharmonic's opera label), 232–33
voice-overs, 50, 60, 113–14, 257
voices, timbre of, 241

Williams, John (composer) (*continued*) 308–16; father, 314; and Herrmann, 310, 311–12; on the Herrmann-Hitchcock rift, 288–89; on H's musical legacy, xvi, 318; on H's musical signatures, 1; non-Hitchcock scores, 212, 243, 308, 310; on *Rebecca*'s ending, 62; on Spielberg and H, 316–17; sudden silence tactic admired, 303, 315

Wilson, Stanley, 217

Wood, Michael, 106, 129

Wood, Robin, 133, 181, 205

Woolrich, Cornell, 219

Wright, Teresa, 89, 90

The Wrong Man (1956), 16, 146, 207–13, *208*, 231, 320

Wrubel, Allie, 119

Wuthering Heights (Wyler; *1939*), 98

Wyman, Jane, 151, 152

Wynn, Keenan, 218

Young, Victor, 232

Young and Innocent (1937), 10, 12, 49–52, 169–70, 322